English - Tagalog
Tagalog - English
Dictionary

Third Edition
Revised & Updated

Compiled by Bigayan Yacapin

 ISBN 1-84356-044-5
Third Edition

First Edition Published 1967
@ Bigayan Yacapin & Alfredo Braganza
Cebu State College
Second Edition Published 2007

Published by The Simon Wallenberg Press

Printed in the United States of America & United Kingdom

Warning and Disclaimer

English - Tagalog
Tagalog - English
Dictionary

Bigayan Yacapin

Simon Wallenberg Press

The Tagalog Language

Tagalog is one of the major languages of the Republic of the Philippines. It is the most spoken Philippine language in terms of the number of speakers.

Tagalog, as its de facto standardized counterpart, Filipino, is the principal language of the national media in the Philippines. It is the primary language of public education. As Filipino, it is, along with English, a co-official language and the sole national language. Tagalog is widely used as a lingua franca throughout the country, and in overseas Filipino communities. However, while Tagalog may be prevalent in those fields, English, to varying degrees of fluency, is more prevalent in the fields of government and business.

History

The word Tagalog derived from tagá-ílog, from tagá- meaning "native of" and ílog meaning "river", thus, it means "river dweller." as coined with the muslim settlement of maynilad, There are no surviving written samples of Tagalog before the arrival of the Spanish in the 16th century. Very little is known about the history of the language. However there is speculation among linguists that the ancestors of the Tagalogs originated, along with their Central Philippine cousins, from northeastern Mindanao or eastern Visayas.

The first known book to be written in Tagalog is the Doctrina Cristiana (Christian Doctrine) of 1593. It was written in Spanish and two versions of Tagalog; one written in Baybayin and the other in the Latin alphabet.

Throughout the 333 years of Spanish occupation, there have been grammars and dictionaries written by Spanish clergymen such as Vocabulario de la Lengua Tagala by Pedro de San Buenaventura (Pila, Laguna, 1613), Vocabulario de la lengua tagala (1835) and Arte de la lengua tagala y manual tagalog para la adminstración de los Santos Sacramentos (1850).

Poet Francisco "Balagtas" Baltazar (1788-1862) is regarded as the foremost Tagalog writer. His most famous work is the early 19th-century Florante at Laura.

In 1937, Tagalog was selected as the basis of the national language by the National Language Institute. In 1959, Tagalog, which had been renamed Wikang Pambansa ("National Language") by President Manuel L. Quezon in 1939, was renamed by the Secretary of Education, Jose Romero, as Pilipino to give it a national rather than ethnicity label and connotation. The changing of the name did not, however, result in better acceptance at the conscious level among non-Tagalogs, especially Cebuanos who had not accepted the selection, the language issue was revived once more,and a compromise solution was worked out — a 'universalist' approach to the national language, to be called Filipino rather than Pilipino. When a new constitution was drawn up in 1987, it named Filipino as the national language. The constitution specified that as that Filipino language evolves, it shall be further developed and enriched on the basis of existing Philippine and other languages.

Classification

Outside the Philippines, the Tagalog language is usually limited to communication within ethnic Filipino groups. Light blue boxes indicate significant Filipino communities where Tagalog is spoken. Tagalog is a Central Philippine language within the Austronesian language family. Being Malayo-Polynesian, it is related to other Austronesian languages such as Indonesian, Malay, Fijian, Maori (of New Zealand), Hawaiian, Malagasy (of Madagascar), Samoan, Tahitian, Chamorro (of Guam and the Northern Mariana Islands), Tetum (of East Timor), and Paiwan (of Taiwan).

It is closely related to the languages spoken in the Bicol and Visayas regions such as Bikol, Hiligaynon, Waray-Waray, and Cebuano.

Languages that have made significant contributions to Tagalog are Spanish, Min Nan Chinese, English, Malay, Sanskrit (via Malay), Arabic (via Malay/Spanish), and Northern Philippine languages such as Kapampangan spoken on the island of Luzon.

Geographic distribution

Tagalog in the world.The Tagalog homeland, or Katagalugan, covers roughly much of the central to southern parts of the island of Luzon - particularly in Aurora, Bataan, Batangas, Bulacan, Cavite, Laguna, Metro Manila, Nueva Ecija, Quezon, and Rizal. Tagalog is also spoken natively by inhabitants living on the islands of Lubang, Marinduque, and the northern and eastern parts of Mindoro. According to the Philippine Census of 2000, 21,485,927 out of 76,332,470 Filipinos claimed Tagalog as their first language. An estimated 50 million Filipinos speak it in varying degrees of proficiency.

Tagalog speakers are to be found in other parts of the Philippines as well as throughout the world; it is the sixth most-spoken language in the United States with over a million speakers

Official status

Predominantly Tagalog-speaking regions in the Philippines.Main article: Filipino language
After weeks of study and deliberation, Tagalog was chosen by the National Language Institute, a committee composed of seven members who represents various regions in the Philippines. President Manuel L. Quezon then proclaimed Tagalog the national language or wikang pambansâ of the Philippines on December 30, 1937. This was made official upon the Philippines' restoration of independence from the United States on July 4, 1946.

From 1939 to 1987, Tagalog was also known as Pilipino.Since 1987, the name Filipino has been used to refer to a de facto Tagalog-based national language that borrows from other languages.

Since 1940, Tagalog has been taught in schools throughout the Philippines. It is the only one out of over 170 Philippine languages that is officially used in schools

Other Languages

More than 180 languages and dialects are spoken in the archipelago, almost all of them belonging to the Borneo-Philippines group of the Malayo-Polynesian language branch of the Austronesian language family.

According to the 1987 Constitution, Filipino and English are both the official languages. Many Filipinos understand, write and speak English, Filipino and their respective regional languages.

Filipino is the de facto standardized version of Tagalog and one of the nation's official languages. English, the other official language, is widely used as a lingua franca throughout the country.

Twelve major regional languages are the auxiliary official languages of their respective regions, each with over one million speakers: Tagalog, Cebuano, Ilocano, Hiligaynon, Waray-Waray, Kapampangan, Bikol, Pangasinan. Kinaray-a, Maranao, Maguindanao and Tausug.

English was imposed by Americans during the U.S. intervention and colonization of the archipelago. English is used in education, churches, religious affairs, print and broadcast media, and business, though the number of people who use it as a second language far outnumber those who speak it as a first language. Still, English is the preferred medium for textbooks and instruction for secondary and tertiary levels. Very few would prefer books in the vernacular. Movies and TV programs in English are not subtitled and are expected to be directly understood, but many films and TV channels are now almost exclusively Tagalog in origin. English is the sole language of the law courts. Written and spoken competence in English among the majority of poor Filipinos has been decreasing in recent years due to the abandonment of English medium free primary education.

The Lan-nang-oe variant of Min Nan Chinese dialect is widely spoken by the country's Chinese minority.

Due to its close proximity as a neighbouring Southeast Asian nation, Indonesian (and some other Malay variants) is also spoken in the Philippines, particularly southern regions. As with Filipino, the Indonesian and Malay languages are also members of the Malayo-Polynesian language branch of the Austronesian language family and represent major languages of Southeast Asia.

Spanish was the original official language of the country for more than three centuries, but was used mainly by the educated illustrados (or self taught natives, including José Rizal) and the Spanish authorities. Spanish was the language of the Philippine Revolution, and the 1899 Malolos Constitution proclaimed it as the official language. Following the American occupation of the Philippines, its use declined, especially after 1940. Currently, only a few Mestizos of Spanish and Mexican descents speak it as their first language, although a few others use it together with Tagalog and English.

Both Spanish and Arabic are used as auxiliary languages in the Philippines. The use of Arabic is increasingly prevalent among Filipino Muslims and taught in madrasah (Muslim) schools.

Part I

English - Tagalog

A a

A *adj.* isang

Aback *adv.* paurong

Abandon *n.* pagpapabaya

Abandon *v.* pabayaan

Abase *v.* pababain,ibaba, hamakin

Abash *v.* lituhin, guluhin

Abate *v.* humulaw, magbawa

Abattoir *n.* matadero

Abbey *n.* abadiya, monasteryo

Abbreviate *v.* daglatin, paikliin, paigsiin

Abbreviation *n.* daglat, abrebysasyon

Abdicate *v.* magbitaw, magdimiti

Abdomen *n.* tiyan, sikmura

Abduct *v.* dukutin, halbutin

Aberrant *adj.* ligaw, naliligaw, lisya

Abet *v.* sulsulan, kampihan

Abettor *n.* manunulsol

Abhorrence *n.* pandidiri, pagkapoot

Abide *v.* maghintay, tumira

Ability *n* kakayahan

Abject *adj.* hamak, mababa

Abjure *v.* iwaksi, itatwa

Ablaze *adj.* nagliliyab, nagaalab

Able *adj.* kaya , maykaya, maalam

Abnormal *adj.* dipangkaraniwan

Aboard *adv.* nakasakay, nakalulan

Abode *n.* tahanan, tuluyan

Abolish *v.* alisin, pawalangbisa

Abolition *n.* pag-aalis

Abort *v.* malaglagan

Abortion *n.* pagpapaagas, pagkaagas, pagkalaglag

Abound *v.* manutiktik, maglipana

About *prep.* tungkol sa, hinggil sa

Above *adj.* sa itaas

Abrade *v.* kuskusin, lihahin, raspahin

Abrasive *adj.* panguskos, pangayod, pangaskas

Abreast *adj.* magkaagapay, magkasabay

Abridge *v.* paikliin

Abroad *adv.* sa ibang lupain

Abrupt *adv.* bigla

Abscond *v.* magtanan, tumalilis, lumayas

Absence *n.* kapalyahan, pagpalya, kakulangan

Absent *adj.* pumalya, liban, absent

Absolute *adj.* lubos, buo, ganap, liban

Absolve *v.* patawarin, absulbihan

Absorb *v.* sipsipin, masipsip, mahithit, saklawin

Abstain *v.* di-lumanhok, magpigil

Abstinence *n.* abstinensiya, pagpipigil

Abstract *adj.* abstrakto, baliwag

Abstract *n.* buod

Abstract *v.* hugutin, ihiwalay, alisin, burahin

Absurd *adj.* baligho, balintuna

Abundant *adj.* sagana, masagana

Abuse *v.* laitin, magmalupit, lapastanganin

Abut *v.* dumait, bumalantay

Abyss *n.* bangin, labing

Academic *adj.* akademiko

Academy *n.* academya, linangan

Accede *v* pumayag, sumangayon

Accelerate *v.* padalin, pabalisin, magpabilis

Accelerator *n.* akselerador, pampatulin

Accent *n.* tuldik, punto, diin

Accept *v* tanggapin, pumayag

Acceptance *n.* pagtanggap, pagkakatanggap

Access *n.* daan, pagpapasok

Accessory *n.* aksesorya, sangkap, kagamitan

Accident *n.* sakuna, disgrasya, aksidente

Acclaim *v.* palakpakan, parangalan, ipagbunyi

Accomodate *v.* pagkalooban, pagbigyan, magkasya

Accomodation *n* matutuluyan, matitirhan, areglo

Accompanist *n.* akompanyente, tagasaliw

Accompany *v.* sumama, saliwan, ihatid

Accomplice *v.* kasapakat, komplise

Accomplish *v.* gawin, isagawa, tapusin

Accord *n.* kasunduan, usapan, pagkakasundo, intindi

According *prep.* alinsunod sa

Accordingly *adv.* Alinsunod, kaya

Account *n.* tuos, tuusin

Account *v.* ipagpalagay, managot, magulat, sulitin

Accountant *n.* kontador, publiko, tagapagtuos

Accredit *v.* paniwalaan, pangtibayin

Accretion *n.* tubo, suloy, talbos

Accrue *v.* magkadagdag, magkatubo

Accumulate *v.* magtipon, dumami

Accumulation *n.* pagtitipon, bunton, pagdami

Accuracy *n.* kawastuan

Accurate *n.* wasto, tama, iksakto

Accuse *v.* ibintang, isakdal, magsakdal, paratangan

Accustom *v.* magsanay, bihasahin

Ace *n.* batikan

Ache *n.* sakit, kirot, hapdi, ankat

Ache *v.* makirot, sumakit

Achieve *v* makamit, kamtan, masapit

Achievement *n.* nagawa, nayari, naganap

Acid *n.* asido

Acidity *n* kaasiduhan

Acknowledge *v.* kilalanin, tanggapin, pananggapan

Acknowledgement *n.* pagkilala, pagtanggap, pagpapasalamat

Acme *n.* sukdulan

Acne *n.* taghawat

Acquaint *v.* ipaalam, ipakilala, ipabatid

Acquaintance *n.* kakilala, kabatiran, kaalaman

Acquire *v.* matamo, makuha, mabili, mamana

Acquit *v.* kalagan ng sagutin

Acrobat *n.* akrobata, sirkero

Across *adv.* patawid, pakabita

Across *adv.* patawid , pakabita

Act *n.* akto, pasiya, yugto

Act *v.* gumawa, kumilos, gumanap, magpasiya, acto, umakto,

Acting *adj.* gumaganap, gumagana, pnsamantala

Acting *n.* Pag-akto

Action *n.* kilos, galaw, labanan, aksiyon,ginawa, kibo

Activate *v.* aktibahin, pagalawin, pukawin

Active *adj.* masipag, maliksi, buhay, masigla

Activity *n.* kilusan, gawain, aktibidad, pagkaktibo

Actor *n.* artista, bituin, istar

Actual *adj.* tunay, kasalukuyan, totoo

Acute *adj.* tulis, matalas, matinis

Adamant *adj.* matimtiman

Adapt *v.* iagpang, ibagay

Add *v.* sumahin, magdagdag, sumahin

Addict *n.* addikto

Addition *n.* dagdag, karagdagan

Address *n.* tinitirahan, direksiyon, tirahan

Address *v.* talumpatian, kausapin

Adequate *adj.* sapat, husto, kainaman

Adhere *v.* manikit, mangapit, kumabit, manghawak

Adherence *n.* paninikit, pangangapit

Adhesive *adj.* malagkit

Adjacent *adj.* karatig, katabi, kalapit, kasanib

Adjective *n.* pang-uri, adhetibo

Adjoining *adj.* kanugnog, kalapit

Adjourn *n.* wakasin, tapusin, itindig

Adjust *v.* itama, iayos, ayusin

Administer *v.* mangasiwa, pangasiwaan

Administration *n.* pangasiwaan, administrasyon

Administrator *n.* Tagapangasiwa, administrador

Admiral *n.* almirante

Admiration *n.* Paghanga

Admire *v.* ihanga, humanga, hangaan

Admission *n.* pagpasok, pasukan, pagtanggap

Admit *v.* aminin, papasukin

Adolescence *n.* adolesensiya, pagbibinata

Adolescent *n/adj* nagbibinata, nagdadalaga, bata

Adopt *v.* ampunin, ugalin, gamitin, angkinin

Adore *v.* sambahin, sumamba, mamintuho, pintuhuin

Adorn *v.* adornohan, palamutian, pagandahin, gandahan

Adrift *adj.* lutang, nakalutang

Adulate *v.* mamuri

Adult *n.* adulto, matanda, maygulang, maykagulangan

Adulterate *v.* haluan, palabnawin, bantuan

Adultery *n.* pakikiapid, adulteryo

Advance *adj.* pauna, antimano

Advance *v.* Pagsulong, punahan, sumikat, isulong

Advantage *n.* pakinabang, kapararakan

Adventure *n* Pakikipagsapalaran, karanasan

Adverb *n.* pangabay, adbrbiyo

Adverse *adj.* pasalunga, nakasasama

Adversity *n.* kasawian

Advertise *v.* Ipagbalita, ilathala, ipaanunsiyo

Advice *n.* Payo, paalaala

Advise *v.* Payuhan, bigayalam, paalam

Adviser *n.* tagapayo

Advocate *n.* tagataguyod, tagapagtanggol

Advocate *v.* itaguyod, tangkilikin, magtanggol

Aerial *n.* antena, eryal

Aerogram *n.* pahatid-radyo

Aeroplane *n.* eruplano

Affair *n.* gawain, asikasuhin

Affect *v.* makapinsala, magkabisa, makasasama

Affection *n* pagkukunwari, pag-ibig

Affectionate *adj.* Malambing

Affidavit *n.* apidabit

Affiliation *n* pag-anib, pagsali

Affirm *v.* patibayan, panindigan

Affix *n* panlapi

Affix *v.* pirmahan, lagdaan

Afflict *v.* pakaguluhin, saktan

Affluence *n.* kasaganaan, kariwasaan, kayamanan

Affluent *adj.* masagana, marisawa, mayaman

Afford *v.* makaya, kayang bilhin

Afraid *adj.* takot

After *adv.* pagkatapos

After *prep.* patapos

Afternoon *n* hapon

Afterwards *adv.* Pagkatapos, matapos, pagkaraan

Again *adv.* Uli, muli

Against *adj.* tutol, labag

Against *prep.* laban sa

Age *n.* gulang, tanda, panahon

Agency *n.* tanggapan, sangay

Agenda *n.* adyenda, ahenda, talausapan, talagawin

Agent *n.* ahente, kinagawa, kintatawan

Aggravate *v.* magpalala, lumala, palalain, palubhain

Aggressive *adj.* marahas, mapandahas, masigasing

Agitator *n.* manunulsol, panghalo

Ago *adv.* kanina, sanakaraan, noong araw

Agony *n.* hapis, aguniya, hingalo

Agrarian *adj.* agraryo, pambukid

Agree *v.* umayon, pumayag, magkaisa, nakabubuti

Agreement *n.* Usapan, kasunduan

Agriculture *n.* pagsasaka, pagpapatanim, agrikultura

Ahead *adv.* nauna, patungo

Aid *n.* saklolo

Aid *v.* tulungin

Aim *n.* Layon, tudla, tukoy

Aim *v.* tukuyin, itudla

Air *n.* Himpapawid, hangin

Airmail *n* koreong panghimpapawid

Airplane *n.* aeroplano

Airport *n.* Paliparan

Airy *adj.* mahangin, masaya

Aisle *n.* pasilyo, koridor

Ajar *adj.* nakaawang

Akin *adj.* kauri, katulad

Akin *adj.* kauri, kamag-anak

Alarm *n* hudyat, alarma, pagkagulat, pangamba

Alarm *v.* mangamba, kabahan, takutin

Album *n.* album

Alchemy *n.* alkimya

Alchohol *n.* alkuhol

Alcohol *n.* alkohol, aguwardiyente

Alert *adj.* handa, listo, maingat

Alibi *n.* dahilan, alibay

Alien *adj.* banyaga, kaiba, dayuhan, estranghero

Alien *n.* dayo

Alight *v.* umbis, bumaba, dumapo

Alight *v.* dumapo

Align *v.* ituwid, pumila, ipila

Alike *adj.* kahawig, kaparis pareho, kamukha

Alike *adv.* Magkapareho

Alimony *n.* sustento

Alive *adj.* gising, buhay, masigla

All *adj.* lahat, buo

Allege *v.* iparatang, sabihin, hinuhain

Allergy *n* taluhiyang

Alleviate *v.* pagaanin, bawahan

Alliance *n.* pagtutulungan, alyansa, liga

Allied *adj.* alyado, magkaugnay

Alligator *n.* buwaya, kayman

Allocate *v.* iukol, ilaan, ipamahagi

Allot *v.* italaga, pag-ayawayawin

Allow *v.* Hayaan, pabayaan, payagan, pahintulutan

Allowance *n.* baon, tustos, panggastos

Allude *v.* ipahiwatig, bumanggit

Allure *v.* painan, akitin, ganyakin

Allusion *n.* banggit, hiwatig

Ally *n.* kaanib, kapanalig

Almond *n.* almendras, pili

Almost *adv.* munti, halos

Alms *n.* limos, tulong, karidad

Aloft *adv.* nasitaas, nakaakyat na

Alone *adj.* Nagiisa, walang kasama

Along *adv.* sabay, patungo

Aloof *adv.* layo, ilag, hiwalay

Aloud *adv.* lakasan, malakas

Alphabet *n.* alpabeto

Already *adv.* tapos na

Also *adv.* Pati, rin, din, man

Altar *n.* dambana, alta

Alter *v.* magbago, baguhin

Alternate *n.* pamalit, kahalili

Although *conj.* bagaman, kahit na, kahiman

Altitude *n* taas, tayog, layog

Altogether *adv.* lubos, buo, puspos, ganap

Alumnus *n.* alumnas, nagtapos

Always *adv.* Palagi, lagi, parati

Amalgamation *n.* pagsasamasama, amalgamasyon

Amass *v.* magbunton, ibunton, magtipon, tipunin

Amateur *n.* baguhan, amatyur

Amaze *v.* magtaka, gulatin, manggulat, papagtakhin

Amazing *adj.* nakakagulat, katakataka

Ambassador *n.* sugo, embahador

Ambiguous *adj.* ambigwo, ditiyak, malabo, alimin

Ambition *n.* Pangarap, hangad, adhika, hangarin

Ambulance *n.* ambulansiya

Ambush *v.* tambangan, abangan, harangin

Amend *v.* iwasto, itama, baguhin, susugan

American *n/adj* Jano, Amerikano

Amiable *adj.* nakaaakit, kaibig-ibig

Amid *prep.* sa gitna ng, sa loob ng

Amiss *adj.* mali, di dapat

Amity *n.* pagkakaibigan, pagkakasundo

Amnesty *n.* pagpapatawad, amnistiya

Amok *n.* huramentado

Among *prep.* sa gitna ng

Amongst *prep.* palaot-laot

Amount *n.* daghan, halaga, kabuuan

Amount *v.* abutin, umabot

Ample *adj.* malawak, malaki, sagana, sapat

Amplifier *n.* pampalaki, pampalakas

Amplify *v.* punan, dagdagan, palakihin, palakasin

Amputate *v.* putulin

Amulet n. galing, amuleto, anting-anting

Amuse *v.* libangin, maglibang, manlibang, aliwin

Amusement *n.* libangan

An *art.* isa

Analogy *n.* pagkakahawig

Analysis *n.* suri, pagsusuri, pagkakasuri

Analyze *v.* magsuri, suriin, analisahin

Anarchy *n.* anarkiya

Anatomy *n.* anatomiya

Ancestor *n.* Ninuno

Ancestor *n.* ninuno

Anchor *n.* angkora, pasangit, angkla

Anchor *v.* pumundo, dumating, dumuong

Ancient *adj.* sinauna

Ancient *adj.* matanda, luma, antigo

And *conj.* at

Anecdote *n.* anekdota

Anemia *n.* kakulangan sa dugo, anemia

Anesthesia *n.* anestesya, pangimay

Angel *n.* anghel

Anger *n.* galit, poot, pagkagalit

Angle *n.* siha, salikop, panig, sulok

Angry *adj.* nagagalit, galit

Anguish *n.* dalamhati, sakit, hapdi, dusa

Animal *n.* hayop, animal

Animate *v.* buhayin, pasiglahin, magpasigla

Ankle *n.* buol, bukung-bukong

Annals *n.* anales, kasaysasayan

Annex *v.* iugnay, ikabit, isanib

Anniversary *n.* kaarawan, anibersaryo

Annotate *v.* anotahan

Announce *v.* ipabalita, magbalita, ipatalastas

Annoy *v.* Abalahin, buwisitin, yamutin

Annual *n.* taunang-aklat, anwal, taunan

Annul *v.* pawalang-bisa, nuluhin

Anonymous *adj.* di-kilala, anonimo, tago, kungsino

Another *adj.* iba, isa pang, ibang

Answer *n.* Sagot, tugon

Answer *v.* sagutin, sumagot, tugunin

Ant *n.* langgam, guyam

Antagonism *n.* antagonnismo, pagsalungat

Antagonize *v.* kalabanin, salangsangin

Antarctic *adj.* antartika

Antecede *v.* mauna, unahan, manguna, pangunahan

Antecedent *adj.* nauna, nanguna

Antenna *n.* antena, eryal

Anthem *n.* awit, kanta, imno

Anthology *n.* antolohiya, katipunan

Anti *prep.* kalaban, kontra

Anticipate *v.* manguna, asahan, umasa, umagap

Anticlimax *n.* pasira sa sukdulan

Antidote *n.* antidot, lunas

Antique *adj.* antigo, matanda

Antique *n.* relikya

Anvil *n.* palihan, pandayan

Anxiety *n.* balino, balisa, bagabag, pagkabagabag

Anxious *adj.* mabalisa, sabik, nababahala

Any *pron.* kahit suno, sinuman, alinman

Anybody *pron.* sinuman, kahit sino

Anyhow *adv.* kahit paano, paano man

Anything *prn.* kahit ano

Anyway *adv.* kahit paano, maski na

Anywhere *adv.* kahit saan, saan man

Apart *adv.* bukodsa, hiwalay, tangi

Apartment *n.* aksesorya

Ape *n.* bakulaw, orangutang

Apex *n.* tuktok, taluktok

Apology *n.* apolohiya, paumanhin

Apostle *n.* alagad, disipulo

Apparatus *n.* aparato, kasangkapan

Apparel *n.* kasuutan, damit

Apparent *adj.* kita, hayag, malinaw

Appeal *v.* umapela, makiusap, ipaghabol

Appear *v.* Lumitaw, kamukha, pakita, humarap

Appearance *n.* ayos, hitsura, anyo, palabas

Appease *v.* payapain, palubagin, patiwasayin

Append *v.* ikabit, itatak, idagdag

Appetite *n.* gana, kumain

Applaud *v.* pumalakpak, purihin

Applause *n.* Palakpak

Apple *n.* mansanas

Appliance *n.* kasangkapan, kagamitan

Applicant *n.* aplikant

Application *n.* aplikasyon, pagtuon, hiling, pagpahid

Apply *v.* ilagay, ituon, umaply, ilipat

Appoint *v.* hirangin, itakda

Appointment *n.* tipanan, tiyapan, paghirang

Appraisal *n.* taya, tantiya, tasa

Appraise *v.* halagahan, tayahin, bintayin

Appreciate *v.* kalugdan, halagahan, malugod

Apprehend *v.* unawain, dakpin, sunggaban

Apprise *v.* pasabihan, balitaan

Approach *v.* lumapit, lapitan

Appropriate *v.* husto, maglaan, magtakda

Approval *n.* pagpapatibay, pagkapatibay

Approve *v.* magpatibay, payagan, masiyahan

Approximate *adj.* malapit

Approximate *v.* maglapit, halos maging

April *n.* Abril

Apron *n.* epron, tapis, tapi

Aptitude n. hilig, kakayahan

Aquarium *adj.* akwaryum

Aquatic *adj.* tubigan

Arbiter *n.* hukom, huwes

Arbitration *n.* pagdinig at pagpapasiya

Arcade *n.* arkada

Arch *n.* arko, balantok

Architect *n.* arkitekto

Archives *n.* artsibo, sinupan

Archway *n.* pasilyo

Ardent *adj.* maalab, maapoy, marubdob

Are *v.* ay

Area *n* lawak, lapad, laki, bahagi

Arena *n.* arena, larangan

Argue *v.* Awayin, makipagtalo, mangatuwiran, magpahiwatig

Argument *n.* argumento, pagtatalo, katwiran

Arid *adj.* tigang, tuyo

Arise *v.* bumangon, umalsa, magkaroon

Arm *n.* bisig, sandata, braso

Arm *v.* sandatahan, armasan

Armor *n.* kalasag, baluti

Army *n.* hukbo, ehersito

Aroma *n.* bango, samyo, halimuyak

Around *adv.* sa paligid, sa palibod, sa tabi tabi, sa malapit

Arouse *v.* gisingin, pukawin

Arrange *v.* ayusin, ihanda, maghanda, iayos

Arrangement *n.* pagaayos, kuntrata

Arrears *n.* atraso sa utang, hulihan

Arrest *n.* dakipan, paghuli, aresto

Arrest *v.* arestuhin, dakpin, bihagin

Arrival *n.* pagdating, dating, pagsapit

Arrive *v.* dumating, sumapit, dumatal

Arrogance *n.* aroganslya, pagpapalalo

Arrow *n.* palaso, pana, tunod

Arson *n.* panununog, arson

Art *n.* ang, sining, arte

Article *n.* abubot, gamit, pahayag, bagay,tinda,pantukoy

Artificial *adj.* pakunwari, aral, huwad, gawagawa

Artist *n.* pintor, artista

As *adv.* Kagaya, katulad

Ascend *v.* umakyat, pumaitaas, sumalunga, umahon, bumarangka

Ascent *n.* dahilig, akyatin

Ascertain *v.* tiyakin, alamin

Ash *n.* abo, upos

Ash tray *n.* Abuhan

Ashamed *adj.* nahiya, napapahiya

Asia *n.* Asya

Aside *adv.* isangtabi, sa tabi, bukod

Ask *v.* hingin, itanong, makiusap, magtanong, humingi, tanungin

Asleep *adj.* natutulog, tulog

Aspect *n.* aspekto, tayo, katayuan, lagay

Aspire *v.* maghangad, maglunggati

Ass *n.* buriko, asno

Assail *v.* dumaluhong, batikusin, tumuligsa, atakihin

Assassin *n.* tagapatay, tagakitil

Assassinate *v.* magtaksil

Assault *n.* pagsalakay, atake, tuligsa, pampbubugbog

Assemble *v.* tipunin, magtagpo

Assembly *n.* asamblea, batasan, pagtitipon

Assert *v.* ipahayag, panindigan

Assert *v.* magsaysay, ipahayag, panindigan

Assess *v.* tayahin, tasahan, magtasa

Asset *n.* pangangari, propyedad

Assign *v.* magtakda, magtalaga, italaga, itoka, ilagay

Assist *v.* tulungan, tumulong

Assistance *n.* saklolo, tulong

Assistant *n.* assistente, katulong, pangalawa

Associate *n.* kasama, katulong, sumana, kasosyo

Association *n.* kapisanan, pagsasamahan, samahan, bakasan

Assort *v.* urtin, klasipikahin

Assume *v.* ipalagay na tunay, magkunwa, kamkamin

Assurance *n.* siguridad, katiyakan

Assure *v.* ipasiguro, tiyakin, ipangako, siguruhin

Asthma *n.* asma, hika

Astir *adj.* aktibo, kumikilos

Astonish *v.* biglain, gulatin, magitla

Astray *adj.* ligaw, namamali, nagkakamali

Astrology *n.* astrolohiya

Asylum *n.* asilo

At *prep.* sa, nasa, saka

Athlete *n.* atleta, manlalaro

Athletic *adj.* malakas, matipuno

Atmosphere *n.* singaw, himpapawid

Atrocious *adj.* napakalupit, tampalasan

Atrocity *n.* katampalasanan, kalupitan, kabuhungan

Attach *v.* ikabit, isama, ilakip, magkapit

Attack *v.* salakayin, lusubin, pagsalakay, atakihin

Attain *v.* matamo, makamtan, maganap, abutin

Attempt *v.* subukan, tangkain, umato, atuhin

Attend *v.* dumalo, kalingain, daluhan, alagaan

Attendance *n.* pagdalo

Attention *n.* pansin, kalinga, pangangalaga

Attest *v.* patunayan, saksihan, patibayan

Attire *n.* bihis, pananamit, damit

Attire *v.* magdamit

Attitude *n.* kilos, ayos, loobin, tayo, palagay

Attorney *n.* atorni, abugado, mananangggol

Attract *v.* umakit, akitin, maakit, hikayatin

Attraction *n.* bighani, gayuma, halina, pang-akit

Attractive *adj.* kaakit-akit, nakahahalina

Auction *n.* subasta, almoneda

Audience *n.* tagapanood, tagapakinig

Audio *adj.* pampadinig

Audit *v.* suriin, sumuri

Auditor *n.* tagasuri, tagapagsuri

Augment *v.* punan, palakihin

August *n.* Agosto

Aunt *n.* tia, ale, nanang

Authentic *adj.* tunay, lehitimo

Author *n.* maykatha, autor

Authority *n.* kapangyarihan

Auto *n.* kotse, auto

Automatic *adj.* kusa

Autumn *n.* taglagas

Avail *n.* pakinabang, benepisyo, kapararakan

Avail *v.* samantalahin, magsamantala

Available *adj.* makukuha, handa

Avenge *v.* ipaghiganti, maghiganti

Avenue *n.* daana, pasyalan

Average *adj.* katamtaman, karaniwan, normal

Average *n.* balasak, kainaman

Avert *v.* umilag, ilagan, agapan

Aviation *n.* abyasyon

Avid *adj.* sabik, matakaw

Avoid *v.* umilag, umiwas, iwasan, panginlagan

Await *v.* Abang, hintayin

Awake *adj.* gising, listo, alisto

Awake *v.* gisingin, magising, pukawin

Awaken *v.* Gisingin

Award *v.* pagkalooban, ipagkaloob, ibigay, ipremyo

Aware *adj.* nainamalayan, batid, nababatid, alam

Aware *v.* may kamalayan

Away *adv.* lumayo, nakalayo, nakaalis

Awe *n.* sindak, hintakot

Awful *adj.* Kakila-kilabot, palakol, nakatatakot

Awkward *adj.* asiwa, mabagal, kahiya-hiya, kalay

Ax /Axe *n.* palakol, puthaw, palathaw

Axis *n.* aksis, painugan

Axle *n.* ehe

B b

Baboon *n.* bakulaw

Baby *n.* sanggol, pasusuhin, bata, batang sumususo

Bachelor *n.* binata, batsilyer

Back *n.* basilo, kabila, likod, likuran

Back *v.* katigan, tumulong, tulungan, pustahan

Background *n.* batayan, kaligran, palibot

Backward *adj.* paurong, pabalik, huli, atrasado

Bacon *n.* bekon, tusino

Bad *adj.* masama, mahigpit, bulok, sira

Badge *n.* dibisa, kondekorasyon, sagisag, tsapa

Badminton *n.* larong, badminton

Baffle *v.* manlito, mambigo, lituhin, biguin

Bag *n.* bayong, maleta, sako, supot

Bag *v.* hulihin, mahuli, mamintog, huli

Baggage *n.* bagahe, daladalahan, dala

Bail *n.* piyansa, lagak

Bail *v.* piyansahan, maglimas, limasan

Bake *v.* hurnuhin, maghurno

Baker *n.* hurnero, panadero

Bakery *n.* panaderya

Balance *n.* Panimbang, timbangan, kalamangan, ekilibriyo

Balance *v.* timbangin

Balcony *n.* balcon, balkonahe

Bald *adj.* Kalbo, panot, kutyog

Ball *n.* bola, sayaw, bayle

Ballet *n.* baley

Balloon *n.* lobo, balun, palintog

Ballot *n.* balota

Balm *n.* pamahid, pabango, balsamo

Bamboo *n.* kawayan

Ban *v.* ipagbawal

Banana *n.* saging

Band *n.* pulutong, kombo, barkada, pangkat

Bandage *n.* benda, bendahe

Bandage *v.* bendahan

Bandit *n.* tulisan, bandido, bandolero

Bane *n.* nakamamatay, nakapupuksa, kamandag, sakuna

Bang *n.* kalabog, putok, bong

Banish *v.* idestiyero, ipatapon, pawliin

Bank *n.* bangko, pampang, bunton

Banker *n.* bangkero

Bankrupt *adj.* bangkarote, insolbente

Banner *n.* Bandera, bandila

Banquet *n.* Kainan, bangkete, piging

Baptism *n.* binyag, pagbinyag, bautismo

Bar *n.* bar, deresto, abugasiya, lingkaw, halang, bareta

Bar *v.* hadlangan

Barbecue *n.* inihaw, barbekyu, litson

Barber *n.* mangugupit, barbero

Bare *adj.* hubad, walang takip, hubo, hayag, lantad

Bare *v.* hubaran, ihayag, ilantad, ibunyag

Barely *adv.* bahagya, munti

Bargain *n.* tawad, kasunduan, baratilyo

Bargain *v.* tawaran, tumawad

Barge *n.* gabara, kasko

Bark *n.* balakbak

Bark *v.* tumahol, tahulan, kumahol, kahulan

Barley *n.* sebada

Barn *n.* kamalig, bangan, tambubong

Baron *n.* baron, baronesa

Barracks *n.* kuwartel, himpilan

Barrel *n.* bariles, kanyon

Barren *adj.* baogay, tigang, tanga, moog

Barter *n.* baligya, palitan, pagpapalitan

Base *adj.* takaran, imbi, hamak, mababa

Base *n.* sandigan, takad, pundasyon

Base *v.* ibatay, pagbatayan

Basement *n.* silong

Basic *adj.* pansimulain, saligan, basiko

Basin *n.* palanggana, batayan, pamantungan

Basis *n.* batayan, saligan

Basket *n.* buslo, pangnan

Bat *n.* paniki, talibatab, bayakan, bumat, pumalo

Batch *n.san* ggawaan, barkada, tungkos

Bath *n.* ligo, paligo, paliguan

Bathe *v.* maligo, paliguan

Bathroom *n.* banyo, paliguan

Battallion *n.* batalyon

Batten *n.* pirasong, tabla

Batten *v.* tumaba, patabain

Battery *n.* bateriya, pila

Battle *n.* labanan, pagbabaka

Bawl *v.* humagulgol, isigaw

Bay *n.* look, alulong, kastanyo

Bazaar *n.* basar, almasen, tindahan

Be *v.* maging, ay

Beach *n.* baybayin, dalampasigan, aplaya

Beacon *n.* hudyat

Bead *n.* butil, abaloryo

Beak *n.* tuka

Beaker *n.* baso

Beam *n.* silaw, sinag, tahilan, biga, sepo

Beam *v.* masilaw, suminag

Bean *n.* bins, abas, lentehas

Bear *n.* oso

Bear *v.* magdala, dalhin, matiis, mamunga

Beard *n.* balbas, misay, bungot

Bearer *n.* maydala, maytaglay

Beast *n.* halimaw, hayop, ganid, bestiya

Beat *n.* palo, tibok, hampas, bugbog

Beat *v.* paluin, hampasin, kumumpas, tugtugin

Beautiful *adj.* maganda, marikit

Beautify *v.* gandahan, gayakan, beatipikahan

Beauty *n.* kagandahan, alindog, ganda, dikit

Because *conj.* dahil sa, mangyari, sapagka't, yayamang

Become *v.* maging, mabagay, bumagay, mangyari

Bed *n.* tulugan, kama, hihigan, higaan

Bedroom *n.* silid-tulugan

Bee *n.* bubuyog, himbubuyog, pukyutan

Beef *n.* karning baka

Beer *n.* serbesa, bir

Before *adv.* dati, nang una, noong araw

Beg *v.* magpalimos, humingi, ipakiusap

Beget *v.* umanak, pagmulan

Beggar *n* pulubi, nagpapalimos

Begin *v.* Umpisa, simulan, magsimula

Beginning *n.* pasimula, simula

Behalf *n.* panig, interes, kapakanan

Behave *v.* magpakaayos, magpakabait

Behavior *n.* asal, gawi, kilos

Behind *adv.* huli, atrasado, sa likod

Behold *v.* tumingin, masdan, tingnan

Being *n.* tao, katauhan, nilalang

Belief *n.* paniniwala, pananalig, pagtitiwala

Believe *v.* maniwala, paniwalaan, magtiwala

Bell *n.* kalembang, batingaw, kampana

Bellow *n.* atungal, ungal

Belly *n.* tiyan, puson, buyon, sikmura

Belong *v.* mapakabit, mapasama, makasama

Beloved *adj.* mahal, sinta, giliw, irog

Below *adv.* ibaba, ilalim

Belt *n.* sinturon, paha, bigkis, kapookan

Bench *n.* bangko, upuan, korte

Bend *v.* baluktutin, hutukin, mamaluktot

Benefit *n.* pakinabang, benepisyo, kagalingan

Benevolence *n.* benebolensiya, loob, kawanggawa

Benign *adj.* benigno, magiliw, mairog

Bequeath *v.* ipamana

Bequest *n.* , pamana, mana

Berth *n.* daungan, puwang, kama, kamarote

Beside *adv.* katabi, bukod

Best *adj.* pinakamabuti, mas mabuti, pinakamainam

Bestow *v.* ipagkaloob, ibigay, maggawad

Bet *n.* pusta, taya

Bet *v.* pumusta, magpustahan, tayaan

Betray *v.* magkanulo, ipagkanulo, pagkanuluhan

Better *adj.* lalong mabuti

Between *prep.* Pagitan

Beverage *n.* inumun

Beware *v.* mag-ingat, pagingatan, mangalaga

Bewitch *v.* kulamin, gawayin

Beyond *prep.* malayo

Bias *n.* bayas, hilig, hiris

Bicycle *n.* bisikleta

Bid *n.* tawad, tampa

Bid *v.* tumawad, tumampa

Big *adj.* malaki, mataas, dakila

Bigamy *n.* bigamya, pagdadawang asawa

Bigot *n.* panatiko

Bilingual *adj.* bilingguwe

Bill *n.* tuka, kuwenta, paskil, kartelon

Bin *n.* balaong, imbakan, pintungan

Bind *n.* Buklurin, buklod, gapos

Bind *v.* gapusin, talian, itali, bigkisin

Bird *n.* ibon

Birth *n.* panganganak, pagsilang, kapanganakan

Birthday *n.* kapanganakan, kaarawan

Biscuit *n.* galyetas, biskotso, biskuwit

Bit *n.* kapiraso, kapiranting, bukado, talim

Bitch *n.* puta

Bite *n.* Kagat, subo, subo

Bite *v.* kagatin, kumagat, nakagat

Bitter *adj.* mapait, masaklap

Black *adj.* itim, luksa, madilim

Blackmail *n.* pasuhol, blakmeil, santahe

Blacksmith *n.* panday

Bladder *n.* pantog

Blade *n.* talim, dahon, sable

Blame *v.* sisihin, manisi, papanagutin

Bland *adj.* suwabe, mayumi, maamo

Blank *adj.* blangko

Blank *n.* puwang

Blanket *n.* blangket, kumot, manta

Blaze *n.* ningas, tala, mantsang, lagablab

Bleach *v.* mamuti, paputiin, kulahin

Bleak *adj.* ilang, mailang

Bleed *v.* dumugo, paduguin, magdugo

Blench *v.* umuklo, umukdo, umigtad

Blend *v.* paghaluin, pagsamahin, timpla

Bless *v.* bindisyunan, basbasan, pagpalain

Blind *adj.* bulag

Bliss *n.* lugod, kaluguran, galak, kagalakan

Blister *n.* lintog, lintos

Bloat *v.* mamaga, bumintog

Blob *n.* patak, bula, labusab

Block *n.* kanto, bara, bloke, marisana

Block *v.* sanggahan, handlangan, sarhan, harangan

Blockade *n.* blokeo, pagkubkob

Blockade *v.* kubkubin

Blood *n.* dugo

Blood *n.* dugo

Bloom *n.* bulaklak, pamumulaklak

Bloom *v.* mamulaklak, manariwa

Blossom *n.* bulaklak

Blot *v.* mantsahan, pawiin

Blouse *n.* blusa

Blow *n.* hihip, suntok, dapyo

Blow *v.* hipan, hinipan, humihip, sumimoy

Blue *adj.* bughaw, asul, matamlay

Bluff *adj.* lapad, prangko

Bluff *n.* talampas, linlang, blap

Blunder *v.* magkadarapa, magkamali

Blunt *adj.* mapurol, dimakapansin

Blur *n.* anagag, bakat, kulabo

Blush *v.* mamula, mahiya, mapahiya

Bluster *v.* magingay

Boar *n.* baboy

Board *n.* kapirasong, kahoy, kasanggunian, lupon, tabla

Boast *n.* pagyabang, pahahambog, kahambugan

Boast *v.* ipagyabang, magyabang, maghambog

Boat *n.* bangka, bapor

Body *n.* katawan, pangangatawan, bangkay, kuwerpo

Bodyguard *n.* bantay, badigard , guwardiya

Boil *n.* pigsa, pagkulo, bukol

Boil *v.* Pakuluin, kumulo, maglaga

Bold *adj.* matapang, pangahas, marahas

Boldly *adv.* malakas ang loob

Bolt *n.* trangka, piyesa, rolyo

Bomb *n.* kanyon, bomba

Bonanza *n.* bonansa, minang, sagana

Bond *n.* tali, bigkis, buklod

Bond *n.* tali, bigkis, buklod

Bondage *n.* kabusabusan, kaalipnan

Bone *n.* buto

Bonfire *n.* siga, bompair

Bonus *n.* bonus, dagdag

Book *n.* aklat, libro

Bookstore *n.* libreriya, tindahan ng aklat

Boom *n.* bung, dagundong

Boon *n.* pabor, pakiusap, kahilingan

Boost *v.* umatang, atangan, ibunsod

Boot *n.* botas

Booth *n.* habong, kuwarto

Border *n.* hangganan, border, gilid, tabihan

Bore *v.* magbutas, butasin, makainip

Born *adj.* nanganak, isinilang, inianak

Borrow *v.* hiramin, sandaliin, manghiram, humiram

Bosom *n.* dibdib, sinapupunan

Boss *n.* amo, boss, panginoon, puno, tagapamahala

Both *pron.* kapuwa

Bother *v.* abalahin, gambalain, mangabala, lituhin

Bottle *n.* bote, botelya

Bottom *n.* lunas, ilalim

Bounce *v.* tumalbog, patalbugin

Bound *adj.* ginapos, nakatali

Bound *n.* lukso, buklod, hangahan

Bound *v.* lumukso, lumundag, pumitlag

Boundary *n.* hanggahan

Bounty *n.* gantimpala, biyaya

Bouquet *n.* palumpon, bukey

Bout *n.* timpalak, kontest, labanan

Bow *n.* pagyukod, panalaso, busog, arko

Bow *v.* yumukod, gumalang

Bowel *n.* bituka

Bowl *n.* mangkok, tason, sulyaw

Box *n.* kahon, kaha, suntok, dagok

Box *v.* suntukin, ikinahon

Boxer *n.* boksingero

Boxing *n.* boksing, suntukan

Boy *n.* batang lalaki, totoy, boy, utusan

Boycott *n.* Welga, boykoteo

Bra *n.* bra, brasyer

Brace *v.* talian, bigkisan, higpitan, suhayan

Bracelet *n.* brasaleta, galang, pulseras

Bracket *n.* modilyon, tukod, braket

Brain *n.* utak, katalinuhan, talino

Brake *n.* preno

Branch *n.* sanga, duklay, sangay

Brand *n.* marka, tatak, hero, uri

Brane *n.* Lamad

Brass *n.* tumbaga, bronse, tanso

Brat *n.* batang malikot

Brave *adj.* matapang

Brawl *n.* takapan, taltalan

Bread *n.* tinapay

Breadth *n.* lapad, luwang, papa

Break *v.* mabasag, bumasag, basagin, labagin

Breakfast *n.* agahan, almusal

Breast *n.* dibdib, pitso, suso

Breath *n.* hininga, hinga

Breathe *v.* hingahan, lumanghap, huminga

Breeze *n.* simoy, hihip

Bribe *n.* Suhol

Bribe *v.* sumuhol, suhulan

Brick *n.* ladrilyo

Bride *n.* nobya, lalaking ikinakasal

Bridegroom *n.* nobyo, lalaking ikakasal

Bridge *n.* tulay, taytay

Brief *adj.* maigsi, maigsingsabi

Brief *n.* alegato, pangangatwiran

Bright *adj.* makislap, maliwanag, masaya, matalino

Brilliant *adj.* maluningning, marilag, matalino

Brilliant *n.* hiyas, brilyante, diyamante

Bring *v.* magdala, dinala, nagdala, dalhin

Broad *adj.* maluwang, malapad

Broadcast *v.* magbalita, ikalat, magsabog, isabog

Brochure *n.* brosyur, pulyeto

Broke *adj.* bangkarota

Broken *adj.* sira, giba, nagambala

Brook *n.* batisan, sapa, batis

Broth *n.* sabaw, kaldo

Brother *n.* lalaking kapatid

Brown *adj.* kayumanggi, moreno

Browse *v.* magbasa-basa

Bruise *n.* pasa, gasgas, bugbog, lamog

Brunt *n.* tindi, lakas, bigat

Brush *n.* eskoba, sipilyo, tindi, brotsa

Brush *v.* eskubahin, sipilyuhin

Brutal *adj.* malupit, makahayop, brutal

Bubble *n.* bula, espuma, bulak

Bucket *n.* timba

Buckle *n.* hebilya

Bud *n.* buko, supang, usbong

Budge *v.* umibo, kumibo, gumalaw

Budget *n.* badyet, presupwesto

Buffalo *n.* kalabaw, tamaraw

Buffer *n.* depensa, tope, pambuli

Buffet *n.* sampal, suntok, bupe, istante

Build *v.* magtayo, gumawa, lumikha, magbuo

Builder *n.* konstruktor, magtatayo

Building *n.* gusali, edipisyo

Bulb *n.* bulbo, bombilya

Bulge *n.* umbok, tambok

Bulk *n.* laki, kalakhan, kabuuan

Bull *n.* bulla pontipisya, toro

Bullet *n* bala, punglo

Bulletin *n.* bulitin, ulat, report

Bullion *n.* bulyon, bara

Bump *v.* mabunggo, mauntog

Bun *n.* kuneho, pusod

Bunch *n.* buwig, kumpol, langkay

Bunch *v.* kumpulin

Bundle *n.* bigkis, tangkas, balutan, tali

Bungalow *n.* bunggalo

Bunk *n.* higaan

Buoy *n.* boya, palutang

Buoyant *adj.* lutang, masaya

Burden *n.* pasanin, sagutin

Bureau *n.* kawanihan, pupitre, eskritoryo

Burglar *n.* manloloob

Burial *n.* libing, paglilibing

Burn *v.* sunugin, nasunog, pasuin, banlian

Burnt *adj.* sunog, tupok, upos

Burst *v.* magputok, pumutok, nagputok

Bury *v.* ilibing, ibaon

Bus *n.* bus

Bush *n.* halaman, damo, talahib, mababang

Business *n.* kalakal, pangangalakal, negosyo, gawain

Busy *adj.* gawain, maraming, abala

But *adj.* kundi, lamang

But *conj.* Nguni't, datapwa't, subali't

Butcher *n.* mangangatay, butser

Butler *n.* mayorodomo

Butter *n.* mantikilya

Butterfly *n.* mariposa, paruparo

Buttocks *n.* puwit

Button *n.* butones, boton

Buy *n.* pagbili, pagkabili

Buy *v.* mamili, bumili, bilhin, ibili

Buyer *n.* mamimili, tagapamili

Buzz *n.* haging, agang

By *prep.* malapit sa, sa tabi ng

By-product *n.* residyo

Bygone *adj.* lumipas, nakalipas

C c

Cab *n.* taksi, piskante

Cabaret *n.* kabaret

Cabbage *n.* repolyo

Cabin *n.* kabanya, kamarote

Cabinet *n.* gabinete, istante, komoda

Cable *n.* kable, kablegrama

Cable *v.* kumbale, kablihan

Cachet *n.* seiyo, kapsula, kasye

Cadet *n.* kadete

Cadre *n.* kadre, balangkas

Caesarian *adj.* sesaryo, sesaryan

Cafe *n.* kapihan, kapiterya

Cage *n.* hawla, kulungan

Cajole *v.* manghibo, hibuin, manghimok, himukin

Cake *n.* puto, bibingka, kalamay, keyk, mamon

Calamity *n.* sakuna, kapahamakan, kalamidad

Calculate *v.* kuwentahin, tayahan, kalkulahin

Calculator *n.* kalkulador, tuusan

Calender *n.* kalendaryo, talaarawan, satinador

Calf *n.* bisiro, bulo

Caliber *n.* kalibre, kakayahan, kaurian

Call *n.* Pagtawag, sigaw, dalaw, pangalan, tawag

Call *v.* tawagin, manawagan, tumawag, dumalaw, ipatawag

Callosity *n.* lipak, kalyo

Calm *adj.* mahinahon, tahimik, payapa, panatag

Calm *adj.* tahimik, mahinahon, payapa, panatag

Calm *v.* lubagin, tiwasayin, huminahon, tumahimik

Calmness *n.* hinahon, katahimikan

Calumniate *v.* paratangan, siraang-puri

Camel *n.* kamelyo

Camera *n.* kamera

Camp *n.* kampo, kamp

Camp *v.* humimpil, magkampamento

Campaign *n.* kampanya, pakikilaban

Campaign *v.* magkampanya, makikampanya

Campfire *n.* siga sa kampo, pugata

Campus *n.* kampus

Can *n.* lata

Can *v.* ilata, latahin

Canal *n.* bambang, daluyan, kanal

Canary *n.* kanaryo

Cancel *v.* kaltasin, kanselahin, bawiin

Cancer *n.* kanser, kangkaro

Candidate *n.* kandidato

Candle *n.* kandila

Candy *n.* kendi

Cane *n.* tungkod, baston, tikin

Cannery *n.* delatahan, kaneri

Canopy *n.* pabelyon, habong

Canteen *n.* kantin, kantina

Canvas *n.* lona, kambas, liyenso

Cap *n.* gora, tapon, takip

Capability *n.* kapasidad, talino, kakayahan

Capable *adj.* kapas, magaling

Capacity *n.* kakayahan, tungkulin, lawak, bulumen, kakayahan

Cape *n.* kapote, kapa, abrigo, balabal, kabo, tangos

Capital *n.* puhunan, pinakalunsod, pangulong, kabisera

Capitulate *v.* sumuko

Capsicum *n.* sili

Capsule *n.* kapsula

Captain *n.* kapitan

Captive *adj.* kaptibo, nabihag, nabighani

Capture *v.* dakpin,, mabihag, bihagin, hulihin

Car *n.* kotse, auto, karo

Carat *n.* kilates

Caravan *n.* karabana, barkada

Card *n.* tarheta, kard, karton, komiko

Cardiac *adj.* kardiyako, pampuso

Cardigan *n.* kardigan

Care *n.* alaga, kandili, kalinga, asikaso

Care *v.* damayin, magmalasakit, alagaan

Career *n.* karera, propesyon, gawaing

Careful *adj.* maingat, maalaga

Careless *adj.* pabaya, halaghag, walang-ingat

Caress *n.* himas, lambing, karinyo, hagpos

Caress *v.* hagpusin, himasin, maglambing, aluin

Cargo *n.* lulan, karga, kargamento

Carnage *n.* patayan, matansa

Carnival *n.* karnabal

Carpenter *n.* karpintero, alwagi

Carpet *n.* alpombra, latag

Carriage *n.* kalesa, dalahan, karwahe, pagdadala, tindig, tikas

Carrot *n.* karot, sanaorya

Carry *v.* bitbitin, buhatin, magdala, dalhin, hakutin

Cart *n.* kareton

Cart *v.* hakutin

Cartage *n.* karitahe

Cartridge *n.* kartutso, punglo

Carve *v.* umukit, lilukin, ukitin, lumilok, manlilok

Case *n.* usapin, kaso, katayuan, kaha, kahon, lalagyan, ukulan

Cash *n.* pera, salapi, hawak, kuwaltang

Cashew *n.* balubad, kasuy

Cashier *n.* kahero

Casino *n.* kasino

Cast *n.* pukol, hagis, itsa

Cast *v.* ihagis, iitsa, ipukol, ibato

Castaway *adj.* itinapon, nabagbag, napadpad

Caste *n.* kasta, lipi

Castle *n.* kastilyo, tore

Casual *adj.* pahapyaw, kaswal, impormal, nagkataon

Casuality *n.* aksidente, sakuna, kapahamakan

Cat *n* pusa

Cataract *n. katarata, talon,* kulaba

Catch *n.* huli, nasilo, pansalo

Catch *v.* hulihin, dakpin, mahuli, maratnain

Cater *v.* magpakain, mangontrata, manustos

Caterer *n.* katerer, abastesedor

Caterpillar *n.* higad, tilas, uod

Cathedral *n.* katedral

Catholic *n.* katoliko

Cattle *n.* ganado, mga baka

Cause *n.* sanhi, dahilan, katwiran, mutibo

Cause *v.* papangyarihin, pagmulan, magbigay, usapin

Caution *n.* babala, ingat

Cave *n.* Yungib, kuweba

Cavity *n.* lugong, uka, butas

Cease *v.* tumigil, matapos, tapusin, tumila, huminto, itigil

Ceiling *n.* kisame, taluktok

Celebrate *v.* magdiwang, ipagdiwang, magpista

Celebration *n.* pagdiriwang

Celibacy *n.* selibato, pagpapakabasal

Cell *n.* piitan, silid, selda

Cement *n.* semento

Cemetary *n.* libingan, sementeryo

Cent *n.* Sentimo, pera

Center *n.* gitna

Central *adj.* sentral, gitna, kalagitnaan

Century *n.* dantaon, siglo

Ceremony *n.* galian, seremonya

Certain *adj.* tiyak, sigurado, totoo, ayos na

Certificate *n.* katibayan, katunayan, sertipiko

Certify *v.* patunayan

Chain *n.* tanikala, kadena

Chair *n.* silya, upuan

Chalk *n.* tisa, yeso, tsok

Challenge *n.* hamon, paghamon

Challenge *v.* hamunin, retuhin, hamitin

Chamber *n.* kuwarto, silid, kamara

Chamberlain *n.* tsambelan

Champ *v.* ngumalot, ngalutin

Champagne *n.* sampan, alak

Champion *n.* kampeon, tagapagtanggol, itaguyod

Chance *adj.* alisaga

Chance *n.* pasumala, pagkakataon

Chance *v.* magbakasakali

Change *n* pagbabago, pagpapalit, pamalit

Change *v*. baguhin, ibahin, magbago, baguhin

Channel *n*. agusan, daanan, tsanel

Chant *v*. umawit, kumanta

Chaos *n*. kaos, kasaligutgutan

Chapter *n*. kabanata, sangay, kapitulo

Character *n*. tauhan, katangian, karakter, letra, titik, uri

Charge *n*. sugod, tablay, pagbintang, karga, dala, kapanag

Charge *v*. sumugod, karga, dala, kapanagutan, tungkulin, magbintang, halaga, paratangan

Chariot *n*. karosa

Charity *n*. kawanggawa, limos, karidad

Charm *n*. bighani, alindog, gayuma, panghalina

Charm *v*. akitin, halinahin, gayumahin

Chart *n*. tsart, karta

Charter *v*. umupa, upahan, umarkila

Chase *v*. habulin, tugisin, hagarin

Chaste *adj*. kasto, basal, dalisay, busilak

Chat *v*. sumatsat, magusap, dumaldal

Chateau *n*. kastilyo

Chauffeur *n*. tsuper

Cheap *adj*. mura

Cheat *v*. mandaya, magdaya, dayain

Check *n*. pagmanman, tseke

Check *v*. tsekan, pigilan, patunayan, ihabilin, hakihin

Cheek *n*. pisngi

Cheer *n*. bunyi, damdamin, saya, buhay

Cheer *v*. pagbunyiin, aliwin, buhayin, aluin

Cheese *n*. keso

Chemist *n*. kimiko

Cherish *v*. mahalin, itangi

Cherry *n*. seresa

Chess *n*. ahedres

Chest *n*. dibdib, baol, kaha, kahon, kaban, pitso

Chestnuts *n*. kastaniyas

Chew *v*. nguyain, ngatain, ngumata

Chew *v*. nguyain, ngatain

Chicken *n*. manok

Chief *n*. hepe, puno, tsip

Chieftain *n*. datu, kabesa, ulo

Child *n* bata

Childhood *n*. kabataan, pagkabata

Childish *adj*. musmos, pambata

Chill *n*. ginaw, ngiki, kaligkig

Chill *v*. panlamigin, ngikihin

Chimney *n*. asuhan, tsiminea, tubo

Chin *n*. baba

Chip *n*. tatal, piraso, hilis, akba

Choice *n*. pagpili, opsiyon, pagkapili

Choke *v.* sakalin, mahirinan, inisin, mainis

Choose *v.* pilin, pumili, napili

Christian *n.* binyagan, kristiyano

Christmas *n.* pasko

Chum *n.* kaibigan, katoto

Church *n.* simbahan

Cigarette *n.* sigarilyo

Cinema *n.* sine, pelikula, sinihan

Cinnamon *n.* kanela

Cinnamon *n.* kanela

Cipher *n.* sero, pamilang

Circle *n.* bilog, sirkulo, paligid, paikot

Circle *v.* umikot, umaligid

Circuit *n.* palibot, paligid, ruta

Circular *adj.* pabilog, paikit, bilugan, paikot

Circulate *v.* kumalat, ilibot

Circulate *v.* umikit, lumigid, ilibot

Circumcise *v.* tuliin, patuli, patulian

Circumference *n.* kabilugan, sirkumperensiya, kabiligan, tikop

Circumstance *n.* tayo, katayuan, lagay

Circus *n.* sirko

Cist *n.* kato

Citizen *n.* mamamayan

City *n.* lungsod, siyudad

Civil *adj.* sibil, pambayan

Civilization *n.* kabihasnan

Clad *adj.* bihis, nagagayakan

Claim *n.* domanda, hiling

Claim *v.* angkinin, mag-domanda, inyuhin, hingin, angkinin

Clamp *v.* grapa, ipitan

Clan *n.* angkan, hinlog

Clap *v.* pumalakpak, mamayagpag

Clarify *v.* magpalinaw, linawin, ipaliwanag

Clash *v.* magkabangga

Clasp *v.* yakapin, yumakap, banggaan

Class *n.* uri, klase, pangkat, lipunan

Classify *v.* uriin

Clause *n.* artikulo, pangkat, sugnay

Claw *n.* kuko, gantso

Clay *n.* luwad, putik

Clean *adj.* malinis, dalisay

Clean *v.* linisin, maglinis

Clear *adj.* malinaw; maliwanag

Clerk *n.* tagasulat, kawani

Clever *adj.* marunong, matalino, suwitik, tuso

Cliff *n.* akyat, talampas

Climate *n.* klima, panahon

Climax *n.* kasukdulan, karurukan

Climb *v.* akyatin, umakyat

Clinch *n.* huling, pukpok, rimatse

Clinch *v.* ipirmi, irimatse, patibayan

Cling *v.* kumapit, dumikit, dumigkit, yapusan

Clinic *n.* klinika

Clip *v.* ikabit, isama, gupitin, putulin, tabasan

Cloak *n.* Kapa, manto

Clock *n.* orasan, relos

Clog *n.* bakya, hadlang

Close *adj.* malapit, tabi, masikip, sarado, malihim, lihim, nakapinid

Close *v.* isara, sarhan, ipinid, wakasan, takpan, yariin

Closet *n.* kloset, munting silid

Clot *v.* mamuo

Cloth *n.* tela, damit, kayo

Clothe *v.* damtan, magdamit, magbihis

Cloud *n.* alapaap, ulap, dagim

Cloud *v.* magdilim, manlabo

Cloudy *adj.* kulimlim, maulap

Clown *n.* bubo, payaso

Club *n.* klub, bambu, pamugbog, kiab

Clue *n.* himaton, bakas, susi, hiwatig

Cluster *n.* Kumpol, langkay, pumpon, buwig

Clutch *n.* hawak, klats, pagkapit

Clutch *v.* sunggaban, kapitan, humawak, kumapit

Coach *n.* kotse, tagasanay

Coal *n.* uling, karbon

Coalition *n.* koalisyon, pagsasama, pagkakaisa

Coarse *adj.* magalas, magaspang

Coast *n.* dalampasigan, baybayin

Coast *v.* padparin, tangayin

Coat *n.* kapa, balat, balok

Coax *v.* himukin, suyuin, utuin

Cobbler *n.* sapatero

Cobra *n.* ulupong, kobra

Cock *n.* tandang, liyabe, tatyaw

Cockpit *n.* sabungan, galyera

Cockroach *n.* ipis

Coconut *n.* niyog

Code *n.* batas, senyal, kodigo

Coffee *n.* kape

Coffin *n.* ataul, kabaong

Coherence *n.* ugnayan, ikaugnayan

Coil *n.* ikid, kidkid, rolyo

Coin *n.* barya, moneda, kuwalta, pera

Coincide *v.* magkasabay, masabay, mataon

Coincidence *n.* pagkakapagsabay, pagkakataon

Cold *adj.* maginaw, malamig, matamlay

Cold *n.* lamig, sipon, ginaw

Collaborate *v.* makipagtulungan

Collapse *v.* gumuho, masira

Collar *n.* kuwelyo, kulyar, kuwintas

Colleague *n.* kasama, kapanalig

Collect *v.* samsamin, tipunin, singilin

Collection *n.* tipon, katipunan

College *n.* kolehiyo, dalubhasaan

Collide *v.* mabangga, magkabanggaan

Colloquial *adj.* kolokyal, pangkaraniwan

Collusion *n.* sapakatan, sabwatan

Colonel *n.* koronel

Colony *n.* kolonya, lupang sakop

Color *n.* kulay, kolor, watawat

Color *v.* kulayan, koloran

Column *n.* pilar, haligi, tudling, hanay

Coma *n.* koma

Comb *n.* suklay, palong

Comb *v.* suklayin, magsuklay, galugarin

Combat *n.* labanan, kumbate

Combat *v.* lumaban, makibaka

Combination *n.* kombinasyon, pagsasama, halo

Combine *v.* pagsamahin, pagisahin

Come *v.* lumapit, dumating, sumapit

Comeback *n.* pagbabalik

Comedian *n.* komiko, payaso

Comfort *n.* ginhawa, kaginhawahan, kaaliwan, kaluwagan

Comfort *v.* aliwin, aluin, paginhawahin

Command *n.* pinagutasan, utos, atas

Command *v.* utasan, atasan, mag-utos

Commence *v.* magsimula, simulan, pumasok

Commend *v.* ihabilin, purihin

Comment *n.* pansin, puna, palagay

Commerce *n.* pangangalakal, kalakal

Commit *v.* gumawa, gawin, ipasok

Committee *n.* lupon, komite

Commodity *n.* kagamitan, tinda, kalakal

Common *adj.* pangkaraniwan, palasak, karaniwan, panlahat

Common sense *n.* muwang, dilidili

Communicate *v.* magsabi, sabihin, magbalita

Community *n.* komunidad, bayan, pook

Commute *v.* , palitan, papalitan

Compact *n.* kompac, baniti

Companion *n.* kasama, kasosyo, kasamahan

Company *n.* kompanya, dalaw, panauhin, pangkat

Compare *v.* ihambing, paghambingin

Compartment *n.* pitak, silid

Compass *n.* aguhon, kompas, palibot

Compassion *n.* awa, habag, simpatiya

Compel *v.* pilitin, pumilit, mamilit

Compensate *v.* bayaran, tumbasan, tapatan, pantayan

Compete *v.* magpaligsahan, sumali, makipagpaligsahan

Competition *n.* paligsahan, tunggalian, paglalaban

Competitor *n.* kasangga, manlalaro

Compile *v.* kompilahin, tipunin

Complain *v.* magsumbong, magreklamo, dumaing, idaing

Complaint *n.* sumbong, reklamo

Complement *n.* komplemento, pampuno, pambuo

Complete *adj.* tapos, ganap, puno, lubos, buo, lahat

Complete *v.* buuin, tapusin, yariin

Complex *n.* hugnayan, magusot, masalimuot

Complexion *n.* kulay, kutis, anyo

Complicate *v.* guluhin, magpagulo, pahirapin

Compliment *n.* papuri, bati, alaalaCondense

Comply *v.* sumunod, tumalima, sundin

Compose *v.* himigan, bumuo, buuin, gumawa

Composer *n.* kompositor, kahista, manunula

Composition *n.* komposisyon, likhain

Compound *adj.* kompuwesto, sangkapan, haluan

Compound *n.* kampo, looban

Comprehend *v.* matanto, manunawaan

Conceal *v.* itago, ikubli

Concede *v.* ipagkaloob, ibigay, sumuko

Conceit *n.* pagmamagaling, siging, ego, banidad

Conceive *v.* maglihi, isaisip, isipin, makaisip

Concept *n.* isip, isipan, palagay

Concern *n.* malasakit, kapakanan, pakialam

Concern *v.* pinagmalasakitan, mabahala, maukol

Concession *n.* kaloob, konsesyon, pagkilala

Concise *adj.* maikli, mahigsi

Conclude *v.* magtapos, tapusin

Concrete *adj.* kongkreto, tunay, nadrama, tahas

Condemn *v.* parusahan, hatulan, sumpain

Condense *v.* kondensahin, pikpikin, paigsiin

Condition *n.* kalagayan, tadhana, kondisyon

Condition *v.* sanayin

Conduct *n.* asal, pamamaraan

Conduct *v.* samahan, pamatnugutan, kumilos, akayin

Cone *n.* kono

Conference *n.* komperensiya, pulong

Confess *v.* mangumpisal, aminin, tapatin

Confidence *n.* tiwala, pagtitiwala

Confirm *v.* patibayan, pagtibayin, patunayan

Confiscate *v.* samsamin, ilitir.

Conflict *n.* pagkakasalungatan, labanan, hidwaan

Confuse *v.* guluhin, lituhin

Congratulate *v.* batiin, bumati

Congratulations *n.* bati, pagbati

Congress *n.* konggreso, kapulungan

Conjunction *n.* , pangatnig

Conjure *v.* magmahiya, magsalamangka

Connect *v.* ikabit, pagugpungin, ugnayin

Conquer *v.* lupigin, manakop, malupig

Conquest *n.* paglupig, kongkista

Conscience *n.* budhi

Conscious *adj.* makamalayaan, nadarama

Consent *n.* pahintulot

Consent *v.* pumayag, payagan

Consequence *n.* konsekwensiya, bunga, kahihinatnan

Conserve *v.* ingatan, pangalagaan, magkonserba

Consider *v.* pinagiisipan, gunamgunamin, isipin, ipalagay

Consideration *n.* pakundangan, pagbibigay, taros

Consign *v.* ibigay, ilipat, dalhin, paalagaan

Consignee *n.* pinagbigyan, pinagpadalhan

Consignment *n.* maypaiwi, maypatinda

Consist *n.* buuin

Console *v.* aliwin, libangin

Consolidate *v.* pagsamahin, palakasin

Constant *adj.* matibay, matapat, pirmihan

Constitute *v.* hirangin, nombrahan, itatag

Constitution *n.* konstitusyon, pagsasabatas, pagtatatag

Constrain *v.* pilitin, igapos, gapusin, pisilin

Construct *v.* yumari, itayo, magtayo, magbuo, gumawa

Consulate *n.* konsulado

Consult *v.* magkonsulta, kumunsulta, isangguni, sanggunlin

Consume *v.* kainin, lamunin, ubusin, lipulin

Consumer *n.* mamimili, tagabili, tagagamit

Consumption *n.* konsumo, kinain, nakain, pakkaubos, nalamon

Contact *n.* kontakto, sagi, hipo, dugtong, pakikitungo

Contact *v.* kontakin, isagi, sagiin

Contain *v.* lakipan, maglaman, lamnan, malaman

Contempt *n.* paghamak, panghihiya

Contend *v.* makiagaw, ikatwiran, imatwid

Content *n.* kapasidad, laman, nilalaman, kahulugan

Content *v.* masiyahan, pairugan, pagbigyan

Conterfeit *v.* manghuwad, huwaran

Contest *n.* timpalak, paligsahan, labanan

Contest *v.* tutulan, labanan

Context *n.* kawawaan, susing, kahulugan

Continue *v.* magpatuloy, ipagpatuloy, tumuloy, ituloy

Continuous *adj.* Panay, parati, tuloy-tuloy

Contract *n.* kasunduan, kontrata

Contradict *v.* salungatin, sumalungat

Contrary *adj.* laban, tutol, kaiba, labag

Contrast *n.* kaibhan, pagiiba

Contravene *v.* salungatin, sumalungat, lumabag

Contribute *v.* mag-ambag, umambag, ambagan, dagdagan

Control *n.* kontrol, katimpian, hunusdili, pangyarihan, makapigil

Control *v.* kontrolin, timpiin, ayusin, supilin, pigilin, magpigil, kotrolin

Controversy *n.* pagtatalo, alitan

Convene *v.* magtipon, paharapin

Convenience *n.* kaginhawahan, kaluwagan, kabagayan, alwan

Convenient *adj.* maginhawa, maalwan

Conversation *n.* usapan, kombersasyon, slitaan

Convey *v.* dalhin, isakay, ipabatid, ilipat

Conveyance *n.* pagdadala, pagsasabi, paglilipat, sasakyan

Convict *n.* bilanggo, preso

Convict *v.* hatulan

Convince *v.* papaniwalain, kumbinsihin, hikayatin

Convoy *n.* kumboy, eskorte, agapay

Cook *n.* kusinero, tagapagluto

Cook *v.* lutuin, iluto, magluto

Cool *adj.* malamig, presko, mahinahon

Cool *v.* lumamig, palamigin

Cooperate *v.* magtulungan, makipagtulungan

Cooperation *n.* kooperasyon, pagtutullungan

Coordinate *adj.* kapantay, kahanay, kauri

Copper *n.* tanso, kobre, tumbaga

Copy *n.* sipi, kopya

Copy *v.* huwarin, sipiin, isalin, kopyahin

Cord *n.* pisi, lubid, tali, panali

Core *n.* ubod, kalagitnaan

Cork *n.* tapon, kortso

Corn *n.* binatog, mais, kalyo, lipak

Corner *n.* sulok, kanto, panulukan

Corner *v.* salukubin

Corpse *n.* bangkay

Correct *adj.* tama, wasto, tuwid

Correct *v.* wastuin, iwasto, itama, itumpak

Correspond *v.* magkatugon, magkabagay, sumulat, magsulatan

Corrupt *adj.* imbi, bulok

Corrupt *v* pasamain, parumihing, budhi

Cosmetic *n.* kosmetiko

Cost *n.* presyo, halaga, bayad, singil

Cost *v.* magkahalaga, ipabayad, ipagasta, napresyuhan, napresyuhan

Costume *n.* kasuutan, damit, pananamit

Cot *n.* tiheras, kubo, dampa, kamilya

Cottage *n.* bahaybahayan, kabanya, kasutsa, dampa

Cotton *n.* bulak, algodon, koton

Couch *n.* higaan, supa, hiligan, silyon

Couch *v.* itago, balutin, takpan

Cough *n.* ubo, tikhim

Cough *v.* inubo, umubo, ubuhin

Council *n.* sanggunian, konsilyo, konseho, kapulungan

Counsel *n.* payo, abugado, konseho, tagapayo

Count *n.* bilang, numero

Count *v.* bilangin, bumilang, asahan, magbilang, isama

Counter *n.* pambilang, numerador, kaha

Counterfeit *adj.* huwad

Country *n.* bayan, kabukiran, distrito, purok, bansa, bukid, lupang

Couple *n.* dalawa, magasawa, pares

Courage *n.* katapangan, tapang

Courier *n.* kuryer

Course *n.* kurso, putahe, karera, ruta, daan

Course *v.* dumaan, paraanin

Court *n.* hukuman, patyo, korte, patyo, husgado, korte

Court *v.* dalawin, ligawin, lumigaw

Courtesy *n.* pitagan, paglilingkod, pagbibigay, kortesiya

Cousin *n.* pinsan

Cover *n.* takip, taklob, kulob, plato

Cover *v.* takpan, takluban, talukbungan, matapos, sumaklaw

Cow *n.* baka

Coward *adj.* naduwag, duwag

Cozy *adj.* maginhawa, maalwan

Crab *n.* alimango, alimasag

Crack *n.* lamat, putok, lagitik, basag,·lamat

Crack *v.* lamatan, basagin, pumutok, batikan

Cracker *n.* kraker, paputik

Cradle *n.* duyan, kuna, aluyan, indanayan

Crash *n.* kalabog, lagapak, tagupak

Crash *v.* kalabugin, bumagsak, kumalabog

Crave *v.* sumamo, mamanhik, naisin

Crawl *v.* gumapang, umusad

Craze *v.* maloko, masiraan ng

Crazy *adj.* loko, ulol, hibang

Cream *n.* krema, kakanggata, gatas

Create *v.* likha, lumikha, likhain, lalangin

Creature *n.* nilikha, nilalang, kinapal

Credit *n.* kredito, mabuting, pangalan, dangal

Credit *v.* maniwala, paniwalaan

Creed *n.* pananampalataya, pananalig, kredo

Crest *n.* palong, plumahe, itaas, taluktok

Crew *n.* tripulante, manggagawa

Crime *n.* krimen, malubhang, pagkakasala

Criminal *adj.* pangsalarin, kriminal

Criminal *n.* salarin, kriminal

Crisis *n.* krisis

Critic *n.* kritiko, mamumuna, tagapuna

Critical *adj.* palapintasin, masuri, malubha, patawirin

Crocodile *n.* buwaya

Crop *n.* ani, tanim, butse, puti

Cross *n.* kurus, dusa, sakripisyo

Cross *v.* tumawid, itawid

Crow *n.* uwak

Crowd *n.* matao, gitgit, pulutong

Crowd *v.* siksikan, gitgitan

Crown *n.* korona, putong

Cruel *adj.* malupit, mabalasik

Crush *v.* pisain, ipitan, durugin, pasukuin, pigain, pipihin, mapisa

Cry *n.* tangis, iyak, sigaw, hiyaw

Cry *v.* iyakan, sumigaw, humiyaw, umiyak

Cuddle *v.* kalungkungin, yumakap, yapusin

Cuff *n.* sampal, punyos, tampal

Cuisine *n.* pangungusina, pagluluto

Cult *n.* kulto, rito

Cultivate *v.* linanging, maglinang, magbungkal

Culture *n.* kultura, kalinangan, pamungkal

Cumbersome *adj.* mabigat, maligalig, nakaaabala

Cunning *adj.* tuso, switik

Cup *n.* tasa, tason, kopa, puswelo

Cupboard *n.* paminggalan, platera

Curb *n.* barbada, pamigil, gilid

Curdle *v.* mamuo, makurta, lumapot

Cure *n.* hilom, lunas, gamot

Cure *v.* pagalingin, gamutin, lunasan

Curious *adj.* mausisa, kuryoso

Curl *adj.* Kulot

Currency *n.* kuwarta, pananalapi, salukuyan

Current *adj.* kasalukuyan, laganap, kumakalat

Current *n.* agos, saloy, kuryente

Curse *n.* panunumpa, sumpa, tungayaw, lait

Curse *v.* sumpain, tungayawin, laitin, manlait

Curtail *v.* pungusan, bawahan

Curtain *n.* tabing, kortina, telon

Curve *n.* kurba, kakurbahan, liko

Cushion *n.* kutson, almuwada, salubayo

Custom *n.* kaugalian, gawi, ugali, asal

Customs *n.* adwana

Cut *n.* putol, hiwa, bawas, gilit, tabas, istilo

Cut *v.* magputol, putlin, pumutol, saksakin, hiwain, iwaan

Cycle *n.* siklo, ikot, ligid, panahon

Cyclist *n.* siklista

Cyclone *n.* siklon, buhawi, bagyo, unos

Cylinder *n.* silindro, bumbungan

Cypher *n.* sipra, sero, wala

Crystal *n.* bubog, kristal

Cyst *n.* kisto, suron, kato

D d

Dad/ Daddy *n.* ama, tatang, tatay, itay

Dagger *n.* sundang, punyal, balaraw, balisong

Daily *adj.* pangarawaraw, arawan, arawaraw

Dainty *adj.* pino, maayos, masarap, maganda

Dairy *n.* pagatasan, letseriya

Dais *n.* pagatasan, letseriya

Dale *n.* labak, lambak

Dam *n.* tabon, pirinsahan

Damage *n.* sira, pinsala, pagkasira

Damage *v.* sirain

Dame *n.* dama, ale, sinyora

Damn *v.* sumpain, laitin

Damp *adj.* basa, mahalumigmig, umedo, matamlay

Dance *n.* sayawan, sayaw

Dance *v.* magsayaw, sumayaw

Dancer *n.* mananayaw

Dandruff *n.* balakubak

Danger *n.* panganib, piligro

Dangerous *adj.* mapanganib, piligroso

Dangling *adj.* bitin, nakalawit, nakabitin

Dare *v.* hamunin, mangahas, pangahasan

Dark *adj.* madilim, maitim, malagim

Dark *n.* paglilihim

Darken *v.* dilimin, padilimin, papagdilimin

Darkness *n.* karimlan, tiniblas, dilim

Darling *n.* giliw, mahal, sinta, irog

Dart *n.* igtad, palaso, hagibis, suligi

Dash *n.* hampas, gatlang, pagkabigo, salpok

Dash *v.* isalpok, ihagis, dumaluhong, ibagsak

Data *n.* datos, bagay-bagay

Date *n.* ligawan, petsa, tiyapan, panahon

Date *v.* dalawin, ligawan, petsahan

Daughter *n.* anak na babae, iha

Dawn *n.* bukang-liwayway

Day *n.* araw, panahon

Daze *v.* tuliruhin, tuligin, matulig, matuliro

Dazzle *v.* silawin, masilaw, mapahanga, magpahanga

Dead *adj.* patay, yumao

Deaf *adj.* bingi

Deal *n.* pamimigay, trato, bilihan, kasunduan

Deal *v.* makipagayos, ipamigay, makitungo, mamigay, nagbibili

Dealer *n.* komersiyante, bangkero, negosyante

Dear *adj.* mahal, masinta, sinta

Dear *n.* giliw, minamahal, sinta, irog

Dearth *n.* kakulangan, kasalatan, kawalan

Death *n.* kamatayan, pagkamatay

Debacle *n.* baha, guho, sakuna

Debate *n.* pagtatalo, diskusyon, pakikipagtalo

Debate *v.* makipagtalo, magtalo

Debit *n.* debito, pagkakautang

Debris *n.* sukal, yabat, guho

Debt *n.* utang, sala, pagkakasala

Debut *n.* dibu, unang, labas, pasinaya

Decade *n.* dekada, sampungtaon

Decade *n.* dekada, sampungtaon

Decant *n.* itigis, isalin

Decay *n.* bulok, pagkasira, pagkagapok

Decay *v.* bulukin, mabulok, masira, mabilasa

Deceased *adj.* patay, nasira, yumao, namatay

Deceit *n.* daya, pagdaraya

Deceive *v.* lokohin, magdaya, dayain, linlangin

December *n.* disyembre

Deception *n.* desepsiyon, daya, lalang, linlang

Decide *v.* hatulan, mapagisipan, pasiyahan, magpasiya

Decimal *n/adj* desimal

Decision *n.* pasiya, hatol, kapasiyahan, disisyon

Decisive *adj.* mapanghatol, disisibo, madali, maagap

Deck *n.* sahig, kubyerta

Declare *v.* ipahayag, magpahayag, ideklara, isaysay

Decline *v.* lumiko, suminsay, tumanggi, tumungo

Decode *v.* desiprahin

Decompose *v.* malansag, magapok, bulukin, bayaang

Decorate *v.* magdekorasyon, magpalamuti, gayakan, gandahan

Decoration *n.* dekorasyon, adorno, gayak

Decoy *n.* pangati, pain

Decrease *n.* bawas, pagunti, panghina, pagliit

Decrease *v.* bawasan, awasin, paliitin, lumiit, umikli

Decree *n.* utos, batas, dekreto

Dedicate *v.* ihandog, ialay, ilaan, itaan

Deduce *v.* maghulo, huluin

Deduct *v.* bawasin, alisin, huluin

Deed *n.* titulo, gawa, asanya, akto, aksiyon

Deem *v.* akalain, ipalagay, isipin

Deep *adj.* malalim, seryo, lubog

Deep *n.* lalim

Deepen *v.* laliman, palaliman

Deer *n.* usa

Deface *v.* dungisan, dispigurahan

Defame *v.* pulaan, manirang-puri

Defeat *n.* katalunan, pagkatalo, pagsuko, pagkalupig

Defeat *v.* talunin, tumalo, lupigin, malupig

Defect *n.* sira, kapintasan, depekto

Defend *v.* ipagtanggol, magtanggol, ipagsanggalang

Defense *n.* tanggulan, depensa, pagtatanggol

Defer *n.* ipagpaliban, antalahin, ibitin, pumayag

Defiance *n.* hamon, panghahamon, paglaban

Deficiency *n.* kakulangan, pagkukulang

Deficit *n.* depisit, pagkukulang

Define *v.* ipaliwanag, ilarawan, uriin

Definite *adj.* tiyak, direkto, eksekto, malinaw

Definition *n.* katuturan, kalinawan

Deflate *v.* paimpisin, makumpis, pakupisin

Deflation *n.* pagkaimpis, pagkakupis

Defraud *v.* mandaya, dayain, ilitin

Defy *v.* manghamon, hamunin, labanan

Degenerate *v.* bumaba, sumama, masira, mabulok

Degrade *v.* ibaba, pababain, itiwalag

Degree *n.* antas, baitang, digri, grado, sidhi

Deity *n.* diyos, bathala

Delay *n.* antala, pagpigil, pagpapaliban

Delay *v.* antalahin, pigilan, bimbinin

Delegate *n.* kinatawan, delegado

Delegation *n.* delegasyon, pagpapakatawan

Delete *v.* kaltasin, alisin, burahin

Deliberate *adj.* sinadya, mahinay, kusa, sadya

Deliberate *v.* bulay-bulayin, wariin, sumangguni

Delicacy *n.* kisig, kapinuhan, dilikadesa, gulusina

Delicate *adj.* marupok, pino, maselang, delikado

Delicious *adj.* masarap, malinamnan

Delight *n.* galak, tuwa, lugod, saya

Delight *v.* nagalak, matuwa, galakin, pasayahin

Delineate *v.* idrowing, iguhit, ilarawan

Deliver *v.* dalhin, ihatid, iligtas, hanguin

Delivery *n.* pagkahatid, dinala, hatid, pagbigkas

Delude *v.* linlangin, manlinlang

Delve *v.* magdukal, dukalin, saliksikin

Demand *n.* hingi, hiling

Demand *v.* hilingin, hingin

Demarcation *n.* patuto, hangganan

Demerit *n.* demerit, kasalanan, kapintasan

Demise *n.* pagyao, pagkamatay, kamatayan

Demobilize *v.* magdemobilisa, demobilisahin

Democracy *n.* demokrasya

Democratic *adj.* demokratiko, pambayan, pangmadla

Demolish *v.* paguhuin, iguho, wasakin, gibain

Demolition *n.* pagpapaguho, paggiba

Demon *n.* demonyo, impakto, diyablo

Demonstrate *v.* ipakita, ituro, ipamalas, mamahayag, ilarawan

Demote *v.* ibaba, idemot

Den *n.* lungga, den, kuweba, selda, yungib

Denial *n.* pagtanggi, pagkakait, pagkakaila

Denominate *v.* ngalanan

Denomination *n.* denominasyon, sekta, uring-tawag

Denotation *n.* palatandaan, himaton, kahulugan

Denounce *v.* isuplong, idinunsiya, isumbong, tuligsain, atakihin

Dense *adj.* kitkit, makapal, masikip, masinsin, malapot

Density *n.* densidad, tanga, katangahan, kasinsinan, kakapalan

Dent *n.* yupi

Dent *v.* mayupi

Dental *adj.* dental, pangngipin

Dentist *n.* dentista

Denude *v.* maagnas, hubaran

Deny *v.* tumanggi, ipagkait, itatwa, tanggihan, pagkaitan itanggi, magtatwa, magkait, tatwaan

Deodorant *adj.* pamawingamoy

Depart *v.* umalis, yumao, lumisan, mamatay

Departed *adj.* lumipas, nakaraan, nasira, panahong

Department *n.* kagawaran, departamento, sangay

Departure *n.* paglisan, umasa, manghawakan

Depend *v.* umasa, magtiwala, manangan, masalig

Deplete *v.* ubusin, sairin, masaid, maubos

Deplore *v.* malungkot, manghinayang

Deploy *v.* mangalat, magsikalat

Deport *v.* ipatapon, idestiyero

Deportment *n.* asal, ugali, kikilos

Deposit *n.* lagak, deposito, tambak, tining

Deposit *v.* ilagak, ilagay, maglagak

Depot *n.* bodega, dipo, lagakan, imbakan

Depreciate *v.* murahan, maliitin

Depreciation *n.* depresyasyon, pagmamaliit

Depress *v.* diinang, pababa, ibaba, patamlayin

Depression *n.* uka, lugong, lumbay, kagipitan

Deprive *v.* alisan, agawan, pagkaitan

Depth *n.* lalim

Deputation *n.* deputasyon, delegasyon

Deputy *n.* diputado, kinatawan

Derail *v.* diskarilin, madiskaril

Derivation *n.* pinagkunan, pinagmulan, pinaghanguan

Derive *v.* kunin, manggaling

Descend *v.* bumaba, lumusong

Descent *n.* pagbaba, paglusong, angkan, lipi, lahi

Describe *v.* ilarawan, maglarawan, iguhit

Description *n.* deskripsiyon, paglalarawan

Desert *n.* desyerto, disyerto, ilang

Desert *v.* iwan, lisanin, tumakas, takasan

Desertion *n.* desersiyon, pagiwan, paglisan, pagtakas

Deserve *v.* magindapat

Deserved *adj.* tapat, lapat, wasto

Design *n.* disenyo, guhit, plano, dibuho

Design *v.* magplano, magdisenyo, magdibuho

Desire *n.* nais, nasa, pita, hangad, lunggati

Desire *v.* magnasa, pitahin, pumita, magnais, naisin

Desist *v.* tumigil, tigilan, huminto

Desk *n.* mesa, sulatan, desk,mesita, pupitre

Desperate *adj.* desperado, maton

Despise *v.* pagmataasan, kamuhian, hamakin

Despite *n.* poot, malisya, kapootan, pagkapoot

Dessert *n.* postre, himagas

Destination *n.* destinasyon, pupuntahan, destino

Destine *v.* idestino, italaga, maukol

Destiny *n.* destino, palad, hantungan

Destitute *adj.* dahop, hikahos

Destitution *n.* kawalan, kasalatan, karukhaan

Destroy *v.* wasakin, patayin, gibain, ibagsak, puksain

Destruction *n.* pagkasira, pagkawasak

Destructive *adj.* nakasisira, panira, mapanira

Detach *v.* kalagin, kalasin, ihiwalay, ibukod

Detail *n.* detalye, bahagi

Detail *v.* italaga

Detain *v.* pigilin, bimbinin, antalahin

Detect *v.* tiktikan, tuklasin, matuklasan

Detective *n.* detektib, tiktik

Detention *n.* pagkaantala, pagkakapigil

Deter *v.* hadlangan

Deteriorate *v.* sumama, manghina

Determine *v.* hangganan, tapusin, wakasan, tiyakin

Detest *v.* mamuhi, kamuhian

Detonate *v.* paputukin

Detour *n.* lihis, ditur, sinsayan, ligiran

Detour *v.* magditur, lumigid, suminsay

Detract *v.* alipustain, kutyain, aglahiin

Detriment *n.* sira, pinsala

Detrition *n.* pagkagasgas

Devaluate *n.* ibaba, babaan ng halaga

Devastate *n.* tupukin, puksain, lipulin

Develop *v.* ihayag, patubuin, lumaki, pakilusin

Development *n.* paglalahad, pagtalakay, paglaki

Deviate *v.* lumihis, lumiko, guminda

Deviation *n.* paglihis, pagliko, pagginda

Device *n.* pamamaraan, imbento, sagisag, pakana, kasangkapan

Devil *n.* diyablo, dimonyo

Devil *v.* paanghangan

Devious *adj.* naliligaw, baluktot, namamali

Devise *v.* magbalak, lumikha

Devolve *v.* malipat, masalin, mapasalin

Devote *v.* iukol, magtalaga, italaga, ihandog,magpakalubog

Devotee *n.* deboto

Devotion *n.* debosyon, panata, pagsinta

Devour *v.* lamunin, sabsabin, laklakin, silain, tapukin

Devout *adj.* mapanata, banal, tapat, taimtim, tapat

Dew *n.* hamog

Dewy *adj.* mahamog

Diabetes *n.* diyabetes

Diagram *n.* dayagram, balangkas

Dial *n.* dayal, mukha

Dial *v.* dumuyal, dayalin

Dialect *n.* diyalekto, wika

Dialogue *n.* diyalogo, salitaan, sagutan

Dialysis *n.* dialisis, pagtunaw, pagbubukod

Diaper *n.* lampin

Diaphragm *n.* diyapragma, binubong, membrana

Diarrhea *n.* kurso, bululos

Diary *n.* talaarawan

Dice *n.* betu-beto

Dictate *n.* utos, atas, mando

Dictate *v.* magdikta, idikta, iutos, utusan

Dictation *n.* pagdidikta

Dictator *n.* diktador

Dictionary *n.* talatinigan, diksiyunaryo

Diddle *v.* magtatarang, magkandirit

Die *n.* dado, molde, estampador

Die *v.* matay, mamatay, mawala, masabik, huminto

Diet *n.* diyeta

Differ *v.* maiba, mabukod, magkaiba

Difference *n.* kahidwaan, kaibahan, diperensiya, pagkakaiba

Different *adj.* iba, magkaiba, hiwalay, sarisari

Differential *n.* diperensiyal

Differentiate *v.* ibahin

Difficult *adj.* mahirap, dimaalwan

Difficulty *n.* kahirapan, kagipitan, kagipitan, krisis

Diffuse *adj.* kalat, laganap

Diffuse *v.* kumalat, mangalat, pakalatin

Dig *n.* hukayan, bungkal

Dig *v.* hukayan, hinukay, maghukay, magdukal, dukalin

Digest *n.* buod, kodigo

Digest *v.* tunawin, matunaw, paigsiin, buurin

Digestion *n.* dihestiyon, panunaw

Digit *n.* numero, pamilang, dali, pigura, daliri

Dignify *v.* dangalin, parangalan

Dignitary *n.* dignitaryo, taong mahal

Dignity *n.* dignidad, kamahalan, karangalan

Dilemma *n.* dilema, linggatong, suliranin

Dilute *v.* labnawin, magbanto, bantuan

Dim *adj.* malamlan, malabo

Dim *v.* palabuin, padilimin, padimlan

Dimension *n.* dimensiyon, sukat , laki, lawak, halaga

Diminish *v.* magbawas, bawasan, lumiit, umunti, humina

Dimple *n.* biloy

Din *n.* linggal

Dindle *n.* kumalating

Dine *v.* mananghalian, maghapunan

Diner *n.* kainan, kumedor

Dingy *adj.* nangingitim, maagiw

Dinner *n.* hapunan, piging, tanghalian

Dint *n.* pukpok, hampas, lakas

Dip *n.* sawsaw, libis, lubog, lusong, tubog, labak, tungo

Dip *v.* isawsaw, ilubog, itubog, basain

Diplomacy *n.* diplomasya

Diplomat *n.* diplomatiko

Dipper *n.* sandok, panalok

Direct *adj.* direkto, tiyakan

Direct *v.* ituro, akayin

Direction *n.* gawi, panuto, turo, hilig, dako

Directly *adv.* tuwiran, kaagad

Director *n.* patnugot, direktor

Directorate *n.* patnugutan

Directory *n.* direktoryo

Dirk *n.* daga, balaraw, punyal

Dirt *n.* dumi, karumhan

Dirty *adj.* marumi, mahalay, masama

Disability *n.* kasalantaan

Disappear *v.* mawala, maparam, maglaho

Disappearance *n.* pagkawala, paglalaho

Disappoint *v.* biguin, mabigo

Disappointed *adj.* nabigo

Disappointment *n.* kabiguan, pagkabigo

Disapprove *v.* di-inaprubahan

Disaster *n.* disastro, sakuna, kapahamakan

Disband *v.* buwagin, tangkalagin

Disburse *v.* magbayad, bayaran, gumugol, gugulan

Discard *v.* itapon, iwaksi, alisin, tapon

Discern *v.* makita, mamalas, makilala

Discharge *v.* madiskarga, kalagan, itiwalag, diskargahin, gumanap magbaba, ibaba

Disciple *n.* disipulo, alagad

Discipline *n.* pasunod, disiplina, panunupil, pagsupil

Discipline *v.* disiplinahin, parusahan

Disclose *v.* ipaalam, ihayag, isiwalat

Discomfort *n.* balisa

Disconnect *v.* paghiwalayin, tanggalin, lagutin, putulin

Discontent *n.* di-nasisiyahan

Discontinue *v.* tumigil, itigil, tigilan

Discord *n.* alitan, labanan

Discount *n.* deskuwento, bawas, tawad

Discount *v.* bawasin, alisin

Discourage *v.* sirain ang loob, pigilin

Discourse *n.* pagpapahayag, paglalahad, panayam, talumpati

Discourse *v.* magpahayag, ipahayag, ilahad, talakayin

Discourteous *adj.* bastos

Discover *n.* tuklas, pagtuklas, pagkatuklas

Discover *v.* tuklasin

Discover *v.* matagpuan, malaman, matuklasan

Discreet *adj.* maalaga, maingat

Discrepancy *n.* kaibahan, pagkaiba

Discrete *adj.* hiwalay, bukod

Discretion *n.* pagkahiwalay, pagkabukod, kabaitan

Discriminate *adj.* iba-iba, nagtatangi, mapagtangi

Discriminate *v.* pagbukudbukirin, itangi

Discrimination *n.* diskriminasyon, pagtatangi

Discuss *n.* diskas

Discuss *v.* magusap, talakayin, magtalo, pagusapan, mangatwiran

Discussion *n.* pagusapan, salitaan, pagtatalakay, pagtatalo

Disease *n.* sakit, pagkakasakit

Disembarkation *n.* paglunsad

Disembarked *v.* lumunsad, bumaba

Disengage *v.* bumitiw, bitiwan, kumalag, kalagin

Disgrace *n.* kahihiyan, kaayupan

Disguise *n.* balatkayo, dispras

Disguise *v.* magdispras, magbalatkayo

Disgust *n.* suya, pagkamuhi, pagkaani

Disgust *v.* nasuya

Dish *n.* pingan, ulam, plato, pagkain

Dish *v.* sandukin

Dishonest *adj.* ditapat, madaya, magdaraya

Dishonor *n.* hiya, kaayupan, kahihiyan

Disillusion *n.* disilusyon, pagkamatay

Disinfect *v.* disimpektáhin, maglanggas, langgasin

Disinfectant *n.* disinpektante, panlanggas

Disintegrate *v.* madurog, mapiraso

Disk *n.* disko, plaka

Dislike *n.* pagayaw, antipatiya

Dislike *v.* ayàwan, umayaw

Dislocated *adj.* linsad, bali, nabalian

Dislodge *v.* maitaboy, matigkal

Disloyal *adj.* sukab, lilo

Dismal *adj.* malagim, nakasisindak

Dismay *v.* gulatin, sindakin, papanlumuhin

Dismiss *v.* itiniwalag, pauwiin, itiwalag, pinaalis, dismisin, paalisin

Disobey *v.* suwayin, sumuway

Disorder *n.* gulo, gusot, kagusutan

Disorganize *v.* guluhin

Disown *v.* itatwa, itawil

Dispatch *n.* mensahe, pahatid, pagpatay

Dispatch *v.* magpadala, palakarin, tapusinagad, ipadala

Dispel *v.* itaboy, iaboy, alisin, pawiin

Dispensary *n.* dispensaryo, pagamutan

Dispense *v.* ilapat, mamahagi, patawarin, ipairal

Disperse *v.* mangalat, ikalat, ihasik, pawiin

Displace *v.* tinagin, paalisin

Display *n.* pakita, pamalas, tanghal, parada

Display *v.* ipakita, iladlad, itanghal, iparada

Displease *v.* galitin

Disposal *n.* ayos, pagsasaayos, pagtatapon

Dispose *v.* iayos, ayusin, italaga, itapon

Dispute *n.* pagtatalo, tutol

Dispute *v.* magtalo, pagtalunan, tumutol, tutulan

Disregard *v.* huwag, pansinin, bayaan

Disrupt *v.* lagutin, guluhin

Dissatisfaction *n.* sama ng loob

Disseminate *v.* maghasik, ipangalat, magsabog, isabog, ikalat

Dissent *v.* sumalungat

Dissert *v.* tumalakay, talakayin

Dissolute *adj.* mabisyo, marawal

Dissolution *n.* pagkasira, pagkatunaw, pagwawakas

Dissolve *v.* tunawin, matunaw, magtunaw, tapusin

Dissuade *v.* pigilan

Distance *n.* agwat, layo, pagitan, distansiya

Distant *adj.* malayo, hiwalay

Distend *v.* lumuwang, mahiklat, lumaki, lumapad, lumawak

Distinct *adj.* iba, kaiba, bukod, tangi

Distinction *n.* kaibahan, pagkaiba, tanda, karangalan

Distinguish *v.* uriin, pinasikat

Distinguish *v.* makilala, kilalanin, itanyag

Distort *v.* ibahin, baguhin, baluktutin

Distract *v.* guluhin, gambalain

Distraction *n.* distraksiyon, kaguluhan, kalituhan

Distress *n.* sakit, bagabag, dusa, takot, pighati

Distribute *v.* ipamahagi, ikalat, ipangalat, mamigay

District *n.* pook, purok, distrito

Disturb *v.* gambalain, abalahin, guluhin

Disturbance *n.* gambala, kaabalahan, gulo, kaguluhan

Dive *n.* talon, pagsisid

Dive *v.* tumalon, sumisid, sumugba

Diverge *v.* mangalat, maghiwalay, magkaiba

Diverse *adj.* iba, magkaiba

Diversion *n.* paglihis, libangan, paglilibang

Divide *v.* bahagihin, hatiin, partihin

Dividend *n.* dibidendo, tubo, pakinabang

Divine *adj.* dibino, banal, makalangit

Division *n.* palahatian, sangay, dibisyon, paghahati

Divorce *n.* diborsiyo, kalagkasal

Divorce *v.* magdiborsiyo

Divulge *v.* ihayag, ibunyag, ipagtapat, isiwalat

Dizziness *n.* hilo, nahihilo, liyo

Do *v.* gumawa, gawin, nagawa

Docile *adj.* masunurin, maamo

Dock *n.* piyer, pantalan

Doctor *n.* manggagamot

Doctor *n.* doktor, paham, pantas

Doctrine *n.* doktrino, simulain, paniniwala

Document *n.* kasulatan, dokumento

Dog *n.* aso

Doing *n.* gawa, kagagawan

Doldrums *n.* lumbay, tamlay, tigil

Domestic *adj.* domestiko, pantahanan

Domicile *n.* tirahan, tahanan

Dominant *adj.* dominante, naghahari, pangunahin

Dominate *v.* dominahan, masupil, supilin

Domination *n.* dominasyon, paghahari, pagsakop

Domino *n.* domino, antipas

Don't huwag, hindi

Donate *v.* magdonasyon, idonasyon, magkaloob, ipagkaloob

Donation *n.* donasyon, bigay, kaloob, gawad

Donkey *n.* buro, buriko

Door *n.* pinsan, pinto

Doorway *n.* pintuan, labasan

Dope *n.* apyan, narkotiko, datos

Dormitory *n.* dormitoryo, tulagan

Dose *n.* disis

Dot *n.* tuldok, puntito

Dot *v.* tuldukan

Double *adj.* ibayo, paris, doble

Double *v.* doblihin, pagdalawahin, ibayuhin, makamukha

Doubt *n.* alinlangan, duda

Doubt *v.* nagalinlangan, magduda, pagdudahan

Down *adv.* ibaba, palalim, pababa, paliit

Dowry *n.* bigay kaya, dote

Doze *v.* umidlip, magtuka

Dozen *n.* dosena, labindalawa

Draft *n.* hila, arastre, lagok, higop

Draft *v.* magbalangkas, magbanghay

Drag *n.* hilahod, hila. arastre, kaladkad

Drag *v.* hilahin, arastrihin, kaladkarin

Drain *n.* tulo, agos, tuluan, agusan, kanal

Drain *v.* patuluin, paagusin, patuyuin, ubusin

Drama *n.* dula, drama

Draw *v.* iguhit, iginuhit, hilahin, batakin

Draw back *n.* pagurong

Drawback *v.* inurong

Drawer *n.* kahon

Drawn *adj.* bunot

Dread *n.* takot, sindak

Dread *v.* matakot, katakutan, masindak, kasindakan

Dream *n.* panaginip, pangarap

Dream *v.* ipanaginip, managinip, managarap

Dress *n.* bihis, bestida, suot, pananamit

Dress *v.* bihisan, damitan, ihanay, gayakan

Drift *n.* direksiyon, tinutungo, hilig, tulak

Drift *v.* lumutang, maanod, mapayid

Drill *n.* pamutas, balibol, barena

Drill *v.* magbutas, butasin, balibulin, sanayin

Drink *n.* inumin, alak, inumin

Drink *v.* inom, uminom, barikin, tumagay

Drip *v.* tulo, pumatak- patak

Drive *v.* magmancho, minaneho

Drizzle *n.* ambon, anggiampiyas

Drizzle *v.* umambon, umanggi

Drop *n.* patak, biglang baba, laglag, tulo

Drop *v.* tumba, ibagsak, pumatak, tumulo

Drown *v.* malunod, lunurin

Drown *v.* lunurin

Drowse *n.* antukin, magtuka, maghikab

Drum *n.* tambol, tuong, dram

Drum *v.* magtambol

Dry *adj.* tuyo, tuyot

Dry *v.* tuyuin, matuyo

Dub *adj.* pipi, tikom, bibig

Duck *n.* bibi, itik, pato

Due *adj.* napapaso, inutang

Dues *N.* butaw

Duet *n.* duwo, duweto, saliwan

Dull *adj.* mapurol, tanga, dungo, mapurol

Dummy *n.* pipi, apaw, taong, tanga

Dump *v.* ibunton, itambak, ibagna

Durable *adj.* matibay, matatag

During *prep.* habang

Dust *n.* alikabok

Dust *v.* paspasan, pagpagin

Duty *n.* katungkulan, tungkulin, buwis

Dwarf *n.* enano

Dwell *v.* nakatira, tumira

Dyanamite *n.* dinamita

Dye *n.* tina

Dye *v.* tinain, dampulin

Dynamic *adj.* dinamiko, mabisa

Dysentery *n.* iti, disenteriya, pag iiti

Dyspeptic *n.* dispeptiko

Dysphonia *n.* panghuhumal

Dyspnea *n.* disnea, hingal

E e

Each *adj.* bawat

Each *pron.* bawat isa

Eager *adj.* sabik, nasasabik, masigla, masigasig, handa

Eagle *n.* agila, banoy

Ear *n.* tainga, pandinig, pakikinig, pagdinig

Earl *n.* konde

Early *adj.* maaga, maagap

Earn *v.* kitain, matamo, tamuhin, kumita, makamit, magtubo, makinabang

Earnest *adj.* taimtim, tapat, marubdob

Earnest *n.* deposito, pauna, mabuting, kalooban

Earnings *n.* kita, kinikita

Earth *n.* lupa, daigdig

Earthly *adj.* makalupa, panglupa

Earthworm *n.* bulati

Ease *n.* kaginhawahan, alwan, ginhawa, kaalwanan

Ease *v.* gaanan, pawiin, padaliin

Easily *adv.* madalian, madali, maluwag, tiyak

East *n.* silangan, kasilanganan

Easy *adj.* madali, magaan, maalwan

Eat *v.* kainin, kumain

Eaves *n.* sibi, sulambi

Ebb *n.* kati, pagkati

Eccentric *adj.* hiwid, kakatwa, kakaiba

Echo *n.* alingawngaw

Eclipse *n.* paglalaho, eklipse

Ecology *n.* ekolohiya

Economics *n.* karunungang, pangkabuhayan

Economy *n.* kabuhayan, pagtitipid, katipiran

Ecstasy *n.* pagtatalik, katalikan

Eden *n.* eden, paraiso

Edge *n.* gilid, bingit, tabihin, talim

Edge *v.* taliman, gumitgit, makagitgit

Edible *adj.* makakain

Edict *n.* edikto, dekreto, utos

Edifice *n.* gusali, edipisyo

Edit *v.* mamatnugot, pamatnugutan, editahan

Edition *n.* edisyon, labas

Editor *n.* editor, patnugot

Editorial *n.* pangulong tudling, editorial

Educate *v.* paaralan, turuan, edukahin, linangin, sanayin

Education *n.* pinagaralan, pagtuturo, edukasyon

Educe *v.* hugutin, hanguin, pagkunan, paghugutan

Eel *n.* igat, palos

Effect *n.* bisa, kalabasan, epekto, bunga, resulta

Effect *v.* maisagawa, umiral, magkabisa

Effective *adj.* mabisa, epektibo, maepekto

Efferent *adj.* palayo, palabas

Efficacy *n.* bisa, bagsik, sidhi

Efficiency *n.* katalaban, kahusayan

Efficient *adj.* matalab, masinop

Effigy *n.* larawan, imahen

Efflorescence *n.* pamumulaklak

Effluence *n.* agos, pag-agos, daloy pagdaloy

Effort *n.* pagpursige, sikap, pagsisikap, punyagi

Effusion *n.* buhos, pagbuhos, bulwak

Egg *n.* itlog

Egg *v.* ulukan, sulsulan, ibuyo, ibunsod

Eggplant *n.* talong

Ego *n.* sarili, pagkamakaako

Eight *adj.* walo

Eighteen *adj.* labingwalo

Eighth *adj.* ikawalo, pangwalo

Eighty *adj.* walumpu

Either *adj.* alinman

Either *adv.* man, din

Either *pron.* isa't isa, bawa't isa sa dalawa

Ejaculate *v.* bumigkas, magpamutawi, ibulalas

Ejaculation *n.* bulalas, hakulatorya

Eject *v.* ihagis, itapon, itaboy

Elaborate *adj.* pinagpakahirapan, sali-saliuout

Elaborate *v.* gawing, detalyado, painamin

Elapse *v.* lumipas, dumaan, magdaan

Elastic *adj*. igkasin, elastiko, nahuhutok

Elasticity *n*. elasticidad, pagkamahuhutok

Elate *v*. paligayahin

Elbow *n*. siko, kodo

Elder *n*. panganay, matanda, apo

Elderly *adj*. maykatandaan, maykagulangan

Eldest *adj*. pinakamatanda

Elect *adj*. halal na, hinirang, pili, pinili, hirang

Elect *v*. ihalal, iboto, piliin, hirangin

Election *n*. halalan, eleksiyon

Electric *adj*. madagitab, dagisikin, elektrika, pandagitab

Electric *n*. elektrik

Electrician *n*. elektrisista, mandaragitab

Electricity *n*. dagitab, kuryente, elektrisidad

Electrocute *v*. elektrokutahin, maelektrokuta, mamatay

Elegance *n*. kisig, kinis, gilas, bikas, kakinisan, gara

Elegant *adj*. makisig, makinis, pihikan, elegante, magara, mabikas, magilas

Element *n*. elemento, sangkap, simulain, arte, sining

Elementary *adj* elementarya, panimula

Elephant *n*. elepante, gadya

Elevate *v*. itaas, pataasin, iasenso, dangalin

Elevation *n*. taas, pagtataas, asenso

Elevator *n*. asensor, elebetor

Eleven *adj*. Labing-isa

Eleventh *adj*. ikalabing-isa

Elf *n*. duwende

Elicit *v*. mahugot, maihayag

Eligible *adj*. maaring hirangin, kaangkupan

Eliminate *v*. alisin, ilabas, iwaksi, iwan, idumi

Ellipse *n*. elipse

Elm *n*. olmo

Elocution *n*. elokusyon, pananalumpati

Elongate *v*. pahabain, habaunatin

Elope *v*. magtanan, tumakas

Eloquent *adj*. maliwanag, elokwente

Else *adj*. pa, iba pa

Else *adv*. sa iba

Else *conj*. kung hindi, kungdi

Elucidate *v*. ipaliwanag, linawin

Elude *v*. tumalilis, umiwas, tumipas, umilag, ilagan

Elusive *adj*. mailap,unawain, madulas, mahirap, hulihin

Emanate *v*. manggaling, magbuhat, magmula

Emancipate *v*. palayain

Emancipation*n*.emansipasyon pagpapalaya, pagliligtas

Embankment *n*. tambak, binundok

Embark *v.* lumulan, sumakay, lumayag

Embarrass *v.* mapahiya, hiyain, hadlangan, gipitin

Embassy *n.* embahada, pasuguan

Emblem *n.* emblema, simbolo, sagisag

Embody *v.* buuin, katawanin

Emboss *v.* patambukin, paalsahin, pabukulin

Embrace *n.* yakop, yapos

Embrace *v.* yakapin, sumaklaw, saklawin

Embroider *v.* magburda, burdahan

Embroidery *n.* burda

Embroil *v.* dalakitin, idalakit, isangkot

Embryo *n.* hermen, embriyon

Emerge *v.* pumaibabaw, sumipot, sumulpot, lumitaw

Emergence *n.* paglitaw, pagsulpot, paggitaw

Emergency *n.* emerhensya, kagipitan

Emigrant *n.* emigrante, mandarayuhan, dayuhan

Emigrate *v.* mandayuhan

Emigration *n.emi* grasyon, pandarayuhan

Eminence *n.* eminensiya, tayog, taas, katayugan

Eminent *adj.* eminente, mataas, dakila, tanyag

Emit *v.* magpalabas, palabasin

Emmission *n.* emisyon, pagpapalabas

Emolument *n.* gantimpagal, sahod, pakinabang, bayad

Emotion *n.* damdamin, emosiyon

Emphasis *n.* diin, empasis

Empire *n.* lupain, imperyo, kaharian

Employ *v.* pinatrabaho, gamitin, gumamit, gugulin

Employee *n.* kawani, mga katulong

Employer *n.* amo, mayari, namumuhunan

Employment *n.* pagkakakitaan

Emporium *n.* emporya, basar

Empty *adj.* walang laman, bakante, basiyo

Empty *v.* todasin, ubusin

Emulate *v.* tularan, parisan, tumulad

Enable *v.* itulot

Enact *v.* isabatas, aktuhin, umakto

Enchant *v.* atikin, bihagin, marahuyo, halinahin, kulamin, ingkantuhin

Encircle *v.pal* ibutan, pabilugan, paligiran

Enclose *v.* maglakip, kulungin, paligiran, ilakip, isama

Enclosure *n.* lakip, bakod

Encompass *v.* pikutin, palibutan, paligiran, bakuran

Encounter *v.* makatagpo, magtagpo, magkalaban

Encourage *v.* udyukan, pasiglahin, pukawin, paasahin

Encouragement *n.* udyok, pasigla

Encumber *v.* kargahan, pabigatan

Encyclopaedia *n.* ensiklopediko

End *v.* wakasan, tapusin, magtapos

Endeavor *n.* pag-ato, sikap, ato, punyagi

Endeavor *v.* pagsikapan, umato, atuhin, magsikap

Endless *adj.* walang-hanggang

Endorse *v.* aprobahan, itaguyod, ilipat

Endorsement *n.* pagpapatibay, taguyod, paglilipat

Endow *v.* pagkalooban, magkaloob, ipagkaloob

Endure *v.* nakakatiis, tiisin, matagalan

Enemy *adj.* magkalaban, magkagalit

Enemy *n.* kalaban, kaaway, kabaka

Energy *n.* enerhiya, sigsa, punyagi

Enforce *v.* ipatupad, magpatupad, ipasunod

Engage *v.* kumuha, lumahok, kumasundo, mangako, upahan, sumali

Engagement *n.* tipan, kompromiso, sagupaan

Engine *n.* makina, motor, aparato

Engineer *n.* inhinyero, makinista

English *n.* ingles

Engrave *v.* iukit, ukitin, ikintal

Engross *v.* maglubog, mahumaling

Engulf *v.* sumakmal, sakmalin, manalikop, salikupin

Enhance *n.* enigma, hiwaga, panlito

Enjoin *v.* iutos, ipagbilin, bawalan

Enjoy *v.* magpakasaya, magtamasa, tamasahin ikalugod, ikatuwa

Enjoyment *n.* kasiyahan, katuwaan

Enkindle *v.* sindihan, pukawin, paalabin

Enlarge *v.* lakhan, magpalaki, palakhin

Enlighten *v.* turuan, ipaalam, pagpaliwangan

Enlightenment *n.* turo, instruksiyon, paliwanag, kabihasnan

Enlist *v.* magpatala

Enmity *n.* enemistad, poot, yamot, galit

Enormity *n.* kalakhan, kasukdulan, kalubusan

Enormous *adj.* napakalaki

Enough *adj.* sapat, tama na, kainaman, katamtaman

Enough *adv.* tama na

Enrage *v.* galitin, magalit, yamutin

Enrich *v.* magpayaman, patabain, pabutihin, pagalingin

Enroll *v.* magpatala, magpalista, ienrol, ilista, itala

Enshrine *v.* idambana, dambanahin

Enslave *v.* alipinin, alilain, busabusin

Ensue *n.* sumunod, humalili

Ensure *v.* magtiyak, tiyakin, akuin, siguruhin

Entail *v.* makailangan, kailanganin

Enter *v.* ipasok, bumaon, pumasok, pasukin, sumapi

Enterprise *n.* empresa, gawain, pakasam

Entertain *v.* pakiharapan, libangin, istimahin, libangin

Entertainment *n.* aliwan, pagtanggap, panlilibang, pangaaliw

Enthusiam *n.* alab, init, sigla, interes

Enthusiast *n.* entusyasta

Enthusiastic *adj.* masigla, maalab, masigasig

Entice *v.* udyukan, hibuin, tuksuhin

Entire *adj.* buo, ganap, lahat

Entirely *adv.* Mabuo

Entirety *n.* kabuuan, kalahatan

Entity *n.* entidad

Entrance *n.* pasukan, pinto, pagpasok, entrada

Entrance *v.* palugdin, papagtalikin, pahangain

Entrap *v.* patibungan, siluin

Entreat *v.* sumamo, magsumamo, mamanhik, pamanhikan

Entrench *v.* magkuta, makialam

Entrepreneur *n.* empresaryo

Entrust *v.* ipagkatiwala, pagkatiwalaan, ihabilin, paghabilinan

Entry *n.* pasukan, pagtatala,entrada, pagpasok, pasimula, lahok, simula

Enumerate *v.* baybayin, bilangin, numeruhan

Enunciate *v.* bigkasin, isaysay, magsalita, ipamalita

Envelope *n.* sobre

Envious *adj.* mainggitin, mapanaghiliin

Environment *n.* kaligiran, palibot, paligid

Envoy *n.* sugo

Envy *n.* ingit, pananaghili

Envy *v.* inggitin, panaghilian

Epic *n.* epiko, darangan

Epidemic *n.* epidemya, salot

Episode *n.* episodyo, pangyayari

Epoch *n.* epoka, panahon

Equal *adj.* katumbas, magkapareho, magkapantay

Equal *v.* tumbasan, pantayan

Equality *n.* katumbasan, pagkakapantaypantay

Equate *v.* ipantay

Equation *n.* pantayan, pagpapantay

Equator *n.* ekwador

Equilibrium *n.* ekilibrio, balanse, kapanuluyan

Equip *v.* bigyan, ihanda

Equipment *n.* kasangkapan

Equitable *adj.* ekitatiboo

Equity *n.* ekidad, katarungan, pagkapantay

Equivalent *adj.* katumbas, ekibalente, kapantay, kawangis

Era *n.* panahon, kapanahunan, era, epoka

Eradicate *v.* lipulin, puksain, bunutin

Erase *v.* burahin, pawiin, katkatin

Erasure *n.* bura, pawi

Ere *prep.* bago

Erect *adj.* tayo, nakatayo, tuwid, tindig

Erect *v.* itayo, magtayo, itindig, magtatag

Erection *n.* pagtayo, pagtindig, pagtuwid

Erose *n.* eros, kupido

Erosion *n.* agnas, pagkaagnas

Erotic *adj.* erotiko, maliyag, malibog, nalilibugan

Err *v.* mamali, magkamali

Errand *n.* sadya, pakay, utos, bilin

Errata *n.* erata

Error *n.* kamalian, mali, pagkakamali

Error *n.* mali, pagkakamali, kamalian

Erstwhile *adv.* dati, datihan, matanda

Erupt *v.* bumuga, sumabog, pumutok

Eruption *n.* pagputok, pagsabog, pagbuga

Escalade *n.* iskalada

Escalator *n.* iskalador

Escape *v.* tumakas,lumayas, umiwas, pumuga, umalis, tumanan

Escort *n.* ihatid, eskolta, bantay, abay

Espionage *n.* pamamatyaw

Esquire *n.* eskudero

Essay *n.* sanaysay, punyagi, pagpipilit

Essay *v.* magpunyagi, magpumilit, pagpumilitan

Essence *n.* buod, sustansiya, pabango

Essential *adj.* kailangan-kailangan, katutubo

Establish *v.* itatag, lumagay, patunayan

Establishment *n.* pagtatatag, pagtatayo, establesimyento

Estate *n.* estado, katayuan, mana

Esteem *n.* pagtingin, pagtatangi

Esteem *v.* bigyanghalaga, pahalagahan, mahalin

Estimate *n.* estimasyon, pahalaga, tuos, taya

Estimate *v.* tantiyahin, tayahin, pahalagahan, bintayin

Estoppel *n.* hadlang, balaksila

Etch *v.* ipaukit sa asido

Etching *n.* etsing, ukit

Eternal *adj.* eterno, walang-hanggan

Eternity *n.* kabilang buhay, walang hanggan

Ethic *adj.* etiko, moral

Ethnic *adj.* etniko, panlahi, panlipi

Evacuate *v.* bakantihin, lisanin, umurong, lumikas, dumumi

Evade *v.* iwasan, umiwas, tumalilis, tumanan

Evaporate *v.* sumingaw, paigahin

Evasion *n.* pag-iwas

Eve *n.* bispiras, gabi

Even *adj.* pantay, patag, buo, eksakto

Even *v.* pantayin

Evening *n.* gabi

Event *n.* pangyayari, pagkakataon, labanan

Eventually *adv.* mangyayaririn, masasapit din

Ever *adv.* pag, kailanman, man, panay, lagi

Every *adj.* tuwig, bawa't

Everybody *adj.* pangaraw-araw

Everybody *prn.* lahat-lahat

Everyone *prn.* bawa't, isa-isa

Everything *prn.* lahat

Everywhere *adv.* lahat ng dako

Evict *v.* paalisin, palayasin

Evidence *n.* ebidensiya, patunay, katunayan

Evident *adj.* malinaw, maliwanag, lantad, halata

Evil *adj.* masama, balakyot, makasalanan

Evoke *v.* makatawag, makapukaw

Evolution *n.* ebulusyon, pagsibol, pagsulong

Evolve *v.* sumibol, tumubo, sumulong, magbuo

Exact *adj.* singkad, husto, eksakto, wasto

Exact *v.* hustuhan, hingan, kunan, singilin

Exaggeration *n.* eksaherasyon, pagmamalabis

Examination *n.* pagsulit, suri

Examine *v.* suriin, butingtingin

Example *n.* halimbawa

Exasperate *v.* inisin, yamutin, galitin

Excavate *v.* hukayin, dukalin

Excavation *n.* hukayan, pagdukal

Excavator *n.* panghukay, tagahukay, manghuhukay

Exceed *v.* lumampas, mahigtan, humigit, makahigit

Excellence *n.* galing, giting, kagalingan

Excellent *adj.* magaling, mahalaga, dalubhasa, dakila

Except *n.* labis, kalabisan

Except *prep.* maliban sa

Except *v.* pinagpaliban

Exception *n.* kataliwasan, tutol

Excerpt *n.* sipi, sinipi

Excess *n.* labis, kalabisan, sobra

Excessive *adj.* lampas

Exchange *n.* pagpalit

Exchange *v.* ipagpalit, magpalitan

Excise *v.* hiwain, putulin

Excite *v.* sinabik

Excitement *n.* pagkalugod, kaguluhan

Exclaim *v.* ibulalas, isigaw

Exclude *v.* alisin, tanggalin

Exclusive *adj.* esklusibo, panarili, solo, buo

Excommunicate *v.* eskumunikahin, itiwalag

Excursion *n.* pagpasyal, pagliliwaliw

Excuse *n.* dahilan, katuwiran, patawad

Excuse *v.* patawarin, ipagpatawad

Execute *v.* ipatupad, patayin, ipaganap, bitayin, isagawa, ganapin

Execution *n.* pagpapatupad, pagpapaganap, pagsasagawa, pagganap

Executive *n.* ehekutibo, tagapagsagawa

Executor *n.* ehekutor, tagapagpaganap

Exempt *adj.* eksento, ligtas, malaya

Exercise *n.* ehersisyo, pagganap, pagsasanay, panunungkol

Exercise *v.* hersisyuhin, gumanap, manungkol

Exert *v.* magpunyagi, pagpunyagian, pagpumilitan

Exertion *n.* pagpupunyagi, pagpupumilit

Exhale *v.* huminga, ihinga, hingahan

Exhaust *n.* palabasan, pasingawan

Exhaust *v.* sairin, ubusin, gasgasin, mahopo

Exhibit *v.* itanghal, ipakita, ihayag

Exhibition *n.* eksibisyon, tanghalan, pagtatanghal

Exile *n.* destiyero, tapon

Exile *v.* ipatapon, idestiyero

Exist *v.* mabuhay, umiral, manatili

Existence *n.* kabuhayan, eksistensiya, buhay, katunayan

Exit *n.* labasan, eksit, salida

Exorbitant *adj.* labis, masyado

Exotic *adj.* kakaiba, kakatwa, banyaga

Expand *v.* lumawak, palawakin, palakihin

Expansion *n.* paglawak, pagkalat, paglaki

Expect *v.* inaabangan, hinagapin, asahan, umasa, maghintay

Expectorate *v.* dumahak, lumura, ilura

Expedite *v.* bilisan, dalidaliin

Expedition *n.* ekspidisyon, paglalakbay, biyahe, agap, kadalian

Expel *v.* espulsahin, tanggalin, itiwalag, paalisin

Expend *v.* gumasta, gastahan, gumugol, gugulan

Expenditure *n.* gastos, gugol, gugulin

Expense *n.* gastos, gugol

Expensive *adj.* mahal, magastos, magugol, gugulin

Experience *n.* karanasan, esperyensiya, pinagdanasan, kaalaman

Experience *v.* dumanas, lasapin

Experiment *n.* esperimento, pagsubak, pagtitikim

Expert *n/adj* esperto, sanay, dalubhasa

Expire *v.* matapos, mamatay, malagutan, huminga, magwakas

Explain *v.* ipaliwanag, magpaliwanag, maglahad, ilahad

Explanation *n.* pagapaliwanag, paliwanag, paglalahad

Explicit *adj.* malinaw, tiyak

Explode *v.* pumutok, sumabog, tumilapon

Exploit *v.* samantalahin, gamitin

Explore *v.* esplorahin, galugarin

Explorer *n.* manggagalugad, esplorador

Explosion *n.* putok, sabog, tilapon, esplosyon

Explosive *adj.* pampaputok, esplosibo

Explosive *n.* paputok

Exponent *n.* esponente, tagapagpaliwanag, tipo, tipiko

Export *n.* esportasyon, luwas, pagluluwas

Export *v.* iluwas, magluwas

Expose *v.* itampak, ihayag, ibunyag, ilantad

Express *adj.* malinaw, tiyak, madali

Express *n.* pagpapahatid

Express *v.* hayag, salitain, sabihin, ipagtapat

Expression *n.* espresyon, pahayag

Exquisite *adj.* eskisito, mainam, pino, napakabuti

Extend *v.* dugtungan, palugitan, paabutin, iabot

Extension *n.* dugtong, karugtong, palugit, sudlong

Extensive *adj.* malawak

Extent *n.* lawak, abot, laki, estensiyon

Exterior *n.* esteryor, labas

Exterminate *v.* lipulin, puksain

External *adj.* panlabas

Extinguish *v.* patayin, tapusin, gibain, puksain

Extra *adj.* labis, ekstra, palabis

Extra *n.* kalabisan, kapalit

Extract *v.* bunutin, katasin, pigainduyuhan

Extreme *n.* sukdulan

Extremely *adv.* sakdal

Eye *n.* mata, tingin, paningin

Eyebrow *n.* kilay

Eyesight *n.* paningin

Eyre *n.* pagligid

F f

Fable *n.* pabula, kasinungalingan, kataka-taka

Fabric *n.* tela, kayo

Fabricate *v.* itayo, gawin

Fabulous *adj.* pabulaso

Facade *n.* patsada, harapan, mukha

Face *n.* mukha, harapan

Face *v.* iharap, humarap, harapin, labanan

Facet *n.* paseta, panig, tapyas

Facilitate *v.* padaliin, paalwanin, pagaanin

Facility *n.* pasilidad, alwan, gaan, dali

Fact *n.* katotohanan, katunayan, pangyayari

Faction *n.* partido, lapian, pangkat

Factitious *adj.* artipisyal, lalang

Factor *n.* kabuo, paktor, sanhi, salik

Factory *n.* gawaan, pabrika, pagawaan

Faculty *n.* pakultad, kapangyarihan, kakayahan

Fade *v.* kumupas, mangupas, malanta

Fag *v.* magpakapagud-pagod

Fail *v.* lumagpak, magkulang, bumagsak, kulangin, mabigo, manghina, biguin, mahulog

Failure *n.* pagkukulang, pagkabigo, pagkabigo

Faint *adj.* mahina, mahiyain, malabo

Faint *v.* himatayin, lumabo

Fair *adj.* maganda, mapusyaw, mabuti

Fairly *adv.* medyo

Fairy *n.* ada, diwata

Faith *n.* paniniwala, tiwala, relihiyon

Faithful *adj.* matapat

Fake *n.* huwad

Fake *v.* magkunwa, manghuwad, mandaya

Falcon *n.* palkon, halkon

Fall *n.* taglagas, talon, pagkahulog, pagbaba, otonyo, taglagas

Fall *v.* bumagsak, malaglag, mahulog, gumuho

False *adj.* bulaan, mali, huwad

Fame *n.* kabantugan, katanyagan

Familiar *adj.* magkakilala, karaniwan

Family *n.* maganak, angkan, pamilya

Famine *n.* gutom, tagsalat

Famous *adj.* bantog, balita, tanyag, bunyi

Fan *n.* pamaypay, abaniko, bentilador

Fanatic *adj.* panatiko

Fancy *adj.* makalakuti, maganda, mainam, magara

Fancy *n.* haraya, kapritso

Fantasy *n.* pantasiya, imahinasyon, guniguni

Far *adv.* malayo, higit

Fare *n.* upa, pilete, pasahe, pagkain

Fare *v.* mangyari, magdanas

Farewell *adj.* paalis, pahimakas

Farewell *n.* pamamaalam

Farm *n.* sakahin, bukid

Farm *v.* magbukid, maglinang

Farmer *n.* magsasaka

Farther *adj.* dulong-dulo

Fascimile *n.* paksimile, kopya, sipi

Fascinate *v.* maakit, akitin, halinahin

Fascist *n.* pasista

Fashion *n.* kayarian, moda, anyo, itsura, tabas

Fashion *v.* hugisan, maghugis, magporma, iporma

Fashionable *adj.* pusturyoso

Fast *adv.* mabilis, matulin, matatag

Fasten *v.* ikabit, pagkabitin

Fastidious *adj.* busisi

Fat *adj.* mataba

Fat *n.* taba, mantika

Fatal *adj.* nakamamatay, patal

Fate *n.* kapalaran, tadhana, suwerte

Father *n.* ama, pare, tatang, padre, tatay, itay

Fathom *v.* arukin, unawain

Fatigue *n.* pagkahapo, hapo, pagod

Fault *n.* kasalanan, pagkukulang, kapintasan, pagkakamali

Fauna *n.* palahayayupan, pauna

Favor *n.* tulong, pabor, lingap, biyaya

Favor *v.* panigan, kampihan, loob

Favorable *adj.* mapalad

Fear *n.* takot, katakutan, sindak, pangamba

Fear *v.* mangamba, matakot

Feasible *adj.* magagawa, maisasagawa

Feast *n.* magpakabusog, pista, bangkete, piging

Feather *n.* balahibo, plumahe, pakpak

February *n.* pebrero

Federal *adj* pederasyon, unyon

Federation *n.* katipunan, pederasyon

Fee *n.* upa, kota, bayad, alkila, butaw

Feeble *adj.* mahina, marupok, masasaktin

Feed *n.* pakain

Feed *v.* pakanin, kumpayan, patukain

Feel *v.* makaramdam, salatin, kapkapin

Feeling *n.* damdamin

Feet *n.* mga paa

Felicitate *v.* pelisitahan, batiin

Felicitation *n.* pelisitasyon, bati

Felicitous *adj.* maligaya, angkop

Fellow *adj.* kapwa

Fellow *n.* mama, kasama, pare, tao, lalaki

Female *n.* babae

Feminine *adj.* pambabae, peminino

Fen *n.* labon, latian, tarlak

Fence *n.* bakod, kural

Fence *v.* bakuran

Fend *v.* manangga, mananggol, sanggahin

Ferment *n.* pahilab, paalsa

Ferment *v.* umasim, pahilabin, paalsa, pahilab

Fermentation *n.* paghilab, ligalig, gulo

Fern *n.* eletso, pako

Ferocious *adj.* mabangis, mabalasik

Ferocity *n.* kabangisan, balasik

Ferry *n.* badeo, tawiran, bantilan

Fertile *adj.* mataba, mabunga, mayaman

Fertile *n.* palmeta, pamalo

Fertility *n.* pertilidad

Festival *n.* pista, piyesta

Festive *adj.* masaya

Festivity *n.* papista, kapistahan, kasayahan

Fetch *v.* kaunin, kumuha, ikuha

Fete *n* pista

Fetus *n.* peto

Feud *n.* alitan, kagalitan

Feudal *adj.* peudal

Fever *n.* lagnat

Few *pron.* kaunti, ilan

Fiance *n.* nobyo, katipan

Fiancee *n.* nobya, katipan

Fiasco *n.* prakaso, kabiguan

Fiber *n.* hilatsa, hibla, sulid

Fibrous *adj.* pibroso, mahilatsa

Fickle *adj.* salawahan

Fiddle *n.* biyolin

Fiddle *v.* magbiyulin, paglaruan, galawin

Fidelity *n.* katapatan

Field *n.* bukid, bukirin, linang, larangan

Fierce *adj.* mabagsik, mabangis, masidhi

Fifteen *num.* Labing-lima

Fifth *adj.* ikalima, panlima

Fifty *num.* limampu

Fig *n.* igos

Fight *n.* labanan, laban, hidwaan

Fight *v.* makilaban

Fighting *n.* laban

Figure *n.* anyo, sagisag, pigura, hugis, itsura

Figure *v.* ilarawan, magtuos, tuusin

Filament *n.* pilamento, lamuymoy

File *n.* tipon, bunton, kikil

File *v.* magharap, kikilin

File *v.* ayusin, iayos, tipuin, itago

Filipino *n.* pinoy, pilipino

Fill *v.* punuin, punuan, tuparin, tupdin

Film *n.* pelikula, plaka

Filter *n.* salaan, panala

Filth *n.* basura, pusali, dumi

Final *adj.* pinal, huli

Final *n.* kahuli-hulihan

Finale *n.* pinale, katapusan

Finally *adv.* sa wakas

Finance *n.* pamimilak, pananalapi

Financial support Tustos

Financier *n.* pinansiyero, mamimilak

Find *v.* mapulot, alamin, makapulot, makita, makuha

Find *v.* makita

Find out Halatain

Fine *adj.* pino, maliit, manipis, mainam

Fine *n.* multa, rekargo

Fine *v.* papagmultahin, multahan

Finesse *n.* pines

Finger *n.* daliri

Finish *n.* wakas, katapusan

Finish *v.* tapusin, mayari

Finite *adj.* limitado

Fire *n.* sunog, apoy

Fire *v.* sisantihin, paputukin, magpaputok

Fireplace *n.* pausukan, tsimenea

Firm *adj.* pirmi, mahigpit, matigas, matatag

Firm *n.* bahay-kalakal, samahan, kapisanan

First *adj.* una, primero, pangunahin

First aid *n.* pangunang lunas

Fiscal *adj.* piskal

Fish *n.* isda

Fish *v.* mangisda

Fisherman *n.* mangingisda

Fist *n.* kamao

Fit *n.* angkop, atake, sumpong

Fit *v.* bumagay, husto

Five *num.* lima

Fix *v.* kumpuniihin, ikabit, itakda, ipirmi, ayusin

Fixture *n.* parte, aksesoryo

Fizzle *v.* sumagitsit, mabigo

Flabby *adj.* luyloy

Flag *n.* bandila, watawat, bandera

Flagellant *n.* nagpepenitensya

Flake *n.* iskama, bulak-bulak

Flame *n.* ningas, liyab, alab

Flannel *n.* pranela

Flap *n.* pardilya, oha

Flare *n.* ansisilaw

Flare *v.* magsiklab

Flash *n.* kislap, silakbo, saglit

Flash *v.* kumislap, magdiklab

Flash v. kumislap, ikalat, sumiklab

Flask *n.* prasko

Flat *adj.* makinis, pipis, pantay, patag, tiyak, sapad

Flat *n.* kapatagan

Flatten *v.* pantayin, patagin

Flatter *v.* utuin, manghibo, kunwari, purihin

Flaunt *v.* ipagparangya

Flavor *n.* linamnam, lasa, lasap

Flaw *n.* mantsa, depekto, pintas, kahunaan, lamat

Flax *n.* lino, sulid

Flay *v.* talupan, parusahan

Flea *n.* pulgas, hanip

Fleck *n.* dungis, amol

Flee *v.* tumakas, layuan, umiwas, lumayo, iwasan

Fleet *adj.* maliksi, matulin

Fleet *n.* plota

Flesh *n.* laman

Flex *v.* pakiluin, hubugin

Flexible *adj.* mahubugin, masunurin

Flick *n.* labtik

Flicker *v.* kumurap, kumisap

Flight *n.* lipad, paglipad, paglayas

Flimsy *adj.* mahuna, mabuway, manipis, dahilan, mahinang

Flinch *v.* umudlot, umukto

Fling *v.* ihagis, ipukol, iitsa

Flirtation *n.* ligaw-biro, limbangan

Float *n.* karosa

Float *v.* lumutang, palutangin, padparin, lutang

Flock *n.* kawan, langkay, ganado, pangkat

Flock *v.* magkatipon, magkalipunpon, magsamasama

Flog *v.* latikuhin, hagupitin, hampasin, paluin, bugbugin

Flood *n.* baha, apaw

Flood *v.* dagsaan, bahain, umapaw, bumaha

Floor *n.* sahig, lapag, palapag

Flop *adj.* bumagsak, bigo, mabagsak, mabigo

Flora *n.* plora

Florescent *adj.* mabulaklak, namumulaklak

Floriculture *n.* plorikultura

Florist *n.* plorero, magbubulaklak

Flour *n.* arina

Flourescent *adj.* makinang, ploresente

Flourish *v.* yumabong, sumibol, umunlad, ikumpas

Flow *n.* anod, balisbis, daloy, agos, tulo

Flow *v.* umagos, dumaloy, tumulo, bumalisbis

Flower *n.* bulaklak

Flu *n.* trangkaso, impluensa

Fluctuate *v.* magpabagu-bago

Flue *n.* tsiminea, pausukan

Fluency *n.* tatas

Fluent *adj.* matatas, madulas

Fluid *n.* likido, tubig, tunaw, lusaw

Flume *n.* paagusan, kanal

Flunk *v.* mahulog, mangalabasa

Fluorescence *n.* panginginang, ploresensiya

Flush *v.* busan, paagusan, mamula, hugasan

Flute *n.* plawta

Flutter *v.* pumagaypay, pumagaspas

Flux *n.* agos, tulo, kurso

Fly *v.* lumipad, nakalipad, magpalipad, tumakas, liparin

Foam *n.* bula, espuma

Foam *v.* bumula, magespuma

Focal *adj.* pokal, panggitna

Focus *n.* tuon, pocus, gitna, sentro

Focus *v.* ituon

Fog *n.* kaaway, kalaban, ulap

Foil *n.* plorete, dahon, asoge

Foil *v.* biguin, daigin

Fold *n.* lupi, tiklop

Fold *v.* tiklupin, itiklop, ilupi, salikupin

Folder *n.* polder, sipitan

Folk *n.* mga tao, kamaganak, katutubo

Folklore *n.* poklor, kaalamangbayan

Follow *v.* sunurin, sumama,tuntunin, sundin, tularan, sumunod, samahan

Follower *n.* tagasunod, alagad

Folly *n.* kaululan, kalokohan

Foment *v.* magbunsod, ibunsod

Fond *adj.* magiliw, mapagmahal, mahilig, maibigin

Fondle *v.* paglamyusan, himasin, hagpusin

Font *n.* puwente, bukal, binditahan

Food *n.* pagkain, ulam

Fool *n.* gaga, gago, bobo, ungas

Fool *v.* lokohin, bolahin, lamangan, maglaro

Foolishness *n.* kagaguhan, kalokohan

Foot *n.* paa, piye, talampakan, paanan

Football *n.* sipang bola, putbol

Footwear *n.* kalsado

For *conj.* kaya

For *prep.* para sa, dahil sa, sa

Forbid *v.* pagbawalan, pinagbawalan, magbawal, ipagbawal

Force *n.* dahas, isig, lakas, puwersa

Force *v.* pilitin, tungkabin

Forceps *n.* pinsas, sipit

Fore *adj.* una

Fore *n.* unahan, bukana

Forearm *n.* bisig, braso

Forecast *n.* prediksiyon, hula, babala

Forecast *v.* manghula, hulaan

Foregone *adj.* dati, nakaraan

Forehead *n.* noo

Foreign *adj.* dayuhan

Foreign *adj.* banyaga, panlabas

Foreigner *n.* banyaga, dayo, dayuhan

Foreman *n.* kapatas, katiwala

Foremost *adj.* pangunahin

Foresee *v.* mahulaan, makinikinita

Forest *n.* gubat, kakahuyan

Forester *n.* manggugubat

Forestry *n.* panggugubat

Foretell *v.* manghula, hulaan

Forever *adv.* kailanman, magpakailanman

Forfeit *v.* magpakatalo, parusa

Forge *n.* pandayan

Forge *v.* magpanday, pandayin, huwaran

Forgery *n.* panghuhuwad, palsipikasyon

Forget *v.* kalimutan, makalimot, limutin, lumimot, malimot, malimutan

Forgive *v.* patawarin, pinatawad, napatawad, magpatawad

Fork *n.* tinidor, sangahan

Form *n.* hugis, anyo, hubog, itsura

Form *v.* hugisan, hulmahin, hubugin, anyuan

Formal *adj.* pormal

Formality *n.* pormalidad

Format *n.* pormat, kaanyuan

Former *adj.* dati, una, nauna

Formidable *adj.* nakatatakot, nakasisindak

Formula *n.* pormula

Formulate *v.* pormulahin, magpormula

Forsake *v.* iwan, pabayaan, talikdan

Fort *n.* kuta, muralya, moog

Forte *n.* galing, katangian

Forth *adv.* tumungo, sa labas

Forthcoming *adj.* darating, nalalapit

Forthwith *adv.* agad, kaagad

Fortify *v.* kutaan, palakasin

Fortnight *n.* dalawang linggo

Fortress *n.* kutang-tanggulan

Fortunate *n.* mapalad, maykapalaran

Fortune *n.* kayamanan, kapalaran, portuna, yaman, palad

Forty *num.* apatnapu

Forum *n.* porum, poro, hukuman

Forward *adj.* mauna, maagap, pangahas

Forward *v.* unahin, ipadala, pasulong, abante

Foster *adj.* pangalawa, ampon, inampon

Foster *v.* tustusan, itaguyod, alagaan

Foul *adj.* masama, marumi, mabaho

Found *v.* magtayo, magtatag, magbuo

Foundation *n.* batayan, simulain, panimula

Founder *n.* tagapagtatag, pundidor

Foundry *n.* pundisyon

Fountain *n.* bukal, balong, pontanya, kadluan

Four *num.* apat

Fourteen *num.* labing-apat

Fowl *n.* maypakpak, manok, gansa, pato, itik, pabo

Fox *n.* sora, soro

Fraction *n.* praksiyon, bahagi

Fracture *n.* bali, lamat, basag, pilay

Fragile *adj.* marupok, mahuna, mahina

Fragment *n.* pragmento, piraso, bahagi

Fragrance *n.* bango, halimuyak, samyo

Fragrant *adj.* mabango, mahalimuyak

Frame *n.* kuwardo, balangkas, bastagan

Frame *v.* ikuwardo

Franchise *n.* prangkisya, karapatan, pahintulot

Frank *adj.* prangko, tapat

Fraternal *adj.* praternal, pangkapatid

Fraternity *n.* praternidad, kapatiran

Fraud *n.* daya, linlang, katiwalian

Fraudulent *adj.* maydaya, mapanlinlang

Fray *n.* taltalan

Fray *v.* manasnas, manisnis, magasgas

Freak *n.* kapritso, sumpong

Freckle *n.* pekas

Free *adj.* malaya, libre, ligtas

Free *v.* palayain, bitawan

Freedom *n.* kalayaan, kaligtasan

Freeze *v.* iyelo, iniyelo, yelado

Freezer *n.* priser, palamigan

Freight *n.* lulan, karga

Freight *v.* magkarga, maglulan

Frequency *n.* limit, dalas, bilis

Frequent *adj.* madalas, malimit

Frequent *v.* pinaglalagian, magdadalaw

Frequently *adv.* kadalasan

Fresh *adj.* sariwa, bago, marahas, bagito

Fret *n.* galit, yamot, balisa, kalado

Fret *v.* gasgasin, magasgas, galitin, yamutin

Friction *n.* priksiyon, kiskis, kuskos, hagod

Friday *n.* biyernes

Fried *adj.* prito

Friend *n.* kabigan

Friendly *adj.* mapagkaibigan

Friendship *n.* palagayan, pakikipagkaibigan

Fright *n.* sindak, takot

Frighten *v.* takutin, sindakin

Frightful *adj.* kakila-kilabot

Frigid *adj.* maginaw, matamlay, napakalamig

Frill *n.* eskote, pileges

Fringe *n.* orla, gilid

Fringe *v.* orlahan

Frock *n.* tuniko, abito, blusa

Frog *n.* palaka

Frolic *n.* pagsasaya, pagdiriwang

From *prep.* buhat, mulasa, sa

Frond *n.* dahon

Front *n.* harapan, unahan, itsura, prontera

Front *v.* humarap, tanawin, bumukana

Frost *n.* yelo

Froth *n.* espuma, bula

Frown *v.* sumimangot, magmasungit, magsungit

Frozen *adj.* ilado, nagyelo

Fruit *n.* bungang-kayhoy, prutas, bunga, anak, kinalabsan

Fruitful *adj.* mabunga, sagana

Frustrate *v.* biguin, talunin

Frustration *n.* kabiguan, pagkabigo

Fry *n.* dulong, kakawag, alamang

Fry *v.* pirituhin, iprito, pritusin

Fudge *n.* kuwento

Fuel *n.* gatong, panggatong

Fugitive *n.* takas, puga

Fulcrum *n.* pulkro, huwitan, katangan

Fulfill *v.* gumanap, gawin, isakatuparan, tuparin, isagawa

Full *adj.* puno, tigib, puspos, lipos

Fume *n.* aso, usok, singaw, silakbo

Fume *v.* umaso, umusok, sumingaw

Fun *n.* katuwaan, kasayahan

Function *n.* umandar, pagganap, pagtupad

Function *v.* tumapad, gumanap, magsagawa

Fund *n.* pondo, kuwalta

Fundamental *adj.* essensiyal, pundamental

Funeral *n.* paglilibing, libing

Fungus *n.* onggo

Funnel *n.* embudo, tsiminea

Funny *adj.* katawa-tawa, nakakatuwa, komiko

Fur *n.* lanilya, katad

Furbish *v.* bulihin, pakinisin

Furious *adj.* mabangis, mabagsik

Furl *v.* balumbunin, ibalumbon, lulunin, ilulon

Furnace *n.* hurno, pugon

Furnish *v.* bigyan, tustusan

Furniture *n.* kasangkapan, muwebles

Furor *n.* gulo, sigya, sigla

Furrow *n.* uka, kanal, kunot, kulubot

Further *adv.* at saka

Further *v.* isulong, ibunsod, itaguyod

Furtive *adj.* palihim, panakaw

Fury *n.* poot

Fuse *n.* mitsa, pusible, piyus

Fuse *v.* matugnaw, mapugnaw, pagsamahin

Fusion *n.* pusyon, unyon, pagsasama

Future *n.* hinaharap, kinabukasan

Fuzz *n.* pelusa

G g

Gab *n.* tabil, tatas, kadaldalan

Gab *v.* magdadaldal, magsasatsat, dumaldal, sumatsat

Gabardine *n.* gabardin

Gabble *v.* dumaldal, sumatsat, magtitilaok

Gabion *n.* gabyon

Gable *n.* gablete, sibi, balisbis

Gad *n.* aguhon, punson

Gad *v.* maggala

Gadfly *n.* bangaw

Gadget *n.* kasangkapan, gadget, kagamitan

Gag *n.* busal, biro

Gag *v.* busalan, sikangan

Gage *n.* ako, hamon, panukat, sangla

Gage *v.* kalkuluhin, sukat, tayahin

Gaiety *n.* kasayahan, saya

Gaily *adv.* masaya

Gain *n.* tubo, pakinabang

Gain *v.* dumami, kitain kumita, makinabang makuha, tubuin makamit, magtubo

Gainsay *v.* salungatin, tuligsain, tanggihan, tutulan

Gait *n.* lakad, paglakad, paso

Gala *adj.* gala

Gala *n.* gala

Galaxy *n.* galaksiya

Gale *n.* silakbo, unos

Galician *n.* Galisyano

Galiot *n.* galyota

Gallery *n.* bulwagan, angpubliko, galeriya, palko, tanghalan

Galley *n.* galera, kusina

Gallivant *v.* maggala, maglibot, maglagalag

Gallon *n.* galon

Gallop *n.* tagbong-kabig

Gallows *n.* bibitayan, bibigtihan

Galore *adj.* kayramirami, saganang-sagana

Galore *adv.* kayramirami, saganang-sagana

Galstone *n.* bato sa apdo

Galvanic *adj.* galbaniko, istimulante

Galvanize *v.* galbanisahan

Galvanometer *n.* galbanometro

Gamble *n.* sugal

Gamble *v.* makipagsapalaran, magsugal, pumus, sugalan

Gambler *n.* hugador, manunugal

Gambling *n.* sugal, pagsusugal

Gambodge *n.* gomaguta

Game *n.* laro, laruan

Gamin *n.* batang-palaboy, kantuboy

Gamut *n.* buong-iskala

Gander *n.* malaking gansa

Gang *n.* barkada, gang, pandilya, pangkat

Ganglion *n.* gangglíyo

Gangster *n.* gangster, kriminal, salarin, mambubutang butangero

Gaol *n.* bilangguan, piitan

Gap *n.* butas, guang, patlang puwang, bangin

Gape *v.* humikab, mapanganga, ngumanga, tumitig

Garage *n.* garahe

Garb *n.* kasuutan, pananamit, suot

Garb *v.* bihisan, damtan

Garbage *n.* basura, layak, yamutmot

Garble *v.* guluhin

Garden *n.* hardin, halamanan

Gardener *n.* hardinero

Gardenia *n.* gardenya

Gardening *n.* ortikultura, paghahardin, paghahalamanan

Gargle *v.* ipagmumog, magmumog, mumugin

Garish *adj.* marangya, mapagparangya

Garland *n.* girnalda, kuwintas na bulaklak

Garlic *n.* bawang

Garment *n.* damit, bistidura, baro

Garner *v.* granero, magtipon tipunin, makatipon

Garnet *n.* garnet, granate

Garnish *v.* gayakan, palamutian

Garrison *n.* garison

Garrote *n.* garote

Garrulous *adj.* masalita, matabil

Garter *n.* garter, ligas

Gas *n* gaas, petroleo, buhog, kabag

Gaseous *adj.* gaseoso

Gash *n.* iwa, laslas, taga

Gasket *n.* gasket

Gaskin *n.* polaynas na balat

Gasoline *n.* gasolina

Gasp *v.* humingal

Gastralgia *n.* gastralhiya

Gastric *adj.* gastriko

Gastrin *n.* gastrin

Gastritis *n.* gastritis

Gastroenteritis *n.* gastroenteritis

Gastronomy *n.* gastronomiya

Gate *n.* entrada, pasukan, tarangkahan

Gatekeeper *n.* portero, bantay-pinto

Gateway *n.* pasukan

Gather *v.* anihin, tipunin, nagkasamasama ipunin, mamitas magtipon, mamulot tipunin, samsamin

Gaud *n.* palamuting mumurahin

Gaudy *adj.* marangya, nagmarangya, nagmamagara, matingkad, masagwa

Gaul *n.* galo, pransiya

Gaunt *adj.* hapis, yayat, patpatin, payat

Gauntlet *n.* guwantelete

Gauze *n.* gasa

Gavel *n.* malyete

Gawk *n.* hangal, gunggong

Gay *adj.* masaya, masigla

Gay *n.* bakla

Gay *n.* albay, suhay, tao

Gaze *v.* titigan, tumitig, tingnan

Gazebo *n.* balkong may bintana

Gazelle *n.* gasela

Gazer *n.* miron

Gazette *n.* gaseta

Gazetteer *n.* gasetero

Gear *n.* engranahe, guwarnisyon, pananamit

Geeko *n.* tuko

Geisha *n.* geysa

Gel *v.* mamuo, manigas

Gelatine *n.* gulaman, helatina

Gelatinous *adj.* helatinoso, malagulaman, malahelatina

Gelation *n.* pamumuo, paninigas

Geld *v.* kapunin, magkapon

Gelded *adj.* kapon, kinapon

Gelder *n.* mangangapon, tagakapon

Gelid *adj.* elado

Gem *n.* alahas, hiyas

Geminate *adj.* paris, doble

Gemini *n.* hemini

Gemma *n.* katawang parang buko

Gendarme *n.* pulisya

Gender *n.* henero, kasarian, tanhin

Genealogist *n.* henealohista, mananalaangkanan

Genealogy *n.* henealohiya, talaangkanan

General *adj.* pangkalahatan, panlahatan kalahatan, karaniwan, kalakaran

General *n.* heneral, lahatan

Generate *v.* lumikha, gumawa, magsupling

Generation *n.* henerasyon, paglikha, paggawa, salinlahi panganganak

Generator *n.* dinamo, henerador

Generatrix *n.* heneratris, ina

Generosity *n.* henerosidad, pagkabukas palad, kabutihang-loob

Generous *adj.* bukaspalad, mapagbigay, maawa

Genesis *n.* henesis, orihen, pinagmulan

Genethliac *adj.* pangkapanganakan

Genetics *n.* henesya, palangkanan

Genial *adj.* grasyoso, henyal, magiliw, masayahin,masintahin

Geniality *n.* pagkagrasyoso, pagkamagiliw

Genital *adj.* henital

Genitive *adj.* henetibo, paari

Genius *n.* henyo, talino

Genre *n.* uri, kategoriya

Genteel *adj.* hentil, mabikas, magalang, mahal

Gentian *n.* hensiyana

Gentle *adj.* butihin, mabait mabini, magiliw marahan, mahinahon, mahinhin

Gentleman *n.* marangal, maginoo

Gentry *n.* gitnang, lipunan

Genuflect *v.* pagluhod

Genuine *adj.* tunay, tapat, autentiko, di-huwad

Genus *n.* henero, klase, uri

Geocentric *adj.* hoesentriko

Geochemistry *n.* heokimika

Geodesy *n.* heodesya

Geodetic *adj.* heodesiko

Geodynamics *n.* heodinamika

Geogeny *n.* heohenya

Geognosy *n.* heognosya

Geographer *n.* heograpo

Geographic *adj.* heograpiko

Geography *n.* heograpiya

Geoid *n.* heoyde

Geologic *adj.* heologiko

Geologist *n.* heologo

Geology *n.* heolohiya

Geomancy *n.* heomansiya

Geometric *adj.* heometriko

Geometrician *n.* heometriko

Geometry *n.* heometriya

Geomorphology *n.* heomorpolohiya

Geophysics *n.* heopisika

Geopolitics *n.* heopolitika

Georama *n.* globoheograpiko, heorama

Geotropism *n.* heotropismo

Geranium *n.* heranyo

Germ *n.* embryon, suloy bakterya, supang semilya, mikrobyo

German *adj.* aleman

German *n.* aleman

Germane *adj.* angkop, kuagnay

Germanium *n.* hermanyo

Germinate *v.* sumuloy, sumupang

Gerontology *n.* herontolohiya

Gerund *n.* herundiyo

Gestate *v.* magbuntis

Gestation *n.* pagbubuntis

Gesticulate *v.* magkukumpas

Gesticulation *n.* hestikulasyon, pagkukumpas

Gesture *n.* galaw, kilos, pahayag, kumpas, pagkumpas

Get *v.* hulihin, kitain, kunin; kumuha, makamit mahuli, makuha matamo, matanggap tamuhin, tanggapin

Gewgaw *n.* laruan

Ghastly *adj.* nakapanghihilakbot

Ghost *n.* multo, anino

Ghoul *n.* bampiro

Giant *adj.* napakalaki

Giant *n.* higante

Gibbet *n.* bibitayan

Gibbon *n.* matsing, gibon

Giblet *n.* menudilyo

Gibous *adj.* bukot, naumbok

Giddy *adj.* hilo, nahihilo, salawahan

Gift *n.* aginaldo, regalo kakayahan, talino, handog

Gifted *adj.* matalino, matalas

Gig *n.* kalisin, lantsa

Giggle *v.* humalikhik, ngumisngis

Gigolo *n.* gigolo

Gild *v.* duraduhin

Gilded *adj.* ginintuan

Gilder *n.* dorador

Gill *n.* hasang

Gimlets *n.* balibol

Gimmick *n.* gimik, pamamaraan

Gin *n.* hinebra

Ginger *n.* luya

Giraffe *n.* hirapa

Girasol *n.* hirasol

Gird *v.* bigkisan, maghanda, sinturunan, talian

Girder *n.* pingga, sepo, tahilan

Girdle *n.* bigkis, kurse paha, sinturon

Girl *n.* batang babae, kasintahan, babae, dalaga

Gist *n.* kakanggata, buod

Give *v.* ibigay, ipagkaloob igawad, magbigay, magkaloob bigyan

Gizzard *n.* balumbalunan

Glace *adj.* makinis at makinang

Glacial *adj.* glasyal

Glacier *n.* glasyer, kimpal ng yelo

Glad *adj.* maligaya, nagagalak, nalulugod, masaya, nutawa

Gladden *v.* magalak, malugod, matuwa

Glade *n.* parang

Gladiator *n.* gladyador

Gladiolus *n.* gladyola

Gladness *n.* galak, lugod, tuwa

Glair *n.* klara ng itlog

Glamorize *v.* alindugan

Glamorous *adj.* maalindog, mapanghalina

Glamorousness *n.* pagka-maalindog

Glamour *n.* alindog, halina, gayuma, panghalina

Glance *n.* sulyap

Glance *v.* masulyapan, sulyapan, tingnan

Gland *n.* glandula

Glare *n.* ningning, panlilisik

Glare *v.* magningning, manlisik

Glaring *adj.* malinaw, nanlilisik, nakasisilaw, maliwanag

Glass *n.* bubog, baso, kristal, salamin

Glaze *v.* salaminan, barnisan

Glazed *adj.* glasyado, satinado

Gleam *n.* sinag, kislap

Gleam *v.* kuminang, kumislap, manginang

Glean *v.* mamulot, manghimalay

Glee *n.* galak, saya, tuwa

Glib *adj.* madulas, maluwag, matatas

Glide *n.* palutang, salimbay

Glide *v.* magpalutang, dumausdos

Glider *n.* glayder

Glimmer *n.* andap, kurap

Glimmer *v.* umandap-andap

Glimpse *n.* siglaw

Glint *n.* kinang, kislap

Glisten *v.* manginang, mangislap

Glitter *n.* kinang, kislap

Glitter *v.* kuminang, kumislap

Gloam *n.* silim

Global *adj.* pambuong-daigdig

Globate *adj.* bilugan

Globe *n.* globo, daigdig, sansinukob

Gloom *n.* kulimlim, lungkot, panglaw lumbay, kalumbayan

Gloomy *adj.* madilim, malungkot

Glorious *adj.* luwalhati

Glory *n.* glorya, kulawalhatian luwalhati, karangalan, pagpupuri

Glory *v.* luwalhatiin

Gloss *n.* kinang, kintab

Gloss *v.* pakintabin, pakinangin

Glossary *n.* glosaryo

Glossy *adj.* makintab, makinang

Glottis *n.* glotis

Glove *n.* glab, guwantes
Glow *v.* magbaga, magningning, magliwanag
Glower *v.* mandilat
Glucose *n.* glukosa
Glue *n.* kola, pandikit
Glue *v.* idikit, ikola
Glum *adj.* malagim, mapanglaw
Glut *v.* lumamon, lumanin
Gluten *n.* gluten
Glutinous *adj.* glutinoso, malagkit
Glutton *n.* taong-masiba
Gluttonous *adj.* masiba, matakaw
Gluttony *n.* kasibaan, matakaw
Gluttony *n.* kasibaan, katakawan
Glycerine *n.* gliserina
Glycerol *n.* gliserol
Glycogen *adj.* glikoheno
Glycogen *n.* glikoheno
Gnarl *n.* buko ng kahoy
Gnarl *v.* umangil
Gnarled *adj.* mabuko
Gnat *n.* niknik
Gnaw *v.* ngatngatin
Gnu *n.* busepalo
Go *v.* lumakad, lumayo, pumunta magpunta, magpatuloy mawala, tumungo umalis, tumulak
Goad *n.* agihon, panundot
Goad *v.* sundutin
Goal *n.* layunin, layon tunguhin, hangad, hantungan
Goat *n.* kambing
Gob *n.* kimpal, marino
Gobble *v.* laklakin, lamunin
Goblet *n.* kopa
Goblin *n.* duwende, tiyanak
Gobo *n.* gobo, panangga
God *n.* bathala, diyos, lumikha
Goddess *n.* diyosa, diwata
Goggle *n.* dilat, sulimpat
Goggle *v.* sumulimpat, magduling, dumilat
Going *adj.* patuloy, umaandar, aktibo
Going *n.* pagalis, pagtungo, pagpunta
Goiter *n.* goiter, bosyo, buklaw
Gold *n.* ginto, oro
Golden *adj.* ginintuan
Golf *n.* golp
Golf *v.* maggolp
Goliath *n.* higante
Gondola *n.* gondola
Gondolier *n.* gondolero
Gone *adj.* wala na
Gong *n.* agong, gong
Gonophore *n.* gonoporo
Good *adj.* kabutihan, kagalingan, mabuti, mabait mahusay
Goodbye *n.* paalam
Goodness *n.* ikabubuti, kabutihan
Goods *n.* mga tinda, bilihin

Goose *n.* gansa

Gore *n.* dugo

Gore *v.* suwagin

Gore *v.* lumamon, magbultak

Gorge *n.* butse, bangin, lalamunan, pagbubultak

Gorgeous *adj.* marilag, maringal

Gorilla *n.* gurilya

Gory *adj.* madugo

Gospel *n.* ebanghelyo

Gossip n. satsat, magtsismis, sumitsit, magsitsit

Goth *n.* godo

Gothic *adj.* gotiko

Gouge *n.* pait na medyakaya

Gouge *v.* dalirutin

Goulash *n.* gulas unggaro

Gourd *n.* bote, inuman, kalabasino

Gourmet *n.* taong mapamiling pagkain

Gout *n.* artritis

Govern *v.* mamahala, pamahalaan, ayusin, sakupin

Governess *n.* yaya

Government *n.* gobyerno, pamahalaan

Governmental *adj.* pampamahalaan

Governor *n.* gobernador

Gown *n.* bestido, toga, tunika

Grab *v.* agawin, daklutin, saklutin, sunggaban

Grabble *v.* maghahalugap

Grace *n.* grasya, kabaitan, biyaya

Grace *v.* palamutian, parangalan, biyayaan

Graceful *adj.* malantik

Gracious *adj.* grasyoso, magiliw, mabait, mapagbiyaya

Gradation *n.* grado, gradasyon

Grade *n.* antas, baitang, grado, hakbang, klase, uri

Grade *v.* pagpantayin, pantayin, uriin

Gradual *adj.* gradwal, dahan-dahan

Gradual *adv.* gradwal

Graduate *n.* gradwado, nagtapos, takalan

Graduation *n.* gradwasyon, pagtatapos

Graft *n.* grapting, katiwalian, paugat, pasupling

Grafter *n.* grapter, manguumit

Grail *n.* kalis

Grain *n.* butil, grano, trigo

Grainy *adj.* butilbutil, granular

Gram *n.* gramo

Grammer *n.* gramatika, balarila

Granary *n.* kamalig, bangan

Grand *adj.* bunyi, dakila, lubusang puno, mahal, malawak maringal,sagana

Grandchild *n.* apo

Grandeur *n.* kadakilaan, karingalan

Grandfather *n.* ingkong

Grandmother *n.* impo

Grange *n.* asyenda, granha

Granite *n.* granito

Granny *n.* lola, lolita, tanda

Granparent *n.* nuno

Grant *v.* ayunan, ibigay, payagan

Granular *adj.* granular

Grape *n.* ubas

Grapefruit *n.* kahel, lukban, suha

Graph *n.* grapika, talangguhit

Graph *v.* magtalangguhit, talangguhitin

Graphic *adj.* grapiko, palarawan

Graphite *n.* grapito

Grapple *v.* bunuin, magbuno, sunggaban, hawakan

Grasp *n.* paghawak, unawa

Grasp *v.* daklutin, hawakan, maunawaan, sunggaban

Grasping *adj.* mapangamkam, matakaw

Grass *n.* damo, sakate

Grasshopper *n.* lukton, balang, tipaklong

Grate *n.* berhas, ngilo, rehas

Grate *v.* kayurin, kudkurin, magkayod, magkudkod

Grateful *adj.* nagpapasalamat

Gratification *n.* gantimpala, kaluguran, kasiyahan

Gratify *v.* pairugan

Gratis *adv.* gratis, libre

Gratitude *n.* gratitud, pagpapasalamat

Gratuitous *adj.* di-hiningi

Gratuity *n.* gantinpagal

Grave *adj.* mahalaga, malala maselan, seryo, malubha

Grave *n.* hukay, libingan, pantiyon

Gravel *n.* graba, kaskaho

Gravitate *v.* grabitasyon, mahulugbigat

Gravitation *n.* grabitasyon, pagkahulogbigat

Gravity *n.* hulugbigat, grabidad, kahalagahan, kalubhaan

Gravy *n.* sarsa

Gray *adj.* gris, abuhin, mapanglaw, senisado kulayabo

Graze *v.* daplisan, dumaplis, manginain, papanginainin

Grazier *n.* ganadero, pastolbaka

Grease *n.* grasa, mantika, sabo

Grease *v.* grasahan, langisan

Great *adj.* dakila, mahal, malaki, makapangyarihan

Greatness *n.* kadakilaan

Greed *n.* katakawan, siba kayamuan, katimawan, imbot

Greedy *adj.* masakim, masiba, masunggab matakaw, sakim

Green *adj.* bastos, baguhan berde, lungti, luntian

Greenhouse *n.* imbernakulo, pasibulan, punlaan

Greet *v.* batiin, bumati, salubungin, kumustahin

Greeting *n.* bati, kumustahan

Grenade *n.* bombagranada, granada

Grenadier *n.* granadero

Grey *adj.* gris, abuhin, mapanglaw

Grey *adj.* abuhin

Greyhound *n.* galgo, lebrel

Grid *n.* berhas, parilya, rehas

Griddle *n.* tortera

Gridiron *n.* parilya, ihawan

Grief *n.* dalamhati, lumbay, pighati, hapis

Grievance *n.* agrabyo, kaapihan, karaingan

Grieve *v.* ipagdalamhati, magdalamhati

Grievous *adj.* nakalulungkot

Griffin *n.* galeon

Grill *n.* parliya, ihawan

Grill *v.* iihaw, pagtatanungin

Grim *adj.* mabangis, mabalasik

Grimace *n.* ngiwi, ngibit, simangot

Grimace *v.* ngumiwi, ngumibit, sumimangot

Grime *n.* uling, dumi

Grimy *adj.* marumi, marungis, madusing

Grin *n.* ngisi, ngiti

Grin *v.* ngumisi, ngumiti

Grind *n.* giniling

Grind *v.* gilingin, durugin ihasa, dinurog itagis, pihitin

Grinder *n.* gilingan, panggiling

Grindstone *n.* hasaan

Grip *v.* hawakan, malatin

Grippe *n.* impluwensa, plu, trangkaso

Grit *n.* buhangin, tibay

Groan *n.* daing, halinghing, haluyhoy

Groan *v.* dumaing, humalinghing, hamuluyhoy

Grocer *n.* groser, abasero

Grocery *n.* groseri, grocery

Grogy *adj.* lango, lasing

Groin *n.* singit

Groom *n.* nobyo, sota

Groom *v.* almusawahin, ayusin, ihanda, iskobahin

Groove *n.* tudling, kanal

Grope *v.* kapain, kumapakapa

Gross *adj.* makapal, magaspang, nakahihiya, buo, mahalay

Gross *n.* gruesa

Grotto *n.* gruta, kuweba, yungib

Ground *n.* lupa, katwiran, paniwala, saligan

Ground *v.* gilingin, sayad

Group *n.* grupo, kuponan pangkat, pulutong, umpok

Group *v.* pagsamahin

Grovel *v.* maggumapang, manikluhod

Grow *v.* dumami, nagtubo lumawak, lumaki sumibol, tumas tumubo, umunlad

Growl *n.* ungol

Growl *v.* umungol

Growth *n.* paglaki, pagsibol, pagtubo, tubo, yabong

Grub *n.* uod, pagkain

Grudge *n.* inggit

Grudge *v.* mahili, mainggit

Gruel *n.* lugaw, niligaw

Gruelling *adj.* mahigpit, mahigpitan

Gruff *adj.* magaspang, masungit, pagalit

Grumble *v.* umungol

Grunt *n.* igik

Grunt *v.* umigik

Guarantee *n.* garantiya

Guarantee *v.* garantiyahan, garantisahan, panagutan, sagutin

Guarantor *n.* garantisador, piyador

Guard *n.* bantay, taliba, tanod

Guard *v.* bantayan, guwardiyahan, tanuran,ipagtanggol pangalaagan, tumanod

Guarded *adj.* binabantayan, maingat, tinatanuran

Guardian *n.* guwardiyan, protektor

Guava *n.* bayabas

Guerilla *n.* gerilya

Guess *n.* hinuha, hula, palagay

Guess *v.* hulaan, isipin, akalain, manghula

Guest *n.* bisita, dalaw, panauhin

Guidance *n.* akay, patnubay, pamamatnubay

Guide *n.* giya, gaybay patnubay, tagaakay

Guide *v.* akayin, patnubayan

Guild *n.* gremyo, kapatiran, unyon

Guilt *n.* kasalanan, pagkakasala

Guilty *adj.* maysala, maykasalanan, nagkasala

Guinea pig *n.* kunehilyo

Guise *n.* anyo, balatkayo, itsura, pananamit

Guitar *n.* gitara

Gulf *n.* kalookan, look

Gull *n.* tagak

Gullet *n.* lalaugan

Gullible *adj.* mapaniwalain

Gully *n.* barangka

Gulp *v.* lulunin

Gum *n.* dagta, gilagid

Gun *n.* baril

Gurgle *v.* lumagaslas, lumagukgok

Gush *v.* bumulwak, bumugalwak, bulwak, sumalagwak sagalwak,tilandoy

Gusset *n.* patigas

Gust *n.* silakbo

Gut *n.* bituka

Gutted *adj.* uka, inuk-ok

Gutter *n.* aluloid, kanal

Guttle *v.* lumamon

Guzzle *v.* maglalangga, magiinom

Gymnasium *n.* himnasyo

Gymnastic *adj.* himnastiko

Gynecologist *n.* hinekologo

Gynecology *n.* hinekolohiya

Gyp *v.* madaya, mandaya mananso, matanso

Gypsum *n.* yeso

Gypsy *n.* hitano

Gyrate *v.* uminog

Gyration *n.* inog

Gyroscope *n.* hiroskopyo

Gyves *n.* pangaw

H h

Ha *intr.* ha, naku,ku

Habiliment *n.* damit, kasuutan, pananamit

Habit *n.* damit, hilig ugali, bisyo gawi, kinagawian

Habit *n.* damit, hilig ugali, bisyo gawi

Habitat *n.* tirahan

Habitation *n.* pagtira, pananahanan, tirahan

Habitual *adj.* kinagawian, kinaugalian

Habituate *adj.* matitirahan

Habituate *v.* ugaliin

Hack *n.* kabayong paupahan

Hack *v.* tadtarin, tabtabin

Haft *n.* hawakan, tatangan

Hag *n.* buruha

Haggard *adj.* hagod

Haggish *adj.* malabruha, bruha

Haggle *v.* magtalo, baratin, magtatawad, makipagt pagtalunan

Haggler *adj.* regatera

Hagiography *n.* talambuhay

Hagiology *n.* hagyolohiya

Hail *n* graniso, ulan

Hail *v.* tawagin, batiin, saluduhan

Hair *n.* buhok, balahibo

Hair-dresser *n.* tagapagkulot, mangungulot

Hairy *adj.* balahibuhin

Hale *adj.* malusog, malakas, walangsakit

Half *adj.* kalahati

Half *n.* kalahati

Halitus *n.* hinga, hininga, singaw

Hall *n.* bulwagan, pasilyo salas, gusali

Hallow *v.* santipikahin, konsagrahin

Hallowed *adj.* konsagrado, pinagpala

Halloween *n.* halowin

Hallucination *n.* kinikita, alusinasyon

Halo *n.* sinag , halo

Halogen *n.* haloheno

Haloid *adj.* haloydeo

Halt *adj.* pilay

Halt *n.* hinto, tigil

Halt *v.* huminto, tumigil, patigilin

Halter *n.* soga, pansuga, silo

Ham *n.* hita, hamon

Hamburger *n.* hamburger

Hammer *n.* martilyo, masilyo pamukpok, malyete

Hammock *n.* hamaka, duyan

Hamper *n.* kanasto, ropero

Hamper *v.* hadlangan, pabigatan, gapusin

Hand *n.* kamay, palakpak kontrol, mano kakayahan

Hand *v.* abutan, ibigay, ipamana

Handbag *n.* kalupi

Handbill *n.* ohaswelta

Handbook *n.* manwal

Handcuff *n.* posas

Handful *n.* sandakot, dakot

Handicap *n.* handikap, palamang, kapansanan

Handicraft *n.* gawaing-kamay

Handiwork *n.* gawang-sining

Handkerchief *n.* panyo, panyolito

Handle *n.* hawakan, tatangnan

Handle *v.* hawakan, tangnan

Handmade *adj.* yaring-kamay

Handout *n.* pamigay

Handrail *n.* pasamano

Handsaw *n.* serutso

Handsome *adj.* maganda, makisig, sagana

Handwriting *n.* sulat-kamay

Handy *adj.* sanay, malapit, katabi

Hang *n.* kahulugan, paraan

Hang *v.* ibitin, bitayin isabit, kumapit isampay

Hanger *n.* sabitan

Hank *n.* likaw, labay, rolyo

Hanker *v.* naisin, lunggatiin

Haphazard *adv.* padaskuldaskol

Haphazard *n.* pagkakataon

Hapless *adj.* sawimpalad

Harmony

Happen *v.* mangyari, magkataon

Happening *n.* pangyayari

Happiness *n.* kaligayahan, luwalhati

Happy *adj.* maligaya, maluwalhati

Harangue *n.* talumpati, diskurso

Harangue *v.* pagdiskursuhan, pagtalumpatian

Harass *v.* pagurin, guluhin pagalin, balisahin

Harbor *n.* daungan, puwerto, kanlungan

Harbor *v.* kupkupin, magkimkim, magdamdam, patuluyin

Hard *adj.* matigas, mahiras matira, malupit

Hare *n.* liyebre, lepus

Harem *n.* harem

Hark *v.* makinig, pakinggan

Harlot *n.* puta, masamang babae, patutot

Harm *n.* pinsala, sakit, kasamaan

Harm *v.* pinsalain, saktan, sugatan

Harmful *adj.* nakapipinsala, nakasasama

Harmless *adj.* di-makakaano, di-makasasama

Harmonic *adj.* kaugma, katunog

Harmonica *n.* silindro

Harmony *n.* armoniya, ugmaan

Harness

Harness *n.* guwarnisyon

Harness *v.* isingkaw

Harp *n.* alpa, lira

Harp *v.* ipahayag, isatinig

Harpy *n.* arpiyas

Harrow *n.* suyod, kalmot

Harrowing *adj.* nakalulungkot, nakapanghihilakbot

Harsh *adj.* magaspang, magaralgal malupit, bastos

Harvest *n.* gapasan, ani

Harvest *v.* gapasin, anihin, umani

Has *v.* may, mayroon

Hasheesh *n.* hasis, kanabis

Hasp *n.* kabitan

Haste *n.* dalos, pagtutulin, pagmamadali

Hasten *v.* dalidaliin, nagmamadali

Hastily *adv.* padalos-dalos

Hat *n.* gora, sambalilo, kupya

Hatch *v.* mamisa, magpakana

Hatchery *n.* pamisaan, ingkubador

Hatchet *n.* palataw, puthaw

Hate *n.* poot, suklam, pagkapoot

Hate *v.* mapoot, kapootan

Hateful *adj.* nakamumuhi, nakagagalit, nakapopoot

Hatred *n.* poot, suklam

Haughtiness *n.* pagmamataas, pagmamalaki

Haughty *adj.* mapagmataas, mapagmalaki

Headless

Haul *n.* batak, hila, hatak

Haul *v* hilahin, arastrihin, remorkihin

Haunt *n.* paboritong pook

Haunt *v.* pagmultuhan

Have *v.* may, hawakan, mayroon, taglayin, ariin

Havelock *n.* panakip ng gora

Haven *n* puwerto, duungan

Haven *n.* duungan, puwerto

Havoc *n.* pagkagiba, pagkapuksa

Hawk *n.* lawin

Hawk *v.* maglako

Hawker *n.* maglalako

Hay *n.* dayami, giniikan

Hayfield *n.* dayamihan

Hazard *n.* panganib, peligro

Hazard *v.* makipagsapalaran, ipagsapalaran

Hazardous *adj.* mapanganib, piligroso

Haze *n.* kulabong, singaw, ulap, paghihirap

Haze *v.* magpahirap, pahirapan

Hazel *n.* abelyano, akstanyo

Hazy *adj.* malabo, maulap

He *pron.* siya

Head *n.* puno, ulo, pinuno, panguluhan

Head *v.* unahan

Headache *n.* sakit ng ulo

Header *n.* panguna

Heading *n.* pamuhatan, pamulaan

Headless *adj.* walang-ulo

Headlight *n.* ilaw sa uluman

Headmaster *n.* prinsipal, punong-guro

Headquarters *n.* himpilan, kuwartel

Headship *n.* pagkapuno

Headstall *n.* busal

Headstone *n.* lapida

Headstrong *adj.* matigas angulo

Headway *n.* pagsulong

Heady *adj.* pangahas, maulo

Heal *v.* palusugin, maghilom, gamutin, pagalingin, gumaling, lunasan

Health *n.* kalusugan

Healthy *adj.* malusog, nakalulusog

Heap *n.* bunton, maramingmarami

Heap *v.* ibunton, magbunton, itambak

Hear *v.* marinig, pakinggan

Hearing *n.* pandinig, bista, paghuhukom

Heart *n.* puso, kalagitnaan, pusod

Heart attack *n.* atake sa puso

Heart-ache *n.* hapdi ng puso

Heartbreak *adj.* dalamhati

Hearth *n.* apuyan, tahanan, pugon, dapugan

Heartily *adv.* masinsinan, buong-puso

Heartless *adj.* walang-puso

Hearty *adj.* magiliw

Heat *n.* init

Heat *v.* painitin, painitan, uminit, magpainit

Heath *n.* parang, matural

Heave *n.* buhat, salya, hagis

Heave *v.* isalya, ihagis, buhatin

Heaven *n.* kalangitan, langit

Heavenly *adj.* makalangit

Heavy *adj.* mabigat, mahalaga, matindi

Hebrew *n.* ebreo

Heckle *v.* mangantiyaw, budyukin

Hectare *n.* ektarya

Hectic *adj.* panunuyot

Hectograph *n.* ektograpo

Hedge *n.* pimpin

Hedge *v.* pimpinan, hadlangan, harangan

Heed *n.* pansin, puna, tingin

Heed *v.* pansinin, puna, tingin

Heel *n.* sakong, sukab, takong

Heft *v.* bintayin, magbintay

Hefty *adj.* mabigat, matipuno

Hegemony *n.* liderato, pamumuno, pamininuno

Height *n.* taas, kataasan, tayog, katayugan

Heir *n.* eredero, tagapagmana

Heirloom *n.* erensiya

Helicopter *n.* helikopter

Heliography *n.* helyograpo, helyograpiya

Helioscope *n.* helyoskopyo

Helium *n.* Helyo

Hell *n.* impiyerno

Hello *intr.* helo, hoy

Helm *n.* ugit, timon

Helmet *n.* helmet, baluti saulo

Help *n.* tulong, adya, saklolo abuloy

Help *v.* tumulong, adyahan, saklolohan abuluyan, tulungan

Helpful *adj.* matulungin

Helpless *adj.* mahina, nakalugmok

Hem *n.* laylayan, lupi, tupi

Hemlock *n.* abeto

Hemoglobin *n.* hemoglobina

Hemophilia *n.* hemopilya

Hemoptysis *n.* hemoptisis

Hemorrhage *n.* emorahiya, pagdurugo

Hemp *n.* kanyamo

Hen *n.* inahin

Hence *adv.* mula rito, mulangayon, sa gayon

Henceforth *adv.* mula ngayon

Henpecked *adj.* dominado, talusaya

Hepatitis *n.* hepatitis

Heptagon *n.* heptagono

Heptagonal *adj.* heptagonal

Her *adj.* kaniya, niya

Her *prn.* kaniya, niya

Herald *n.* taliba, tagapagbalita

Herb *n.* damo, yerba

Herbalist *n.* yerbalista

Herbarium *n.* erbaryo

Hercules *n.* herakleo

Herd *n.* kawan, ganado

Here *adj.* dito, dini

Hereafter *adv.* pagkatapos nito, sa darating, sa hinaharap

Hereby *adv.* sa pamamagitan nito

Hereditary *adj.* namamana, minamana

Hereditary *n.* erensiya, mana, pagmamana

Heredity *n.* pagkakamana

Herein *adv.* sa loob nito

Hereof *adv.* nito

Hereon *adv.* dito

Heretic *n.* erehe

Heretical *adj.* eretiko

Hereto *adv.* dito

Herewith *adv* kalakip nito

Heritage *n.* mana, minana, erensiya

Hermetic *adj.* ermetiko

Hermit *n.* ermitanyo

Hermitage *n.* ermita

Hernia *n.* luslos

Hero *n.* bayani, bida

Heroine *n.* bidang babae, bayaning babae

Heroism *n.* kabayanihan

Heron *n.* tikling, tagak, kandanggaok

Herpes *n.* erpes, buni

Hers *adj.* kanyang, niya, kaniya

Herself *pron.* sarili niya, kanyang sarili, siya na rin

Hesitant *adj.* atubili, alinlangan, urung-sulong

Hesitate *v.* mag-atubill, magalinlangan, mag-alangan, matigilan

Hesitation *n.* pag-aatubili, pag-aalinlangan

Heterogramous *adj.* heterogramo

Heterogramy *n.* hetorogramya

Hew *v.* tagpasin, palakulin

Hex *n.* ingkanto, gaway

Hex *v.* manngaway

Hexagon *n.* heksagono

Heyday *n.* kasikatan, kapanahunan

Hibernate *v.* umiberna

Hiccup *n.* sinok

Hick *n.* tagabukid, probinsiyano

Hide *n.* balat, katad, kuwero

Hide *v.* itago, ilingid, magtago, ipaglihim

Hideous *adj.* napakapangit

Hideout *n.* taguan

Hie *v.* daliin, magmadali

Hierarchy *n.* herarkiya

High *adj.* mataas, matayog

Highborn *n.* anak-mahal

Highland *n.* kabundukan, paltok, kataasan

Highway *n.* karetera, haywey, daang-bayan

Hike *n.* paglalakad

Hike *v.* maglakad nang mahaba, pataasin, dagdagan

Hilarious *adj.* masayang maingay

Hill *n.* burol, punso, tugatog

Hillock *n.* munting burol

Hillside *n.* libis

Hilly *adj.* maburol

Hilt *n.* puluhan

Hilum *n.* mata

Him *pron.* kaniya

Himself *pron.* siya na rin

Hind *adj.* huli, likuran, hulihan

Hinder *v.* hadlangan, pigilan, antalahin

Hindi *n.* hindi

Hindrance *n.* sagabal, balaksila, hadlang

Hinge *n.* bisarga, batayan

Hinge *v.* bisagrahan, pagbatayan

Hint *n.* hiwatig, pahiwatig, paramdam

Hint *v.* ipahiwatig, ipamalay, iparamdam

Hip *n.* pigi, baywang, balakang

Hipbone *n.* balakang

Hipopotamus *n.* hipopotamus, ipopotamo

Hire *n.* alkila

Hire *v.* upahan, umalkila umupa, kamasundo alkilahin, tumawag bumayad

His *adj.* kanyang, niya

His *pron.* kaniya

Hiss *n.* sutsot, singasing, hingasing

Histology *n.* histolohiya

Historian *n.* istoryador, mananalaysay

Historic *adj.* istoriko, makasaysayan

Historical *adj.* pangkasaysayan

History *n.* istorya, kasaysayan

Hit *v.* hampasin, paluin hinampas, nahampas, tumama, tamaan

Hitch *n.* sagabal, hadlang

Hitch *v.* itali, isuga, isingkaw

Hither *adv.* dini, dito

Hive *n.* bahay-pukyutan

Hives *n.* urtikarya, tagulabay, imunimom

Hoard *n.* tinipon

Hoard *v.* magtipon, tipunin, magtinggal

Hoarder *n.* maniningal

Hoarding *n.* panininggal

Hoarse *adj.* malat, namamalat, paos

Hoax *n.* daya, lalang, linlang

Hobble *v.* umika, isuga

Hobby *n.* libangang-gawain

Hobgoblin *n.* duwende

Hobnob *v.* makihalubilo

Hock *n.* tarso, korba

Hodgepodge *n.* bahog, haluhalo

Hoe *n.* asarol

Hoe *v.* asarulin

Hog *n.* baboy

Hoist *v.* itaas

Hold *n.* taban, hawak, kapit

Hold *v.* hinwakan, humawak hawakan, magdaos tumaban, nahawakan

Hole *n.* butas

Holiday *n.* pista, pistang opisyal

Holiness *n.* kasagraduhan, kasantuhan, kabanalan

Holland *n.* olanda

Hollow *adj.* humpak, hungkag, buaw, hupyak

Hollow *n.* guwang

Holocaust *n.* holokosto, pagkapugnaw

Holster *n.* kaluban

Holy *adj.* banal, pinagpala, sagrado

Homage *n.* pitagan, parangal

Home *adj.* pantahanan

Home *n.* tahanan, pamamahay, tirahan, bahay, ampunan

Homeopath *n.* homyopata

Homeopathy *n.* homyopatiya

Homework *n.* araling-bahay, gawaing-pantahanan

Homicide *n.* omisidyo

Homogeneous *adj.* omoheneo, kasangkap, kauri

Homosexual *adj.* omoseksuwal

Homosexuality *n.* omoseksuwalidad, kaomoseksuwalan

Hone *n.* tagisan, lagisan

Hone *v.* itagis, ihasa, ilagis

Honest *adj.* matapat, marangal, tapat

Honesty *n.* katapatan, dangal, karangalan

Honey *n.* pulut-pukyutan

Honeybee *n.* pukyutan

Honeymoon *n.* pulut gata

Honor *n.* dangal, karangalan

Honor *v.* dakilain, iginalang, parangalan

Honorary *adj.* pandangal

Hood *n.* pandong, pindong

Hoodlum *n.* butangero, gangster

Hoodwink *v.* mandaya, manlinlang, dayain, linlangin

Hook *n.* pangalawit, kawit, kalawit, sabitan

Hookworm *n.* bulati

Hooligan *n.* bagabundo, butangero

Hop *n.* buklod, anilyo

Hop *v.* lundagin, lumundag, kumandirit

Hope *n.* pagasa, tiwala

Hope *v.* umasa, pagasa, tiwala

Hopeful *adj.* maasa

Hopeless *adj.* walang pagasa

Horde *n.* horda

Horizon *n.* kagiliran, orisonte

Horizontal *adj.* orisontal, pahiga

Hormone *n.* hormon

Horn *n.* busina, tambuli, sungay, torotot

Hornet *n.* putakti

Horny *adj.* masungay, sungayan

Horoscope *n.* oroskopyo

Horrible *adj.* nakagagalit

Horrify *v.* sindakin, takutin

Horror *n.* sindak, takot

Horror *v.* sindak, takot

Horse *n.* kabayo

Horsepower *n.* lakas-kabayo

Horticulture *n.* holtikultura, paghahalaman

Horticulturist *n.* hortikultor

Hose *n.* medyas

Hospitable *adj.* mapagtanggap

Hospital *n.* ospital, pagamutan

Hospitality *n.* ospitalidad

Hospitalize *v.* ospitalin, iospital

Host *n.* hukbo, mayhanda, ostiya

Hostage *n.* prenda

Hostel *n.* tuluyan, panuluyan

Hostess *n.* hostes

Hostile *adj.* ostil, laban, kalaban

Hostility *n.* ostilidad, pagkakalaban, labanan, pagkakagalit

Hostler *n.* establero, sota

Hot *adj.* mainit, masilakbo, maanghang

Hour *n.* oras

House *n.* bahay, tahanan, tirahan

Hovel *n.* silungan, habong, dampa

Hover *v.* magpaligid-ligid

How *adv.* paano, papano, gaano, magkano

Howl *n.* tambaw, alulong, angal

Howl *v.* tumambaw, umangal

Hub *n.* kuko, sentro, kalagitnaan

Hubbub *n.* linggal, hiyawan, gulo

Huddle *n.* umpukan, siksikan

Huddle *v.* sumiksik, magsiksikan

Hue *n.* kulay, kolor, sigaw, hiyaw

Hue *n.* kolor, kulay

Hug *n.* yakap, yapos

Hug *v.* yapusin, yakapin

Huge *adj.* malaking-malaki

Hull *n.* balok, kasko, balat, bayna

Hum *n.* ugong, higing, ungol, huni

Hum *v.* umugong, humiging, umungol, humuni, ihuni

Human *adj.* pantao, makatao, tauhan

Human *n.* tao

Humanitarian *adj.* makatao

Humble *adj.* aba

Humid *adj.* umedo, halumigmig

Humidity *n.* kahalumigmigan

Humiliate *v.* hiyain, halayin

Humiliating *adj.* nakahihiya

Humiliation *n.* pagkahiya

Humorous *adj.* nakakatawa

Humour *n.* umor, kalooban, pagpapatawa

Humour *v.* bagayan

Hump *n.* umbok

Humpback *n.* kuba, bukot

Humus *n.* lupang-itim

Hunch *n.* bukol, umbok

Hunchback *n.* kuba, bukot

Hundred *n./ad* sandaan

Hungarian *n.* unggaro

Hunger *n.* gutom, pasal, hayok

Hunger *v.* mapasal, mahayok

Hungry *adj.* gutom

Hunk *n.* piraso, tigkal

Hunt *v.* manugis, hanapin, maghanap, mangaso, paghanapin

Hunter *n.* kasador, mamamaril

Hunting *n.* kaseriya, pangaso, pamamaril

Hurdle *n.* lundagan

Hurdle *v.* lumundag, lundagin

Hurl *v.* ihagis, ipukol, ibarog

Hurricane *n.* unos, buhawi

Hurry *v.* magmadali, dalasin, habulin, kahog

Hurt *v.* saktan, masakit, sinaktan, nasaktan

Husband *n.* esposo, asawa, asawang lalaki

Hush *v.* patahimikin

Husk *n.* bunot, upak, balak, balok

Husky *adj.* agas, matipuno

Hustle *v.* pangatawanan, balikatin

Hut *n.* dampa, kubo, kamalig

Hybrid *n.* hibrido

Hydra *n.* hidra

Hydrant *n.* boka-insendiyo

Hydrate *n.* hidrato

Hydraulic *adj.* hidraulika

Hydrogen *n.* hidroheno

Hygene *adj.* iheyene

Hymen *n.* himen

Hymn *n.* dalit, imno, awit

Hyphen *n.* gitling, giyon

Hypnotic *n.* hipnotiko

Hypnotism *n.* hipnotismo

Hypnotize *v.* hipnotisahin

Hypocrisy *n.* hipokresiya, pagkukunwa, pagpapaimbabaw

Hypocrite *n.* ipokrita, mapagkunwari

Hypodermis *n.* hipodermis

Hysteria *n.* histerya

I i

I *n.* kaakuhan, ego

I *pron.* ako

Ice *n.* yelo

Ice Cream *n.* sorbetes

Iceberg *n.* yelong lutang

Icing *n.* aysing, kapang matamis

Icon *n.* larawan, imahen

Icy *adj.* mayelo

Idea *n.* idea, akala, plano, palagay, haka, munukala, pakana, isip

Ideal *adj.* ideal, huwaran, tularan, uliran

Idealism *n.* idealismo

Idealist *n.* idealista

Identical *adj.* pareho, magkauri, pantay, magkatulad

Identification *n.* identipikasyon, pinagkakakilanlan

Identify *v.* identipikahin, kilalanin, ituro, turulin, makisama, makiisa

Identity *n.* identidad, kaisahan, kasarilinan

Ideology *n.* ideolohiya, isip, pangingisip

Ides *n.* kalagitnaan ng buwan

Idiocy *n.* katangahan, kahangalan

Idiom *n.* idyoma, kawikaan

Idiot *n.* idyota, hangal, tanga, tulala

Idle *adj.* tamad, walang-trabaho, walang-empleo, walang-ginagawa

Idleness *n.* katamaran

Idol *n.* idolo

Idolatry *n.* idolatriya

Idyl *n.* idilyo

If *conj.* kung, sakali

Igneous *adj.* igneo, malaapoy, mayapoy

Ignite *v.* sindihan, paningasin, sumiklab

Ignition *n.* ignisyon, pagsisindi, pagpapamngas

Ignoble *adj.* imbi, mababa, hamak

Ignominious *adj.* nakahihiya, walangdangal

Ignorance *n.* kamangmangam

Ignorant *adj.* mangmang

Ignore *v.* pabayaan, huwag pansinin

Iguana *n.* bayawak

Ileum *n.* ilyon

Iliac *adj.* ilyako

Ilk *n.* angkan, hinlog, pamilya, uri

Ill *adj.* masama, may sakit, may karamdaman

Illegal *adj.* ilegal, labang sa batas

Illegible *adj.* di-mabasa

Illegitimate *adj.* bastardo, ilehitimo

Illicit *adj.* di-ipinahihintulot

Illimitable *adj.* di-masusukat

Illinium *n.* ilinyum

Illiteracy *n.* kamangmangan

Illiterate *adj.* mangmang

Illness *n.* karamdaman, sakit

Illumine *v.* magliwanag, paliwanagan, tanglawan

Illusion *n.* ilusyon, malikmata, guniguni, kahibanan

Illusive *adj.* madaya, mapanlinlang

Illustrate *v.* ilarawan

Illustration *n.* larawang paliwanag

Illustrative *adj.* naglalararawan

Illustrator *n.* disenyador, dibuhante

Illustrious *adj.* bantog, dakila, ilustrado

Image *n.* imahen, larawan, anino

Imagery *n.* alaala, haraya, imahinasyon, paghaha

Imaginable *adj.* mahahaka, maiisip

Imagination *n.* haraya, hinagap, imahinasyon, pagpapaharaya, guniguni

Imagine *v.* isipin, hakain, gunigunihin, magnuniguni, mahaka

Imaginery *adj.* sa guni guni

Imam *n.* imam, pari

Imbalance *n.* pagka-di-timbang

Imbecile *adj.* imbesil, mulala, ungas

Imbecility *n.* imbesilidad, kagunggungan, kamulalaan

Imbibe *v.* lumanghap, lumagom, sumipsip, uminom

Imbroglio *n.* hidwaan, pagkakagulo

Imbue *v.* ikintal, itanim, kintalan, tamnan

Imitate *v.* manghuwad, gagarin, huwaran, gayahin, tularan, tumulad, parisan

Imitation *n.* huwad, gagad, gaya, imitasyon, kopya, panggagagad

Immaculate *n.* busilak, puro

Immanence *n.* pamumuspos, pananatili

Immanent *adj.* imanente, likas, namumuspos

Immaterial *adj.* di-kailangan

Immature *adj.* mura, bubot

Immaturity *n.* kabataan, kabubutan, kamuraan

Immeasurable *adj.* di-masusukat

Immediacy *n.* kakagyatan

Immediate *adj.* kagyat, madalian, pagdaka

Immediately *adv.* agad, kaagad, karakaraka, kapagdaka

Immense *adj.* dakilangdakila, napakalaki

Immerse *v.* ilubog, ibabad, itubog

Immigrant *n.* imigrante, mandarayuhan, nandarayuhan

Immigrate *v.* mandayuhan

Immigration *n.* imigrasyon, pandarayuhan

Imminence *n.* pagka-napipinto

Imminent *adj.* nalalapit, napipinto

Immobile *adj.* panatilihan

Immobility *n.* pagka-di-mapagalaw

Immobilize *v.* ipirmi, patigilin, pahintuin

Immoderate *adj.* labis, mabilis

Immodest *adj.* pangahas, mahalay, magaspang, magaslaw

Immolate *v.* ipagsakrispisyo

Immolation *n.* sakripisyo

Immoral *adj.* imoral, mahalay, masagwa

Immorality *n.* inmoralidad, kahalayan

Immortal *adj.* inmortal

Immortality *n.* inmortalidad

Immovable *adj.* di-matinag, di-mapatinag, walang-tigatig

Immune *adj.* liway,di-tinatablan, ligtas

Immunity *n.* inmunidad, kaliwayan

Immunization *n.* inmunisasyon, pagliliway, pagpapaliway

Immunize *v.* inmunisahin, liwayin

Imortalize *v.* inmortalisahin

Imp *n.* batang pilyo, munting diyablo

Impact *n.* bagsak, lagpak, bangga, banggaan, bunggo, bungguan, tama

Impair *v.* makasira, pahinain, humina, pasamain

Impale *adj.* tuhugin

Impale *v.* tuhugin

Impanation *n.* transub-stansiyasyon, pananapay

Impart *v.* ibigay, ipabatid, idulot, ipaalam, ituro, magturo, magbigay, magdulot

Impartial *adj.* imparsiyal, makatarungan

Impassable *adj.* di-madaraa-nan

Impasse *n.* daang-putol, kagipitan

Impassionate *adj.* madam damin

Impassive *adj.* impasibo, walang-buhay

Impatience *n.* pagkainip

Impatient *adj.* mainipin

Impeach *v.* isakdal, ihabla, usigin

Impeachment *n.* pagsasak-dal, paghahabla

Impeccable *adj.* impekable

Impedance *n.* impedans

Impede *v.* hadlangan,pigilin, humadlang

Impediment *n.* hadlang, balaksila, sagabal

Impel *v.* itulak, isulong, ibunsod, pagalawin, itaboy, mabunsod, mapilitan, magtangay

Impend *v.* magbala, magbanta, malapit

Impending *adj.* nagbabala, nagbabanta,nalalapit

Impenitent *adj.* impenitente

Imperative *adj.* imperatibo, pautos, sapilitan

Imperator *n.* emperador

Imperceptible *adj.* di-halata, di-mapapansin

Imperfect *adj.* di-ganap

Imperfection *n.* pagka-di-ganap, imperpeksiyon

Imperial *adj.* imperyal, supremo

Imperialism *n.* imperyalismo

Imperil *v.* isapanganib

Imperious *adj.* makahari, mapagmataas, mapanlupig, makapangyarihan

Imperishable *adj.* di-mawala, walang-pagkawala, walang-kamatayan

Impermanent *adj.* di-panati-lihan, di-permanente

Impermeable *adj.* di-tablan, di-talaban

Impersonal *adj.* di-personal

Impersonate *v.* magpanggap

Impersonation *n.* personipikasyon,imitasyon

Impertinent *adj.* imperti-nente, bastos, pangahas

Imperturbable *adj.* mahinahon, panatag

Impervious *adj.* di-tablan, di-malusutan

Impetous *adj.* palasubo, mapusok

Impetus *n.* bulas, bunsod, impetus, impulso

Impiety *n.* kalapastanganan

Impigne *v.* banggain, bundulin., panghimasukan

Impious *adj.* lapastangan, suwail

Implacable *adj.* di-magam-otloob

Implant *v.* itanim,ibaon, ihasik, ikintal, ituro

Implement *n.* kasangkapan, kagamitan

Implement *v.* ganapin, ipagawa, isagawa, isakatuparan, tuparin

Implementation *n.* imple-mentasyon, pagsasakatuparan

Implicate *v.* iugnay, ikabit,idawit, isangkot

Implication *n.* dalawit

Implore *v.* sumamo, lumuhog, magmakaamo, pamanhikan

Imply *v.* mangahulugan, ipahiwatig, imungkahi

Impolite *adj.* bastos

Import *n.* angkat

Import *v.* angkatin, umangkat

Importance *n.* kahalagahan, bigat

Important *adj.* mahalaga, mabigat

Importer *n.* mang-aangkat

Importtation *n.* pang-aangkat

Importunity *v.* panggagam-bala

Impose *v.* lapatan,maglapat, patawan, magpataw, papanaigin

Imposition *n.* imposisyon, pataw, buwis

Impossibility *n.* imposibilidad

Impossible *adj.* di-maaari

Impost *n.* buwis

Imposter *n.* impostor

Imposture *n.* pagpapaganap, pandaraya

Impotence *n.* kahinaan, katuyuan

Impotent *adj.* impotente, mahina, tuyo

Impound *v.* ikulong, magtipon

Impoverish *v.* parukhain, pulubihin

Impoverishment *n.* paghihi-rap, pamumulubi, paghihikahos

Impracticable *adj.* di-magagamit

Impractical *adj.* di-praktikal, walang-kagamitan

Imprecate *v.* sumpain

Imprecation *n.* sumpa

Impregnable *adj.* di-masasalakay, di-malulupig, di-magapi

Impresario *n.* impresaryo

Impress *v.* tablan, ilimbag, mapukaw, itatak, magkabisa, ikintal

Impression *n.* impresyon, kakintalan,marka

Impressionism *n.* impres-yonismo

Impressionist *n.* impres-yonista

Impressive *adj.* nakakap-upukaw loob

Imprint *n.* limbag, tatak

Imprint *v.* maglimbag, limbagin

Imprison *v.* ibilanggo, ikalabos, kulungin, ikulong

Imprisonment *v.* pagkakabil-anggo, pagkakapiit

Improbability *n.* pagka-di-matapat

Improbable *adj.* mahirap mangyari

Improper *adj.* di-dapat, di-bagay, di-angkop

Improve *v.* bumuti, gumaling, pabutihin, magpakagaling, magpakabuti, napagbago

Improvement *n.* pagbuti,pagpapabuti, paghusay, pagkakabago

Improvided *adj.* improbisado

Improvident *adj.* pabaya

Improvisation *n.* improbisasyon

Improvise *v.* improbisahin

Imprudence *n.* pagka-imprudente

Imprudent *adj.* imprudente

Impudent *adj.* pangahas, dinahihiya., walanghiya

Impulse *n.* impulso, bunsod,tulak, simbuyo

Impulsion *n.* impulsiyon, tulak,budlong

Impulsive *adj.* masimbuyo

Impunity *n.* impunidad

Impure *adj.* mahalay, marumi

Impurity *n.* karumihan

Imputation *n* Pagbibintang

Impute *v.* ibintang, iparatung, iugnay

In *prep.* sa, nasa

Inability *n* kawalang-kaya, Kawalang-lakas

Inaccessible *adj.* di-maabot, di-malapitan

Inaccurate *adj.* di-wasto, dieksakto

Inaction *n.* kawalang-kilos

Inactive *adj.* walang-ginagawa, walang-galaw, matamlay

Inadequate *adj.* di-sapat, kulang

Inadmisible *adj.* di-matatanggap

Inadvertent *adj.* di-napansin

Inanimate *adj.* walang-sigla

Inanition *n.* kawalang-laman

Inapplicable *adj.* di-maaari, di-bagay

Inappreciable *adj.* di-halata, di-mahalata

Inapproachable *adj.* di-malapitan

Inappropriate *adj.* di-angkop, di-tumpak

Inapt *adj.* bi-bagay, di-handa

Inarticulate *adj.* pipi, umid

Inaugurate *v.* pasinayaan, magpasinaya, inagurahan

Inauguration *n.* inagurasyon, pasinaya

Inauspicious *adj.* sinasama

Inborn *adj.* katutubo

Inbound *adj.* papasok, papaloob

Inca *n.* inka

Incalculable *adj.* di-maulatan, di-mataya, di-tayak

Incapable *adj* Walang-kaya

Incapacity *n.* pagka-walangkaya

Incarcerate *v.* ikarsel

Incarnate *v.* magkarne, maglaman, magkalaman

Incarnation *n.* engkarnasyon, paglalaman, pagkakatawan

Incendiary *adj.* pampasunog

Incendiary *n.* manununog

Incense *n.* insenso

Incense *v.* galitin, sulsulan

Incentive *adj.* pamukaw, pampasigla, pangganyak

Inceptive *adj.* pansimula

Incessant *adj.* patuloy

Incest *n.* insesto

Incestuos *adj.* insestuwoso

Inch *n.* pulgada, dali

Incidence *n.* Pagkapangyari

Incident *n.* pangyayari

Incinerate *v.* sunugin, tupukin

Incineration *n.* insinirasyon, pagsunog

Incinerator *n.* insinirador

Incipient *adj.* panimula, nagsisimula

Incise *v.* hiwain

Incisive *adj.* nakakahiwa, matalas, matalim

Incite *v.* ibuyo, ibudlong, paiyahan

Incivility *n.* kabastusan

Inclination *n.* ingklinasyon, hilig, kiling

Incline *n.* dahilig

Incline *v.* humilig, kumiling, yumukod

Inclined *adj.* mahilig, hilig

Inclose *v.* ipaloob, ilakip, kulungin, palibutan, maglakip

Inclosure *n.* lakip

Include *v.* isama, ibilang, ilakip, isali

Incognito *adj/a* inkognito

Incombustible *adj.* di-magniningas

Income *n* Kita, Kinita

Income *n.* kita, kinita

Incomparable *adj.* walang-kapantay

Incompatible *adj.* inkompatible, di-magkabagang

Incompetent *adj* Inkompetente

Incomplete *adj* di-kompleto, di-tapos

Inconceiveable *adj.* di-sukat maisip

Inconsiderate *adj* di-mabuting, makipagkapwa

Inconsistent *adj* di-nagkakatugmaan

Inconstant *adj* salawahan

Inconvenience *n.* kagipitan, pagkagipit, sagabal, kaabalahan

Inconvenience *v.* mak-asagabal, makagipit, makaaabala

Inconvenient *adj* pang-abala, panggulo, di-maginhawa

Incorporate *adj* pinagsama

Incorporate *v.* pagsamahin, ilakip, isama

Incorrect *adj* di-wasto, mali, di-dapat, di-tama

Incorrupt *adj.* dilisay, puro

Increase *n.* dagdag, karagdagan, pakinabang, tubo

Increase *v* dagdagan, damihan, dumami,lumaki, tumubo, lakihan, madagdagan, patubuin

Incredible *adj* di-mapaniwalaan, di-kapani-paniwala

Increment *n* dagdag, karagdagan

Increscent *adj.* palaki

Incriminate *v.* idamay, idawit, isakdal, isangkot

Incubate *v.* humalimhim, ingkubahin, lumimlim

Incubator *n.* ingkubador, pamisaan

Incubus *n.* bangungot, ingkubo, uum

Inculcate *v.* ikintal, itanim, ituro

Inculpate *v.* ibintang, iparatang, isangkot

Incumbent *adj.* nakahiga

Incur *v.* mahita, matagpuan, magkasagutin

Incurable *adj.* di-mapagaling

Indebted *v.* may utang

Indebtedness *n.* pagkak-autang

Indecent *adj.* mahalay

Indecision *n.* pag-uulik-ulik

Indeed *adv.* talaga, siyanga

Indefinite *adj.* di-tiyak

Indemnify *v.* magbayad-pinsala

Indent *n.* palugit

Indent *v.* ipasok, palugitan, ikintal

Independence *n.* indepen-densiya, kasarinlan, kalayaan, pagsasarili

Independent *adj.* malaya, sarilining

Index *n.* indise, talatuntunan

Indian *n.* indiyan, indiyano

Indic *adj.* indo, indiko

Indicate *v.* ilagay, ituro, ipakita, ipamalas, ipahiwatig magpakilala

Indication *n.* indikasyon, marka, palatandaan, tanda

Indicative *adj.* indikatibo, nagpapakilala

Indicator *n.* indikador

Indict *v.* ihabla, isakdal

Indifferent *adj.* walang-bahala, patay-damdamin

Indigence *n.* karukhaan, pagdadahop

Indigenous *adj.* katutubo

Indigent *adj.* aba, dukha

Indigestion *n.* indihestiyon, impatso

Indignant *adj.* galit, nagagalit

Indignity *n.* kaalipustaan, kaduhagian

Indigo *n.* anyil, indigo, nilad

Indirect *adj.* indirekto, dituwiran

Indiscreet *adj.* di-matino, walang-bait

Indiscrete *adj.* ig-ig, kitkit

Indiscretion *n.* indiskresyon, imprudensiya

Indite *v.* isulat, sulatin

Individual *adj.* sarili, panarili

Individual *n.* isang tao

Individualism *n.* indibiwal-ismo

Individuality *n.* kasarilinan, kakaniyahan

Indivisible *adj.* di-mahahati

Indolence *n.* indolensiya, katamaran

Indolent *adj.* batugan, tamad

Indoor *adj.* sa loob ng bahay

Induce *v.* himukin, hikayatin, kayagin, maghinuha, hinuhain

Induct *v.* italaga, bigyangsimula

Induction *n.* induksiyon, pagtatalaga

Indulge *v.* magpairog, magpakalabis, pairugan, palayawin, palamangin

Indulgence *n.* indulhensiya, pagpapalayaw

Indulgent *adj.* mapagpalyaw, mapagbigay

Industrialize *v.* industriyal-isahin

Industrious *adj.* masipag, masikap, masikhay

Industry *n.* sikap, sipag, industriya, kalalang kapamuhayan

Indwell *v.* manahanan, panahanan, tirhan, tumira

Inebriate *adj.* lasing

Inebriate *n.* maglalasing

Inebriate *v.* languhin, lasingin

Ineffective *adj.* walang-bisa, di-mabisa

Inefficient *adj.* walang-kaya

Inequality *n.* pagka-di-pantay-pantay

Inert *adj.* walang-galaw

Inertia *n.* inersiya

Inessential *adj.* di-kailan-gang-kailangnan

Inevitable *adj.* di-mailwasan, di-maiilagan

Inexact *adj.* di-eksakto, ditunay na tunay

Inexcusable *adj.* di-mapatatawad

Inexhaustible *adj.* di-mauubos

Inexpensive *adj.* dimahal, mura

Inexperienced *adj.* bagito, walang-karanasan

Inexpressible *adj.* di-maipahayag

Infallible *adj.* impalible

Infammable *adj.* madaling, magsiklab

Infancy *n.* kamusmusan, kasanggulan, pagkabata

Infant *n.* sanggol, paslit, musmos

Infanticide *n.* impantisidyo

Infatuated *adj.* halig, nahahalig

Infect *v.* hawahan, lalinan, manghawa

Infection *v.* impeksiyon, pagkakalalin, pagkakahawa

Infectious *adj.* nakakalalin, nakakahawa

Infer *v.* huluin, hinuhain, maghulo

Inference *n.* imperensiya, hulo, hinuha

Inferior *adj.* mababa, mahina

Inferiority *n.* kababaan

Inferno *n.* impiyerno

Infertile *adj.* asteril, basal

Infest *v.* pagdamihan, pagdumugan

Infidel *n.* impiyel, erehe

Infidelity *n.* kataksilan

Infiltrate *v.* pagsalingitan, sumalingit

Infinite *adj.* walang hanggan, walang hangganan

Infinitive *n.* pawatas

Infinity *n.* pagka- walang hanggan

Infirm *adj.* mabuay, mahina, mahuna

Infirmary *n.* pagamutan

Infirmity *n.* kabuayan, kahinaan

Infix *n.* gitlapi

Inflame *v.* apuyan, mamaga, paningasin, palalain, sindihan, sulsulan, mamula

Inflammable *adj.* siklabin

Inflammation *n.* pamamaga

Inflate *v.* pabintugin, papintugin, palakihin

Inflation *n.* pamimintog, implasyon

Inflexible *adj.* matigas, di-maibaluktot

Inflict *v.* manakit, saktan, magparusa, parusahan

Inflorescence *n.* pamumu-laklak

Inflow *n.* agos na paloob, agos na papasok

Influence *n.* impluensiya, impluho, bisa, palakasan

Influence *v.* magpabago, makabuti, makasama, pasunurin

Influential *adj.* maimpluho, makapangyarihan

Influenza *n.* trangkaso

Infold *v.* balutin, yakapin

Inform *v.* magpabatid, ipabatid, paalam, sabihin, patalstatasan

Informal *adj.* impormal, di-porr ıal

Information *n.* impormasyon, kabatiran, kaalaman

Infraction *n.* pagsira, paglabag

Infrequency *adj.* kadalangan, kabihiraan

Infrequent *adj.* madalang, bihira

Infringe *v.* labagin, lumabag, makialam

Infuriate *v.* galitin, papagngalitin

Infuse *v.* iukit, ikintal, punuin, tigmakin

Ingenous *adj.* inhenwo, matapat

Ingenous *adj.* magaling, mapanlikha

Ingenuity *n.* inhenyosidad, katalinuhan, pagkamatalino

Ingrate *n.* ingrato

Ingratiate *v.* manuyo

Ingredient *n.* panangkap, panahog, panrikado, rikado

Inguinal *adj.* inggínal

Inhabit *v.* tahanan, tirhan

Inhabitant *n.* maninirahan, nakatira

Inhalant *adj.* panlanghap

Inhalation *n.* paglanghap

Inhalator *n.* inhalador, paglanghap

Inhale *v.* langhapin, lumanghap

Inharmonious *adj.* di-magkaugma

Inherent *adj.* likas, katutubo

Inherit *v.* magmana, manahin

Inheritance *n.* mana, erensiya

Inheritor *n.* tagapagmana

Inhibit *v.* magbawal,pigilan, ipagbawal, magpigal

Inhibition *n.* pagbabawal, pagpipilan

Inhospitable *adj.* di-mapagtanggap, ayaw magpapasok

Inhuman *adj.* di-makatao, malupit

Inimical *adj.* di-kaayon, salungat

Iniquitus *adj.* balakyot, imbi

Initial *adj.* panimula, inisyal, muna, una

Initial *v.* inisyalan

Initiate *v.* umpisahan, pinasimulan, simulan, pasimula, inisyahan, tanggapin

Initiation *n.* inisyasyon

Initiative *n.* insyatiba, kusa, pagkukusa

Inject *v.* ipasok,iniksiyunan, itusok,tusukan, isuksok

Injection *n.* iniksiyon

Injunction *n.* utos, atas, batas

Injure *v.* manakit,sirain, saktan, pinsalain, sugatan

Injurious *adj*. nakapipinsala

Injury *n*. kapinsalaan

Injustice *n*. kawalang-katarungan, pang-aapi

Ink *n*. tinta

Inkling *n*. hiwatag, akala, haka

Inkstand *n*. tinteruhan

Inlaid *adj*. maylabor

Inland *n*. ilaya, ibaba, libis

Inlander *n*. taong-ilaya, tagahulo

Inlaw *n*. pinagbiyanan

Inlay *n*. labor

Inlay *v*. laburan

Inlet *n*. ilug-ilugan

Inmate *adj*. maninirahan, bilanggo

Inmost *adj*. kaibuturan

Inn *n*. posada

Innate *adj*. katutubo, likas

Innocence *n*. insosensiya

Innocent *adj*. inosente, walang-kasalanan, walang-malay

Innovation *n*. pagbabago, kabaguhan, inobasyon

Innuendo *n*. parunggit, invendo, insinwasyon

Innumerable *adj*. di-mabilang, napakarami

Inoculate *v*. inukulahan, bakunahan, liwayan, imunisahan

Inordinate *adj*. di-ayos , labis

Inorganic *adj* inorganika, walang-buhay

Input *n*. puwersa, lakas

Inquest *n*. sayasig, pagsisiyasat

Inquire *v*. itanong, imbestigahin, pagtanungan, usisain,tanungin, magtanong, ipagtanong siyasatin, usigin

Inquiry *n*. pagsisiyasat, pag-uusisa, usig

Inquisitive *adj*. mausisa, matanong

Inquisitor *n*. ingkisidor

Inroad *n*. pasok, pagpasok

Insane *adj*. baliw, loko, ulol

Insanity *n*. kabaliwan, kaululan

Insatiable *adj*. walang-pagkabusugan

Inscribe *v*. isulat,limbagin,ikintal, sulatin, ilimbag

Inscription *n*. inskripsiyon, limbag, sulat, ukit

Insect *n*. insekto, kulisap

Insecticide *n*. , insektisida

Insecure *adj*. di-tiwasay, di-panatag

Inseminate *v*. maghasik, magtanim, inseminahan, tamarun

Insemination *n*. insem-inasyon

Inseminator *n*. inseminador

Insensible *adj*. di-makaramdam, walang-pandama

Inseparable *adj*. di-mapaghihiwalay

Insert *n.* lakip, singit

Insert *v.* ipasok,ipaloob, isingit,, isuksok, magsingit, magpaloob

Inside *adj.* sa loob, panloob

Inside *adv.* sa loob

Inside *n.* loob, interyor, ang loob

Insider *n.* taga-loob

Insight *n.* katalasan, katalusan

Insignia *n.* insigniya, sagisag

Insignificant *adj.* walang-ka-hulugan,munti, walang-kawa-waan, di-mahalaga, munti

Insincere *adj.* di-tapat, di-matapat

Insinuate *v.* magpahiwatig, ipahiwatig

Insinuation *n.* pahiwatig, paramdam

Insist *v.* igiit, ipilit, ipanindigan

Insistence *n.* pagpipilit

Insistent *adj.* mapilit

Insolent *adj.* insolente,bastos, mapagmataas

Insoluble *adj.* di-matunaw

Insolvable *adj.* di-malutas, walang-kalutasan

Insolvency *n.* , insolbensiya

Insolvent *adj.* insolbente

Inspect *v.* tingnan, suriin, siyasatin

Inspection *n.* ispeksiyon, inspeksiyon, pagsisiyasat

Inspector *n.* inspektor

Inspiration *n.* inspirasyon, sigya, paglanghap

Inspire *v.* bigyan ng inspirasyon, pukawan ng sigla

Instability *n.* pagka-di-pirmihan, kawalang-kapanatagan

Install *v.* iluklok,italaga, magkabit, ikabit

Installation *n.* instalasyon

Installment *n.* hulog, hurnal

Instance *n.* hiling, pagkakataon, pakiusap, halimbawa, mungkahi

Instancy *n.* kadalian, kadaglian

Instant *adj.* madalian, kagyat

Instant *n.* kisapmata, takna

Instantaneous *adj.* biglaan

Instantly *adj.* bigla

Instead *adv.* sa halip

Instigate *n.* manulsol, sulsulan

Instigation *n.* instagasyon

Instigator *n.* instigador

Instill *v.* ibuhos na patak-pakat, iturong unti-unti

Instinct *n.* galing, hilig, instinto, talino

Institute *n.* instituto, linangan, surian

Institute *v.* magtatag, simulan, itatag, magsimula

Instruct *v.* magturo,atasan, ituro, utusan

Instruction *n.* instruksiyon, turo, pagtuturo

Instructive *adj.* may itinuturo

Instructor *n.* instruktor, tagapagturo

Instrument *n.* instrumento, aparato, kasangkapan

Insubordinate *adj.* masuwayin, suwail

Insufficient *adj.* di-sapat

Insular *adj.* insular, pampulo, pangkapuluan

Insulate *v.* aislahan

Insulation *n.* aislasyon, insulasyon

Insulator *n.* aislador, insulador

Insult *n.* paglait, minamura, paghamak

Insult *v.* laitin,hamakin, tungayawin, alipustain, murahin

Insuperable *adj.* di-mapangibabawan

Insurance *n.* seguro

Insure *v.* magpaseguro, ipaseguro

Insurgence *n.* insureksiyon, pagbabangon, paghihimagsik

Intact. *adj.* di-naaano, buopa

Intaglio *n.* intaglio

Intake *n.* pasukan

Integer *n.* bilang na buo

Integral *n.* kabuo, pambuo

Integrate *v.* buuin, pag-isahin, pagsama-samahin

Integration *n.* pagbubuo

Integrator. *n.* tagabuo

Integrity *n.* pagka-buo , integridad

Integument *n.* balot, balat, takip

Intellect *n.* dunong, talino, katalinuhan, kaalaman

Intellectual *adj.* pangkatalinuhan

Intellectual *n.* ang matalino

Intelligent *adj.* matalino, marunong

Intelligentsia *n.* pangkat-matalisik

Intemperate *adj.* labis, nagmamalabs, masagwa

Intend *v.* binabalak, magbalak, balakin, tangkain, sadyain

Intense *adj.* masidhi, marubdob, matindi

Intensify *v.* pasidhiin, patindihin

Intension *n.* kasidhian, katindihan, balak

Intensity *n.* pagka-masidhi, pagka-matindi

Intensive *adj.* masidhi, matindi

Intention *n.* hangarin, intensiyon, layon, layunin, tangka, nasa, hangad

Intentional *adj.* sinasadya, tinikis, sinạdya, tinitikis

Intercede *v.* mamagitan

Intercept *v.* harangin, hadlangan

Interception *n.* pagharang, paghadlang

Interceptor *n.* tagaharang, tagahadlang

Intercession *n.* pamamagitan

Intercessor *n.* tagapamagitan

Interchange *v.* magpalitan, pagpalitin

Intercom *n.* interkom

Intercourse *n.* pagsasamahan

Intercrop *v.* maghulip

Interdict *v.* magbawal, ipagbawal

Interest *n.* kapakanan,tubo, hilig, patong, interes, kawilihan, patubo,pagkawili, wilihin, pakinabang

Interest *v.* akitin, papagkagustuhin

Interfere *v.* manghimasok, makagulo, makialam, pakialaman, makasagabal

Interference *n.* himasok, pakialam

Interior *n.* interyor, loob, sa loob

Interjection *n.* pandamdam

Interlock *v.* pagkabit-kabitin, pagkawing-kawingin

Interlude *n.* interludyo

Intermediary *n.* tagapama-gitan

Intermediate *n.* adj., interm-edya, panggitna

Interment *n.* paglilibing, libing

Intermission *n.* intermisyon, intermedyo

Intermittent *adj.* paulit-ulit, pabalik-balik

Intermix *v.* paghalu-haluin

Intern *n.* interno, residente

Intern *v.* antalahin, bimbinin

Internal *adj.* panloob

International *adj.* inter-nasyonal, sabansaan, pandaigdig, sansinukubin

Interpolate *v.* magpasok, singitan, pasukan, magsingit

Interpose *v.* isingit, mamagitan

Interpret *v.* ipakahulugan, pakahuluganan, ipaliwanag

Interpretation *n.* inter-pretasyon

Interpretative *adj.* palarawan

Interpreter *n.* interprete, tagapagsalin

Interregnum *n.* interegno

Interrogate *v.* tanungin

Interrogation *n.* tanong, pagtatanong

Interrupt *v.* abalahin, gambalain, sumabad, pinahinto

Interruption *n.* pagkaabala, pagkagambala, abala, pagkakahinto

Interruptive *adj.* nakak-aabala

Intersection *n.* krosing, tawiran

Intersectional *adj.* pangkat-pangkat

Intersperse *v.* isabog, ikalat, ibudbod

Interstice *n.* ngingi, pagitan

Interval *n.* pagitan, patlang, tigil

Intervene *v.* mamagitan, makialam, makihalo

Intervention *n.* interbensiyon, pamamagitan, pakikialam

Interview *n.* pakikipagpanayam, pakikipag-interbiyu

Interview *v.* kapanayamin,makipag-interbiyu, interbiyuhin, makipagpanayam

Interviewer *n.* tagapanayam, tagainterbiyu

Intestate *adj.* intestado, abintestado

Intestine *n.* bituka

Intimacy *n.* pagpapalagayang-loob, pagka-malapit

Intimate *adj.* matalik, malapit

Intimate *v.* ipaunawa, ipabalita

Intimidate *v.* manakot, takutin

Intimidation *n.* pananakot, pagbabala, pagbabanta

Intimidator *n.* mananakot

Into *prep.* sa, sa loob ng

Intolerable *adj.* di-mababata, di-matitiis

Intolerance *n.* intoleransiya, pagka-di-makapagbata

Intolerant *adj.* di-makapagbata

Intonation *n.* intonasyon, himig, pagkanta, tono

Intone *v.* himigin, awitin

Intoxicant *adj.* nakalalasing, nakalalango

Intoxicate *v.* lasingin, languhin, malasing, malango

Intoxication *n.* pagkalasing, kalasingan

Intramural *adj.* , intramural

Intramuscular *adj.* , intramuskular

Intransitive *adj.* katawanin

Intravenous *adj.* intrabena

Intricate *adj.* masalimout

Intrigue *n.* intriga

Intriguing *adj.* nakakapukaw-suri

Intrinsic *adj.* kalikas, katutubo

Introduce *v.* ipagamit, ipakilala,ipasok, ipauso, magsimula, iharap,simulan, pinakilala

Introduction *n.* introduksiyon, paghaharap, pagpapasok, prepasyo, panimula, pagpapakilala, pambungad

Introductory *adj.* panimula, pansimula

Introit *n.* introito

Introspect *v.* manalamisim

Introspection *n.* salamism, pananalamisim

Introvert *n.* taong-mapanarili

Intrude *v.* makialam, pakialaman

Intrusion *n.* pakikialam

Intuition *n.* intuwisyon, andam

Intuitive *n.* intuwitibo, mayandam

Intumescence *n.* pamamaga, pamumukol

Inundate *v.* magsanaw, magbaha

Inundated *adj.* lumubog, sinanaw, binaha

Inundation *n.* sanaw, baha

Inured *adj.* bantad, bihasa

Invade *v.* lumusob,salakayin, lusubin, sumalakay

Invalid *adj.* inbalido

Invalid *n.* maysakit, salanta, baldado, lumpo

Invalidate *v.* nuluhin

Invalidation *n.* pagwaw-alang-saysay

Invalidity *n.* kawalang-saysay

Invaluable *adj.* napakam-ahalaga

Invariable *adj.* , panatilihan, pareho

Invective *n.* upasala

Inveigle *n.* ibuyo, ulukan, udyukan

Invent *v.* lumikha, lumubid, imbentuhin, kumatha, likhain, magimbento

Invention *n.* imbensiyon, likha, imbento

Inventor *n.* imbentor, manlilikha

Inventory *n.* imbentaryo

Invert *n.* itaob, baligtarin, itiwarik, saliwain

Invest *v.* mamuhunam, pamuhunanan

Investigate *v.* imbestigahan, magsiyasat, siyasatin

Investigation *n.* imbesti-gasyon, pagsisiyasat

Investigator *n.* imbestigador, tagasiyasat

Investiture *n.* imbestidura

Investment *n.* pamumu-hunan

Investor *n.* mamumuhunan

Invigorant *n.* pampalakas

Invigorating *adj.* nakapag-papalakas

Invigoration *n.* pagpapalakas

Invincible *adj.* di-masupil, di-madaig, di-mapasuko, di-magagapi

Inviolable *adj.* di-malalabag

Invisible *adj.* imbisible, di-nakikita, di-kita, di-makita

Invitation *n.* anyaya, imbitasyon, paanyaya

Invite *v.* imbitahan, anyayahan, kumbidahin, yayain, pumarito

Invocation *n.* panawagan, imbokasyon

Involuntary *adj.* di-kusa, di-sinasadya, di-sinadya

Involve *v.* idawit, ilakip, isangkot, madawit, isama, masangkot

Inward *adj.* paloob, papasok, kalooban

Iodate *n.* yodado

Iodide *n.* yoduro

Iodine *n.* yodo

Iodize *v.* yodurahan

Ion *n.* ion

Ionic *adj.* ioniko

Ionization *n.* ionisasyon

Ionosperic *adj.* ionosperika

Ionosphere *n.* ionospera

Iota *n.* katiting, kapurat

Irascible *adj.* magagalitin, madaling, magalit

Irate *adj.* galit, nagagalit

Ire *n.* galit, pagkagalit

Irelevant *adj.* di-kaugnay, walang kaugnayan

Iris *n.* iris,bahaghari, arkoiris, balangaw

Irish *n.* Irlandes

Irk *v.* makayamot, makainip

Irksome *adj.* nakayayamot, nakalinip

Iron *n.* bakal, yero, plantsa

Iron *v.* mamalantsa, mamirinsa, ayusin, plantsahin, pirinsahin

Iron *v.* mamalantsa, mamirinsa

Ironical *adj.* balintuna

Irony *n.* ironiya, panunuya, tuya

Irrational *adj.* irasyonal

Irreconcilable *adj.* irekonsil-yable

Irredeemable *adj.* di-matubos, mahirap matubos

Irregular *adj.* aliwaswas, tiwali, baku-bako

Irrelevant *adj.* malayo, di-kaugnay

Irreligious *adj.* , lapastangan

Irreparable *adj.* ireparable, di-mapagtatakpan

Irreplaceable *adj.* di-mapalitan, walang maipapalit

Irreproachable *adj.* di-mapipintasan, walang maipipintas

Irresistible *adj.* di-mapaglabanan

Irresolute *adj.* urong-sulong, bantulot

Irresponsible *adj.* irespons-able

Irretrievable *adj.* di-mababawi, walang pagkabawi

Irreverent *adj.* walang pitagan, lapastangan

Irreversible *adj.* di-maibabaligtad

Irrevocable *adj.* di-mababawi, di-matatalikdan

Irrigable *adj.* mapatutubigan

Irrigate *v.* magpatubig, sumpitin, patubigan, magsumpit

Irrigator *n.* tagapagpatubig, pangenema, irigador,labatiba, panumpit

Irritable *adj.* mainipin,, mayamutin, magagalitin

Irritate *v.* bugnutin, yamutin, inipin, pakatihin, galitin, pagalitin

Irritating *adj.* nakayayamot, nakagagalit

Irritation *n.* iritasyon, pagkayamot, pagkagalit

Is *v.* ay

Island *n.* pulo

Isle *n.* pulo

Islet *n.* munting pulo

Ism *n.* ismo

Isogloss *n.* , isoglosa

Isolate *v.* ibukod, ihiwalay, ilayo

Isolation *n.* pagbubukod, paghihiwalay

Isometric *adj.* isometriko

Isomorphous *adj.* isomorpo

Issue *n.* bilang,labas,bunga, paglabas,tubo, kinalabasan, isyu

Issue *v.* bigyan, tumulo, magsupling, umagos, magbunga, lumabas,ilathala, maglathala, maglabas

Isthmus *n.* tangway

It *pron.* ito

Italian *adj.* Italyano

Italic *adj.* italika, bastardilya

Italicize *v.* italikahin

Itch *n.* kati, paghahangad

Itchy *adj.* makati

Item *n.* aytem, balita, kasangkapan, detalye, gamit, paksa, sangkap, bagay

Itinerant *adj.* pagala

Itinerary *n.* iteneraryo, talalakbayan

Its *pron.* kaniya, kanya, nito, niya, niyan, niyon

Itself *pron.* kaniyang sarili, itong sarili

Ivory *n.* garing, nakalinip

J j

Jab *n.* sapok, sundot

Jab *v.* dunggulin, sapukin, diyabin, sunduttin

Jabber *v.* sumatsat, dumaldal

Jack *n.* diyak, gato

Jackass *n.* buriko, uto-uto

Jacket *n.* diyaket, tsaketa

Jackfruit *n.* langka

Jacknapes *n.* matsing, barumbado

Jacknife *n.* lanseta, kortapluma

Jade *n.* jade, batong-ihada

Jagged *adj.* uka-uka

Jail *n.* karsel, kulungan, piitan, kalaboso, bilangguan

Jail *v.* ikulong, ikalabos, ipiit, ibilanggo

Jalopy *n.* lumang kotse

Jam *n.* halea, kaguluhan, siksikan, gusot

Jam *v.* mangsiksikan, siksikan, barahan, guluhin, gu

Jamboree *n.* diyambori

Janitor *n.* diyanitor

January *n.* Enero

Japanese *n.* Hapon, Hapones

Jar *n.* tapayan, banga, gusi, taro

Jar *v.* kulugin, igain, ugain, yanigin

Jargon *n.* wikang walang kawawaan

Jasmin *n.* hasmin

Jaundice *n.* ikterisya, paninilaw

Jaunt *v.* magpalibut-libot, magpagla-gala

Javanese *n.* adj., Habanes

Javelin *n.* habelina, diyablin

Jaw *n.* panga, sihang

Jaw *v.* ngawngaw

Jay *n.* ibong europeo

Jazz *n.* jazz, diyas

Jealous *adj.* panibughuin, panahili, seloso, panibugho

Jealousy *n.* panibugho, pagseselos

Jeans *n.* diyins , jeans

Jeep *n.* diyip, dyip, jeep

Jeer *n.* aglahi, pang-aaglahi

Jeer *v.* tuyain, aglahiin

Jehovah *n.* Heoba

Jell *v.* mamuo, magdiyeli

Jelly *n.* halea

Jeopardize *v.* isapinsala, ipanganyaya, ipahamak, isapanganib

Jerk *n.* baltak, tangtang

Jerk *v.* baltakin, tangtangin, batakin

Jersey *n.* jersey

Jest *n.* siste, biro

Jest *v.* magbiro, magpatawa

Jesting *n.* pagbibiro

Jesuit *n.* Hesuwita

Jesus *n.* Hesus

Jet *n.* asabatse,dyet, tilandoy, diyet

Jet *v.* tumilandoy

Jetsam *n.* lutang

Jetty *n.* piyes, malekon, pantalan

Jew *n.* hudyo

Jewel *n.* hiyas, batong brilyante, alahas, rubi, kayamanan

Jeweler *n.* alahero, mag-aalahas

Jewelry *n.* alahas, hiyas

Jezebel *n.* babaing bisyoso

Jibe *v.* , magkasundo, magkaugma

Jiffy *n.* sandali, saglit

Jig *n.* indak

Jigger *n.* kopita

Jilt *n.* mananakwil

Jilt *v.* magtakwil

Jimmy *n.* maikling bareta

Jingle *n.* kalansing, kililing, tugma-tugma

Jingle *v.* kumalansing, kumililing, pakalansingin

Jingo *n.* hinggoista

Jinx *n.* buwisit

Jitney *n.* dyitne, dyipne

Jitters *n.* nerbiyos, labis na pagkatakot

Job *n.* trabaho,tungkulin, empleo, hanapbuhay, gawain

Jockey *n.* hinete

Jocose *adj.* mabiro, palabiro, mapagbiro

Joggle *v.* maniko, sikuhin

Join *v.* idugtong, ikabit, sumama, pagdugtungin, pagkab mapagbiro, sumapi, u

Joint *adj.* pinagsama, pinagtambal, magkaanib

Joint *n.* dugtong, kasukasuan, pinagdugtungin, sugpong

Joist *n.* suleras

Joke *n.* biro

Joke *v.* biruin, magbiro, mambiro, biruin

Joker *n.* diyoker, taong mapagbiro

Jolly *adj.* masaya, masigla

Jolt *n.* biglang kalog, bigwas

Jostle *v.* sumiksik, maniksik, maniko

Jot *n.* punto, tuldok, katiting

Jot *v.* itala, isulat, ititik

Journal *n.* diyurnal, talaarawan

Journalism *n.* peryodismo, pamamahayag, pamahayagan

Journalist *n.* mamamahayag, peryodista

Journalize *v.* itala sa talaarawan

Journey *n.* lakbay, paglalakbay, lakbayin

Journey *v.* maglakbay, lakbayin

Joust *n.* magturneo, paligsahan

Joust *n.* turneo

Jove *n.* Hupiter

Jovial *adj.* masaya, masigla

Joviality *n.* kasayahan

Joy *n.* galak, kagalakan, lugod, kaluguran, katuwaan, tuwa

Joyful *adj.* nalulugod, malugod, masaya, maligaya

Joyous *adj.* nalulugod, malugod

Jubilant *adj.* nakasasaya, nakatutuwa, nakagagalak

Jubilation *n.* hubilasyon, pagkakatuwaan

Jubilee *n.* hubileo

Judaism *v.* Hudaismo

Judge *n.* hukom, huwis

Judge *v.* hukuman, hatulan, humatol, magpasiya

Judgement *n.* hatol, bait, kurukuro, pasiya, pagpapasiya, paghato

Judicature *n.* hukuman

Judicious *n.* mabuting humatol

Judo *n.* dyudo, judo

Jug *n.* pitsel, galong

Juggle *v.* magsalamangka, manlinlang

Juggler *n.* salamangkero

Jugglery *n.* pagsasalamangka

Juice *n.* katas

Juicy *adj.* makatas

July *n.* Hulyo

Jumble *n.* paghahalu-halo

Jumble *v.* paghalu-haluin, guluhin

Jumbo *adj.* malaking-malaki

Jump *n.* lundag,igpaw, lukso, talon

Jump *v.* lumukso, lundagin, tumalon, lumundag, talunin

Junction *n.* pinagdugtungan, pinaghugpungan, salikop

Juncture *n.* sugpungan

June *n.* Hunyo

Jungle *n.* gubat, dawag, kagubatan

Junior *adj.* diyunyor, preparatorya, anak, bata

Junk *n.* sampan,basura, tapon, luma

Junk *v.* itapon

Junket *n.* diyanket, paseoreal

Jurisdiction *n.* hurisdiksiyon, sakop, nasasakupan

Jurisprudence *n.* hurisprudensiya

Jurist *n.* hurista, huriskonsulto

Juror *n.* hurado

Juvenile *n.* bata

Juxtaposition *n.* pagkakatabi-tabi

Jury *n.* sanggunian hurado, inampalan, panghukumang lupon

Just *adj.* husto, makatarungan, tapat, matuwid

Just *adv.* lamang, halos

Justice *n.* hustisya, hukom, katarungan, mahistrado

Justify *v.* bigyang- matuwid

Justly *adv.* makatarungan

Jut *v.* umungos, umusli

Jute *n.* yute, kanyamo, lang gotse

Juvenile *adj.* bata, pangkabataan, mura, pambata

K k

Kafir *n.* kapre

Kaleidoscope *n.* kaleydoskopo

Kamikaze *n.* kamikase

Kangaroo *n.* kangguro, kanggaro

Kapok *n.* kapok, buboy

Karma *n.* karma, tadhana

Katharsis *n.* katarsis

Keel *n.* kilya

Keel *v.* kumilya, tumagilid

Keen *adj.* matalas, mahapadi, matindi, matalim, masidhi

Keep *v.* bantayan, ingatan, iligpit, itago, magingat, tin ilingid, magtago, tu

Keeper *n.* nangangasiwa, tagapagtago, katiwala

Keeping *n.* pag-iingat

Ken *n.* unawa, pagkatanto

Kennel *n.* bahay-aso

Kerchief *n.* alampay, bandana, panyo, panuwelo, talukbong

Kernel *n.* butil, ubod, buod

Kerosene *n.* pitrolyo, gas

Kettle *n.* kaldero

Key *n.* susi, liyabe

Keyboard *n.* teklado

Keyhole *n.* butas na susian

Keynote *n.* simulaing bata-yan

Keystone *n.* klabe

Khaki *n.* kaki

Khan *n.* lakan

Kibitz *v.* magkibits, makialam

Kibitzer *n.* kibitser, pakialam

Kick *n.* sipa, sikad, tutol

Kick *v.* manipa,sikaran, sipain sumipa, magsipa, manikad

Kickback *n.* sauli, kikbak

Kickup *n.* gulo

Kid *n.* anak ng kambing, bata, paslit

Kid *v.* biruin, magbiro

Kidnap *v.* dukutin

Kidnapper *n.* mandurukot

Kidney *n.* bato

Kill *v.* pumatay,magpatay, patayin, kitilin

Killer *n.* mamamatay

Kiln *n.* hurno, patuyuan

Kilo *n.* kilo

Kilocalorie *n.* kilokaloriya

Kilocycle *n.* kilosiklo

Kilogram *n.* kilogramo

Kiloliter *n.* kilolitro

Kilometer *n.* kilometro

Kilometric *adj.* kilometriko

Kilowatt *n.* kilobatiyo, kilokilowat

Kilt *n.* enagwilyas

Kimono *n.* kimono

Kin *n.* kamag-anak, hinlog, kaangkan

Kind *n.* uri,mabait, tipo, klase, mapagpala

Kindergarten *n.* kindergarten

Kindhearted *adj.* maawain, mahabagin

Kindle *n.* magpaningas, papagningasin, sindihan

Kindle *v.* magningas, sindihan, pagningasin

Kindly *adj.* magiliw

Kindred *n.* kaanak

Kinfolks *n.* hinlog

King *n.* hari

Kingdom *n.* kaharian, lupain

Kingfisher *n.* peskador, lumbas

Kingly *adj.* makahari

Kingship *n.* pagkahari

Kink *n.* pilipit,kulubot, sulupot, kulot

Kinky *adj.* kulot

Kinship *n.* pagka-kamag-anak

Kiosk *n.* kiyosko, kubol

Kismet *n.* tadhana

Kiss *n.* halik

Kiss *v.* humalik, halikan, hagkan

Kit *n.* huwego, lote, kit

Kitchen *n.* kusina, batalan, lutuan

Kitchenware *adj.* kagamitan pangkusina

Kite *n.* buradol, guryon, saranggola

Kitten *n.* kuting, malit na pusa

Kleptomania *n.* kleptomaniya, makating-kamay

Knack *n.* kasanayan, galing, kabihasnan

Knapsack *n.* alporhas, kabalyas

Knave *n.* taong-barumbado, saramulyo, sota

Knavery *n.* kabarumbaduhan

Knavish *adj.* barumbado

Knead *n.* magmasa

Knead *v.* magmasa, masahin

Knee *n.* tuhod

Kneel *v.* lumuhod, luhod, nakaluhod

Knell *n.* agunyas

Knickers *n.* nikers

Knicknack *n.* kalukati

Knife *n.* kutsilyo, lanseta, kortapluma

Knight *n.* kabalyero

Knit *n.* maglala, maggantsilyo, lalahin, magniting

Knit *v.* ikibot, ikunot, magniting

Knob *n.* bukong, hawakan, puluhan

Knock *n.* katok, tuktok

Knock *v.* kumatok, tuktukin, tumuktok, katukin, suntukin, paluin

Knock-knee *adj.* piki

Knockabout *v.* maglagalag

Knockout *n.* nak-aut, lugpo, tumba

Knoll *n.* munting gulod

Knot *n.* buhol,tali, hirap, buko

Knot *v.* ibuhol, talian

Know *v.* malaman, maunawaan, makilala, matutuhan, kilalanin

Knowledge *n.* kaalaman, nalalaman, karunungan, pagkakil

Knuckle *n.* buko ng daliri

Kodak *n.* kodak, kamera

Komintern *n.* komintern

Koran *n.* Koran, Kuran

Korean *n.* Koreano

Kowtow *v.* yumukod

Kudos *n.* papuri

L l

Label *n.* etiketa

Label *v.* etikitahan, lagyan ng etiketa

Labial *adj.* labyal

Labor *n.* gawa,panganganak, trabaho, gawain

Labor *v.* gumawa, magtrabaho, magdamdam bago manga

Laboratory *n.* laboratoryo

Laborer *n.* manggagawa, trabahador

Laborious *adj.* mahirap gawin

Labyrinth *n.* labirinto, daang salimuot

Lace *n.* puntas,sintas, tiras, engkahe

Lace *v.* itali

Lacerate *v.* pilasin, punitin, munglayin

Laceration *n.* laserasyon

Lachrymal *adj.* panluha, lakrimal, hinggil

Lack *n.* kulang, kakulangan, pangangailangan

Lack *v.* magkulang, kailanganin, kulangin, mawalan, mangailangan

Lackadaisical *adj.* matamlay, mamamanglaw

Lackey *n.* alila, utusan

Lackluster *n.* lamlam, labo

Laconic *n.* lakoniko, matipid sa salita

Lacquer *n.* laka, barnis, laker

Lactary,Lacteal *adj.* lakteo

Lactate *n.* laktato

Lactation *n.* laktasyon, pagtulo ng gatas, paggibik

Lacteous *adj.* parang gatas, malagatas

Lactescence *n.* pagmamal-agatas

Lactescent *adj.* malagatas

Lactoscope *n.* laktoskopyo

Lactose *n.* laktosa

Lacuna *n.* lakuna, puwang, huyo

Lad *n.* binatilyo, bagong-tao

Ladder *n.* hagdan

Laden *adj.* maykarga, maylulan, maypasan

Ladle *n.* kutsaron, sandok

Lady *n.* ginang, sinyora, dalaga, babae

Ladyfighter *n.* bruas

Ladykiller *n.* palikero

Lag *v.* mahuli, magtagal

Lagard *adj.* mabagal, mahina, mapag-aligando

Lager beer *n.* serbesang lager

Lagoon *n.* lanaw, lawa

Lair *n.* pahingahan, tulugan, kubil

Laity *n.* lego

Lake *n.* lawa, dagatan

Lam *v.* lumayas, tumakas

Lamb *n.* kordero

Lambaste *v.* tuligsain, atakihin

Lambent *adj.* paandap-andap, malamlam, mapungay

Lame *adj.* pilay, tumitikod

Lame *v.* mapilay,malumpo, mapilayan,lumpuhin, pilayan

Lament *n.* panaghoy, panambitan

Lament *v.* ikalungkot, ipamighati, ipagdalamhati, managhoy

Lamentation *n.* toghoy, daing

Lamina *n.* lamina

Laminate *v.* laminahin, laminahan

Laminated *adj.* laminado, nilamina, nilaminahan

Lamination *n.* laminasyon, paglalamina

Lamp *n.* ilawan, lampara

Lampoon *n.* tuligsa

Lampoon *v.* manuligsa, tuligsain

Lampshade *n.* pantalya

Lanai *n.* lanay, ebranda, asotea

Lanate *adj.* buhukan

Lance *n.* lansa, sibat, suligi, tulag

Lanceolate *adj.* hugissibat

Lancet *n.* lanseta, laseta

Lancinate *v.* sibatin

Land *n.* lupa,bayan, lupain, bansa

Land *v.* sumadsad,lumapag, lumunsad,dumaong, bumaba, makahuli, manalo

Landlady *n.* kasera

Landlord *n.* kasero

Landmark *n.* muhon

Landscape *n.* paysahe, tanawin

Lane *n.* landas, daanan, ruta

Language *n.* wika,pananalita, lengguwahe, pahayag

Languid *adj.* mahina, matamlay

Lanky *adj.* mahagway

Lanoline *n.* lanolina

Lantern *n.* parol

Lap *n.* kalungan, kandungan, sinapupunan

Lap *v.* humimod, himurin

Lapel *n.* sulapa

Lapidary *n.* lapidaryo

Lapse *n.* lapso, pagkakamali

Larce *adj.* malaki, malawak

Larceny *n.* urto, pagnanakaw

Lard *n.* mantika

Larder *n.* paminggalan

Large *adj.* malaki, pangkalahatang, pagtuturing

Lariat *n.* reata

Larithmic *adj.* laritmiko

Larithmicist *n.* laritmisista

Larithmics *n.* laritmika

Lark *n.* langaylangayan

Larva *n.* larba

Larval *adj.* panlarba

Larvicide *n.* pamatay-larba

Larygitis *n.* laringhitis

Laryngeal *adj.* panlalamunan

Laryngologist *n.* laringgologo

Laryngology *n.* laringgolohiya

Laryngoscope *n.* laringgos-kopyo

Laryngotomy *n.* laringgoto-miya

Larynx *n.* lalamunan

Lascivous *adj.* mahalay, malibog

Lash *v.* hagupit,ihagupit, hagupitin,ilatigo, latiguhin, tuligsain igapos, hagupitin

Lass *n.* binibini, dalagita

Lassitude *n.* kapagalan, kapaguran

Lasso *n.* silo, reata

Lasso *v.* siluin

Last *adj.* huli, wakas, matibay, matagal

Last *n.* hulmahan

Last *v.* itagal, magluwat, magpatuloy, magtagal, tumagal

Latch *n.* tarankahan, trangkilya, aldaba, trangka

Latch *v.* itrangka,aldabahan, trang-kahan, ialdaba

Late *adj.* huli, nasira, nahuli, atrasado, yumao, namatay

Lately *adv.* kamakailan

Latent *adj.* latente,nakabitin, di-kita, nakatigil

Lateral *adj.* lateral, patagilid

Lath *n.* listong kahoy

Lathe *n.* torno, lilukan, lalikan

Lather *n.* bula ng sabon

Lather *v.* pabulain

Latin *n.* Latin

Latitude *n.* latitud

Latria *n.* latria

Latrine *n.* latrina, palikuran

Latter *adj.* huli

Laud *v.* purihin, dakilain

Laudable *adj.* kapuri-puri

Laudanum *n.* laudano

Laudation *n.* pagbibigaypuri

Laudatory *adj.* nagbibi-gaypuri

Laugh *n.* tawa

Laugh *v.* tumawa, tawanan, pagtawanan

Laughingstock *n.* tampulan ng tawa

Laughter *n.* tawanan, pagtatawa, halakhak

Launch *n.* lantsa

Launch *v.* ibunsod,lumansa, ibuyo, ilunsad, maglansa

Launder *v.* maglaba, labhan

Launderer *n.* maglalaba

Laundress *n.* labandera

Laundry *n.* labanderya, labahin, labada

Laundryman *n.* labandero

Laureate *adj.* laureado

Laurel *n.* laurel

Lava *n.* laba, kumukulon putik

Lavaliere *n.* kuwintas labalyer

Lavander *n.* labanda

Lavatory *n.* hugasan, lababo

Lave *v.* maghugas, hugasan, maligo

Lavee *n.* pilapil, saplad, tambak

Lavish *adj.* sagana, damak-damak

Lavish *v.* buntunan

Law *n.* batas, tuntunin, reglamento

Lawful *adj.* legal

Lawgiver *n.* mambabatas

Lawless *adj.* labag sa batas

Lawn *n.* damuhan

Lawsuit *n.* pleyto, litigasyon

Lawyer *n.* abugado, manananggol

Lax *adj.* maluwag, di-mahigpit, pabaya

Laxative *adj.* pampaluwag, laksatiba

Laxative *n.* pampaluwag, laksatiba

Laxity *n.* kaluwagan, kapabayaan

Lay *adj.* lego, sekular

Lay *n.* awit, himig

Lay *v.* ilagay, maglatag, mangitlog, ilapag, iharap

Layer *n.* mangingitlog, patong, suson

Layman *n.* lego, layko

Layout *n.* ayos, pagkakaayos, latag

Lazar *n.* leproso, ketungin

Lazareto *n.* lazareto

Laziness *n.* katamaran

Lazy *adj.* tamad, batugan

Lea *n.* damuhan, pastulan

Lead *n.* pagsakay, pangunguna, pang, pagtunton,pamumuno, pagtuturo,unang tala

Lead *v.* akayin, turuan, pamunuan, ihatid, pangunahan, pa itunton, mamuno, mang dalhin, patungo

Leaden *adj.* may pabigat, namimigat

Leader *n.* lider, patnugot, direktor, puno

Leading *adj.* nangunguna, pangunahin

Leaf *n.* dahon

Leaflet *n.* uhilya

League *n.* liga, kompederasyon

Leak *n.* tulo, pagkabunyag, kayat,singaw, tagas

Leak *v.* mabunyag, masiwalat, tumagas, tumulo

Lean *adj.* butuhan, balingkinitan, payat

Lean *n.* taba, lamang walang

Lean *v.* sumandal, sumandig, humilig, kumiling

Leap *v.* lumundag, lumukso, lundagin

Leap year *n.* taong bisyesto

Leapfrog *n.* biyola

Learn *v.* matuto, mabatid, matutuhan,matuklasan maunawaan, malaman

Learned *adj.* marunong

Learner *n.* mag-aaral

Learning *n.* dunong, alam

Lease *v.* paupahan, arendahin, ipaarenda, upahan

Leash *n.* tali

Leash *v.* talian, itali

Least *adj.* pinakamaliit, pinakamunti, pinakamunsik

Leather *n.* kuwero, katad, balat

Leave *v.* makaiwan, iwan,pabayaan, iwanan, umalis

Leaven *n.* lebadura, paalsa

Lectern *n.* atril

Lecture *n.* panayam

Lecture *v.* magpanayam, pagunitaan, magsalita

Lecturer *n.* tagapanayam

Ledge *n.* tangwa, bingit

Ledger *n.* libro-mayor, ledyer

Lee *n.* latak

Leech *n.* linta, manghuhuthot

Leeway *n.* luwag

Left *adj.* kaliwa

Left *n.* ang kaliwa

Left-handed *n.* kaliwete

Left-over *n.* tira

Leftist *n.* iskiyerdista

Leg *n.* binti, pata

Legacy *n.* erensiya, pamana

Legal *adj.* legal, ayon sa batas

Legality *n.* legalidad, pagkalegal

Legalize *n.* legalisahin

Legate *n.* legado, sugo, embahador

Legation *n.* pasuguan

Legato *n.* legato, ligado

Legend *n.* alamat, leyenda

Legible *adj.* nababasa

Legion *n.* lehiyon, hukbo, kuyog

Legislate *v.* magbatas gumawa ng batas

Legislation *n.* lehislasyon, pagbabatas

Legislative *adj.* pampagba-batas, lehislatibo

Legislator *n.* lehislador, mambabatas

Legislature *n.* lehislatura, batasan

Legitimacy *n.* pagka-lehitimo

Legitimate *adj.* lehitimo, tunnay, ayon sa batas, legal

Legume *n.* legumbre

Leguminous *adj.* leguminoso

Leisure *n.* oras na malaya, luwag ng panahon, ginhawa

Lemon *n.* limon, kalamanse

Lemonade *n.* limunada

Lend *v.* magpahiram, magpautang, ipahiram, pautangin, pahiramin, magbigay

Length *n.* haba, kahabaan, tagal

Lengthen *v.* pahabain, habaan

Lengthiness *n.* kahabaan

Lengthwise *adv.* sa pahaba

Lengthy *adj.* napakahaba

Lenient *adj.* nakapag-papalambot, maawain, nakapagpapaginhawa, d malambot

Lens *n.* lente

Lent *n.* kuwaresma

Lenticel *n.* lentehuwela

Lentil *n.* lenteha

Leo *n.* leo, leon

Leocoma *n.* leukoma, pamu-muti ng busilig

Leopard *n.* leopardo

Leper *n.* leproso, ketungin

Lepidoptera *n.* lepidoptera

Lepidopteron *n.* lepidopteron

Lepidopterous *adj.* lepidoptero

Leprosarium *n.* leprosaryo

Leprosy *n.* lepra, ketong

Leprous *adj.* may lepra, may ketong

Lesion *n.* lesyon

Less *adj.* maliit, di-gaano, kakaunti, mababa

Lessee *n.* ang nangungupahan, ingkilino

Lessen *v.* pauntiin, bawasan

Lesson *n.* liksiyon, aral, aralin

Lessor *n.* ang maypaupa

Lest *conj.* baka, at baka

Let *v.* tulutan, hayaan, pahintulutan,payagan bayaan, pabayaan

Lethal *adj.* letal, patal, nakamamatay

Lethargy *n.* himbing, kawalang-galaw, kahimbingan, kawalang-bahala

Letter *n.* titik, sulat, letra,kalatas, liham

Lettuce *n.* litsugas

Leucocyte *n.* leukosito

Leucocytis *n.* leukositis, pagdami ng leukosito

Leukemia *n.* labis na puting dugo

Levee *n.* pilapil, saplad, tambak

Level *adj.* patag, pantay

Level *n.* taas, kapantayan, patag,nibel, kapatagan

Level *v.* patagin, pantayin, ipantay

Level-headed *adj.* matali-nong magpasiya

Leveler *n.* pamatag

Lever *n.* pansuit, palangka, pingga

Levitate *v.* palutang sa hangin

Levitation *n.* lebitasyon, paglutang sa hangin

Levity *n.* kagaanan, pagka masayahin

Levy *n.* pataw, impuwesto

Levy *v.* patawan, lagyan ng impuwesto

Lewd *adj.* malibog, mahalay

Lewdness *n.* kalibugan, kahalayan

Lexical *adj.* leksikal, panalita, pantalasalitaan

Lexicographer *n.* leksikog-rapo, diksiyunarista

Lexicography *n.* leksikog-rapiya

Lexicon *n.* leksikon, diksiyunaryo, talahuluganan

Liability *n.* kapanagutan, obligasyon, utang

Liable *adj.* obligado, nanganganib, sapilitan, nananagot

Liaison *n.* liayson, ugnayan, alunyaan

Liar *n.* taong sinungaling, sinungaling

Libation *n.* buhos, libasyon

Libel *n.* libelo, paninirangpuri

Libelous *adj.* libeloso

Liberal *adj.* liberal, bukas-kamay, may magandang kaloob bukas-isip,malay

Liberate *v.* palayain, bigyang kalayaan

Liberation *n.* liberasyon

Liberator *n.* libertador, tagapagpalaya

Liberty *n.* libertad, independensiya, kasarinlan

Libidinal *adj.* pangkalibugan

Libido *n.* libido, kalibugan, libog

Libra *n.* libra, timbangan

Librarian *n.* bibliotekarya, laybraryan

Library *n.* aklatan, biblioteka

Librettist *n.* libretista

Libretto *n.* libreto

Lice *n.* mga kuto

Licence *n.* lisensiya

Licence *v.* bigyang, lisensiya, lisensiyahan

Licentiate *adj.* lisensiyado

Lichee *n.* litsiyas

Lichen *n.* liken, lumot

Lick *v.* dilaan, daigin, himurin, talunin

Licorice *n.* regalis

Lid *n.* takip, panaklob, panakip, saklob

Lie *n.* kasinungalingan

Lie *v.* magsinungalingan

Lie *v.* humiga, mahiga

Lien *n.* grabamen

Lieu *n.* halip

Life *n.* buhay, pamumuhay, kabuhayan

Lift *n.* asensor, pag-angat, pagtaas,tulong, pagbuhat

Lift *v.* itaas, angatin, buhatin, iangat

Ligament *n.* ligamento, balamban

Ligature *n.* ligadura, pangangkop

Light *adj.* magaan, di-mahigpit, di-mariin

Light *n.* liwanag, ilaw

Light *v.* magsindi, sindihan ilawan buhɔ pasiglahin

Lightning *n.* kidlat, illuminasyon, pag-iilaw

Lightweight *n.* timbaang na magaan

Like *adj.* katulad, magkapa-reho, magkatulad, pareho

Like *cong.* gaya ng, tulad ng

Like *prep.* parang, animo'y

Like *v.* maibagan, magu-stuhan

Lilác *n.* lila

Lilliputian *adj.* liliput-yense, enano

Lilliputian *n.* liliput-yense, enano

Lilt *n.* indayog, indak

Lilty *adj.* maindayog, mataldik

Lily *n.* liryo, asusena

Lima bean *n.* patani

Limb *n.* sanga, bisig, paa

Limbo *n.* limbo

Lime *n.* apog

Limelight *n.* kalantaran sa bayan

Limerick *n.* maigsing tulang-pampatawa

Limestone *n.* batong apog

Limit *n.* hangganan, saklaw, patuto, abot

Limit *v.* magtakda, takdaan, itakda

Limn *v.* ilarawan, iguhit, iukit

Limousine *n.* limosina

Limp *adj.* malata, mahina, mahuna

Limp *v.* tumikod

Limpid *adj.* malinaw

Line *n.* guhit, kawad, linea,hanay, raya

Line *v.* guhitan, ihanay, humanay

Lineage *n.* linahe, angkan

Lineament *n.* pagmumukha

Linen *n.* linen, linso

Linger *v.* magtagal, magluwat

Lingerie *n.* lingerie

Linguist *n.* dalubwika, lingguwista

Linguistic *adj.* lingguwistikal

Liniment *n.* linimento, panghaplas

Link *n.* kawing, kaugnayan, hugpong

Link *v.* ikabit, ikawil, iugnay

Linoleum *n.* linolyum

Linotype *n.* linotipya

Linseed *n.* linga, linasa

Lint *n.* lamuymoy

Lintel *n.* lintel, katel, katangan

Lion *n.* leon, liyon

Lip *n.* labi, gilid

Liquate *v.* lusawin, tunawin

Liquefacient *adj.* pampalikido

Liquefy *v.* lusawin, tunawin

Liquescent *adj.* nalulusaw, natutunaw

Liquid *adj.* lusaw, tunaw, likido

Liquid *n.* likido

Liquidate *v.* likidahin

Liquidation *n.* likidasyon

Liquidity *n.* kalikiduhan

Liquor *n.* likor, alak

Lisip *v.* mautal, mag-utal, magaril

Lissome *adj.* maliksi

List *n.* listahan, tala, talaan, lista

List *v.* ilista, itala, magtala

Listen *v.* makinig, manainga, dinggin, pakinggan

Listless *adj.* walang sigla, walang bahala

Litany *n.* litaniya

Liter *n.* litro

Literacy *n.* pagkamarunong

Literal *adj.* literal, tunay, likas, karaniwan

Literary *adj.* pampanitikan

Literature *n.* literatura, panitikan

Litharge *n.* literhiryo

Lithe *adj.* may malambot na katawan

Lithograph *n.* limbag na litograpiya

Lithographer *n.* litograpo

Lithography *n.* litograpiya

Lithoid *adj.* malabato, parang bato

Litigant *n.* litigante

Litigate *v.* maglitis

Litigation *n.* litigasyon

Litigatious *adj.* mapaglitis

Litmus *n.* litmus, turnasol

Litter *n.* kamilya, kalat, sukal

Litter *v.* magkalat

Little *adj.* maliit, munti, kaunti

Littoral *n.* litoral, tabing-dagat, baybayin

Liturgy *n.* liturhiya, rito, ritwal

Live *adj.* buhay

Live *v.* mabuhay, manirahan, manatiling, magdanas tumira, nagbabaga

Livelihood *n.* ikinabubuhay

Lively *adj.* masigla

Liver *n.* atay

Livestock *n.* hayupan

Livid *adj.* pasa, putlang-abo

Lizard *n.* lagarto

Load *n.* dala, karga, dalahin,sunong, lulan,pasan

Load *v.* maglulan, kargahan, lulanan, magkarga

Loaf *v.* magbagabundo, mag-ansikot, magbulakbol

Loafer *n.* haragan, bulakbulero

Loan *v.* ipahiram, ipautang, pautangin, pahiramin

Loan *n.* pagpapahiram, pagpapautang, pahiram, pautang, utang

Loath *adj.* di-nagkakagusto, ayaw

Loathe *v.* mandiri, pandirihan, kamuhian, kasuklaman mamuhi

Loathing *n.* pagkaani

Lobby *n.* bestibulo, lobi, bulwagan

Lobby *v.* maglobi

Lobbyism *n.* panlolobi

Lobbyist *n.* manlolobi

Lobe *n.* lobulo

Lobster *n.* ulang

Local *adj.* lokal

Local *n.* pampook, lokal, katutubo

Locale *n.* pook

Locate *v.* bigyang-pook, makita

Location *n.* pook, lugar, lunan, kinalalagyan

Locative *adj.* lokatibo, panlunan

Locator *n.* panghanap-pook

Lock *n.* kandado, seradura, susian

Lock *v.* isusi, kandado, putol, kandaduhan, magkulon ikandado, seradura, susian

Locker *n.* aparador, laker

Locket *n.* laket, kuwardapelo

Lockjaw *n.* tetano

Lockout *n.* pagsasara ng pabrika

Locksmith *n.* panday-kaban

Lockup *n.* bilangguan

Locomotion *n.* lokomosyon

Locomotive *n.* lokomotora, lokomobil

Locomotive *adj.* nakakikilos

Locust *n.* balang, lukton

Lode *n.* pilon

Lodge *n.* lohiya, kabanya

Lodge *v.* tumuloy, ilagak, maglagak, maghain, manuluyan, paglagaka tumira, tumigil, tum manirahan, magharap,

Log *n.* kalap, koredera, tala, *troso*

Logarithm *n.* logaritmo

Logic *n.* lohika

Logical *adj.* lohikal, makatuwiran

Logician *n.* lohiko

Logos *n.* berbo

Loin *n.* lomo, balakang, pigi

Loincloth *n.* bahag

Lollipop *n.* lolipap

Lone *adj.* nag-iisa, kaisa-isa

Lonely *adj.* nag-iisa, nalulumbay

Lonesome *adj.* malungkot, mapanglaw

Long *adj.* mahaba, matagal, nakaiinip

Long *v.* masabik, kauhawan, pitahin

Look *v.* asahan, makita, tingnan, tumingin, umasa

Looks *n.* asta, ayos, mukha

Loom *n.* habihan

Loom *v.* bumadha, lumitaw, sumipot

Loop *n.* liko, bilog, silo, ikot

Loose *adj.* alpas, buhaghag, kalag, nakawawala, malaya, tanggal, maluwag, umuuga

Loose *v.* alpasan, kalagan, kalagin, palayain, paluwagan

Loosen *v.* luwagan, buhaghagin, pakawalan

Loot *v.* mandambong

Loot *n.* botin, pinagdambungan

Looter *n.* mandarambong

Lop *v.* lumuyloy, magtabas, putulin, tabasin

Lope *n.* kabig, marahang, paso

Lopsided *adj.* kiling, tagilid

Lord *n.* poon, panginoon

Lordly *adj.* matayog

Lore *n.* karunungan, kaalaman

Lose *v.* mawala, iwala, mawalan, matalo, malagaw, malugi, aksayahin

Loss *n.* pagkawala, kalugihan, kawalan

Lost *v.* nawala

Lot *n.* kalahatan, kapalaran, lote, suritido

Lotion *n.* losyon

Lottery *n.* loteriya

Lotus *n.* loto

Loud *adj.* malakas, maingay, matunog, matingkad

Loudspeaker *n.* laudspiker

Lounge *n.* pahingahan

Louse *n.* kuto

Lousy *adj.* nakasusuya

Love *v.* umibig, ibigin

Love *n.* pag-ibig, pagsinta, pagmamahal, paggiliw

Loveliness *n.* kariktan

Lovely *adv.* kaibig-ibig

Lover *n.* manliligaw, mangingibig

Low *adj.* mahaba, mahina, matamlay

Low *n.* unga

Lower *v.* babaan, ibaba, hinaan

Loyal *adj.* tapat, matapat

Loyalty *n.* katapatan

Lubricant *n.* pampadulas, lubrikante

Lubricate *n.* lubrikahan

Lubrication *n.* lubrikasyon

Luck *n.* kapalaran, suwerte

Lucrative *adj.* lukratibo

Lug *v.* dalhin, hilahin

Luggage *n.* bagahe, kargada

Lukewarm *adj.* malahininga

Lull *v.* aluin, ipaghele

Lumber *n.* kahoy, tabla

Lumen *n.* lumen

Luminary *adj.* ilaw

Lumination *n.* iluminasyon, pailaw

Lump *n.* bukol, kimpal, masa

Lunch *n.* tanghalian, pananghalian

Lung *n.* baga, pulmon

Lurch *v.* gumiwang, tumagilid

Lure *v.* akitin, hibuin, rahuyuin

Lure *v.* akitin, hibuin, rahuin

Lure *n.* pangati, pain

Lurid *adj.* barak, namamarak

Lurk *v.* abatan, magtago

Luscious *adj.* masarap

Lush *adj.* malago, malabay, sagana

Lust *n.* pananabik, kasabikan, magtamasa

Luster *n.* kintab, kinang, kislap

Lustful *adj.* malibog, mahalay

Lusty *adj.* masigla, malakas, matapang

Lute *n.* laud

Luxuriant *adj.* madohan, malabay, malago, masagana

Luxuriate *v.* marangya, mariwasa

Luxurious *adj.* marangya, mariwasa, maluho, malusog

Luxury *n.* karangyaan, luho, rangya

Lycanthrope *n.* aswang

Lyceum *n.* liseo

Lye *n.* lihiya

Lymph *n.* limpa

Lymphadenitis *n.* limpadeni-tis

Lynch *v.* lintsahin, manlintsa

Lynx *n.* linse

Lyre *n.* lira

Lyric *adj.* lirika, lirikal

Lysol *n.* lisol

M m

Ma *n.* inay, inang, mama, mami

Macaroni *n.* makaroni

Mace *n.* masa

Macerate *v.* maserahin, ibabad

Maceration *n.* maserasyon, binabad

Macerator *n.* maserador, tagababad

Machete *n.* matsete, gulok, pantabas

Machine *n.* makina

Machinery *n.* makinarya

Mackintosh *n.* kapote

Macro *pref.* mahaba, matagal

Macrobian *adj.* makrobyano

Macrobiotics *n.* makrobyotika

Macrocosm *n.* makrokosmo

Macron *n.* makron

Macroscopic *adj.* makro-skopika

Mad *adj.* ulol, loko, haling, nahahaling

Madam *n.* sinyora, madam

Madcap *adj.* pugosa

Madcap *n.* pugoso

Madden *v.* galitin, hibangin, pagalitin

Maddening *adj.* nakahihibang , nagagalit, nahihibang

Made *v.* ginawa

Madhouse *n.* manikomyo

Madman *n.* loko, loka

Madness *n.* kahibangan, pagkaloko, pagkaloka

Madonna *n.* madona

Madrigal *n.* madrigal

Magazine *n.* magasin, rebista

Magi *n.* mago

Magic *adj.* mahika, mahiwaga, makapagtataka

Magic *n.* mahiya, salamangka, kababalaghan

Magician *n.* mago, madyisyan, salamangkero

Magistrate *n.* mahistrado, hukom

Magnate *n.* magnate

Magnesium *n.* magnesyo

Magnet *n.* magneto, batobalani

Magnetic *adj.* magnetiko, kaakit-akit

Magnetism *n.* magnetismo

Magnetize *v.* magnetisahan, balanian

Magnificence *n.* karingalan, kadakilaan, karilagan

Magnificent *adj.* maringal, dakila, marilag, kahangahanga

Magnifier *n.* pampalaki, ampliador

Magnify *v.* palakhin, lakhan

Magnolia *n.* magnolya

Maguey *n.* magey

Maharajah *n.* maharaba

Maharani *n.* maharaha

Mahatma *n.* mahatma

Mahogany *n.* kamagong

Maid *n.* dalaga, birhen, utusang babae

Maidenhead *n.* kadalagahan, kabirhinan

Maidenly *adj.* mahinay, mahinhin

Mail *n.* koreo, lingkurang postal, sulat

Mail *v.* ikoreo, ihulog sa koreo

Mail box *n.* buson

Mailman *n.* kartero, koreo

Main *n.* daluyang prinsipal, bahaging prinsipal, lakas, kalawakan, karagatan

Mainland *n.* lupalop

Maintain *v.* magpatuloy, tustusan, panindigan, ipagpatuloy, pagapatuluyan, papanatilihin

Maintenance *n.* pagbuhay, sustento, taguyod, tustos, tangkilik, pagtatanggol

Maize *n.* mais

Majestic *adj.* mahestuwoso

Majesty *n.* mahestad, kadakilaan, kamahalan

Major *adj.* mayor, malaki, mahalaga

Major *n.* komandante, medyor

Majority *n.* mayoriya, nakararami

Majuscule *n.* mayuskula

Make *v.* gawin, igawa, gumawa, ganapin, gampanan, buuin, yariin, gumanap

Maker *n.* manggagawa, pabrikante

Makeshift *adj.* pansamantala, takip-butas

Maladjustment *n.* pagka-diahustado

Maladroit *adj.* kalay

Malady *n.* sakit

Malaria *n.* malarya, lagnat

Malcentent *adj.* di-nasisiyahan, di-kontento

Male *adj.* lalaki

Malediction *n.* maldisyon, sumpa

Malefaction *n.* pananam-palasan

Malfeasance *n.* katiwalian

Malformation *n.* tawisi

Malice *n.* malisya

Malicious *adj.* malisyoso

Malign *v.* manirang-puri, siraang-puri, alipustain

Malignant *adj.* makasasakit, makapipinsala, malubha, makamamatay

Malignity *n.* kalubhaan

Malleable *adj.* pitpitin, mapipitpit, mahuhubog, hubugin

Malleolus *n.* bukungbukong

Mallet *n.* maso, maseta, malyeta

Mallow *n.* malbas, kulutkutan

Malnutrition *n.* nutrisyong di-wasto

Malodor *n.* , antot, ban'ot

Malposition *n.* posisyong di-wasto, katayuang di-wasto

Malpractice *n.* di-wastong gawi, masamang gawi

Malt *n.* malta

Maltreat *v.* pagmalupitan, apihin, pagmalabisan

Maltreatment *n.* pag-api, pang-aapi

Mamma *n.* inay, inang, nanay, ima, ina

Mammal *n.* manunuso, mamipero

Mammiferous *adj.* mami-pero, maysuso

Mammilla *n.* utong

Mammon *n.* mamon

Mammoth *adj.* napakalaki

Mammoth *n.* mamut, dambuhala

Man *n.* tao, lalaki, sangkatauhan, esposo, tauhan

Man *v.* tauhan, patauhan

Manacle *n.* posas

Manacle *v.* posasan

Manage *v.* pangasiwaan, patnugtan, pangangasiwa

Management *n.* pangasi-waan, patnugutan

Manager *n.* tagapangasiwa, manedyer

Mandamus *n.* mandamus

Mandarin *n.* mandarin

Mandate *n.* mandato, utos

Mandatory *adj.* sapilitan

Mandible *n.* panga

Mandolin *n.* bandolin

Maneuver *n.* maniobra

Manganese *n.* mangganeso

Mange *n.* dusdos

Manger *n.* sabsaban

Mangle *n.* hiwagin, durugin, munglayin, salantain

Mango *n.* mangga

Mangy *adj.* dusdusin

Manhandle *v.* saktan

Manhood *n.* pagkalalaki, kalalakihan

Mania *n.* kahibangan, maniya, sumpong, hangal

Maniac *adj.* lunatiko, loko, luku-luko

Manicure *n.* manikyur

Manifest *adj.* halata, kita

Manifest *v.* ipakita, ipakilala, ihayag

Manifestation *n.* manipesta-syon, pakita

Manifesto *n.* manipesto, pahayag sa madla

Manikin *n.* maniki

Manila *n.* maynila

Manipulate *v.* kamayin, manipulahir, pamahalaan

Manito *n.* anito

Mankind *n.* sangkatauhan

Manly *adv.* maginoo, marangal

Manna *n.* mana

Manner *n.* paraan, asal, ugali

Mannerism *n.* gawi

Manor *n.* asyenda

Mansion *n.* mansiyon

Mansuetude *n.* kamansuhan

Mantis *n.* sasamba

Mantle *n.* manto, kapa

Manual *n.* manwal

Manufacture *v.* gumawa, yumari, pabrikahin

Manufacturer *n.* pabrikador, pabrikante

Manumission *n.* manumisyon, pagtitimawa

Manure *n.* manyur, patabasa lupa

Manuscript *n.* manuskrito, sulat-kamay

Many *adj.* marami

Map *n.* mapa

Map *v.* gumawa ng mapa, magbalak, planuhin, magplano

Mar *v.* pinsalain, sirain, saktan, dumhan, mantsahan

Maraschino *n.* maraskino

Marasmus *n.* pangangayayat

Marathon *n.* maraton, takbong mahabaan

Maraud *v.* manduwit, mandambong

Marauder *n.* manduduwit, mandudduit

Marble *n.* marmol, batong marmol

March *n.* marso

March *n.* martsa, pag-unlad

March *v.* magmartsa, umunlad, magpatuloy

Marchioness *n.* markesa

Mardigras *n.* karnabal

Mare *n.* kabayong babae, putrangka

Margarine *n.* margarina

Margin *n.* marhen, tabihan, hangganan, palugit

Marian *adj.* maryano

Marijuana *n.* mariwana

Marimba *n.* marimba

Marinade *n.* eskabetse

Marinate *v.* eskabetsihin

Marine *adj.* marino, pandagat

Marine *n.* marinero, marino

Marionette *n.* maryonet, papet, titires

Maritime *adj.* maritima, tabing-dagat, pandagat

Mark *n.* target, tudlaan, puntiryahan, marka, kahalagahan

Mark *v.* markahan

Market *n.* palengke, pamilihan

Market *v.* dalhin sa merkado, ipagbili

Marl *n.* marga, margal

Marline *n.* merlin

Marmalade *n.* mermelada, marmalada

Marmoset *n.* unggo, unggoy

Maroon *n.* kastanyong magulang, marun

Maroon *v.* mapadpad

Marquetry *n.* ukit, labor

Marquis *n.* markes

Marriage *n.* pag-aasawa, paglagay sa estado, kasal, pagkakasal

Marry *v.* ikasal, pakasal, mag-asawa, pakasalan

Mars *n.* marte

Marsh *n.* latian, labon

Marshal *n.* mariskal

Martial *adj.* marsiyal, pandigma, panghukbo, militar

Martingale *n.* gamara

Martyr *n.* martir

Martyrdom *n.* martiryo

Marvel *n.* kababalaghan, pagtataka

Marvel *v.* magtaka, mamangha

Marvelous *adj.* kataka-taka

Marvelousness *n.* pagka-kataka-taka

Mary *n.* Maria, Mariam, myrna

Mascot *n.* maskot, wisit, galing

Masculine *adj.* maskulino, panlalaki, lalaki

Masculinity *n.* pagkalalaki

Mash *n.* masa

Mash *v.* masahin

Masher *n.* pangmasa

Mask *n.* maskara, takip sa mukha, balatkayo

Masochism *n.* masokismo

Mason kantero, prankmason

Masonic *adj.* masonika

Masonry *n.* masoneriya

Masquerade *n.* Maskarada, pagmamaskara

Mass *n.* masa, materya, bulto, taong-bayan

Mass *v.* masahin

Massacre *n.* pamumuksa

Massacre *v.* puksain

Massage *n.* masahe

Massage *v.* masahihin

Masseur *n.* masahistang lalaki

Masseuse *n.* masahistang babae

Massive *adj.* masibo, malaking-malaki, mabigat na mabigat

Mast *n.* labor, palo, mastil

Master *n.* panginoon, amo, maestro, guro

Master *v.* maging panginoon, maging magaling, masupil, makapangyari

Mastermind *n.* punong-utak

Masterpiece *n.* obramaestra, lakang-akada

Mastery *n.* kapangyarihan, kadalubhasaan, kahigpitan

Masticate *v.* nguyain, ngatain, ngalutin

Mastication *n.* pagnguya

Masticator *pangn* guya

Mastitis *n.* mastitis

Mastodon *n.* mastodonte

Masturbate *v.* magsalsal

Masturbation *n.* pagsasalsal

Mat *n.* nilala, tinirintas

Match *n.* puspuro, pareha, kalaban

Match *v.*makalaban, ipantay, ibagay

Matchless *adj.* walang kapantay, di-mapapantayan

Matchmaker *n.* tulay

Mate *n.* kapares, asawa, piloto

Material *adj.* materyal, mabigat, pangkatawan

Material *n.* materya, kagamitan, lahok, panlahok, datos

Materialist *n.* materyalista

Materialistic *n.* materyal-istiko

Materialization *n.* materyal-isasyon

Materialize *v.* matupad, mangyari, lumitaw

Maternal *adj.* maternal, pangina

Mathematics *n.* matematika

Matinee *n.* matine

Matriarch *n.* matriarka

Matriarchy *n.* matriarkiya

Matricide *n.* matrisidyo

Matriculate *v.* magmatrikula, magpatala

Matrimony *n.* matrimonyo

Matrix *n.* matris, molde

Matron *n.* matrona

Matter *n.* materya, materyal sangkap , kahalagahan

Mattock *n.* patik

Mattress *n.* kutson

Maturate *v.* mahinog, magnana

Mature *adj.* hinog, magulang na, pagadero

Mature *v.* gumulang

Maturity *n.* kagulangan

Maul *v.* gulpihin, bugbugin

Mauler *n.* manggugulpi

Mausoleum *n.* mausoleo

Maw *n.* butse

Mawkish *adj.* nakasusuya

Maxilla *adj.* panga

Maxim *n.* sawikain

Maximal *adj.* pinakamataas, pinakadakila

Maximize *v.* palakhin hanggang sa maaari

Maximum *n.* maksimo, pinakamatayog, pinakadakila

May *n.* mayo

May *v.* maaari

Maybe *adj.* marahil, siguro

Mayhem *n.* mutilasyon, pananalanta

Mayonnaise *n.* mayonesa

Mayor *n.* alkalde

Mayoress *n.* alkadesa

Maze *n.* labirinto

Mazurka *n.* masurka

Me *pron.* ako, sa akin

Mead *n.* idromel, agwamyel

Meager *adj.* , payat, kakaunti

Meal *n.* pagkain, galapong

Mealy *adj.* durog, pulbos

Mean *adj.* ordinaryo, pangkaraniwan, mumurahin, mababa

Mean *adj.* panggitna, promedyo

Mean *n.* kagitnaan

Mean *v.* hangarin, layunin, tangkain, ipakahulugan

Meander *v.* magpakilu-kilo

Meantime *adj.* samantala

Measles *n.* tigdas, sarampiyon

Measly *adv.* may uod, hamak, kahamakhamak

Measure *n.* lawak, hangganan, panukat, abot, sukat, grado, kaya, bülumen, ramedyo

Measure *v.* sukatin, takalin

Measurement *n.* sukat

Meat *n.* karne, laman

Meatus *n.* daanan, butas

Mechanic *adj.* manwal, pangkamay, mekaniko, pangmakina

Mechanical *adj.* mekanical

Mechanician *n.* mekaniko

Mechanics *n.* mekaniko

Mechanism *n.* mekanismo

Mechanization *n.* mekanisasyon

Mechanize *v.* mekanisahin

Medal *n.* medalya, agnus

Meddle *v.* makialam, pakikialam, manghimasok, panghimasukan

Meddlesome *adj.* pakialam

Mediacy *n.* pamamagitan

Medial *adj.* panggitna

Median *n.* mediyana

Mediate *v.* mamagitan

Mediation *n.* pamamagitan

Mediator *n.* tagapamagitan

Mediatrix *n.* medyatris

Medic *n.* mediko, manggagamot

Medicable *adj.* magagamot

Medical *adj.* medikal

Medicament *n.* gamot, panlunas

Medicate *v.* gamutin

Medication *n.* paggamot

Medicinal *adj.* medisinal, nakalulunas

Medicine *n.* medisina

Medicolegal *adj.* medikolegal

Medieval *adj.* medyoebal

Mediocre *adj.* medyokre, pangkaraniwan

Meditate *v.* magnilay-nilay, magwari-wari, mag-isip

Meditation *n.* pagninilay-nilay

Meditative *adj.* mapagnilay-nilay

Mediterranean *adj.* mediteraneo

Medium *n.* panggitna, paraan, pamamaraan, kainaman katamtaman

Medusa *n.* medusa

Meed *n.* gantimpala, premyo

Meek *adj.* mahinahon, matiisin, mapagpakumbaba

Meet *v.* makita, matagpuan, makasalubong, sumalubong

Mega *pref.* mega

Megacycle *n.* megasiklo

Megaphone *n.* megapon

Megapod *adj.* malaking paa

Megascope *n.* megaskopyo

Melancholic *adj.* mapanglaw, malungkot

Melee *n.* labu-labo

Meliorate *v.* magmehora, mehorahin, pagbutihin

Melliferous *adj.* mapulot

Mellow *adj.* lunot, hinog na hinog

Melodious *adj.* melodyoso, mahimig

Melodrama *n.* melodrama

Melody *n.* melodiya, himig

Melon *n.* muskmelon, milon

Melt *v.* matunaw, tunawin, malusaw, lusawin

Member *n.* kasapi, kaanib

Membership *n.* pagkakasapi, pagkakaanib

Membrane *n.* membrana, lamad

Membraneous *adj.* malamad, membranoso

Memento *n.* memento

Memoir *n.* memoryas

Memorable *adj.* memorable

Memorandum *n.* memorandum

Memorial *adj.* memoryal

Memorization *n.* pagsasaulo

Memorize *v.* sauluhin, isaulo

Memory *n.* memorya, alaala, gunita

Menace *n.* bala

Menace *v.* pagbalaan, magbala

Menage *n.* pamamahay

Menaret *n.* minarete

Mend *v.* bumuti, mahkumpuni, kumpunihin,, magwasto, pagalingin iwasto, pabutihin

Mendacious *adj.* bulaan, magpasinugaling

Mendacity *n.* pagbubulaan, pagsisinungaling

Mendicant *n.* magpapalimos, pulube

Menial *adj.* pampanilbihan, mababa, aba

Menial *n.* menyal, alila

Meninges *n.* meninghes

Meningitis *n.* meninghitis

Meniscus *n.* medyaluna

Menopause *n.* menopawsiya

Menorrhagia *n.* menorahiya, labis na menses

Menses *n.* menses, panaog ng dugo

Menstrual *adj.* buwanan, menstrual

Menstruation *n.* mentruasyon

Mental *adj.* mental, pangkaisipan, pang-utak

Mentality *n.* mentalidad

Menthol *n.* mentol

Mentholated *adj.* mentolado

Mention *n.* banggit

Mention *v.* banggitin, mabanggit, tukuyin

Mentor *n.* mentor, patnubay, giya, tagapayo

Mentrum *n.* panunaw, panlusaw

Menu *n.* menu

Mephitic *adj.* mabantot, maantot

Mephitis *n.* bantot, antot

Mercantile *adj.* merjantil, komersiyal

Mercantilism *n.* merkanti-lismo

Mercenary *adj.* mersanaryo, nagpapaupa

Mercer *n.* mersero, magtetela

Mercerize *v.* merserahin

Mercery *n.* merseriya, merkaderiya

Merchandise *n.* kalakal

Merciful *adj.* maawain, mahabagin

Merciless *adj.* pagkawal-angawa

Mercury *n.* merkuryo, asoge

Mercy *n.* awa, habag

Mere *adj.* lamang

Meretricious *adj.* meretrisyo, nagmamagara

Merge *v.* pag-isahin, pagsa-mahin, pagpisanin, paghaluin

Merger *n.* konsolidasyon, kombinasyon

Meridian *adj.* meridyano, tanghali, katanghalian

Meridian *n.* meridyano, tanghali, katanghalian

Meringue *n.* merengge

Merit *n.* merito, kagalingan, galing

Mermaid *n.* sirena

Merriment *n.* saya, pagsasaya, kasayahan

Merry *adj.* massaya

Merry-go-round *n.* tiyubibo

Merrymaking *n.* pagsasaya

Mescal *n.* kaktus, hagdambato, surusuru, magey

Mesenchyma *n.* mesenkima

Mesentery *n.* mesenteryo, balamban

Mesh *n.* lambat, engrane

Mesial *adj.* gitna, kalagitnaan, hinati, hati

Mesmerism *n.* mesmerismo, hipnotismo

Mesne *n.* panggitna, pampagitan

Mesoblast *n.* mesoblasto

Mesocarp *n.* mesokarpiyo

Mesoderm *n.* mesodermo

Mesogastrium *n.* meso-gastrio, kapusuran

Mesomorph *n.* mesomorpo

Mesozoic *adj.* mesosoyko

Mess *n.* plato, salu-salo, gulo

Message *n.* mensahe, pasabi, pahatid, kalatas

Messiah *n.* mesias, mesiyas

Metabolism *n.* metabolismo

Metacarpus *n.* metakarpo

Metacentre *n.* metasentro

Metachromatism *n.* pagbabagong-kulay

Metagenesis *n.* metahenesis

Metal *n.* metal

Metalize *v.* metalisahin

Metallic *adj.* metalika

Metalliferous *adj.* metalipero

Metallography *n.* metalograpiya

Metallurgy *n.* metalurhiya

Metalware *n.* yaring-metal

Metamorphic *adj.* metamorpiko

Metamorphose *v.* magbagong-anyo

Metamorphosis *n.* metamorposis, banyuhay

Metaphor *n.* metapora, paghahambing

Metaphrase *n.* saling-wika

Metaphrase *v.* magsaling-wika, isaling-wika

Metaphysician *n.* metapisiko

Metaphysics *n.* metapisika

Metatarsal *n.* metatar-siko

Metathesis *n.* metatesis, palit-tayo

Metazoa *n.* metasoa

Mete *v.* sukatan, takalan

Metempsychosis *n.* metempsikosis

Meteor *n.* bulalakaw

Meteorite *n.* meteorito

Meteorologist *n.* meteorologo

Meteorology *n.* meteorolohiya

Meter *n.* metro, indayog

Method *n.* metodo, paraan, sistema, pamamaraan, ayos

Methodical *adj.* methodikal, sistematiko

Methodist *n.* metodista

Methodology *n.* metodolohiya

Methyl *n.* metilo

Meticulous *adj.* metikuloso, makuriri

Metier *n.* propesyon, espesiyalidad, linea

Metric *adj.* metrika

Metronome *n.* metronomo

Metropolis *n.* metropoli

Metropolitan *adj.* metropolitano

Metropolitan *n.* metropolitano

Metrorrhagia *n.* metrorahiya, pagdurugo ng bahay

Mettle *n.* tibay, tigas, tapang, init, sigla

Mew *n.* ngiyaw, ingaw

Mexican *adj.* mehikano

Mexican *n.* mehikano

Mexico *n.* mehiko, meksiko

Mezzanine *n.* entreswelo

Miaow *v.* ngumiyaw, umingaw

Miasma *n.* singaw

Mica *n.* mika

Mice *n.* daga

Micrify *v.* palinggitin, pauntiin

Micro *pref.* , mikro

Microampere *n.* mikroamperyo

Microbe *n.* mikrobyo

Microbiology *n.* mikrobyolohiya

Micrococcus *n.* mikrokoko

Microcosm *n.* mikrokosmo

Microcyte *n.* mikrosito

Microdetector *n.* mikro-detektor

Microfilm *n.* mikropilm

Micrography *n.* mikrograpiya

Micrology *n.* mikrolohiya

Micrometer *n.* mikrometro

Micron *n.* mikron

Microphone *n.* mikropono

Microscope *n.* mikroskopyo

Microscopy *n.* mikroskopiya

Microscosmic *adj.* mikro-kosmiko

Micturate *v.* umihi

Micturation *n.* pag-ihi

Mid *adj.* gitna

Mid *pref.* gitna

Midday *n.* katanghalian

Midden *n.* agsaman, bunton ng basura

Middle *n.* gitna, sentro, kalagitnaan

Middle aged *adj.* nasa gitnang gulang

Middle ear *n.* timpano, gitnang tainga

Middleman *n.* ahente

Middleweight *n.* gitnang-bi-gat

Middling *adj.* kainaman, katamtaman

Midget *n.* enanilyo

Midnight *n.* hatinggabi

Midrib *n.* tingting ng dahon

Midshipman *n.* guwarda-marina

Midst *n.* gitna

Midsummer *n.* gitnang-tagaraw

Midway *n.* hating-daan

Midweek *n.* hatinlinggo, gitnanlinggo

Midwife *n.* hilot

Midwifery *n.* panghihilot

Midyear *n.* hatintaon

Mien *n.* itsura, pagmumukha, kiya kiyas

Might *n.* kapangyarihan, poder, lakas

Mighty *adj.* makapangyarihan

Migrant *n.* mandarayuhan

Migrate *v.* mandayuhan, mangibang-bayan

Migration *n.* pandarayuhan

Migrator *adj.* padayu-dayo, pagala-gala

Mild *adj.* maamo, mabini, mahinay, suwabe

Mildew *n.* tagulamin

Mile *n.* milya

Mileage *n.* milyahe

Milepost *n.* milyarya

Milestone *n.* milyarya

Militant *adj.* militante, nanlalban, mapanlaban

Military *adj.* militar

Military *n.* militar

Militia *n.* milisya

Milk *n.* gatas

Milk *v.* gatasan

Mill *n.* gilingan, mulino, makina, gawaan, pabrika

Millenium *n.* milenaryo

Milleped *n.* ulahipan, alupihan

Miller *n.* mulinero

Millet *n.* miho

Milli *pref.* libo, sanlibo, ikasanlibo

Milligram *n.* miligramo

Millimeter *n.* milimetro

Milliner *n.* modista

Million *n.* milyon

Millionaire *n.* milyunaryo

Milt *n.* baso

Mime *n.* mimo, pantomina

Mimeo *n.* mimyo

Mimeograph *n.* mimyograp

Mimesis *n.* mimesis, panunulad, panggagaya

Mimic *adj.* gaya, gagad

Mimicry *n.* mimika

Mimosa *n.* mimosa, makahiya

Mince *v.* tadtarin, durugin, pikadilyuhin

Mincemeat *n.* pikadilyo

Mind *n.* unawa, alaala, isip, hangad, kaisipan, talino

Mindful *adj.* maasikaso

Mine *n.* mina

Mineral *adj.* mineral

Mineral *n.* mineral

Mineralogist *n.* mineralogo

Mineralogy *n.* mineralohiya

Mingle *v.* makihalubilo, makisama, makihalo

Miniature *adj.* minyatutura, munsing

Miniature *n.* minyatutura, munsing

Minimal *adj.* minimal

Minimize *v.* paliitin

Minimum *adj.* minimo, pinakamaliit, pinakamababa

Minimum *n.* minimo, pinakamaliit, pinakamababa

Minister *n.* ministro, kinatawang, diplomatiko, sugo

Ministerial *adj.* ministeryal

Ministry *n.* ministeryo

Minor *adj.* menor, mababang-uri, maynor

Minority *n.* minoriya

Minster *n.* monestaryo

Minstrel *n.* trobador, kantor, manganganta

Mint *n.* monedera

Mint *n.* menta, yerbabwena

Mint *v.* gumawa, kumatha

Mintage *n.* monederiya

Minter *n.* akunyador, imbentor

Minus *adj.* pabawas, wala

Minus *prep.* menos, bawasan ng

Minuscule *n.* minuskula, munting titik

Minute *adj.* menudo, munsing, munsik, napakaliit

Minute *n.* minuto, sandali

Minutes *n.* minutas, katitikan

Miracle *n.* himala, milagro

Miraculous *adj.* mapaghimala, milagroso

Mirage *n.* kinikinita

Mire *n.* lusak, putik

Mirror *n.* salamin

Mirth *n.* tuwa, saya, pagkatuwa, pagsasaya

Miry *adj.* malusak, maputik

Mis *pref.* mali, masama, sala

Misadventure *n.* desbentura, sakuna, disgrasya

Misappropriate *v.* magkamali sa paggamit

Misappropriation *n.* misa-propriasyon

Misbegotten *adj.* bastardo, ilheitimo

Misbelief *n.* maling panini-wala

Miscalculation *n.* maling pagkakataya

Miscarriage *n.* pagkalaglag, pagkaagas

Miscellanea *n.* miselanea

Miscellaneous *adj.* sarisari, samutsari

Mischief *n.* kalikutan, kapilyuhan

Mischievous *adj.* malikot, pilyo

Misconception *n.* maling akala

Misconduct *n.* di-mabuting asal, masamang pag-aasal

Miscreant *adj.* buhong

Misdeed *n.* masamang gawa, maling gawa

Miser *n.* abaro

Miserable *adj.* miserable, kaaba-aba

Misery *n.* pagdurusa, paghihirap

Misfire *v.* pumaltos

Misfit *n.* taong di-akma

Misfit *v.* di-magkahusto

Misfortune *n.* kasawian

Misgiving *n.* sagimsim, salagimsim

Misgovernment *n.* maling pa-mamahala

Misguidance *n.* maling akay

Mishap *n.* kapahamakan

Misinformation *n.* maling kabatiran

Misinterpretation *n.* maling pakahulugan

Misleading *adj.* nakaliligaw

Mismanagement *n.* maling pangangasiwa

Misogamist *n.* misogamo

Misogamy *n.* misogamya

Misologist *n.* misologo

Misplaced *adj.* wala sa lugar

Misprint *n.* maling pagkakalimbag

Miss *n.* binibini

Miss *v.* di-tamaan, di-makita, di-marinig, di-magkita, di-matagpuan, di-makuha

Missal *n.* misal

Missil *n.* proyektil, pansalipad, misil

Mission *n.* misyon, pakay, sadya

Missionary *n.* misyunero

Missive *n.* sulat, liham, kalatas

Misspelling *n.* maling bay-bay

Mist *n.* ulap

Mistake *n.* mali, kamalian, pagkamali

Mister *n.* ginoo

Mister(Mr) *n.* ginoo(G)

Mistiness *n.* pagkamaulap

Mistletoe *n.* miselto

Mistress *v.* ama, sinyora, kalunya, katiwala

Mistress (Mrs) *n.* ginang(Gng)

Mistrust *n.* kawalang-tiwala

Misty *adj.* maulap

Misunderstanding *n.* maling pakahulugin, di-pagkakasundo

Misuse *n.* maling pagkakagamit

Mitigate *v.* paginhawahin, hawahan

Mitosis *n.* mitosis, karyokinesis

Mix *v.* isama, maghalo, mahlahok, pagsamahin, lumahok, ihalo, haluan, paghaluin

Mixture *n.* mistura, halo

Mmassotherapy *n.* masoterapya

Mmaterialism *n.* materyalismo

Moan *n.* taghoy, daing, panambitan, haluyhoy

Moan *v.* tumaghoy, managhoy, dumaing, humaluyhoy

Mob *n.* taong-bayan, ang masa, libumbon

Mob *v.* pagdumugan

Mobility *n.* mobilidad

Mobilization *n.* mobilisasyon

Mobilize *v.* mobilisahin

Moblie *adj.* mobil, naikikilos, naigagalaw

Mock *v.* tuyain, kutyain

Mocker *n.* manunuya

Mockery *n.* tuya

Mockingly *adv.* patuya

Mode *n.* paraan, moda, panagano, uso

Model *n.* modelo, huwaran

Moderate *adj.* kainaman, katamtaman, mahinahon

Moderate *v.* pahinaan

Moderation *n.* moderasyon, hinahon

Moderator *n.* tagapamagitan

Modern *adj.* moderno, makabago

Modernize *v.* modernisahin

Modest *adj.* mahinhin, mabini, basal

Modestly kahinhinan, kabinian

Modification *n.* modipikasyon, pagbabago

Modify *v.* baguhin

Modular *adj.* modular

Modulate *v.* modulahin

Modulation *n.* modulasyon

Module *n.* modulo

Mogul *n.* mogul

Mohammedan *adj.* mahometano

Mohammedan *n.* mahometano

Mohammedanism *n.* mohamedanismo, islamismo

Moist *adj.* halumigmig

Moisten *v.* basa-basain

Moisture *n.* umido, halumigmig

Molar *n.* bagang

Molassess *n.* pulot, melasa

Mole *n.* nunal, taling

Molecular *adj.* molekular

Molecule *n.* molekula

Molest *v.* gambalain, guluhin

Mollify *v.* patahimikin, patiwasayin

Moment *n.* saglit sandali

Momus *n.* momo, mamumuna

Monachal *adj.* monakal, monastiko

Monanthous *adj.* mananto

Monarch *n.* monarka

Monarchical *adj.* monarkiko

Monarchist *n.* monarkista

Monarchy *n.* monarkiya

Monastery *n.* monasteryo

Monday *n.* lunes

Monetary *adj.* monetaryo, pamimilak

Monetization *n.* monetisasyon, pagmomoneda

Monetize *v.* monetisahin, monedahin

Money *n.* salapi, kuwarta, kuwalta, pilak

Monger *n.* trapikante

Mongering *adj.* nagtatrapikante

Moniker *n.* moniker, palayaw

Monitor *n.* monitor

Monk *n.* monghe

Monkey *n.* unggo, tsonggo

Monocle *n.* monokulo

Monogamist *n.* monogamo

Monogamy *n.* monogamya

Monogram *n.* monograma

Monograph *n.* monograpiya

Monographer *n.* monograpo

Monolith *n.* monolito

Monopolism *n.* monopolismo

Monopolistic *adj.* monopolista

Monopolize *v.* monopolisahin

Monopoly *n.* monopolyo

Monotheism *n.* monoteismo

Monotheist *n.* monoteista

Monotonous *adj.* monotono

Monotony *n.* pagka-monotono

Monsoon *n.* monson

Monster *n.* monstruo, halimaw, dambuhala

Monstrance *n.* kustodya

Monstruous *adj.* monstruoso, napakalaki

Month *n.* buwan

Monthly *adj.* buwan-buwan, bawa't buwan, buwanan

Monument *n.* munumento, bantayog

Monumental *adj.* munumental, bantayugin

Mood *n.* disposisyon , panagano

Moody *adj.* malungkutin

Moon *n.* buwan

Moonbeam *n.* sinag ng buwan

Moor *n.* latin, labon, moro, muslim

Moor *v.* dumuong, iduong, magduong

Moose *n.* anta

Moot *n.* pagtatalakayan, pagtatalo

Mop *n.* panlampaso

Mop *v.* maglampaso, lampasuhin

Mope *v.* mamanglaw

Moral *adj.* moral, marapat , marangal

Morale *n.* sigla, diwa

Moralism *n.* moralismo

Morality *n.* moralidad, kasanlingan

Moralize *v.* mangaral

Morals *n.* kabudhian

Morbid *adj.* malagim

Morbidity pagkamalagim

Mordent *adj.* mordente

More *adj.* higit, lalo pa

Mores *n.* kustumbre, ugaling-bayan

Morganatic *adj.* morganatiko

Morgue *n.* morge

Morion *n.* moryon

Morning *n.* umaga

Moron *adj.* moron, tanga

Moron *n.* moron, tanga

Morpheus *n.* morpeo

Morphia *n.* morpina

Morphology *n.* morpolohiya

Mortal *adj.* mortal, may kamatayan, nakamamatay, patal

Mortality *n.* mortalidad, pagkakamatay

Mortar *n.* lusong, mortar

Mortgage *n.* sangla, pagsasangla, ipoteka

Mortgage *v.* magsangla, isangla

Mortification *n.* mortipikasyon, pagpipigil, kahihiyan, gangrena

Mortify *v.* magpigil, hiyan, magkagangrena, gangrenahin

Mortise *n.* aab, ukit

Mortise *v.* aaban, ukitan

Mortuary *n.* morge, punerarya

Mosaic *n.* mosayko

Moslem *n.* muslim

Mosque *n.* meskita

Mosquito *n.* lamok

Moss *n.* lumot, musgo

Mossy *adj.* malumot

Most *adj.* pinaka, pinakamarami, pinakamalaki, kalaki-lakihan

Most *n.* , karamihan, halos kabuuan

Mostoid *adj.* mastoyde

Motel *n.* motel

Moth *n.* polilya

Mother *n.* ina, pinagmulan

Mother *v.* alagaan

Motile *adj.* motil, umiibo, gumagalaw, kumikilos, kumikibo

Motility *n.* mobilidad

Motion *n.* galaw, takbo, kilos, takbo, kibo, mosyon, ibo

Motionless *adj.* walang-galaw, walang-kibo

Motivate *v.* ibuyo, ganyakin, kayagin

Motivation *n.* motibasyon, ganyak, pagganyak, pangganyak

Motive motibo, hangarin

Motor *n.* motor, makina

Motorboat *n.* autobote

Motorcycle *n.* motorsiklo

Mottled *adj.* bakat-bakat

Motto *n.* moto, bansag

Mould *n.* molde, hulma, hulmahan

Mound *n.* tambak, puntod

Mount *n.* bundok, umbok

Mount *v.* dumani, sakyan, tumaas, ipatong,umakyat, ikama,umahon, sumakay

Mourn *v.* magdalamhati, ipagdalamhati

Mouse *n.* daga

Mouth *n.* bibig

Move *n.* galaw, kilos, sulong, hakbang

Move *v.* kumilos, pukawin, ilipat, itaboy, pagalawin, imungkahi umunlad, pakilusin, iaboy

Mow *v.* gumapas, gapasin

Mower *n.* panggapas, manggagapas

Much *adj.* marami, malaki

Much *adv.* napakalaki, halos, lalo, higit

Muck *n.* burak, pusali

Mucous *adj.* malauhog

Mucus *n.* uhog

Mud *n.* putik

Muddy *adj.* maputik

Mudguard *n.* tapalodo

Mudstone *n.* tapya

Muezzin *n.* muesin

Muffler *n.* bupanda, mapler

Mug *n.* pitsel

Mule *n.* mula

Muleteer *n.* muletero

Mull *v.* magmuni, magkuro

Muller *n.* pandikdik

Mullet *n.* banak

Multifarious *adj.* sarisari, iba-iba

Multilateral *adj.* mapanig

Multimillionaire *n.* multimil-yunaryo

Multiple *adj.* multiplo, marami

Multiplicand *n.* multi-plikando

Multiplication *n.* multipli-kasyon. pagpaparami

Multiplier *n.* multiplikador

Multiply *v.* multiplikahin, paramihin

Multitude *n.* multitud

Mum *adj.* tahimik
Mummification *n.* momipi-kasyon
Mummify *v.* momipikahin
Mummy *n.* momya, mumo
Mumps *n.* baiki, biki
Munch *v.* ngalutin
Mundane *adj.* mundano, makalupa
Municipal *adj.* munisipal
Municipality *n.* munisipyo
Munificent *adj.* mapagbigay, liberal
Mural *adj.* mural, pandingding
Murder *n.* sadyang pagpatay
Murderer *n.* mamamatay-tao
Murk *n.* dilim, lagim
Murky *adj.* malagim, madilim
Murmur *v.* bumulong, bumulung-bulong
Muscle *n.* muskulo, kalamnan, laman
Muscular *adj.* muskular
Muse *n.* musa
Muse *v.* magnilaynilay
Museum *n.* museo
Mushroom *n.* kabute
Music *n.* musika, tugtugin
Musical *adj.* musikal
Musician *n.* musikero, musiko, manunugtog
Musk *n.* almiskle
Musket *n.* moskete, pusil
Musketeer *n.* mosketero
Muskmelon *n.* milon
Muslin *n.* muselina, perkal
Mussel *n.* kabibi, tikhan
Must *n.* lubhang kailangan
Must *v.* dapat, marapat, nararapat, kailangan
Mustache *n.* bigote, misay
Mustang *n.* kabayong mustang
Mustard *n.* mustasa
Muster *v.* tipunin, tawagin
Mute *adj.* pipi
Mute *n.* pipi
Mutilate *n.* gutayin, gibain
Mutilation *n.* mutilasyon, paggutay, paggiba
Mutiny *n.* pag-aalsa, pagbabangon, himagsik
Mutter *v.* umungol
Mutton *n.* karning-tupa
Mutual *adj.* mutwo, resiproko, gantihan, palitan
Muzzle *n.* nguso, busal
My *pron.* akin, ko
Myopia *n.* myopya
Myriad *n.* sanlaksa
Mysterious *n.* misteryoso, mahiwaga
Mystery *n.* misteryo, hiwaga
Mystic *adj.* mistiko
Mysticism *n.* mistisismo
Mystification *n.* mistipikasyon
Myth *n.* mito, alamat
Mythologist *n.* mitologo
Mythology *n.* mitolohiya

N n

Nab *V.* dakpin, sunggaban, hulihin

Nacre *n.* nakar, madreperla

Nag *n.* haka, hako

Nag *v.* magnanag, mangnag

Nagger *n.* nager

Nags *v.* kagalitang malimit

Nail *n.* kuko, pako

Nail *v.* magpako, ipako, pakuan

Naitionalize *v.* nasyonalisahin

Naive *adj.* naib, natural, walang pakunwari

Naked *adj.* hubo't habad, walang damit

Name *n.* pangalan, ngalan, pamagat, kabantugan

Nameless *adj.* hindi kilala, walang pangalan

Namely *adv.* gaya ng

Nap *n.* idlip

Nap *v.* maidlip, umidlip, matulog

Nape *n.* batok

Napkin *n.* serbilyeta

Napthelene *n.* naptalina

Narcotic *n.* narkotiko

Narrate *v.* isalaysay, magsalaysay, salaysayin

Narration *n.* salaysay, pagsasalaysay

Narrative *adj.* pasalaysay, salaysayin

Narrative *n.* pasalaysay, salaysayin

Narrow *adj.* makipot, makitid, maigsi

Nasty *adj.* marumi, masagwa, mahalay

Natal *adj.* katutubo, natibo

Natant *adj.* lutang, nakalutang, lumalangoy

Nation *n.* bansa, nasyon

National *adj.* pambansa

National *n.* mamamayan

Nationalism *n.* nasyonalismo

Nationality *n.* nasyonalidad, kabansaan, kabansahan

Native *n.* katutobo, natibo

Natural *adj.* likas, natural

Nature *n.* kalikasan, likas, naturalesa

Naught *n.* wala, sero

Naughty *adj.* pilyo, masama

Nausea *n.* duwal, pagduduwal, lula, pagkaani

Nautical *adj.* marina, nautiko

Naval *adj.* nabal, pandagat

Navel *n.* pusod

Navigate *v.* maglayag

Navigation n. paglalayag

Navigator *n.* manlalayag, tagapaglayag

Navy *n.* hukbong-dagat

Nay *n.* pagtanggi, pagpapahindi

Nazi *n.* nazi, nasi

Near *adj.* malapit
Nearby *adv.* sa tabi-tabi
Nearly *adv.* halòs
Neat *adj.* maayos, malinis
Necessary *adj.* kailangan, dimaiiwasan
Necessity *n.* pangan-gailangan, karukhaan
Neck *n.* liig, leeg
Neck *v.* magyapusan
Necklace *n.* kuwintas
Nectar *n.* nektar
Nee *adj.* anak, nee
Need *n.* pangangailangan, kasalatan, karukhaan
Need *v.* mangailangan
Needle *n.* aguha, karayom
Needlework *n.* burda, tahi
Needy *adj.* dahop
Negate *v.* tanggihan
Negation *n.* pagpapahindi, pagtanggi
Negative *n.* negatibo
Neglect *v.* magpabaya, pabayaan
Negligence *n.* kapabayaan
Negotiate *v.* makipagkasundo
Negotiation *n.* negosasyon
Negrito *n.* itA, agta, ayta, negrito
Negro *n.* negro
Neigh *n.* halinghing
Neigh *v.* humalinghing
Neighbor *n.* kapitbahay
Neighborhood *n.* paligid
Nematode *n.* bulati, nematoda
Nemesis *n.* nemesis, katarungan
Neon *n.* neon
Nephew *n.* pamangking lalaki
Neptune *n.* neptuno
Nerve *n.* nerbiyo, ugat, nerbiyos
Nervous *adj.* ninenerbiyos
Nest *n.* pugad
Nest *v.* magpugad, mamugad
Nestle *v.* pakalong, pakalungkong
Net *n.* net, neto, lambat
Net *v.* magneto, numeto
Nether *adj.* ibaba, ilalim
Nettle *n.* baluhan
Neurologist *n.* neurologo
Neurology *n.* neurolohiya
Neutral *adj.* neutral
Never *adv.* hindi kailanman
New *adj.* bago, makabago, sariwa
News *n.* balita
Newsman *n.* peryodista
Newspaper *n.* diyaryo, peryodiko
Next *adj.* kasunod,.susunod
Next *adv.* kasunod, susunod
Nexus *n.* bigkis, kawing, koneksiyon
Nibble *v.* ngumatngat, ngatngatin
Nice *adj.* angkop, mainam, marikit, magiliw, nakalulugod

Nick *n.* bungi, gatla, hiwa
Nickle *n.* nikel
Nickname *n.* palayaw
Nickname *v.* palayawan
Nickname *v.* palayawan
Niece *n.* pamangking babae
Niggard *adv.* kuripot
Nigh *adv.* malapit
Night *n.* gabi
Nightfall *n.* takipsilim
Nightmare *n.* bangungot
Nimble *adj.* maliksi, matalas, mabilis, gumanap
Nine *n.* siyam
Nineteen *adj.* labinsiyam
Nineteen *n.* labinsiyam
Nineteenth *adj.* ikalabin-siyam
Ninety *adj.* siyamnapu
Ninety *n.* siyamnapu
Ninth *adj.* ikasiyam
Nip *v.* kumurot, kumagat, sugpuin, ipitin
Nipple *n.* utong
No *adj.* hindi, wala
Nobility *n.* noblesa
Noble *adj.* noble, mahal, maharlika, marangal
Nobody *pron.* walang tao
Nocturnal *adj.* panggabi
Nocturne *n.* nokturno
Nod *v.* tumango
Node *n.* buko
Noise *n.* ingay
Noiseless *adj.* tahimik
Noisy *adj.* maingay
Nomad *n.* taong layas
Nominal *adj.* nominal, sa pangalan lamang
Nominate *v.* nominahan, ipasok ang pangalan
Nomination *n.* nominasyon
None *pron.* wala
Nonsense *n.* kahunghangan, kaululan
Nonstop *adj.* walang-hinto
Noodle *n.* miki, bihon, misua
Nook *n.* sulok
Noon *n.* katanghalian, tanghaling tapat
Noose *n.* likaw, silo
Norm *n.* norma, pamantayan, tuntunin
Normal *adj.* normal, karaniwan, katamtaman
Normalcy *n.* kanormalan
Normality *n.* kanormalan
Normalize *v.* normalisahin
Normative *adj.* normatibo
North *adj.* hilaga, norte
North *n.* hilaga, norte
Northeast *n.* hilagang-silangan
Northerly *adv.* pahilaga
Northward *adj.* pahilaga
Northward *adv.* pahilaga
Northwest *n.* hilagang-kanluran
Nose *ilong* pangamoy
Nosebleed *n.* balinguyngoy
Nostalgia *n.* nostalhiya, galimgim, hidlaw
Nostril *n.* butas ng ilong

Not *adv.* hindi, wala

Notable *adj.* kapansin-pansin, katangi-tangi, kilalang tao

Notarize *v.* notaryuhin, notaryuhan

Notary *n.* notaryo

Notation *n.* notasyon

Notch *n.* ukit, gitgit

Note *n.* nota, marka, palatandaan

Note *v.* punahin

Notebook *n.* kuwederno

Noted *adj.* tanyag, bantog, kilala

Noteworthy *adj.* katangitangi

Nothing *n.* wala

Nothing *pron.* wala

Notice *n.* pabatid, paunawa, puna, asikaso

Notice *v.* abisuhan, asikasuhin, banggitin, pagmasdan, punahin

Noticeable *adj.* hayag, lantad, litaw

Notification *n.* abiso

Notify *v.* abisuhan, pasabihan, balitaan, papagsabihan

Notion *n.* haka, idea, paniwala, kuro

Notorious *adv.* bantog sa kasamaan

Nought *n.* wala

Noun *n.* pangngalan

Nourish *v.* magpakain, pakanin, magtaglay

Nourishment *n.* pagkain

Novel *adj.* bago, naiiba

Novel *n.* nobelo, kathambuhay

Novelette *n.* maikling nobela

Novelist *n.* nobelista

Novelty *n.* kabaguhan

November *n.* Nobyembre

Novena *n.* nobena

Novice *n.* baguhan, nobisyo

Now *adv.* ngayon

Noxious *adj.* nakapipinsala

Nozzle *n.* bokilya

Nuclear *adj.* nuklear

Nucleus *n.* nukleo, ubod

Nude *adj.* hubu't-hubad

Nude *n.* hubu't-hubad

Nudge *n.* paniniko

Nudge *v.* sikuhin

Nugget *n.* tigkal

Nuisance *n.* panggulo, panligalig

Null *adj.* walang-bisa

Nullify *v.* nuluhin

Numb *adj.* manhid, namamanhid

Numb *v.* pamanhirin

Number *n.* numero, bilang

Number *v.* numeruhan, bilangin

Numeral *adj.* numeral

Numerical *adj.* numeriko

Numerous *adj.* marami

Numismatics *n.* numismatika

Numismatist *n.* numismatiko

Nun *n.* mongha, madre

Nunnery *n.* kumbento ng mga mongha

Nupital *adj.* nupsiyal, pangkasal

Nuptials *n.* kasal, pagkakasal

Nurse *n.* nars

Nurse *v.* magpasuso, magyaya, alagaan

Nursemaid *n.* ama, yaya

Nursery *n.* narsery

Nurture *v.* alagaan, pakanin, palakihin, hubugin, turuan

Nut *n.* nuwes, tuwerka, pili

Nutrient *adj.* nakapagpapalusog

Nutrition *n.* nutrisyon, pagpapakain, pagkain

Nylon *n.* naylon

Nymph *n.* nimpa

O o

Oak *n.* roble

Oar *n.* gaod, sagwan

Oar *v.* gumaod, sumagwan

Oarlock *n.* orkilya

Oasis *n.* oasis

Oath *n.* sumpa, panunumpa

Oats *n.* abena

Obbligato *adj.* obligato

Obbligato *n.* obligato

Obdurate *adj.* may matigas na puso, di-matinag

Obedience *n.* pagkamasunurin, pagsunod

Obedient *adj.* masunurin, madaling akayin

Obese *adj.* mataba

Obesity *n.* katabaan

Obey *v.* sumunod, sundin

Obfuscate *v.* padilimin, padimlan, guluhin, lituhin

Obfuscation *n.* pagpapadilim, panlilito

Obi *n.* obi

Obituary *n.* obitwaryo

Object *n.* bagay, layon, puntahin, sadya

Object *v.* tutulan, tumutol

Objection *n.* tutol, protesta

Objectionable *adj.* may kapintasan, di-mabuti

Objective *adj.* palayon

Objective *n.* , layunin

Objector *n.* ang tumututol, ang sumasalungat

Oblate *adj.* nakaalay, nakahandog, deboto

Oblation *n.* pag-aalay, paghahandog

Obligate *v.* obligahin, ipatungkol

Obligation *n.* obligasyon, tungkulin, pananagutan, kautangan

Obligatory *adv.* sapilitan

Oblige *v.* pilitin, pagbigyan

Obliging *adj.* matulungin, magiliw

Oblique *adj.* hiris, pahilis

Oblique *v.* humulig

Obliterate *v.* katkatin, pawiin, kayurin

Oblivion *n.* limot, pagkalimot, paglimot

Obloquy *n.* alipusta

Oboe *n.* oboe

Obscene *adj.* mahalay, magaspang, malaswa

Obscenity *n.* kahalayan

Obscurantism *n.* obskurantismo

Obscure *adj.* madilim, malagim, baliwag, malabo

Obscurity *n.* dilim, karimlan

Obsequious *adj.* serbil, mapanuyo, mapangayupapa

Observance *n.* pagtalima, pagdiriwang, seremonya

Observant *adj.* mapagmasid

Observation *n.* pagmamasid

Observatory *n.* obserbatoryo

Observe *v.* pagmasdan, tumalima, umayon, ipagdiwang, masdan

Observer *n.* tagamasid, ang nagmamasid

Obsess *v.* mahumaling

Obsession *n.* obsesyon

Obsolete *adj.* di na gamit, lipas; laos

Obstacle *n.* hadlang, sagwil, sagabal, balakid

Obstetrician *n.* obstetrisyan

Obstetrics *n.* obstetrisya

Obstinacy *n.* katigasan ng ulo

Obstruct *v.* hadlangan, sarhan, harangan

Obstruction *n.* sagabal, balakid

Obstructionist *n.* manghahadlang

Obstrusion *n.* pakikialam

Obstrusive *adj.* pakialam

Obstuse *adj.* pulpol, pudpod, salsal

Obtain *v.* makuha, matamo, kunin, tamuhin, makamit, magtamo, kamitin, makakuha

Obtainable *adj.* maaaring makuha

Obtrude *v.* makialam

Obverse *n.* harapan, kabila, pinaka-mukha, kara

Obviate *v.* umiwas, iwasan, maiwasan

Obvious *adj.* maliwanag, madaling maunawaan, hayag, lantad

Occasion *n.* pagkakataon, pangyayari, okasyon, pagdiriwang

Occasional *adj.* manaka-naka

Occident *n.* oksidente, kanluran

Occidental *adj.* oksidental, kanluranin

Occult *adj.* tago, lingid, mahiwaga

Occult *v.* itago, ilingid, mapatago, mapalingid

Occultism *n.* okultismo, alimuwang

Occupant *n.* nakatira, naninirahan

Occupation *n.* pag-okupa, hanapbuhay, pagtira

Occupy *v.* okupahan, tirhan, tahanan

Occur *v.* mangyari, matagpuan, makita, lumitaw

Occurence *n.* pangyayari

Ocean *n.* oseano, malaking dagat, karagatan

Oceanic *adj.* oseaniko

Oceanographer *n.* oseanograpo

Oceanographic *adj.* oseanograpiko

Oceanography *n.* oseanograpiya

Ochre *n.* okre

Octagon *n.* oktagono

Octave *n.* oktaba

Octavo *n.* tiklop oktabo

October *n.* oktubre

Octogenarian *n.* oktohenaryo

Octopus *n.* pugita, oktopus

Ocular *adj.* okular, pangmata

Ocular *n.* silipan

Oculist *n.* okulista

Odd *adj.* gansal, di-karaniwan, samut-samot, nagkakasalungatan

Ode *n.* oda

Odious *adj.* nakamumuhi, nakapopoot

Odium *n.* poot, kamuhian, pagkamuhi

Odontology *n.* odontolohiya

Odor *n.* amoy

Odorous *adj.* mahalimuyak

Oestrus *n.* kandi, pangangandi

Of *prep.* ng

Off *adv.* mula rito , palayo, pahiwalay

Offence *n.* kasalanan, ataka, tuligsa, pagkakasala

Offend *v.* magkasala, upasalain, manggalit, galitin, insultuhin

Offer *n.* alay sakripisyo, mungkahi, handog, tulong

Offer *v.* ihandog, ialok, ialay, isakripisyo, magsakripisyo

Offering *n.* alay, handog

Offertory *n.* opertoryo

Offhand *adj.* biglaan, di-handa

Office *n.* opisna, tanggapan, tungkulin, katungkulan

Officer *n.* pinuno

Official *adj.* opisyal, pampamahalaan

Official *n.* opisyal, pinuno, puno

Officiate *v.* manungkulan, manuparan, gumanap

Offing *n.* laot, darating

Offish *adj.* malayo

Offset *n.* sanga, katumbas, katimbang, opset

Offset *v.* tapatan, timbangan, tumbasan, iopset

Offshoot *n.* sanga, angkan binga

Offspring *n.* supling, anak, bunga

Often *adv.* malimit, madalas

Oh *intr.* o

Ohm *n.* omyo

Ohmmeter *n.* omimetro
Oil *n.* langis, aseyte
Oil *v.* langisan, maglangis
Oily *adj.* malangis
Ointment *n.* ungguwento
Okra *n.* okra
Old *adj.* laon, antigo, matanda, antigwa, gulang, dati, luma
Oleaster *n.* asebutse
Oleoresin *n.* oleoresina
Olfaction *n.* pangamoy, pagamoy
Oligarch *n.* oligarka
Oligarchy *n.* oligarkiya
Olive *n.* olibo, oliba, aseytunas
Olympiad *n.* olimpiada
Olympian *n.* olimpiko
Olympic *n.* olimpiko
Olympus *n.* olimpo
Omega *n.* omega, huli, wakas
Omelet *n.* tortilla
Omen *n.* pangitain, palatandaan, babala, tanda
Omentum *n.* omento
Ominous *adj.* nagbabala
Omission *n.* omisyon, di-pagkakasama
Omit *v.* iwan, kaltasin, pabayaan, ligtaan
Omnibus *n.* bus, omnibus
Omniscience *n.* lubos na karunungan
Omniscient *adj.* lubos na marunong, alal ang lahat
Omnivorous *adj.* omniboro, kaing lahat
On *prep.* sa
Onanism *n.* onanismo
Once *adv.* minsan
Once *conj.* pag, kapag, sa minsang
Oncoming *adj.* nalalapit, palapit
One *adj.* isa, nag-iisa
One *n.* isa, nag-iisa
One *pron.* sinumang tao
One-sided *adj.* may pinapanigan
Onemastic *adj.* onomastiko, pampangalan
Oneness *n.* pagka-iisa, pag-ka-nag-iisa, kaisahan
Onerous *adj.* mabigat, malupit, mahigpit
Oneself *n.* sarili
Onion *n.* sibuyas, lasuna
Onlooker *n.* manonood
Only *adj.* lamang, tangi, bugtong
Only *adv.* lamang, tangi, bugtong
Only *conj.* nguni't
Onomatopoeic *adj.* onomato-peyiko
Onrush *n.* pagsunod
Onset *n.* salakay, atake, umpisa, simula
Ontology *n.* ontolohiya
Onus *n.* karga, dala, tungkulin, kapanagutan
Onward *adj.* pasulong

Onward *adv.* pasulong

Onyx *n.* onise

Ooze *n.* tagas, kayat

Ooze *v.* tumagas, kumayat

Opacity *n.* opasidad, kalabuan

Opague *adj.* malabo, kulabo

Opal *n.* opalo

Open *adj.* bukas, tapat, lantad, libre, prangko

Open *v.* buksan, ibuka, ibunyag, ilatag, iladlad, ihayag

Open-handed *adj.* bukas-kamay

Open-hearted *adj.* bukas-puso

Opener *n.* pambukas

Opening *n.* butas, siwang, puwang, bakante

Opera *n.* opera

Operate *v.* gumawa, magbisa, magtrabaho, gumanap, magpalakad, tumupad

Operation *n.* pagmamaneho, operasyon, pagpapalakad, pamamahala, pagtistis

Operative *adj.* maybisa

Operator *n.* makinista, operetor

Ophanage *n.* ampunan ng mga ulila

Ophthalmia *n.* optalmiya

Ophthalmologist *n.* optal-mologo

Ophthalmology *n.* optal-molohiya

Opiate *adj.* may-apyan, narkotiko, nakagiginhawa

Opiate *n.* may-apyan, narkotiko, nakagiginhawa

Opine *v.* magpalagay, akalain, isipin

Opinion *n.* palagay, pananaw, paniwala

Opium *n.* apyan, opyo

Oponent *n.* kalaban, kaaway, katalo

Opportune *adj.* napapanahon

Opportunist *n.* oportunista, mapagsamantala

Opportunity *n.* oportunidad, pagkakataon

Oppose *v.* sumalungat, labanan, salungatin, sumalangsang, salangsangin

Opposite *n.* kasalungat, kabaligtaran

Opposition *n.* pagtutol, oposisyon

Oppress *v.* pahirapan, mangapi, apihin

Oppressive *adj.* mapang-api

Oppressor *n.* opresor, mangaapi

Opprobrious *adj.* oprobyoso

Optic *adj.* optiko

Optician *n.* optika

Optics *n.* optika

Optimism *n.* optimismo, pagka-maasahin

Optimistic *n.* optimista, maasahin

Option *n.* opsiyon

Optional *adj.* opsiyonal, di-sapilitan

Optmist *n.* optimista, taong maasahin

Optometer *n.* optometro

Optometrist *n.* optometra

Opulence *n.* yaman, kayamanan, kasanganaan

Opulent *adj.* mayaman, mariwasa

Opus *n.* opus

Or *conj.* o

Oracle *n.* orakulo

Oral *adj.* pasalita, oral, pambibig

Orange *n.* dalandan, sintunis, dalanghita, kahel

Orangutan *n.* orangutang

Orate *v.* manalumpati

Oration *n.* talumpati

Orator *n.* orador, mananalumpati

Oratory *n.* pananalumpati, dalanginan

Orb *n.* orbe

Orbit orbita, ligiran

Orchard *n.* looban, halamanan, gulayan, lagwerta

Orchestra *n.* orkesta

Orchid *n.* orkidea, dapo

Ordain *v.* italaga, ipag-utos, itadhana, iatas

Ordeal *n.* mahigpit na pagsubok

Order *n.* orden, kaurian, kautusan, pabilin, kaayusan, panunuran

Order *v.* mag-ayos, iayos, isaayos, pag-ugnay-ugnayin

Orderly *adj.* maayos

Ordinal *adj.* bilang panunuran, numero ordinal

Ordinal *n.* bilang panunuran, numero ordinal

Ordinance *n.* ordinansa, kautusan

Ordinary *adj.* ordinaryo, karaniwan, pangkaraniwan

Ore *n.* kiho, inang-mina

Organ *n.* organo, sangkap, kasangkapan, pahayagan

Organic *adj.* organiko

Organism *n.* organismo

Organist *n.* organista

Organization *n.* organisasyon, pagbubuo, pagtatatag, asosyasyon, samahan, kapisanan

Organize *v.* mag-organisa, magbuo, magtatag

Organized *adj.* organisado

Organizer *n.* organisador

Orgy *n.* orhiya, lasingan

Orient *n.* oryente, silangan, silanganan

Orient *v.* humarap sa silangan, iwastong-dako, isilangan, manilangan

Oriental *adj.* oryental, silanganin

Orientalism *n.* oryentalismo

Orientate *v.* ipanilangan

Orientation *n.* oryentasyon, paninilangan, pag-aangkop

Orifice *n.* butas, siwang

Origin *n.* orihen, pinagmulan

Original *adj.* orihinal

Original *n.* orihinal

Originality *n.* orihinalidad, kasarilinan

Originate *v.* magsimula

Originator *n.* ang nagbigaysimula

Oriole *n.* oryol

Orion *n.* oryon, kasador

Orison *n.* orasyon, plegarya, dalangin, panalangin

Ornament *n.* palamuti

Ornamental *adj.* ornamental, pampalamuti

Ornate *adj.* maadorno, mapalamuti

Orologist *n.* orologo, dalub-bundok

Orology *n.* orolohiya

Orotund *adj.* mataginting

Orphan *n.* ulila

Orphan *v.* maulila, ulilahin

Orphaned *adj.* naulila

Orpheus *n.* orpeo

Orthodox *adj.* ortodokso

Orthodoxy *n.* ortodoksiya

Orthography *n.* ortograpiya, palabaybayan, palatitikan

Orthopedics *n.* ortopedya

Oscillate *v.* magpa-tayuntayon, magpaurung-sulong

Oscillation *n.* osilasyon

Oscillator *n.* osilador

Osculate *v.* halikan, humalik, hagkan

Osculation *n.* paghalik

Osmosis *n.* osmosis

Osmotic *adj.* osmotiko

Ostensible *adj.* hayag, pakita

Ostensibly *adv.* diumano, dikuno

Ostentation *n.* karangyaan, pagmamarangya

Ostentatious *adj.* marangya, mapagparangya

Osteologist *n.* osteologo, dalubbuto

Osteology *n.* osteolohiya

Ostracism *n.* ostrasismo

Ostrich *n.* abestrus, ostrik

Other *adj.* iba

Other *pron.* isa, ikalawa

Otiose *adj.* namamahinga, nagpapahingalay, nagtatamad

Ouch *intr.* aray

Ought *v.* dapat, nararapat

Ounce *n.* onsa

Our *adj.* atin, amin

Our *pron.* atin, amin

Oust *v.* paalisin, palayasin

Ouster *n.* pagpapaalis

Out *adv.* sa labas, patungo sa labas, palayo

Out *n.* sa labas, patungo sa labas, palayo

Out *v.* lumitaw, mabunyag

Outbreak *n.* silakbo, siklab

Outburst *n.* putok, sabog

Outcast *n.* taong itinapon, taong desterado, taong itinakwil

Outcome *n.* kinalabasan, bunga, resultado

Outcry *n.* kaingay, sigawan

Outdistance *v.* lampasan

Outdo *v.* mahigtan, madaig

Outfit *n.* ekipo, kasangkapan

Outgoing *adj.* palabas, paalis, salyente

Outgrow *n.* pagkalakhan

Outgrowth *n.* labas na tubo

Outing *n.* eskursiyon, hira

Outlaw *n.* tulisan

Outlaw *v.* ilabas sa batas

Outlay *n.* gastos, gugol

Outlay *v.* gumasta, gumastos, gumugol

Outlet *n.* salida, labasan, palabasan, eksit

Outline *n.* hugis, tabas, guhit, balangkas

Outlook *n.* bista, tanawin

Outplay *v.* talunin

Outpost *n.* abansada

Output *n.* kabuuang produkto, kabuuang nayayari

Outrage *n.* kahalayan, paghalay

Outrage *v.* manghalay, halayin

Outrageous *adj.* kahalay-halay

Outright *adj.* lahatan

Outset *n.* simula, umpisa

Outside *adj.* panlabas, mula sa labas

Outside *n.* labas

Outsider *n.* tagalabas

Outspoken *adj.* prangko

Outspread *v.* kumaiat, lumaganap

Outstanding *adj.* umungos, tanyag

Outward *adj.* palabas, patungo sa labas

Oval *adj.* obalo, obalado, taluhaba, habilog

Oval *n.* obalo, obalado, taluhaba, bilog-haba

Ovary *n.* obaryo

Ovate *adj.* hugis-itlog

Ovation *n.* pagbubunyi, pagbibigay-puri

Oven *n.* hurno, hurnuhan

Over *adv.* higit, uli, muli, lampas

Overbear *v.* manupil, manaig, mangibabaw

Overboard *adv.* sa dagat, mula sa bapor

Overcoat *n.* gaban, sobretodo, abrigo

Overcome *v.* manaig, pangibabawan, pagtagumpayan

Overdo *v.* magmalabis, lumabis, pagmalabisan

Overdose *n.* labis na dosis

Overdraft *n.* lampas na lagak, lampas na kredito

Overdue *n.* atrasado, bansido

Overflow *v.* umapaw, bumaha

Overgrow *v.* lumamba, lumabay, lumago, pagkalakhan

Overhand *adj.* pabulada, papalo, pababa

Overhang *v.* ibitin, bitinan, magbitin

Overhaul *v.* mag-oberhol, oberholim

Overhead *adv.* sa itaas, sa ibabaw, oberhed, gastospihos

Overhear *v.* maulinigan , inggan

Overlap *v.* magkasanib-sanib, magkasudlung-sudlong

Overlook *v.* di-mapuna, makaligtaan, bantayan

Overnight *adj.* magdamag

Overpower *v.* mapipilan, madaig, magahis

Overseas *adj.* sa kabilang dagat, sa kabilang ibayo

Overseas *adv.* sa kabilang dagat, sa kabilang ibayo

Oversee *v.* pamanihalaan, bantayan

Overseer *n.* katiwala, tagapamanihala

Overshadow *v.* liliman, malililiman

Oversight *n.* ligta, pagkaligta

Overt *adj.* kita, lantad, hayag

Overtake *v.* abutin, abutan, maabutan

Overthrow *v.* talunin

Overture *n.* obertura

Overturn *v.* tumaob, itaob, mapataob

Overweening *adj.* palalo

Overweight *n.* labis na bigat

Overwhelm *v.* madaig, daigin, magapi, gapiin

Ovine *adj.* malatupa, parangtupa

Ovulate *v.* mangitlog

Ovulation *n.* pangingitlog

Ovule *n.* munting itlog

Ovum *n.* itlog

Owe *v.* magkautang

Owl *n.* kuwago, bahaw

Own *adj.* sarili

Own *v.* mananggap, tanggapin, ariin, umamin, aminin

Owner *n.* may-ari, propietaryo

Ownership *n.* pangangari, pagka-may-ari

Ox *n.* toro, baka

Oxygen *n.* oksiheno

Oxygenate *v.* oksihenihan

Oyster *n.* talaba

Ozonation *n.* osonisasyon

Ozone *n.* osono

Ozonic *adj.* osonisado

P p

Pace *n.* hakbang, lakad, bilis
Pace *v.* magmartsa
Pachyderm *n.* pakidermo
Pacific *adj.* tahimik, pasipiko
Pacific ocean *n.* dagat pasipiko
Pacificate *v.* patahimikin, pasipikahin
Pacification *n.* pagpapatahimik
Pacifier *n.* pampatahimik, tagapagpatahimik
Pacifism *n.* pasipista
Pacify *v.* patahimikin, pasipikahin
Pack *n.* kasunduan, pakto
Pack *n.* pakete, balutan, pulutong, kawan
Pack *v.* paketehin, pikpikin, empakihin, balutin, siksikin
Package *n.* pakete, balutan
Packer *n.* empakador
Packet *n.* pakete
Pad *n.* sapin
Padding *n.* pading
Paddle *n.* gaod, sagwan
Paddle *v.* gumaod, sumagwan
Paddler *n.* manggagaod, mananagwan
Paddock *n.* , dehesa
Paddy *n.* palayan
Padlock *n.* kandado
Padlock *v.* kandaduhan, ikandado
Pagan *adj.* pagano
Pagan *n.* pagano
Paganism *n.* paganismo
Page *n.* pahina, pahe
Page *v.* ipatawag nang malakas
Pageant *n.* pedyant
Pageantry *n.* dingal, karingalan
Paginate *v.* pahinahin
Pagoda *n.* pagoda
Pai *n.* pal, katoto
Pail *n.* timba
Pain *n.* parusa, multa, sakit
Painful *adj.* masakit, makirot, mahapdi
Painless *adj.* walang-sakit
Painstaking *adj.* mapagsumakit
Painstaking *n.* pagsusumakit
Paint *n.* pinta, pintura
Paint *v.* magpinta, pintahan, magpintura, pinturahan
Painter *n.* pintor
Painting *n.* pagpipinta, pintura, kuwadro
Pair *n.* pares
Pajama *n.* padyama
Palace *n.* palasyo, mansiyon
Paladin *n.* paladin
Palatable *adj.* masarap
Palate *n.* ngalangala
Pale *adj.* maputla, namumutla
Pale *n.* bakuran, looban

Paleness *n.* kaputlaan

Paleography *n.* paleograpiya

Paleolith *n.* paleolitiko

Paleontologist *n.* paleontologo

Paleontology *n.* paleontolohiya

Palette *n.* paleta

Palindrome *n.* palindromya

Pall *n.* lambong

Pall *v.* kulubungan, lambungan

Pall *v.* magsawa, masuya

Pallet *n.* kamilya, banig

Palliate *v.* paginhawahin

Palliation *n.* pagpapaginhawa

Palliative *adj.* nakagiginhawa

Palluim *n.* palyo

Palm *n.* palad, palma, palaspas

Palmist *n.* manghuhula sa palad

Palmistry *n.* panghuhula sa palad

Palpable *adj.* nahihipo, nadarama

Palpate *v.* pakiramdaman

Palpation *n.* pakikiramdam

Palpitate *v.* tumibok

Palpitation *n.* tibok, pagtibok

Pamper *v.* magpalayaw, palayawin

Pamphlet *n.* polyeto, librito, munting aklat, pamplet

Pan *n.* bandeha

Panacea *n.* panasea

Pancake *n.* pankek

Pancreas *n.* lapay, pankreas

Panda *n.* panda

Pandanus *n.* pandan

Pandemic *adj.* pandemiko

Pander *n.* bugaw

Pander *v.* magsilbing bugaw

Pane *n.* oha, dahon, pohas

Panegyric *n.* panegiriko, papuri

Panel *n.* panig, panel, lupon

Panic *n.* biglang sindak, biglang takot, panik

Panic *v.* masindak matakot, magpanik

Panorama *n.* panorama

Pant *n.* hingal, tibok

Pant *v.* humingal, magiliw, masabik, tumibok

Pantheism *n.* panteismo

Pantheon *n.* panteon, pantiyon

Panther *n.* pantera

Pantograph *n.* pantograpo

Pantomine *n.* pantomina

Panty *n.* panti, panty

Papa *n.* papa, tatay, tatang

Papacy *n.* papado

Papal *adj.* papal, pontipikal

Paper *n.* papel, papeles, kasulatan, pahayagan

Papilla *n.* papila

Paprika *n.* paminton

Papule *n.* tagihawat

Par *n.* par, paridad, nimel, par

Parable *n.* parabula

Parabola *n.* parabola

Parachute *n.* parakayda, parasyut

Paraclete *n.* paraklito

Parada *v.* magparada

Parade *n.* parada

Paradigm *n.* paradigma, huwaran

Paradise *n.* paraiso

Paradox *n.* paradoha, balintunay

Paraffin *n.* parapina

Paragon *n.* uliran, modelo, huwaran

Paragraph *n.* talataan, parapo

Parakeet *n.* parakit, lorong munti

Paralelogram *n.* paralelogramo

Paralitic *adj.* paralitiko

Paralize *v.* paralisahin, alisan ng bisa

Parallax *n.* paralahe

Parallel *adj.* paralelo, kaagapay

Paralysis *n.* paralisis

Paramecium *n.* paramisyum

Parameter *n.* parametro

Paramnesia *n.* paramnesya

Paramount *adj.* pinakamataas, puno

Paramour *n.* kaapid

Paranoia *n.* paranoya

Parapet *n.* kuta

Parasite *n.* parasito

Parasitic *adj.* parasito

Parasitologist *n.* parasitologo

Parasitology *n.* parasitolohiya

Parasol *n.* parasol, payong

Parcel *n.* pakete, kalipunan, bahagi

Parcel *v.* baha-bahaginin, ipamahagi

Parch *v.* isalab, salabin, tuyuing, tuyung-tuyo

Parchment *n.* pergamino

Pardon *n.* patawad, pagpapatawad, paumanhin, pagpapaumanhin

Pardon *v.* magpatawad, patawarin, magpaumanhin, pagpaumanhinan

Pardonable *adj.* mapatatawad

Parent *n.* magulang, ama'tina

Parentage *n.* parentela, angkan

Parenthesis *n.* parentesis, panaklong

Parenthood *n.* pagkamagulang

Parish *n.* parokya

Parity *n.* paridad, pagkamagkapantay

Park *n.* parke, liwasan

Park *v.* pumarada, iparada

Parkway *n.* lansangang-parke

Parlance *n.* pananalita, paguusap, salitaan

Parley *n.* komperensiya

Parliament *n.* parlamento, batasan

Parliamentarian *adj.* parlamentaryo

Parliamentarian *n.* parlamentaryo

Parliamentary *adj.* parlataryo

Parlor *n.* salon, salas

Parnassus *n.* parnaso

Parody *n.* parodya, karikatura

Parole *n.* pangako

Parotid *n.* parotida

Parotitis *n.* baiki

Paroxysm *n.* paroksismo, atake, pagsasal

Parrot *n.* loro

Parry *v.* umilag, ilagan, manalag, salagin

Parse *v.* magparsing, parsingin

Parsing *n.* pagpaparsing

Parsley *n.* parsley, perehil

Parson *n.* pari

Part *n.* bahagi, papel, sangkap, praksiyon, hati

Part *v.* bahaginin, hatiin, umalis, lumisan

Partake *v.* lumahok, makilahok, makibahagi, bumahagi

Partial *adj.* mahilig, bahagi, parsiyal

Partiality *n.* parsiyalidad

Participant *n.* kalahok, kasali

Participate *v.* makibahagi, lumahok, sumali

Participation *n.* pakikiba-hagi, paglahok, pakikilahok

Participator *n.* kalahok

Particle *n.* katiting, butil, kataga, tapik

Particular *adj.* bukad, magatod, hiwalay, namumukod, tangi, sadya

Particular *n.* detalye, kabatiran

Partner *n.* kasama, kasosyo, kapareha, kakopon

Partnership *n.* bakasan, samahan

Partridge *n.* pugo

Parturient *adj.* buntis

Party *n.* partido, pagtitipon, lapian, panig, pulutong, party

Pasch *n.* pasko

Pascha *n.* baha

Pass *n.* landas, pagpasa, hagpos, daanan, hagod, himas pases, paglipat

Pass *v.* dumaan, tumawid, magdaan, tawirin, makaraan, makalipas,makalampas

Passage *n.* daan, daanan, pasahe

Passbook *n.* libreta

Passenger *n.* pasahero, sakay, luhan

Passerby *n.* mga dumaraan

Passion *n.* pagdurusa, pagtitiis, damdamin

Passionate *adj.* masimbuyo sa damdamin

Passive *adj.* pasiba, balintiyak, tahimik, walang-biko, mapagtiis, matiyaga

Passport *n.* pasaporte, tulotlakbay

Passtime *n.* libangan

Password *n.* kontra-senyas

Past *adj.* kararaan, nagdaan, dati, kalilipas

Paste *n.* pasta, pandigkit, koia

Paste *v.* magdigkit, idigkit, digkitan

Pasteboard *n.* karton

Pastel *n.* pastel

Pasteurize *v.* pasteurisahin

Pastile *n.* pastilyas, tabletas

Pastime *n.* paglilibang, libangan

Pastor *n.* pastor, pastol

Pastoral *adj.* pastoral

Pastoral *n.* pastoral

Pastorale *n.* kantata

Pastry *n.* pastel

Pasture *n.* pastulan

Pasture *v.* manginain, magpastol, pastulan

Pat *n.* tapik, tampi, tapikin

Patch *n.* tagpi, tutop

Patch *v.* magtagpi, tagpian

Patchy *adj.* tagpi-tagpi

Paten *n.* patena

Patent *adj.* malinaw, hayag, patentado

Patent *n.* patente, titulo, karapatan

Pater *n.* ama

Paternal *adj.* ng ama

Paternity *n.* pagka-ama

Path *n.* landas, daan

Pathetic *adj.* nakakaawa, nakalulungkot, nakapupukaw

Pathfinder *n.* manggagalugad

Pathologist *n.* patologo

Pathology *n.* patolohiya

Pathos *n.* pamukaw-awa, pamukaw-habag

Patience *n.* tiyaga, pagtitiyaga, katiyagaan

Patient *adj.* pasyente, matiyaga, mapagtiis

Patient *n.* pasyente, maysakit

Patio *n.* patyo

Patois *n.* diyalekto

Patriarch *n.* patriarka

Patriarchal *adj.* patriarkal

Patriarchy *n.* patriarkado

Patrician *n.* patrisyo, mahal, aristokrata

Patricide *n.* pariside, parisidyo

Patrimony *n.* patrimonyo, mana

Patriot *n.* patriota, makabayan

Patriotic *adj.* patriotiko, makabayan

Patriotism *n.* patriotismo

Patristic *adj.* patristiko

Patrol *n.* patrulya, ronda, taliba, guwardiya

Patrol *v.* pumatrulya, rumonda, tumaliba, gumuwardiya

Patroller *n.* tagapatrulya, tagaronda

Patrolling *n.* pagpapatrulya, pagroronda

Patrolman *n.* pulisyang patrulya, pulisyang rondador, patrolman

Patron *n.* patron, tagataguyod, tapagpagtanggol, suki

Patronage *n.* patrosinyo, pagtangkilik, patronato

Patroness *n.* patrona

Patronize *v.* tangkilikin

Patten *n.* bakya, suwekos

Patter *n.* taguktok, tunog ng patak

Pattern *n.* patern, tularan, disenyo, huwaran

Pattern *v.* itulad, tularan

Paucity *n.* pagka-kakaunti, kakulangan

Paunch *n.* buyon

Pauper *adj.* dahop, hikahos, salat

Pauper *n.* abukanin, pulubi

Pause *n.* tigil , pahinga, ulik-ulik

Pause *v.* sandaling tumigil, sandaling huminto, magpahinga

Pave *v.* latagan ng bato, latagan ng semento

Pavement *n.* pabimento, bangketa

Pavilion *n.* pabelyon

Paw *n.* paang may pangalmot, paa ng hayop

Pawn *n.* piyon, sangla, prenda

Pawnage *n.* pagsasangla

Pay *n.* suweldo, bayad, upa

Pay *v.* magbayad, gumanti, bayaran, gantihan, umupa, upahan

Payable *adj.* pagadero, mababayaran

Payee *n.* ang pagbabayaran, ang pinagbabayaran

Paymaster *n.* pagador, tagabayad

Payment *n.* bayad, kabayaran

Pea *n.* gisantes

Peace *n.* kapayapaan

Peaceful *adj.* payapa, tahimik

Peacemaker *n.* pasipikador, tagapamayapa

Peach *n.* melokoton

Peacock *n.* paboreal

Peak *n.* tugatog, taluktok, ituktok, karurukan

Peanut *n.* mani

Pear *n.* peras

Pearl *n.* perlas, mutya

Peasant *n.* taong-bukid, magbubukid, magsasaka

Pebble *n.* munting bato, graba

Peck *v.* tumuka, tukain, manuka

Pectoral *adj.* pektoral, pandibdib

Peculiar *adj.* pekulyar, pambihira, kakatwa, kakaiba

Peculiarity *n.* pekulyaridad

Pedagogue *n.* pedagogo, guro

Pedal *adj.* pedal

Pedal *n.* pedal

Pedant *adj.* pedante

Pedantic *adj.* pedantesko

Pedantism *n.* pedantismo

Peddle *v.* maglako, ilako, paglakuan

Peddler *n.* maglalako, tagapaglako

Pedestal *n.* pedestal

Pedestrian *n.* taong naglalakad

Pediatrics *n.* pedyatriya

Pedigree *n.* linahe, angkan

Peek *n.* sumilip, silipin

Peek *n.* silip, sulyap, siglaw

Peel *v.* magtalop, talupan, mabakbak

Peeler *n.* pantalop

Peelings *n.* pinagtalupan

Peep *n.* siyap, huni, silip

Peep *v.* sumiyap, humuni, sumilip

Peeper *n.* maninilip

Peer *n.* kapantay, kauri, taong mahal

Peer *v.* masdan

Peeress *n.* sinyora

Peerless *adj.* walang kapantay

Peeve *v.* galitin, yamutin

Peevish *adj.* magagalitin, mayamutin

Peg *n.* kalabiha, pasak, sabitan, pangkuhit

Peg *v.* lagyan ng kalabiha

Pejoration *n.* paninira, panghahamak

Pelf *n.* yamang, ninakaw

Pelican *n.* pelikano

Pellagra *n.* pelagra

Pellet *n.* pildoras, perdigones, bolitas

Pellucid *adj.* malinaw, nasisinag

Pelt *n.* balat, kuwero

Pelvis *n.* balakang, buto ng baywang

Pen *n.* pluma, panulat, panitik

Penal *adj.* penal

Penalize *v.* multahan

Penalty *n.* parusa, kastigo, multa

Penance *n.* penitensiya, pagsisisi

Penchant *n.* hilig, pagkagusto

Pencil *n.* lapis

Pendant *n.* hikaw, palamuti

Pending *adj.* nakabitin, nakalawit

Pending *prep.* samantala, habang, hanggang

Pendulum *n.* pendulo

Penetrant *adj.* tumatagos, matalas

Penetrate *v.* pumasok, lumusot, mapasok, tumusok, maglagos, tumimo, lagusan

Penetrating *adj.* matalas, matalim, matulis

Penetration *n.* katalasan, pagtagos, pagpasok

Penguin *n.* pengguwin

Penicillin *n.* penisilin

Peninsula *n.* peninsula, tangway

Penitence *n.* pagsisisi, penitensiya

Penitent *adj.* nagsisisi

Pennant *n.* penant, banderola

Penniless *adj.* walang-kuwarta, dahop

Penny *n.* pera, sentimos

Penology *n.* penolohiya

Penon *n.* bandera, bandila, watawat, pendon

Pension *n.* pensiyon

Pensioner *n.* pensionado

Pent *adj.* nakakulong

Pentagon *n.* limang panig, pentagon

Penthouse *n.* sibi, aneks

Penult *n.* una na huli, penultima

Penumbra *n.* penumbra

Penurious *adj.* maramot, yayat, tigang

Peon *n.* piyon, manggagawa

People *n.* mga tao, taong bayan, mamamayan

Pep *n.* brio, sigla

Pepper *n.* sili

Peppermint *n.* menta, yerbabwena

Peppy *adj.* mabrio, masigla

Per *prep.* sa pamamagitan', bawa't

Perambulate *v.* maglakad-lakad

Perceive *v.* madama, mapansin, matanto, mahulo

Percent *n.* bahagdan, pursiyento

Percentage *n.* pursiyento, persentahe, bahagdan, kumisyon

Percentile *adj.* persentil, pamahagdan

Percentile *n.* persentil, pamahagdan

Perceptible *adj.* nadarama, napapansin

Perception *n.* pagkadama, pagdama

Perceptive *adj.* matalas, dumama

Perceptual *adj.* ukol sa pandama

Perch *n.* hapunan, dapuan, katangan

Perch *v.* humapon, dumapo, ipatong

Percolate *v.* salain, patagasin, patigmakin

Percolation *n.* pagsasala, pagtatagas

Percolator *n.* perkolador

Percuss *n.* tapikin

Percussion *n.* perkusyon, tapik

Peregrinate *v.* magperegrino, maglakbay, maglagalag

Peregrination *n.* peregrina-syon, paglalakbay

Peregrinator *n.* peregrino, manlalakbay

Perennial *adj.* pansantaon, walang tigil, pangmatagalan

Peretuate *v.* papamalagiin, papanatilihin

Perfect *n.* ganap, lantay, buo, kumpleto, eksakto

Perfect *v.* dalisayin

Perfection *n.* perpeksiyon, kahigpitan

Perfidious *adj.* lilo

Perfidy *n.* paglililo, kaliluhan

Perforate *v.* pagbutas-butasin

Perforation *n.* perporasyon

Perforator *n.* perporador, pambutas

Perform *v.* gumawa, matapos, gawin, tapusin, gumanap, ganapin

Performance *n.* pagganap

Performer *n.* tagaganap

Perfume *n.* pabango, perpume

Perfume *v.* pabanguhan, lagyan ng pabango

Perfumery *n.* perpumeriya

Perhaps *adj.* marahil, kaypala

Periapt *n.* amuleto

Pericardium *n.* perikardiyo

Peril *n.* panganib, kapanganiban

Perilous *adj.* mapanganib

Perimeter *n.* perimetro, paligid

Perineum *n.* perineo

Period *n.* punto, tuldok, panahon, hangganan

Periodic *adj.* paulit-ulit, pabalik-balik

Periodical *n.* peryodiko, pahayagan

Periphery *n.* ibabaw, superpisye , sirkumperensiya

Periphrasis *n.* pagpapaliguyligoy

Periscope *n.* periskopyo

Perish *v.* mapuksa, magiba, mamatay, pumanaw, maparam

Perishable *adj.* madaling masira

Peritonium *n.* peritoneo

Perjure *v.* magsinungaling

Perjury *n.* perhuryo

Perk *v.* magtuwid ng katawan, tumayo, lumindig, maglumindig

Permanence *n.* kapanatili-han, permanensiya, pagkapalagian

Permanent *adj.* panatilihan, permanente, palagian

Permanganate *n.* perman-gganato

Permeate *v.* sumulop, pumawis, tumalab, tumulus, talaban, mangalat, tumagas

Permissible *adj.* maipahihin-tulot

Permission *n.* pahintulot, permiso

Permit *n.* pahintulot, permiso

Permit *v.* pahintulutan

Permutation *n.* permutasyon

Permute *v.* baguhin

Peroxide *n.* peroksido

Perpendicular *adj.* patayo, perpendikular

Perpetrate *v.* gumawa ng kasalanan, gumawa ng masama

Perpetual *adj.* perpetwo, habang panahon

Perpetuation *n.* pagpapamalagi, pagpapanatili

Perquisite *n.* dagdag ng kita

Persecute *v.* usigin, pag-usigin, ipahamak, saktan

Persecution *n.* pag-uusig

Persecutor *n.* mang-uusig

Perseverance *n.* tiyaga, pagtitiyaga, kasigasigan

Persevere *v.* magtiyaga, magpumilit, magsigasig

Persian *n.* persa

Persist *v.* magpumilit, pagpumilitan, magtiyaga, pagtiyagaan

Persistence *n.* pagpupumilit, pagmamatigas

Persistent *adj.* mapagpumilit

Person *n.* tao, sinuman, pagkatao, katauhan

Personality *n.* katauhan, personalidad, pagkatao

Personification *v.* pagtatao

Personnel *n.* personel, tauhan

Perspective *n.* perspektiba, tunay na larawan, padamang layo

Perspiration *n.* pawis

Perspire *v.* pawisan, pagpawisan

Persuade *v.* papaniwalain, hikayatin, himukin

Persuasive *adj.* mapanghi-kayat, mapanghimok

Persussion *n.* hikayat, himok

Pertain *v.* maukol, mahinggil

Pertinent *n.* nauukol, nahihinggil, kaugnay

Perturb *v.* gambalam, magambala, magulumihanan

Perusal *n.* maingat na pagbabasa

Peruse *v.* magbasa, basahin

Peruser *n.* mambabasa

Pervade *v.* laganapan, malaganapan, mangalat, mangalatkat

Perverse *adj.* sinsay, lisya, mail, balakyot

Pervert *v.* isinsay, ilisya, iligaw

Perverted *adj.* sinsay, lisya, pilipit

Peso *n.* piso

Pessary *n.* pesaryo

Pessimism *n.* pesimismo, hilig sa pagmamasama

Pessimist *n.* pesimista

Pessimistic *adj.*. pesimista, mahilig-magmasama

Pest *n.* peste, epidemya, salot

Pester *v.* mangyamot, yamutin, buwisitin

Pestle *n.* halo, pambayo

Pet *adj.* paborito

Pet *n.* alagang hayop, mahal, irog

Pet *v.* hagpusin, himasin

Petal *n.* talulot, petalo

Petiole *n.* palapa, balaba

Petition *n.* petisyon, hiling, kahilingan

Petition *v.* magpetisyon, humiling, hilingin

Petrifaction *n.* petripak-siyon, pagiging bato

Petroleum *n.* pitrolyo, gas

Petticoat *n.* nagwas, petikot
Petulant *adj.* sumpungin, madaingin
Phantasm *n.* pantasma
Phantasmagoria *n.* pantasmagoriya
Phantasy *n.* pantasiya
Phantom *n.* manlalabas
Pharaoh *n.* paraon
Pharisee *n.* pariseo
Pharmaceutical *adj.* parmaseutiko
Pharmacist *n.* parmaseutiko
Pharmacology *n.* parmakolohiya
Pharmacy *n.* parmasya, butika
Pharmocologist *n.* parmakologo
Pharyngology *n.* paringgolohiya
Pharynx *n.* paringhe, lalaugan
Phase *n.* pase, aspekto, anyo, panig
Phenomenal *adj.* penomenal
Phenomenon *n.* penomena
Philander *v.* manlimbang, limbangin
Philanteopist *n.* pilantropo
Philantrophy *n.* pilantropiya
Philatelic *adj.* pilatelika
Philately *n.* pilateliya
Philharmonic *adj.* pilarmoniko
Philippics *n.* tuligsa, pilipiko
Philological *adj.* pilolohiko
Philologist *n.* pilologo
Philology *n.* pilolohiya
Philosopher *n.* pilosopo
Philosophical *adj.* pilosopiko
Philosopy *n.* pilosopiya
Philter *n.* gayuma
Phlegm *n.* plema, kalaghala
Phlegmatic *adj.* maplema, walang sigla
Phobia *n.* pobya, takot, sindak
Phone *n.* telepono
Phonetic *adj.* ponetiko
Phonetician *n.* ponetista
Phonetics *n.* ponetika, palatinigan
Phonogram *n.* ponograma, plaka ng ponograpo
Phonologist *n.* ponologo
Phosphorescent *adj.* posporesente, nanginginang
Phosphoric *adj.* posporiko
Phosphorous *n.* posporo
Photogenic *adj.* potoheniko, maganda sa retrato
Photograph *n.* retrato
Photographer *n.* potograpo
Photography *n.* potograpiya
Photostat *n.* potostat
Photosynthesis *n.* potosintesis
Phototherapy *n.* pototerapya
Phrase *n.* prase, parirala
Phraseology *n.* praseolohiya, pamamarirala

Phylon *n.* tribu, lipi, lahi

Phylum *n.* pilum, kalapian, kalahian

Physic *n.* lunas

Physical *adj.* pisikal, materyal, pangkatawan

Physician *n.* manggagamot

Physicist *n.* pisika

Physics *n.* pisika

Physiognomy *n.* pisonomiya, mukha, pagmumukha

Physique *n.* pangangatawan, tikas, bikas

Pianist *n.* pianista

Piano *adj.* suwabe

Piano *n.* piyano

Piazza *n.* piasa

Piccolo *n.* plawtin

Pick *n.* piko, patik

Pick *v.* pikuhin, pumitas, magpiko, piliin, magpatik, patikin

Pick-up *n.* pagbuti, paggaling, pagtulin

Picket *n.* istaka, piket, urang, tulos

Pickle *n.* salmuwera, atsara, kagipitan

Picnic *n.* picnic, kura

Pictograph *n.* piktograpiya

Pictorial *adj.* maylarawan, malarawan

Picture *n.* larawan, retrato

Picture *v.* ilarawan

Picturesque *adj.* pintoresko

Pie *n.* pastel, pay, gulo, sabog

Piece *n.* piraso, piyesa, kaputol, bahagi, rolyo

Pier *n.* piyer, patungan, pantalan, lunsaran

Pierce *v.* duruin, tuhugin, saksakin, lumusot

Piety *n.* debosyon, piyedad, awa, habag, kabanalan

Pig *n.* baboy

Pigboat *n.* submarino

Pigeon *n.* palomar, kalapatihan

Piggery *n.* babuyan

Pigment *n.* pigmento, kulay, kolor

Pigmy *n.* pigmeo, enano

Pigskin *n.* balat ng baboy, putbol

Pike *n.* tulos, sibat

Pile *n.* bunton, pila

Pile *v.* magbunton, ibunton, buntunan

Piles *n.* almuranas

Pilfer *v.* mang-umit, umitin, magnakaw, nakawin

Pilgrim *n.* peregrino

Pilgrimage *adj.* perigrina-syon, paglalakbay

Pill *n.* pilduras

Pillage *n.* pandarambong, sakeo

Pillage *v.* mandambong, dambungin

Pillar *n.* pilar, kolumna, haligi

Pillow *n.* unan, sapin, almuwadon

Pillowcase *n.* punda

Pilot *n.* piloto, tagaugit, giya, patnubay, abyador

Pilot *v.* magpiloto, pilotohan, magugitan, patnubayan

Pimp *n.* bugaw

Pimple *n.* tagihawat

Pin *n.* klabiha, tarugo, trangka, aspile

Pin *v.* aspilihan

Pinch *n.* kurot

Pinch *v.* pumisil, kumurot, kurutin

Pine *n.* pino

Pine *v.* tumamlay, mangayayat, hanap-hanapin, kasabikan

Pineapple *n.* pinya

Ping-pong *n.* ping-pong

Pinhole *n.* butas na munsing

Pinion *n.* bagwis, pakpak

Pinion *v.* putulan ng bagwis, balitiin, posasan

Pink *n.* klabel, rosas

Pinnacle *n.* taluktok, ituktok

Pinpoint *n.* tilos ng aspile

Pinpoint *v.* tiyakin

Pint *n.* pinta

Pioneer *n.* ang una

Pioneer *v.* manguna

Pious *adj.* leal, matapat, banal, relihiyoso

Pipe *n.* pito, kuwako, plawta, tubo, pipa

Pipeline *n.* tuberiyas

Piper *n.* plawtista

Pipette *n.* pipeta, pampatak

Pipit *n.* pipit

Piquancy *n.* anghang, kaanghangan

Pique *n.* galit, yamot

Pique *v.* manggalit, galitin

Piracy *n.* panunulisan sa dagat, pirateriya

Pirate *n.* tulisang-dagat, pirata

Piscary *n.* pangisdaan, palaisdaan

Pisces *n.* pisces, mga isda

Pisciculture *n.* pisikultura

Pistil *n.* pistilo, ubod

Pistol *n.* pistola, rebolber, automatiko

Piston *n.* piston

Pit *n.* hukay, balon, bangin, patibong

Pitch *n.* itsa, hagis, taluktok, ituktok

Pitch *v.* iitsa, ihagis, ilagay sa tono

Pitcher *n.* pitser

Pitchfork *n.* orkilya

Pitchy *adj.* malaalkitran, malaaspalto

Pith *n.* ubod

Pity *n.* awa, habag

Pity *v.* maawa, mahabag, kaawaan, kahabagan

Pivot *n.* pibote, ikutan

Placable *adj.* mapapapayapa, mapatatahimik

Placard *n.* kartelon, paskil

Placate *v.* payapain, patahimikin

Placatory *adj.* pampapayapa, pampatahimik

Place *n.* pook, lalagyan, lugar, puwesto, puwang, tayo

Place *v.* iayos, ilagay, ilapag

Placement *n.* bigay-empleo, pagbibigay-empleo

Placenta *n.* plasenta, inunan

Placid *adj.* walang tigatig, payapa, tahimik, mahinahon

Placket *n.* plaket

Plagiarist *v.* plahiyaryo, mamamlahiyo

Plague *n.* plaga, peste, salot

Plague *v.* magkapeste, magkasalot, salutin

Plain *adj.* yano, simple, maliwanag, liso, malinaw, pantay, patag

Plain *n.* lupang patag, kapatagan

Plaint *n.* daing, hibik

Plaintiff *n.* ang maysakdal

Plaintive *adj.* madaing, mahibik

Plait *n.* pleges, pileges, tupi, pliting, lupi

Plan *n.* plano, balak

Plan *v.* magplano, planuhin, magbalak, balakin

Plane *adj.* patag, pantay

Plane *n.* eruplano, katam

Planet *n.* planeta

Planetarium *n.* planetaryum

Plankton *n.* plankton, palutang

Plant *n.* halaman, tanim, pananim

Plant *v.* magtanim, itanim, magtatag, ikintal, itatag, iukit

Plantation *n.* taniman, pataniman, asyenda

Planter *adj.* pansakong, hinggil sa sakong, pantalampakan

Planter *n.* magtatanim

Plaque *n.* plak

Plash *n.* lamaw, sanaw, tubog

Plasma *n.* plasma

Plaster *n.* emplasto, pantapal, plaster

Plastic *adj.* plastik, plastiko

Plasticity *n.* plasticidad

Plate *n.* elektrodo, plato, plantsa, ohas, anodo

Platen *n.* platina, rodilyo

Platform *n.* plataporma, andamyo, entablado, tuntungan

Platonic *adj.* platoniko

Platoon *n.* pulutong

Platter *n.* bandeha, bandehado

Play *n.* galaw, dula, laro, biro, likot, huwego, drama

Play *v.* maglaro, paglaruan, kalantariin, tumugtog, magsugal

Player *n.* manlalaro

Playful *adj.* malaro, malikot

Playhouse *n.* dulaan, bahaybahayan

Playmate *n.* kalaro

Plaything *n.* laruan

Playwright *n.* mandudula

Plaza *n.* plasa, liwasan

Plea *n.* dahilan, panawagan, luhog, pakiusap

Pleasant *adj.* nakalulugod

Pleat *n.* tupi, lupi, tiklop

Plebe *n.* plebeyo

Plebiscite *n.* plebisito

Plectrum *n.* plektro, pua

Pledge *n.* prenda, sangla, pangako

Pledge *v.* iprenda, isangla, mangako, pangakuan, ipangako

Plenary *adj.* buo, plenaryo

Plenty *adj.* masagana

Plenty *n.* kasaganaan

Pleonasm *n.* ligoy, kaliguyan

Plethora *n.* pagkakatusak, pletora

Plexus *n.* plekso

Plight *n.* katayuan, kalagayan, kagipitan, pakikipagkasundo

Plink *v.* kumalantog

Plod *v.* gumayod

Plot *n.* balangkas, lote, intriga, sabwatan

Plot *v.* mag-intriga, magsabwatan, magplano, magpakana

Plough *n.* araro

Plough *v.* mag-araro

Pluck *n.* tapang, tigas ng loob, bunot, labnot

Pluck *v.* bunutin, kalbitin, labnutin, maghimulmol, himulmulan

Plug *n.* pasak, siksik

Plum *n.* sirwelas

Plumage *n.* plumahe

Plumate *n.* antena, sungot

Plumb *n.* plumada

Plumber *n.* plomero

Plumbing *n.* plomeriya

Plume *n.* plumahe

Plump *adj.* bilugan, mataba

Plunder *n.* pandarambong

Plunder *v.* mandambong

Plunge *v.* sumugba, lumubog, sumisid

Plural *adj.* pangmarami, plural

Plural *n.* maramihan, plural

Plus *prep.* dagagan ng, at saka

Plush *n.* pelpa

Pluvious *adj.* maulan

Ply *n.* pleges, play, kapal

Pneumatic *adj.* neumatiko, hinggil sa hangin, panghangin

Pneumatics *n.* neumatika

Pneumonia *n.* neumonya, pulmonya

Pocket *n.* bulsa

Pocket *v.* ibulsa

Pocupine *n.* porkoespin
Poem *n.* tula
Poet *n.* poeta, makata
Poignancy *n.* hapdi, kirot
Poignant *adj.* mahapdi
Point *n.* tulis, dulo, puntos, tuldok
Pointer *n.* puntero, patnubay
Poise *n.* ekilibrio, timbang, tikas, tindig
Poison *n.* lason, kamandag
Poison *v.* manlason, lasunin
Poisonous *adj.* nakakalason
Poke *v.* manundot, sundutin
Poker *n.* poker
Poland *n.* polonya
Polar *adj.* polar
Polarization *n.* polarisasyon
Polarize *v.* polarisahin
Pole *n.* polo, tikin, polako
Police *n.* pulisya
Police *v.* bantayan
Policeman *n.* pulis
Policy *n.* palakad, pamamaraan, patakaran, polisa
Poligamist *n.* poligamo
Poligamous *adj.* poligamo
Polish *adj.* polako, plones
Polish *n.* pagbuli, kultura, pakintab, kintab, kinang, kapinuhan
Polish *v.* magbuli, bulihin, pakintabin
Polite *adj.* pino, pulido, magalang
Politic *adj.* pampamahalaan, pampolitika, matalisik, mapamaraan
Political *adj.* pampolitika
Politician *n.* politiko
Politicize *v.* mamulitika, pamulitikahan
Politics *n.* politika
Polka *n.* polka
Poll *n.* pagboto, paghahalal
Pollen *n.* polen
Pollex *n.* hinalaki
Pollinate *v.* magpolen, magbulo, mamluo
Pollination *n.* pagpopolen, pagbubulo, pamumulo
Pollute *v.* parumihin, dumhan, hawahan, lalinan
Polluted *adj.* marumi, nahawahan, nalalinan
Pollution *n.* karumhan, kasalaulaan
Pollux *n.* poluk
Polo *n.* polo
Polyandrous *adj.* poliandro, poliandriko
Polyandry *n.* poliandria
Polychromatic *adj.* makulay
Polyclinic *n.* polikilinika
Polytechnic *adj.* politekniko
Polytechnik *n.* politeknika
Pomade *n.* pomada
Pomegranate *n.* granada

Pommel *n.* pomo, kulata

Pomp *n.* dingal, karingalan, rangya, karangyaan

Pompous *adj.* maringal, marangya

Poncho *n.* pontso, kapote

Pond *n.* lanaw

Ponder *v.* magnuynoy, nuynuyin

Pontoon *n.* ponton

Pony *n.* kabayong munti

Pooch *n.* aso

Poodle *n.* asong delanas

Pool *n.* samahan, bakasan, monopolyo, lawa, sanaw, bilyar

Poor *adj.* mahirap, dukha

Pop *n.* pusngat, putok

Pop *v.* pumusngat, pumutok

Popcorn *n.* binusang mais

Pope *n.* papa

Popgun *n.* pamusngat, barilbarilan

Poplin *n.* paplin

Popular *adj.* popular, balita, bantog

Popularity *n.* pagka-popular

Popularize *v.* popularisahin

Populate *v.* tauhan

Population *n.* kabuuan ng mga mananahanan

Populous *adj.* matao

Porcelain *n.* porselana, losa

Porch *n.* portiko, beranda

Pork *n.* karning baboy

Porker *n.* alagang baboy

Pornography *n.* pornograpiya

Porosity *n.* porosidad

Porous *adj.* poroso

Porridge *n.* lugaw, nilugaw

Port *n.* puwerto, daungan, portal, bintanilya

Portable *adj.* bitbitin, dalahin

Portage *n.* portahe, pagkakarga

Portend *v.* magbabala, magbadha, magbala

Portent *n.* babala

Portfolio *n.* portpolyo

Portion *n.* porsiyon, bahagi, bulos, kapalaran

Portrait *n.* retrato, larawan

Portray *n.* maglarawan, ilarawan

Portrayal *n.* paglalarawan

Portuguese *n.* portuges

Pose *n.* pusisyon, anyo, tayo

Pose *v.* pumusisyon, pumuwesto, mag-anyo

Position *n.* puwesto, lugar, paglalagay, katayuan tungkulin, katungkulan

Position *v.* ilagay sa lugar

Positive *adj.* positibo, pasulong, tiyak, paayon, tunay

Possess *v.* magtaglay, mangibabaw, magari, magtamo, magkaroon

Possession *n.* pag-aari, pagmamay-ari, ar-arian

Possessive *adj.* mapang-angkin, mapangabig

Possessor *n.* may-ari

Possibility *n.* posibilidad

Possible *adj.* maaari, maaaring mangyari

Possibly *adv.* marahil, kaypala

Post *n.* poste, puwesto, koreo, haligi, tukod, distino

Post-mortem *adj.* posmortem

Postdate *n.* atrasuhan ng petsa

Poster *n.* poster, kartelon, paskil

Posterior *adj.* posteryor, huli, hulihan, likod, likuran

Posterity *n.* posteridad

Postern *adj.* sa likod, sa likuran

Postgraduate *adj.* postgradwet, lampastapos

Posthumous *adj.* postumo

Postman *n.* kartero

Postmark *n.* tatak ng koreo

Postmaster *n.* postmaster

Postpone *v.* ipagpaliban

Postponement *n.* pagpapaliban

Postposition *n.* paghuhuli

Postscript *n.* habol, dagdagsulat

Posture *n.* tayo, tindig, tikas

Pot *n.* palayok, anglit, agio

Potable *adj.* maiinom

Potassium *n.* potasa

Potato *n.* patatas

Potency *n.* bisa, lakas

Potent *adj.* mabisa

Potentate *n.* potentado, hari, monarka

Potential *adj.* potensiyal, posible

Potentiality *n.* potensiyalidad

Pother *n.* alboroto, kuskusbalungos, kagulo

Potion *n.* sanglagok, posiyon

Potpourri *n.* potpourri, halu-halo, samutsari

Potter *n.* manggagawa ng palayok

Pouch *n.* supot

Poultry *n.* manukan

Pounce *v.* manila, silain, sumagpang, managpang, dakluttin sagpangin, sumila

Pound *n.* kulungan, piitan

Pound *n.* libra

Pound *v.* ikulong, ipiit

Pound *v.* bugugin, magbayo, bayuhin

Pour *n.* buhos, pagbuhos, pagbubuhos, salinan, magsalin, isalin

Pour *v.* bumuhos, magbuhos, ibuhos, buhusan

Pout *v.* lumabi, magmungot

Poverty *n.* karukhaan, karalitaan

Powder *n.* pulbos

Powder *v.* pulbusin, pulbusan

Power *n.* kontrol, poder, kasaklawan, kapangyarihan, lakas, kakayahin

Powerful *adj.* makapangyarihan

Practicable *adj.* magaganap , magagamit

Practical *adj.* praktiko, maykagamitan

Practice *v.* sanayin, isagawa, magpraktis, magsanay, magpraktika

Pragmatic *adj.* pragmatiko

Praise *n.* puri, papuri

Praise *v.* pumuri, purihin

Praiseworthy *adj.* kapuripuri

Prate *v.* sumatsat, dumaldal

Pratice *n.* praktika, ugali, gawi, ehersisyo, pagsasanay

Prawn *n.* ulang

Pray *v.* sumamo, magsumamo, pagsamuan, lumuhog

Prayer *n.* dasal, dalangin, panalangin

Preach *v.* mangaral, magsermon

Preamble *n.* preambulo, pambungad, panimula

Precaution *n.* ingat, pagiingat, alaga

Precede *v.* umuna, manguna, unahan, mauna

Precedence *n.* pagkauna

Precedent *n.* una, nauna

Precept *v.* utos, turo, tuntunin

Preceptive *adj.* nagtuturo

Preceptor *n.* guro

Precinct *n.* presinto, pook, distrito

Precious *adj.* mamahalin-mahal, mahalaga

Precipice *n.* talampas

Precipitant *adj.* bigla, sumusugba, humahagibis

Precipitate *n.* dalas-dalas, pabigla-bigla

Precipitation *n.* pagpapa-bilis, pagpapatulin, pagpapatining

Precis *n.* buod

Precise *adj.* presisyo, tiyak, eksakto

Precision *n.* presisyon

Preconceive *v.* umagap-isip

Preconception *n.* agap-isip

Predecessor *n.* predesesor , ninuno

Predestination *n.* predes-tinasyon , katalagahin

Predestine *v.* italaga

Predicable *adj.* maisaysay, mapanagurian

Predicable *n.* panaguriin, kaurian, kaibhan

Predicament *n.* suliranin, dilema

Predicate *adj.* panaguri

Predicate *v.* ipanaguri

Predication *n.* pananaguri

Predict *v.* manghula, hulaan

Predictable *adj.* mahuhulaan

Prediction *n.* hula, panghuhula

Predictor *n.* manghuhula

Predominant *adj.* mapanaig

Predominate *v.* manaig

Preface *n.* prepasyo

Prefect *n.* prepekto

Prefer *v.* hirangin, piliin

Preference *n.* preperensiya, pili, hirang

Preferential *adj.* preperensiyal, namimili, mapili

Prefix *n.* unlapi, prepiho

Prefix *v.* unlapian, iunlapi

Pregnancy *n.* pagbubuntis , kabuntisan

Pregnant *adj.* buntis, uno ng kabuntisan

Prehistoric *adj.* preistoriko

Prehistory *n.* preistorya

Prejudice *n.* prehuwisyo

Prejudicial *adj.* nakapipinsala

Prelate *n.* prelado

Preliminary *adj.* pauna, preparatoryo, panghanda

Prelude *n.* preludyo, pauna, pambungad, pambukas

Premature *adj.* maaga, maagap

Premier *adj.* una, puno, prinsipal, pangunahin

Premier *n.* premyer, unang ministro

Premise *n.* premisa

Premise *v.* ipremisa , premisahin

Premises *n.* palibot

Premium *n.* gantimpala, gantimpagal, tubo prima, interes

Prenatal *adj.* antenatal

Preoccupation *n.* kaabalahan

Preparation *n.* paghahanda, preparasyon

Preparatory *adj.* preparatorya

Prepare *v.* maghanda, paghandaan

Prepetration *n.* paggawa ng kasalanan, pagkakasala

Preposterus *adj.* balintuna, di-likas, tiwali, kakatwa

Prerequisite *adj.* kailangan, kinakailangan

Prerogative *n.* karapatan, pribilehiyo

Prescribe *v.* ipanuto, itakda, resetahan, idikta, iutos

Prescription *n.* reseta, preskripsiyon

Presence *n.* presensiya, tikas, pagharap, bikas, pagdalo

Present *adj.* kaharap, dumalo, kasalukuyan

Present *n.* regalo, alaala

Present *v.* iharap, regaluhan, itanghal, ipakita

Presentable *adj.* presentable

Presentation *n.* paggagawad, donasyon, regalo

Presently *adj.* di na maglalaon, ngayon

Preservation *n.* preserbasyon, konserbasyon

Preservative *n.* preserbatibo

Preserve *v.* pangalagaan, konserbahin, ipagsanggalang, papanatilihin, imbakin

Preside *v.* mangulo, mamatnugot, patnugutan

Presidency *n.* panguluhan

President *n.* pangulo

Presidium *n.* presidyum

Press *n.* diin, presyon, prensa, imprenta

Press *v.* diinan, pikpikin, prinsahin, igiit, pisilin, daganan, pindutin, pigain

Pressman *n.* manlilimbag

Pressure *n.* presyon, diin

Prestige *n.* prestihiyo, kagitingan, kabantugan

Presto *adv.* madali, madalian, agad-agad, kagyat

Presume *n.* mangahas, pangahasan, manghimasok, panghimasukan

Presuppose *v.* hakain, sapantahain, akalain

Pretend *v.* magkunwa, magkunwari, magbalabala, magpanggap

Pretense *n.* pagkukunwa, pakitang-tao

Pretext *n.* dahilan, pretesto, pagkukunwa

Pretty *adj.* nakalulugod, nakaiigaya, makisig, maganda

Prevail *v.* manaig, makapanaig, makapangyari, mangibabaw

Prevalence *n.* pangingibabaw, kalaganapan, pagiral

Prevaricate *v.* magbulaan, magsinungaling

Prevent *v.* hadlangan, ilayo, ilagan, pigilan, agapan, sawatain

Preview *n.* pribyu

Previous *adj.* una, nauna, nauuna, nangunguna

Prey *n.* biktima

Prey *v.* manloob, manulisan, biktimahin

Price *n.* presyo, halaga

Priceless *adj.* mahalagangmahalaga, mamahalin

Prick *n.* butas, tudlok

Prick *v.* sundutin, duruin, manayo, papanayuin

Prickle *n.* tinik, tibo

Prickly *adj.* matinik

Pride *n.* orgulyo, banidad, ego, kaakuhan,pagmamalaki

Priest *n.* pare, padre, saserdote

Priesthood *n.* pagka-pari

Prim *adj.* mabikas, makisig

Primacy *n.* pangunguna

Primary *adj.* nangunguna, pangunahin, primarya

Prime *adj.* una, maaga, simula

Primer *n.* kartilya, katon

Primitive *adj.* primitibo, kauna-unahan, sauna

Primrose *adj.* mabulaklak, masaya

Prince *n.* prinsipe

Princess *n.* prinsesa

Principal *adj.* prinsipal, puno, pinakamataas

Principal *n.* prinsipal, namumuno, puno, ulo, puhunan

Principle *n.* simulain, prinsipyo

Print *n.* limbag, tatak

Print *v.* ilimbag, itatak

Printer *n.* manlilmbag

Prior *adj.* una, nauna, nauuna

Prior *n.* prior

Priority *n.* kaunahan

Prism *n.* prisma

Prison *n.* piitan, karsel, kulungan, bilangguan, bilibid

Pristine *adj.* pristiho , busilak

Privacy *n.* , kalingiran, kalihiman

Private *adj.* pribado, panarili, bukod, sarili, pansarili

Privilege *n.* pribilechiyo, karapatan

Prize *n.* gantimpala, premyo

Prize *v.* mahalagahin, kalugdan, mahalin

Pro *adv.* pro, paayon

Pro *n.* pro, propesyonal

Pro rata baha-bahagi, proporsiyonal

Probability *n.* probabilidad

Probably *adv.* marahil nga

Probe *n.* sundol, siyasig, panundol, imbestigasyon, pagsisiyasat

Probe *v.* imbestigahin, siyasatin, sundulin

Probity *n.* kabaitan, katapatan, karangalan

Problem *n.* problema, suliranin

Procedure *n.* prosedimyento, pamamaraan, palakad

Proceed *v.* magpatuloy, umabante, magbanat, sumulong, manggaling

Proceeds *n.* pinagbilhan, benta

Process *n.* proseso, pagsusunud-sunod, pamamaraan

Procession *n.* prusisyon

Proclaim *v.* iproklama, ibando, ipahayag

Procreate *v.* magsupling, umanak, ipagpaliban

Procreate *v.* magsupling, umanak, manganak

Procreator *n.* manunupling

Proctor *n.* proktor, prokurador

Procure *v.* makuha, kunin, makakuha, kamtin, matamo, makamit, tamuhin

Procurement *n.*· pagkuha, pagtamo, pagkamit

Procurer *n.* tagakuha

Prod *n.* panundot, panduro, duruan

Prod *v.* sundutin, duruin, pakilusin, ibunsod, sulsulan

Prodigal *adj.* alibugha, labusak, labusaw, mapagtapon

Prodigy *n.* kababalaghan

Produce *v.* ilanted, isilang, ianak, yariin, ipakita, psibulin, itanghal, magbunga, ilabas,ibunga, gawin

Producer *n.* produktor

Product *n.* produkto, bunga, ani, anak, supling

Production *n.* produksiyon

Productive *adj.* produktibo, mabisa, mabunga

Productivity *n.* produktibidad

Profess *v.* ipahayag, magkunwa, aminin, manalig

Profession *n.* propesyon

Professional *adj.* propesyonal

Professor *n.* propesor, guro

Proficiency *n.* pagbuti, paggaling, pagkasanay, kabutihan

Proficient *adj.* mabuti, magaling, sanay, dalubhasa

Profile *n.* perpil

Profit *n.* tubo, pakinabang, gana

Profit *v.* makinabang, pakinabangan, gumana, magtubo

Profitable *adj.* mapakikinabangan

Profiteer *n.* manghuhuthot

Profound *adj.* baliwag, malalim

Profound *v.* ipasaalangalang

Profuse *adj.* masagana, saksa, magkakatusak, malago

Profusion *n.* kasaganaan, kasaksaan, pagkakatusak

Prognosis *n.* prognostiko, prediksiyon, hula

Program *n.* programa, palatuntunan

Progress *n.* progreso, kaunlaran, pagsulong

Progress *v.* umunlad, sumulong, umadelanto

Progressive *adj.* pagbawalan, ipagbawal

Prohibition *n.* pagbabawal

Prohibitive *adj.* mapagbawal

Project *n.* proyekto, balak, plano

Project *v.* umungos, paungusin, umusli, pausliin, balakin

Projection *n.* usli, proyeksiyon, ungos

Projector *n.* proyektor

Prolate *adj.* banat, tangtang

Prolific *adj.* mabunga, mabungahin, palaanak, malikhain

Prologue *n.* prologo

Prolong *n.* pahabain, palawakin, patagalin, ituloy, ipagpatuloy

Promenade *n.* pasyal, pagpapasyal, pasyalan

Prominent *adj.* tanyag, kita, bantog, lanted, katangi-tangi

Promise *n.* pangako, pagasa

Promise *v.* mangako, pangakuan

Promote *v.* iasenso, itaas, iuna, itaguyod

Promoter *n.* promoter

Promotion *n.* promosyon, pagtaas, pagpasa

Prompt *adj.* maliksi, daglian, madalian

Prompt *n.* takdang panahon

Prompt *v.* magdikta, diktahan, udyukan

Promptness *n.* kadalian, kaliksihan

Promulgate *v.* ipaalam, ibunyag, ihayag, isaysay

Promulgation *n.* pagbibigayalam, pagbubunyag, paghahayag

Prone *adj.* mahilig, nakataob, nakadapa

Pronoun *n.* panghalip

Pronounce *v.* sabihin, bumigkas, bigkasin, isaysay, patunayan, panindigan

Pronunciation *n.* bigkas, pagbigkas

Proof *n.* patunay, katunayan, patibay, katibayan, pruweba

Prop *n.* tukod, suhay

Prop *v.* tukuran, suhayan

Propaganda *n.* propaganda

Propagate *v.* magparami, paramihin, magpalaganap, palaganapin

Propagation *n.* pagpapalaga-nap

Propagator *n.* tagapagpalaga-nap

Propel *v.* isulong, itulak

Propeller *n.* elise

Proper *adj.* natural, katutubo, pantangi, tumpak, nauukol, wasto

Prophecy *v.* manghula, hulaan

Prophet *n.* propeta, manghuhula

Propitiate *v.* payapain, papagkasunduin

Proportion *n.* proporsiyon, iyakis, kaugnayan, simetriya, ugmaan

Proportional *adj.* propor-siyon, mungkahi, alok, balak

Propose *v.* imungkahi, tangkain

Proprietor *n.* may-ari, propetaryo

Propriety *n.* katumpakan, kabagayan

Propulsion *n.* propulsiyon, pagsusulong, pagtulak

Prorogation *n.* proroga, pataan, palugit

Prosaic *adj.* prosaiko, malatuluyan, nakaiinip

Prose *n.* prosa, tuluyan

Prosecute *v.* isagdal, magsakdal, usigin, maghabla, ihabla

Prosecution *n.* pag-uusig

Prosecutor *n.* tagausig

Prospect *n.* tanawin, pagasa

Prospective *adj.* inaasahan

Prospectus *n.* prospektus, prospekto

Prosper *v.* magtagumpay, umunlad, sumagana

Prosperity *n.* tagumpay, kaunlaran

Prosperous *adj.* maunlad, prospero

Prostate *n.* prostata

Prosthesis *n.* prostesis, pagdaragdad

Prostitute *n.* puta, patutot

Prostitute *v.* gamitin sa masama

Prostrate *adj.* subsob ang ulo, nakadapa, lupaypay

Prostrate *v.* magpatirapa

Protect *v.* ipagtanggol, ipagsanggalang, pangalagaan, kupkupin

Protection *n.* proteksiyon

Protective *adj.* mapagtanggol

Protector *n.* protektor, tagapagtanggol

Protectorate *n.* protektorado

Protein *n.* proteina

Protest *n.* protesta, tutol

Protest *v.* tumutol, tutulan, sumalungat, salungatin

Protestant *n.* protestante

Protocol *n.* protokolo, protokol

Proton *n.* proton

Protoplasm *n.* protoplasma

Prototype *n.* prototipo, tularan, uliran

Protozos *n.* protosoa, protosoo

Protract *n.* pagtatagal, patagalin, lumawig, palawigin

Protractor *n.* protraktor

Protrude *v.* umusli, unungos

Proud *adj.* palalo, mapagmalaki, lugod na lugod, kahanga-hanga

Prove *v.* subukin, tikman, patunayan, ipamalas

Proverb *n.* salawikain

Provide *v.* maglaan, magtakda, paglaanan, itakda, bigyan, itadhana, tustusan

Providence *n.* katalagahan

Provident *adj.* mapaglaan, matipid

Providential *adj.* probidensiyal, mapalad

Province *n.* probinsiya, lalawigan

Provincial *adj.* probinsiyal

Provision *n.* probisyon, tadhana, takda, tustos, panustos, handa

Provisional *adj.* probisyonal, pansamantala

Provocation *n.* hamon, hamit, pagpukaw

Provocative *adj.* nanghahamit

Provoke *v.* pukawin, galitin

Proximal *adj.* kalapit, kapanig, puno

Proximate *adj.* kasunod

Proximity *n.* kalapitan

Proxy *n.* kinatawan, kahalili, proxy

Prude *n.* santuron

Prudence *n.* bait, kabaitan, kasanayan

Prudent *adj.* mabait

Prudential *adj.* may pagkamabait

Prudery *n.* kasanturunan

Prune *n.* pruns

Prune *v.* talbusan, tagpasin

Pry *n.* panunubok, paninilip, maninilip

Pry *n.* pansuit, pansikwat

Pry *v.* suitin, sikwatin

Psalm *n.* salmo

Pseudo *adj.* seudo, palso

Pseudonym *n.* seudonimo, ngalang-sagisag

Psoas *n.* pigi, lomo

Psychiatrist *n.* psikyatrista

Psychiatry *n.* psikyatriya

Psychic *adj.* psikiko

Psychologic *adj.* psikolohiko

Psychologist *n.* psikologo

Psychology *n.* psikolohiya

Puberty *n.* pubesensiya, pagbabaguntao, pagdadalaga

Public *adj.* publiko, tao, taong-bayan, madla

Publication *n.* lathala, paglalathala

Publicity *n.* publisidad

Publicize *v.* bigyang publisidad

Publish *v.* maglathala, ilathala

Publisher *n.* publikador

Pucker *v.* sumangoy, ngumibit, ngumiwi

Pudding *n.* puding

Puddle *n.* sanaw, lamaw, tubog

Puddle *v.* pagputikin, labusawin

Pudgy *adj.* himandak

Puff *n.* buga , alsa, espongha

Puff *v.* bumuga, ibuga, bugahan, sumingasing

Pull *n.* hila, lakas, hatak, bunot, hugot

Pull *v.* hilahin, hatakin, bunutin, hugutin

Pullet *n.* dumalaga, dumalagang manok

Pulley *n.* pulea, moton, kalo

Pulp *n.* sapal, pulpa

Pulpit *n.* pulpito

Pulsate *v.* tumibok, pumitok, pumintig

Pulsation *n.* tibok, pitok, pintig

Pulse *n.* pulso, tibok

Pump *n.* bomba, pamp

Pump *v.* bombahan, bombahin

Pumpkin *n.* kalabasa

Pumpkinseed *n.* isdang ruweda

Pun *n.* pun

Punch *n.* pontse

Punch *n.* suntok, pambutas, punson, bisa

Punch *v.* manundot, sundutin, magbutas, butasin

Punctual *adj.* maagap, nasa wastong oras, puntuwal

Punctuality *n.* kapuntuwalan

Punctuation *n.* bantas

Puncture *n.* butas

Puncture *v.* butasin

Pundit *n.* pantas

Pungent *n.* maanghang

Punish *v.* parusahan, kastiguhin, supilin

Punishment *n.* parusa

Punt *n.* gabara

Puny *adj.* munti, munsing, mahina

Pup *n.* tuta, kuwa

Pupa *n.* higad, uod

Pupil *n.* eskuwela, disipula, estudyante, mag-aaral

Puppet *n.* manika, papet, maryonet, titeres

Purchase *n.* pagbili, binili, pinamili

Purchase *v.* bumili, bilhin

Pure *adj.* dalisay, ganap, puro, basal, wagas, lubos

Puree *n.* pure

Pureness *n.* kadalisayan

Purgation *n.* pagpupurga

Purgatory *n.* purgatoryo

Purge *v.* purgahin, linisin

Purification *n.* puripikasyon

Purifier *n.* puripikador

Purify *v.* dalisayin

Puritan *adj.* puritano

Purity *n.* kadalisayan

Purl *n.* saluysoy, sapa

Purl *v.* mamuyo, mamusod, sumaluysoy, umalun-alon

Purple *n.* murado, purpura

Purport *n.* kahulugan, kabuluhan

Purport *v.* magpanggap

Purpose *n.* layon, layunin, tangka

Purse *n.* pitaka, portamoneda, lukbutan

Purser *n.* sobrekargo

Pursuance *n.* pagsasagawa, pagsasakatatuparan

Pursuant *adv.* ayon sa, alinsunod sa

Pursue *v.* tugisin, hagarin, magpatuloy

Pursuit *n.* pagtugis, gawain, paghabol, paghagad, pagpapatuloy

Purulence *n.* pagnanana

Purvey *v.* manustos, tustusan

Purview *n.* saklaw, nasasaklaw

Pus *n.* nana

Push *n.* tulak

Push *v.* itulak

Puss *n.* pusa

Pustule *n.* butlig

Put *v.* ilagay

Putrefaction *n.* pagkabulok

Putrefy *v.* mabulok

Putrid *adj.* bulok

Putt *n.* putt

Putty *n.* masilya

Puzzle *n.* suliranin, hiwaga, palaisipan

Puzzle *v.* guluhin ang isip, lituhin, hirahin

Pyjama *n.* padyama

Pyramid *n.* piramide, tagilo

Pyre *n.* siga

Pyrite *n.* pirita

Pyrophobia *n.* takot sa apoy

Pyrotechnics *n.* pagkukuwitis

Python *n.* sawa

Pythoness *n.* babaylan

Q q

Quack *adj.* huwad, palsipikado

Quack *n.* kuwak, pagkuwak, albularyo

Quack *v.* kumakak

Quadrangle *n.* patyo

Quadrant *n.* kuwadrante, kapat

Quadrate *n.* kuwadrado, parisukat

Quadrilateral *adj.* kuwadri-lateral, kuwadranggular

Quadrile *n.* rigodon

Quadruped *adj.* apatang paa, kuwadrupedo

Quadruplet *n.* apatang kambal

Quadruplicate *adj.* kuwadruplikado

Quagmire *n.* kuminoy

Quail *n.* pugo

Quail *v.* umuklod

Quaint *adj.* kakaiba, katangitangi, kakatwa

Quake *n.* lindol

Quake *v.* manginig, mangatal, lumindol, yumanig

Qualification *n.* katangiang, kailangan

Qualified *adj.* may katangi ang kailangan

Qualify *v.* magkaroon ng katangiang kailangan

Qualitative *adj.* kalitatibo

Quality *n.* kalidad, uri, katangian

Qualm *n.* pagkahilo, panimdim, pagkabahala

Quandary *n.* linggatong, suliranin, kagipitan

Quantity *n.* kantidad, dami, kabuuan

Quarantine *n.* kuwarentenas, ibukod, ihiwalay

Quarrel *n.* away, babag, alitan

Quarrel *v.* magkagalit, magaway, awayin, magbabag

Quarrelsome *adj.* palaaway

Quarry *n.* tibangan

Quarry *v.* tumibag, magtibag, tibagin

Quart *n.* kuwarto, galon

Quarter *n.* kapat, sampaa, ikaapat, kuwarto, tirahan

Quarter *v.* hiwagin, kuwartuhin

Quarterly *adj.* , trimestral

Quartette *n.* kuwarteto

Quartile *n.* kuwartil, kuwadrado

Quartiz *n.* kuwarso

Quarto *n.* aklat-kuwarto

Quash *v.* sugpuin, nuluhin,' pigilan, supilin

Quasi *pref.* animo, mala

Quatrain *n.* quwarteto

Quaver *v.* manginig, mangatal

Quay *n.* muwelyo, desembarkadero

Queasy *adj.* maselang, dilikado

Queen *n.* reyna

Queer *adj.* kaiba, kakaiba, kakatuwa

Quell *v.* mapasuko, masugpo, pasukuin, sugpuin, masupil, payapain, supilin

Quench *v.* patayin, patdin, tapusin, itubog, supilin, sugpuin

Quern *n.* munting gilingan

Querulous *adj.* mapamintas, mapintasin, mayamutin, palaangil

Query *n.* tanong, ususa, alinlangan

Quest *n.* paghahanap, abentura

Quest *v.* maghanap, magabentura

Question *n.* tanong, pagtatanong, usisa, suliranin

Question *v.* magtanong, mag-usisa, tanungin

Questionnaire *n.* talatanungan, kuwestiyonaryo

Queue *n.* tirintas, pila, hanay

Queue *v.* pumila, humanay

Quible *n.* isuiso, pagpapaisuiso

Quick *adj.* maagap, matulin, maliksi, mabilis, matalas, madali, handa

Quicken *v.* daliin, bilisan, pakilusin, tulinan, liksihan

Quicklime *n.* apog

Quickly *adj.* madalian, madali, agad

Quicksand *n.* kumunoy

Quid *n.* ngatain

Quiddity *n.* kaanuhan

Quiescence *n.* katimikan

Quiescent *adj.* walang-kibo, walang-salaw, timik

Quiet *adj.* tahimik, panatag, payapa, mahinahon

Quiet *v.* patahimikin, payapain

Quill *n.* pluma

Quilt *n.* kubrekama, sobrekama

Quinine *n.* kinina

Quinone *n.* kinona

Quinsy *n.* anghina

Quintal *n.* kintal, sandaang kilo

Quintessence *n.* kaanu-anuhan

Quintet *adj.* kinteto, limahan

Quintet *n.* kinteto, limahan

Quintuplet *n.* kintuplo, lima sa kambal

Quip *n.* siste, biro, tukso

Quit *v.* lisanin, tumigil, huminto, magtigil, maghinto, umalis

Quiver *n.* pangangatal, pangangatog

Quiver *v.* manginig, mangatal, mangatog

Quiz *n.* maikling pagsusulit

Quorum *n.* korum

Quota *n.* kota, takda

Quotation *n.* sipi

Quote *v.* sumipi, sipiin, magsabi, sabihin

R r

Rabbit *n.* kuneho

Rabid *adj.* masugid, masidhi

Race *n.* karera, takbuhan, labanan, lahi, lipi

Race *v.* magtumulin, makipagkarera

Rack *n.* sabitan, pangawan

Rack *v.* istrahin, pahirapan, batakin

Racket *n.* pangungulimbat, raket

Radiant *adj.* makinang, maliwanag, maaliwalas

Radish *n.* labanos

Raffle *v.* pagparipahan

Raft *n.* balsa

Raft *v.* magbalsa

Rag *n.* basahan

Rage *n.* galit, poot

Rage *v.* magalit, magngalit, manalanta

Raid *v.* salakayin, sumalakay

Railing *n.* barandilya

Railroad *n.* perokaril

Railroad *v.* madaliin, agarin

Rain *v.* umulan

Raincoat *n.* kapote

Rainy *adj.* maulan

Raise *v.* lumikha, magtayo, itaas, dagdagan, pataasin, gumawa, angatin, taasan, magtans

Raisin *n.* pasas

Raja *n.* raha, hari

Rake *n.* kalaykay

Rake *v.* kalaykayin

Rakish *adj.* masagwa

Rally *n.* rali

Rally *v.* magtipon, pakilusin

Ram *n.* murweko , martinete

Ram *v.* pagikpikin, pikpikin sa bayo

Ramble *v.* pasyal, paglilibot

Rambutan *n.* rambutan

Ramie *n.* rami

Ramification *n.* pagsasanga, ramipikasyon

Ramp *n.* daag hilig

Ramp *v.* sumyinta, suminta

Rampage *n.* alboroto

Rampant *adj.* nakasinta, nagbbabala, laganap

Rampart *n.* kuta

Ramrod *n.* baketa

Ranch *n.* rantso, asyenda

Rancher *n.* rantsero, asendero

Rancid *adj.* maanta

Random *adj.* laya, ligaw

Range *n.* hanay, saklaw, dako, linea, layo, abot, ayos, tagal, uri

Range *v.* ihanay, ihelera, isaayos, libutin, galain, gaygayin

Rank *adj.* malago, pusakal, mabaho, magaspang, mahalay, masangsang

Rank *n.* hilera, klase, patong, katayuan, ranggo, pila, taas

Rank *v.* ihanay, klasihin, ihelera, pahanayin, pahelerahin, uriin

Rankle *v.* magpakirot, magpahapdi

Ransack *v.* halughugin, saliksikin, dambungin, pandambungan

Ransom *n.* tubos

Ransom *v.* tubusin, sagipin

Rant *v.* maghumiyaw, magmura, manuligsa

Rap *n.* katok, tuktok

Rap *v.* katok

Rapacious *adj.* mangangamkam, masiba

Rape *n.* panggagahasa

Rape *v.* gahasain

Rapid *adj.* matulin, maliksi, mabilis

Rapid *n.* lagaslasan

Rapier *n.* espadin

Rapine *n.* dambong, pandarambong

Raport *n.* armoniya, ugmaan, pagkakasundo

Rapture *n.* pagtatalik, katalikan

Rare *adj.* malasado, pambihira

Rarefy *v.* palabnawin, panipisin, papinuhin

Rarely *adv.* bihira

Rarity *n.* kadalangan

Rascal *adj.* pilyo

Rash *adj.* padalus-dalos, walang-taros

Rash *n.* abang-abang, butlig-butlig, pantal-pantal

Rash *n.* pantal

Rash *n.* abang-abang, butlig-butlig, pantal-pantal

Rasp *v.* kikirin, kayurin, kaskasin

Raspberry *n.* prambuwesas

Raspy *adj.* maagas-as

Rat *n.* daga

Ratchet *n.* tringkete

Rate *n.* halaga, presyo, proporsiyon, singil, tasa

Rate *v.* halagahan, ipalagay, pahalagahan, tasahan, ihanay

Rather *adv.* manapa, lalong mabuti, medyo

Ratification *n.* ratipikasyon, pagpapatunay

Ratify *v.* ratipikahan

Rating *n.* grado, ranggo, uri, tasa

Ratio *n.* rasyon, proporsiyon, kaugnayan

Ration *n.* rasyon, kaparti

Ration *v.* magrasyon, irasyon

Rational *adj.* maykatwiran, rasyonal

Rationale *n.* paliwanag

Rationalize *n.* pangatwiranan

Ratoon *n.* taad, pasupling

Rattan *n.* ratan, yantok

Rattle *n.* kalantog, kalampag

Rattle *v.* kalampagin

Raucous *adj.* pagaw, namamagaw

Ravage *n.* pamumuksa, pamiminsala, panlilipol, pagkasira, pinsala

Ravage *v.* gibain, wasakin, lipulin

Rave *v.* magdiliryo, magmangmang

Raven *n.* uwak

Ravenous *adj.* masiba, mapanagpang, gutom, dayukdok

Ravine *n.* bangin, labing, talabis

Ravish *v.* gabutin, manggabot, dukutin, mandukot, magtalik

Ravishment *n.* pagtatalik

Raw *adj.* hilaw, mahapdi, makirot, magaspang, maginaw, katutubo, baguhan, taal

Rawboned *adj.* yayat

Ray *n.* sinag, sikat

Ray *n.* page

Ray *v.* magbigay-sinag

Rayon *v.* gibain, wasakin, iwalat

Raze *v.* iwasak, wasakin

Razor *n.* labaha

Re *n.* re

Re *n.* tungkol, hinggil

Reach *v.* umabot, sumapit, , dukwangin, abutin, dumating

React *v.* magtauli, magtamuli, manugon, mamalik

Reaction *n.* reaksiyon, pagtatauli, pagtatamuli

Reactor *n.* reaktor

Read *v.* bumasa, magbasa, basahin

Reader *n.* mambabasa, akalat

Reading *n.* pagbabasa

Readmit *v.* tanggapin uli, papasukin uli

Ready *adj.* handa, nalalaan, maliksi, madali

Reaffirm *v.* patibayan, patunayan

Reagent *n.* reaktibo

Real *adj.* tunay, aktuwal, totoo

Realism *n.* realismo

Realist *n.* realista

Realistic *adj.* realistiko

Reality *n.* katunayan

Realization *n.* realisasyon

Realize *v.* maisakatuparan, pangilakan, mapaghulo, makinabang

Realm *n.* kaharian, lupang sakop, rehiyon, daigdig

Realty *n.* pingkas

Ream *n.* resma

Reap *v.* anihin, gumapas, pumuti, gapasin, mamuti, umani, putihin, magani

Reaper *n.* mag-aani

Reappear *v.* muling lumitaw

Rear *n.* likod, likuran, hulihan

Rear *v.* itayo, itaas, mag-alaga, magpalaki

Reason *n.* katwiran, matuwid

Reason *v.* mangatwiran, magmatuwid

Reasonable *adj.* makatuwiran

Reassurance *n.* pagmumuling-tiwala

Rebate *n.* sauli, rebaha, deskuwento

Rebel *n.* maghihimagsik, manghihimagsik

Rebel *v.* maghimagsik, manghimagsik

Rebellion *n.* panghihimagsik, pagbabangon

Rebellious *adj.* mapanghimagsik

Rebirth *n.* muling pagsilang, pagmumuling-silang

Rebound *n.* talbog, sikad, umalingawngaw

Rebuff *n.* pagtanggi, pagayaw

Rebuff *v.* tumanggi, umayaw

Rebuild *v.* magtayo uli, magmuling tatag

Rebuke *v.* murahin, pagsabihan, pagwikaan

Rebut *v.* pabulaanan, pasinungalingan, sumalungat, salungatin

Rebuttal *n.* pagpapabulaan

Recalcitrant *adj.* suwail

Recalcitrant *n.* suwail

Recall *v.* pabalikin, bawiin, pauwiin, iurong, alalahanin, maalaala

Recant *v.* iurong, bawiin, itakwil

Recap *v.* magrikap, rikapin

Recapitulate *v.* lumagom, lagumin

Recapitulation *n.* rekapitulasyon, paglalagom

Recapture *v.* alalahanin

Recede *v.* umurong, manliit, manghina, kumati

Receipt *n.* resipe, resibo, pagtanggap

Receive *v.* tumanggap, maglaman, danasin, tanggapin, lamanin, magpapasok, magtamo, papasukin, tamuhin

Receiver *n.* tagatanggap

Recent *adj.* kapangyayari

Receptacle *n.* lalagyan, sisidlan

Reception *n.* resepsiyon, pagtanggap

Receptionist *n.* resepsiyonista, tagatanggap, tagasalubong

Receptive *adj.* mapagtanggap

Receptor *n.* reseptor, tagatanggap

Recess *n.* alkoba, tigil, lugong, urungan, sandaling

Recess *v.* magrises

Recession *n.* urong, pagurong

Recessive *adj.* paurong

Recipe *n.* resipe, pormula

Recipience *n.* pagtanggap

Reciprocal *adj.* gantihan, palitan

Reciprocate *v.* gumanti, gantihan

Reciprocation *n.* pakikipaggantihan

Reciprocity *n.* resiprosidad, paggagantihan

Recital *n.* pagsasalaysay, pagbigkas, resital

Recitation *n.* resitasyon, pagliksiyon

Recitative *adj.* pasalaysay

Recite *v.* magsalaysay, isalaysay, bumigkas

Reckless *adj.* pabaya, walang-bahala, walang-ingat

Reckon *v.* bilangin, isipin, tuusin, umasa, tayahin, asahan, ipalagay

Reckoning *n.* pagbilang, pagtaya, pag-iisip, pag-asa

Reclaim *v.* paamuin, iligtas, sagipin, bawiin

Reclamation *n.* reklamasyon

Recline *v.* sumandal, humilig

Recluse *adj.* bukod, ligpit, layo, solo

Recluse *n.* ermitanyo

Reclusion *n.* pagbukod, pagbibilanggo

Recognition *n.* pagkilala, pagkakilala

Recognizable *adj.* kilala, nakikilala

Recognize *v.* makilala, kilalanin

Recoil *n.* urong, pangungurong

Recoil *v.* umurong, mapaurong, umudlot, sumikad, umilag

Recollect *v.* magunita, gunitain, isipin, maisip

Recollection *n.* alaala, gunita

Recommend *v.* itagubilin, irekomenda, magtagubilin, purihin magrekomenda, ipayo

Recommendation *n.* tagubilin, rekomendasyon

Recommit *v.* ibalik

Recompense *n.* gantimpala, upa, bayad

Recompense *v.* gantihin, upahan, ibayad, bayaran

Reconcile *v.* makipagkasundo, papagkasunduin, iayos, ayusin

Reconciliation *n.* pagkakasundo, rekonsilyasyon

Recondite *adj.* tago, lingid , baliwag

Recondition *v.* magkumpuni, kumpunihin, magpanibagong-buti

Reconnaissance *n.* pagmamatyag, paggalugad

Reconsider *v.* muling isaalang-alang

Reconsign *v.* muling ibigay

Reconstitute *v.* muling buuin uli

Reconstitution *n.* muling pagbubuo

Reconstruct *v.* muling itayo, uli, muling buuin, buuin uli

Reconstruction *n.* pagbabagong-tatag

Reconvey *v.* isauli

Record *n.* tala, rekord, kasulatan

Record *v.* magtala, itala, nagrekord, irekord

Recorder *n.* rekorder

Recount *v.* isalaysay, ikuwento

Recoup *v.* makabawi, mauyanan

Recoupment *n.* pagkabawi, uyan

Recourse *n.* dulugan, takbuhan , rekurso

Recover *v.* mabawi, gumaling, bumuti, masagip, maligtas

Recovery *n.* pagkabawi

Recreant *adj.* di-tapat, sukab, duwag

Recreate *v.* pasiglahing muli, muling buhayin, magpaalwan, mag-aliw

Recreation *n.* pag-aaliw, paglilibang

Recrement n. lawang, taingmetal

Recriminate *v.* manggantin-gratang

Recruit *n.* rekluta

Recruit *v.* mangalap ng tauhan

Recruitment *n.* pagrerekluta

Rectal *adj.* rektal, pampuwit

Rectangle *n.* rektanggulo, parihaba

Rectification *n.* rekipika-syon, pagtutuwid, pagwawasto

Rectify *v.* rektipikahin, ituwid, iwasto

Rectilinear *adj.* tuwid

Rectitude *n.* kawastuan, katarungan

Rector *n.* rektor

Rectory *n.* rektoriya

Rectum *n.* tumbong

Recumbent *adj.* nakasandal, nakahilig, nakahiga

Recuperate *v.* gumaling, bumuti, makabawi, magpalakas

Recur *v.* umulit , magbalik

Red *n.* pula, namumula sa hiya, kumunista

Redden *v.* mamula

Redeem *v.* tubusin, hanguin

Redeemer *n.* manunubos

Redemption *n.* katubusan, kaligtasan

Redirect *n.* pagmumulin-tanong

Redirect *v.* mulintanungin

Rediscover *v.* matuklasan uli, magmulintuklas

Redolence *n.* halimuyak, mabango, maypahiwatig

Redouble *v.* pag-ibayuhin, ulitin, magbalik, pagbalikan

Redoubt *n.* kuta, muralya

Redoubtable *adj.* napakala-kas , kapitapitagan

Redound *n.* magbunga, humantong, paghantungan, magbisa, magkabisa

Redress *n.* pagwawasto, pagtutuwid, pagbabago

Redress *v.* iwasto, ituwid, bayaran, lunasan

Reduce *v.* magbawa, ibaba, magbawas, pababain, magpaliit, babaan, paliitin, bawasan

Reduction *n.* Reduksiyon, bawas

Redundance *n.* kaliguyan, kalabisan

Reduplicate *adj.* dinoble, inulit

Reduplicate *v.* doblihin, ulitin, pagulitin

Reduplication *n.* reduplikasyon, pag-uulit

Reed *n.* lingguweta, dila-dilaan, tambo, bukawe

Reek *v.* mangamoy

Reel *n.* ikiran, karete, rolyo

Reel *v.* mag-iikot, mag-inikot, gumiray, sumuray

Reelect *v.* muling ihalal, ihalal uli

Reelection *n.* muling pagkakahalal, reeleksiyon

Reeve *v.* isulot

Reexamination *n.* muling ikasamin, muling suri, muling sulit

Reexamine *n.* muling iksaminin, muling suriin, muling tanungin

Refectory *n.* bulwagang kainan, komedor

Refer *v.* iugay, banggitin,sumangguni itukoy, bumanggit

Reference *n.* reperensiya, sanggunian, pagtukoy

Referendum *n.* reperendum

Referent *adj.* reperente

Refill *n.* muling punuin

Refill *n.* pangmumulimpuno

Refine *v.* pinuhin, gilingin, dalisayin

Refined *adj.* pino, kulto, malinang, repinado

Refinement *n.* kapinuhan, kadalisayan, kalinisan

Refinery *n.* repineriya

Refit *v.* , kumpunihin, baguhin

Reflect *v.* umisip, ikasirang-puri, ibalik, ikapuri, italbog

Reflectance *n.* kahunaban

Reflection *n.* pag-iisip, pagbubulay-bulay

Reflector *n.* replektor

Reflex *n.* repleks

Refluent *adj.* kumakati

Reflux *n.* kati, pagkati

Reforestation *n.* pagmumulinggubat, pagmumulingpagubat

Reform *n.* reporma, pagwawasto, pagpapabuti

Reform *v.* repormahin, baguhing-anyo, papagbaguhinganyo

Reformation *n.* reporma, pagbabagong-anyo, pagpapabuti

Reformatory *n.* repormatoryo

Reformer *n.* repormador

Refract *v.* repraktahin

Refraction *n.* repraksyon kalihisan

Refrain *n.* ulit, koro

Refresh *v.* sariwain, palamigin, magrepresko, buhayin

Refresher *n.* inumin, paalaala

Refreshment *n.* pagpapapresko, pagpapanariwa

Refreshments *n.* pamatiduhaw, pamawing-gutom

Refrigerant *adj.* repriherante

Refrigerant *n.* repriherante

Refrigerate *v.* repriherahin, palamigan

Refrigeration *n.* repriherasyon

Refrigerator *n.* repridyeretor

Refuge *n.* kanlungan, silungan, ampunan

Refugee *n.* repuhiyado, manlilikas

Refund *n.* pagsasauli ng kuwarta

Refund *v.* isauli, bayaran, ibalik

Refundable *adj.* mapapasauli

Refusal *n.* pagtanggi, pagayaw

Refuse *n.* labis, agsaman, basura

Refuse *v.* tumanggi, tanggihan, umayaw, ayawan

Refutation *n.* pabulaan, pagpapabulaan

Refute *v.* pasinungalingan, pabulaanan

Regain *v.* mabawi, makabalik

Regal *adj.* makahari, real

Regale *v.* pigingin, bangketihin

Regalia *n.* sagisag, makahari

Regard *n.* tingin, alangalang, paggalang, pagtingin

Regard *v.* pagmasdan, igalang, itangi, gumalang

Regardful *adj.* maasikaso, magalang

Regarding *adj.* hinggil sa

Regardless *adj.* walang-asikaso, walang-pansin

Regency *n.* rehensiya

Regeneration *n.* rehenerasyon

Regenerator *n.* rehenerador

Regent *n.* rehente

Regime *n.* rehimen, pamamahala, pamahalaan

Regiment *n.* rebimyento

Regimentation *n.* rehimentasyon

Regina *n.* reyna

Region *n.* rehiyon, purok

Regional *adj.* rehiyonal

Regionalism *n.* rehiyonalismo

Regionalist *n.* rehiyonalista

Register *n.* aklat-talaan, rekord

Register *v.* itala, irehistroirekord, magpatala, magparehistro

Registrar *n.* tagatala

Registration *n.* patalaan

Registry *n.* rehistro

Regress *v.* magpaurong

Regression *n.* pagbabalik-kababaan

Regressive *adj.* paurong, pabalik

Regret *n.* pagdaramadam, pagsisisi

Regret *v.* ipagdalamhati, ikalungkot, magsisi

Regretful *adj.* nagdaramdam

Regrettable *adj.* kalungkut-lungkot

Regular *adj.* regular, karaniwan, kainaman, likas

Regulate *v.* areglahin, isaayos

Regulation *n.* alituntunin

Regulator *n.* regulador

Regurgitate *v.* bumulbok, bumulubok, bumulukabok

Rehabilitate *v.* ibalik sa dati, reabilitahan

Rehabilitation *n.* reabilita-syon

Rehash *v.* ibahing-anyo, ulitin

Rehearsal *n.* ensayo, pag-iinsayo

Rehearse *v.* ulitin, insayuhin, kademyahin, mag-insayo

Reify *v.* isatunay

Reign *n.* kaharian, paghahari

Reign *v.* maghari, mamayani, umiral, mangibaw

Reimburse *v.* pagbayaran, magbayad, bayaran

Rein *n.* renda

Rein *v.* hilahin ang renda

Reincarnate *v.* magreen-karnasyon, maglaman uli, magsatao uli

Reincarnation *n.* reen-karnasyon

Reindeer *n.* usang reno

Reinforcement *n.* palakas, patibay

Reins *n.* bato

Reintroduce *v.* ipakilala uli, ipasok uli

Reissue *n.* muling limbag, muling lathala

Reissue *v.* muling limbagin, muling ilathala

Reiteration *n.* muling-sabi

Reject *v.* tanggihan, di-paniwalaan, iwaksi

Rejection *n.* pagtanggi

Rejoice *v.* magalak, malugod

Rejoin *v.* sumama uli, magsama uli

Rejoinder *n.* tugon, sagot

Rejuvenate *v.* pabatain, muling, palakasin, papagbaguhin

Rejuvenation *n.* pagpapa-bata, rehubenasyon

Rekindle *v.* muling papagalabin

Relability *n.* pagka-mapagkakatiwalaan

Relapse *n.* binat

Relapse *v.* mabinat

Relate *v.* magsalaysay, isalaysay, mag-ugnay, iugnay

Relation *n.* kaugnayan, pagsasalaysay

Relative *adj.* may kaugnayan, relatibo

Relative *n.* kamag-anak

Relator *n.* mananalaysay, tagapagsalaysay

Relax *v.* magpahingalay, maglibang-libang, paluwangin, luwagan

Relaxation *n.* pagpapahingalay

Relay *n.* relebo, relebador

Relay *v.* relebuhan, magrelebador

Release *n.* ginhawa, kalag, paglaya, pagk.:alpas

Release *v.* pakawalan, palayain, ibsan, kalagan

Relegate *v.* , kalimutan, itapon, paalisin

Relevance *adj.* pagkakaugnay, pagkakaukol

Relevant *adj.* kaugnay, nauukol

Reliable *adj.* mapapagkatiwalaan

Reliance *n.* tiwala, kumpiyansa

Reliant *adj.* may tiwala

Relic *n.* relikya, bakas, alaala

Relict *n.* biyuda, balo

Relief *n.* ginhawa, adya, alwan, relebo

Relieve *v.* ibsan, paginhawahin, pagaanin, halinhan

Religion *n.* relihiyon, pananampalataya

Religious *adj.* relihiyoso

Relinguish *v.* iwan

Relish *n.* lasa, linamnam, kagustuhan, panlass

Relish *v.* masarapan, ganahan, kalugdan, katuwaan

Reluctance *n.* kawalang-gusto, pagka-di-gusto

Reluctant *adj.* walang-gusto, di-gusto

Rely *v.* umasa, asahan, magtiwala, pagkatiwalaan

Remain *v.* maiwan, manatili, paiwan, matira, magpatira

Remainder *n.* tira, natira

Remains *n.* labi, bangkay

Remand *v.* pabalikin

Remark *n.* pansin, puna, pagmamasid, banggit, pananalita

Remark *v.* mapansin, pansinin, punahin, isaysay

Remarkable *adj.* katangitangi

Remarry *v.* pakasal uli, magasawa uli

Remediable *adj.* malulunasan, magagamot

Remedial *adj.* panlunas, panggamot

Remedy *n.* gamot, lunas, remedyo

Remember *v.* alalahanin, gunitain, maalaala, isipin, magunita, maisip, matandaan, tandaan

Remembrance *n.* alaala, gunita

Remind *v.* paalalahanan, ipaalaala

Remindern. paaalaala, pagunita

Remindful *adj.* mapag-alaala

Reminisce *v.* maggunamgunam, alaala

Reminiscence *n.* gunamgunam, alaala

Reminiscent *adj.* nagpapaal-aala

Remiss *adj.* pabaya, bulagsak

Remissible *adj.* mapatatawad

Remission *n.* patawad, bawa, pagpapadala

Remit *v.* patawarin, ipadala, bawahan, ibalik

Remittance *n.* padalang kuwarta

Remitter *n.* ang maypadala

Remnant *n.* tira, retaso, bakas

Remodel *v.* magbagung-yari, baguhing-yari, kumpunihin

Remonstrance *n.* tutol, paggtutol

Remonstrant *adj.* tumututol

Remonstrate *v.* tumutol, sumalungat

Remorse *n.* pagsisisi, penitensiya, balisa

Remorseful *adj.* nagsisisi, nagtitika

Remote *adj.* malayo, banyaga

Removable *adj.* maaalis, matatanggal

Removal *n.* pag-aalis, pagtatanggal

Remove *v.* alisin, tanggalin, ilipat

Remover *n.* tagapag-alis, pang-alis

Remunerate *v.* upahan, bayaran, gantimpagalan

Remuneration *n.* upa, bayad, gantimpagal

Remunerative *adj.* pinag-kakakitaan

Renaissance *n.* muling-silang, renasimyento

Rename *v.* ngalanan uli

Renascent *adj.* muling isinisilang

Rend *v.* bigtalin, pigtasin, punitin, sirain

Render *v.* ibigay, iabot, ipadala, isalin

Rendezvous *n.* tagpuan, tipanan

Rendition *n.* rendisyon

Renegade *n.* apostata, taksil, sukab

Renew *v.* magpanibago, papanariwain, ulitin

Renewal *n.* pagpapanibago

Rennet *n.* kuwaho

Renominate *v.* muling nominahan, muling hirangin

Renounce *v.* magrenunsiya, pabayaan, magbitiw, itakwil

Rent *adj.* sira, punit, gisi

Renunciation *n.* renunsiyen-siya, pagrerenunsiya

Reorganization *n.* pagmu-muling-ayos, reorganisasyon

Reorganize *v.* magmulinga-yos, reorganisahin

Reorganized *adj.* magmulin-gayos, reoganisado

Repaint *v.* pintahan uli

Repair *v.* magkumpuni, kumpunihin, lunasan, remedyuhan

Reparation *n.* reparasyon

Repartee *n.* repartee

Repast *n.* pagkain, komida

Repatriation *n.* repatriasyon

Repay *v.* magbayad, bayaran, isauli, gumanti

Repeal *n.* pagpapa-walang-bisa

Repeal *v.* iurong, bawiin

Repeat *n.* repitisyon

Repeat *v.* mag-ulit, ulitin

Repel *v.* mapaurong, paurungin, malabanan, tumanggi, tanggihan

Repellent *adj.* mawaksi, nagwawaksi

Repent *v.* magsisi, pagsisihan

Repentance *n.* pagsisisi

Repentant *adj.* nagsisisi

Repercussion *n.* alingawn-gaw, balik-bisa

Repercussive *adj.* maalin-gaw, umaalingawngaw

Repertoire *n.* repertoire, talatanghalan

Repertory *n.* repertoryo, katipunan, imbakan, kabangyaman

Repetition *n.* repitisyon, ulit

Repetitious *adj.* paulit-ulit

Repine *v.* dumaing, maghinaing

Replace *n.* isauli, iuli, palitan

Replacement *n.* palit, halili

Replant *v.* itanim uli

Replay *v.* tugtugin uli

Repletion *n.* kapunuan, kabusugan

Replica *n.* replika, sipi, kopya

Reply *n.* tugon, sagot

Reply *v.* tumugon, sumagot

Report *n.* sumbong, salaysay, ulat, report

Report *v.* mag-ulat, iulat, magsumbong, isumbong

Repose *n.* pahingalay, pahinga, kapayapaan, hinahon

Repose *v.* magpahingalay, nakalibing, mahiga

Reposeful *adj.* tahimik, maalwin

Repository *n.* lagakan, ingatan

Reprehend *v.* pagsabihan, bigyang-sala, punahin

Reprehension *n.* pagsasabi, mura, wika

Represent *v.* ipakilala, katawanin, kumatawan, sagisagin, magsagisag

Representation *n.* represent-asyon

Representive *n.* kinatawan

Repress *v.* magpigil, pigilin, supilin

Repression *n.* pagpipigil, pagsansala

Repressive *adj.* nagpipigil, mapagpigil

Reprieve *n.* palugit, tayong

Reprieve *v.* ipagpaliban, palugitan

Reprimand *n.* suat

Reprimand *v.* suatan, masuatan

Reprint *n.* muling limbag

Reprint *v.* muling ilimbag

Reprisal *n.* ganting-salakay, higanti

Reproach *n.* sisi, mura

Reproach *v.* sisihin, murahin

Reproachable *adj.* masisisi

Reproachless *adj.* walang-masisisi

Reprobate *adj.* imbi, balakyot

Reprobate *n.* masamang tao, balawis, salanggapang

Reprobate *v.* tanggihan, ayawan, kondenahin

Reproduce *v.* kopyahin, papagsuplingin, isalarawan, retratuhan

Reproduction *n.* reproduksiyon, pagpaparami, kopya, duplikado

Reproductive *adj.* reproduktibo

Reproof *n.* sisi, suat, mura

Reprove *v.* sumbatan, sisihin, suatan, murahin

Reptile *n.* reptil, ahas

Republic *n.* republika

Repudiate *v.* itakwil, iwaksi, itatwa

Repugnance *n.* kaayawan, kainisan, pangangani

Repugnant *adj.* nakaiinis, kaani-ani

Repulse *v.* mapaurong, paurungin, tanggihan

Repulsion *n.* pagpapaurong, pagkainis

Repulsive *adj.* nakaiinis

Reputable *adj.* itinatangi, kapuri-puri, palasak

Request *n.* pakiusap, hiling

Request *v.* makiusap, humiling, hilingin

Require *v.* hingin, hilingin, hingan, kunan

Requirement *n.* kailangan, kinakailangan, rikisito, kailangan

Requisition *n.* rikisisyon

Requisition *v.* magriksisyon

Rescript *n.* kabatasan, kautusan

Rescue *n.* pagtubos, pagsagip

Rescue *v.* iligtas, tubusin, sagipin

Research *n.* pananaliksik, pagsisiyasig, paniniyasig

Research *v.* magsaliksik, manaliksik

Researcher *n.* mananaliksik, tagasalksik

Resemble *v.* makatulad, makamukha

Resent *v.* isama ng loob, masamain, ikagalit

Reservation *n.* pataan, reserba, pareserba

Reserve *n.* reserba, timpi

Reserve *v.* ilaan, ireserba, itago, impukin

Reservoir *n.* tangke ng tubig, deposito

Reshape *v.* muling hugisan

Reside *v.* tumahan, manahanan

Residence *n.* residensiya, tirahan, tahanan, tinitirahan

Resident *n.* residente, ang nakatira, ang naninirahan

Residential *adj.* residensiyal

Residual *adj.* labi, latak

Residue *n.* labi

Resign *v.* magbitiw

Resignation *n.* pagbibitiw

Resilience *n.* kaelastikuhan

Resilient *n.* elastiko

Resin *n.* resina, sasahingin

Resinous *adj.* resinoso, sasahingin

Resist *v.* lumaban, labanan, salungatin, sumalungat

Resistance *n.* resistensiya

Resistant *adj.* resistente, sumasalungat, lumalaban

Resolute *adj.* yari ang loob

Resolution *n.* resolusyon, kapasiyahan, katatagan

Resolve *v.* magpasiya, ipasiya, ipasiya, lutasin

Resonance *n.* alalad

Resonant *adj.* maalalad, matunog

Resort *n.* bakasyunan, pook-aliwan

Resort *v.* pumuntang malimit, dumulog, dulugan

Resound *v.* tumunog

Resource *n.* pagka-maparaan, rekurso, pagkukunan, mapagkukunan

Resourceful *adj.* mapama-raan

Respect *n.* galang paggalang, pitagan, pamimitagan

Respect *v.* gumalang, igalang, pagpitaganan, mamitagan

Respectable *adj.* kagalang-galang

Respectful *adj.* magalang, mapamitagan

Respective *adj.* kani-kaniya, kani-kanila

Respiration *n.* paghinga, hininga

Respirator *n.* respirador, hingahan, pampahinga

Respiratory *n.* respiratoryo

Respire *v.* huminga, makahinga, makaasa uli

Respite *n.* paliban, pagpapaliban, sandaling tigil

Respite *v.* antalahin, ipagpaliban

Resplendence *n.* kaluning-ningan

Resplendent *adj.* makinang

Respond *v.* sumagot, sagutin, umayon, makiayon

Respondence *n.* sagot, tugon, pagsagot, pagtugon

Respondent *n.* respondiyente

Response *n.* sagot, tugon, pagsagot, pagtugon

Responsibility *n.* kapana-gutan, sagutin

Responsible *adj.* respons-able, maykapanagutan

Responsive *adj.* katugon, nakikiayon

Rest *n.* pahinga, pahingalay, patungan, tigil

Rest *n.* tira, labi, labis

Rest *v.* magpahinga, magpahingalay

Restaurant *n.* restauran

Restful *adj.* tahimik

Restitution *n.* pagsasauli, pagpapanumbalik, bayadpinsala

Restoration *n.* restorasyon, pananauli

Restore *v.* ibalik, iuli, isauli

Restrain *v.* paurungin, pigilin, supilin, higpitan

Restraint *n.* pagpipigil, pagtitimpi

Restrict *v.* hanggahan, higpitan

Restricted *adj.* limitado

Restriction *n.* restriksiyon, paghihigpit

Restrictive *adj.* nagbibigay-hanggahan

Result *v.* magbunga, bunga, bisa, ibunga, magbisa, magtapos

Resume *n.* buod, lagom

Resume *n.* simulan uli, magpatuloy

Resumption *n.* pagsisimula uli, pagpapatuloy

Resurge *v.* lumitaw uli

Resurgence *n.* muling paglitaw

Resurgent *adj.* muling lumilitaw

Resurrect *v.* mabalik sa buhay, muling ilabas

Resurrection *n.* resureksiyon

Resuscitate *v.* ibalik sa buhay, pahimasmasan

Ret *v.* ibabad

Retail *adj.* tingian

Retail *n.* tingi

Retain *v.* pumigil, tandaan, mamigil, magpanatili, itago

Retake *v.* mambawi, bawiin

Retaliate *v.* gumanti , maghiganti, paghigantihan

Retaliation *n.* retalyasyon, ganti, higanti

Retard *v.* pabagalin, papagbagalin, antalahin, hadlangan

Retardation *n.* kabagalan

Retention *n.* pamimigil

Retentive *adj.* matandain

Reticent *adj.* matimpi

Reticulate *adj.* parang lambat

Reticule *n.* suput-suputan

Retina *n.* retina, bilot ng mata

Retinitis *n.* retinitis

Retire *v.* umurong, mamahinga, magretiro, matulog

Retired *adj.* bukod, nag-lisa, retirado

Retirement *n.* retiro, pagurong

Retiring *adj.* mahiyain, mahinhin, matimpi

Retort *n.* pakli, balik-sabi

Retort *v.* ipakli, pagbalik-sabihan

Retouch *v.* ayusin, ritokihin

Retouching *n.* ritoke

Retrace *v.* magkuli, pagkulian, iurong, itakwil

Retractile *adj.* naiuarong

Retraction *n.* retraksiyon , pagbawi, pag-talikwas

Retread *v.* magritred, retredan

Retreat *n.* pag-urong, taguan

Retreat *v.* umurong, magretirada

Retrench *v.* magbawas, bumawas, bawasan, magtipid

Retrenchment *n.* pagbaba-was, pagtitipid

Retribution *n.* retribusyon, ganti

Retrieve *v.* muling makuha, mabawi

Retroactive *adj.* retroaktibo

Retrocede *v.* bumalik, umurong

Retrograde *adj.* paurong, pasama, pababa

Retrograde *v.* umurong, sumama, bumaba

Retrogress *v.* umurong

Retrogression *n.* pag-urong, pagbabalik sa dati, pagsama

Retrospect *n.* gunamhunam

Retrospect *v.* gunamgunamin

Return *n.* pagbabalik, pagsasauli

Return *v.* bumalik, magbalik, isauli, gumanti

Reunion *n.* reunyon

Reunite *v.* magsama uli, magkaisa uli

Revamp *v.* baguhin, magbagong-anyo

Reveal *v.* isiwalat, ipagtapat, ihayag, ibunyag

Reveille *n.* rebeli

Revel *n.* pagsasaya, pagpipista

Revel, *v.* magpistahan, magkasayahan

Revelation *n.* pagbubunyag, paghahayag

Revenge *n.* higanti, paghihiganti

Revenge *v.* maghiganti, paghigantihan

Revengeful *adj.* mapaghiganti

Revenue *n.* kita, pinagkakakitaan

Reverberate *v.* umalin-gawngaw

Revere *v.* pagpitaganan, sambahin

Reverence *n.* reberensiya, pamimitagan

Reverend *adj.* reberendo, kapita-pitagan

Reverent *adj.* mapitagan, magalang

Reverie *n.* salamisim, pangangarap

Reversal *n.* pagbabalik sa dati, pagbabaligtad

Reversible *adj.* baligtaran

Revert *v.* magbalik sa dati

Review *n.* muling pagsusuri, balik-aral, repaso

Review *v.* magsuri uli, magbalik-aral, pagbalik-aralan, repasuhin

Revile *v.* alimurahin, alipustain

Revilement *n.* pang-aalimura

Revise *v.* rebisahin, baguhin, iwasto

Revision *n.* rebisyon, pagwawasto

Revisit *v.* muling dalawin

Revitalization *n.* pagbabagung-buhay, pagmumulingsigla

Revitalize *v.* papagbagungbuhayin

Revival *n.* muling-buhay, pagmumuling-buhay

Revive *v.* muling buhayin

Revocable *adj.* mabawi, maiuurong

Revocation *n.* pagbawi, paguurong

Revoke *v.* bawiin, iurong

Revolt *n.* paghihimagsik, pagbabangon, pag-aalsa

Revolt *v.* maghimagsik, magbangon, mag-alsa

Revolting *adj.* nakaani, nakaririmarim

Revolution *n.* pag-inog, paghihimagsik

Revolutionize *v.* magbagunglubos

Revolve *v.* uminog, pagbulaybulayin

Revolver *n.* rebolber

Revulsion *n.* rebulsiyon

Reward *n.* gantimpala, premyo, pabuya

Reward *v.* gantimpalaan, premyuhan, pabuyaan

Rewind *v.* muling iikid

Rewrite *v.* sulatin

Rex *n.* hari

Rhapsody *n.* rasodya

Rheostat *n.* reostato

Rhetoric *n.* retorika, sayusay

Rheumatism *n.* reumatismo, reuma, rayuma

Rhinestone *n.* hiyas, puwit ng baso

Rhinitis *n.* rinisis, korisa, sipon

Rhinoceros *n.* rinoseros, rinoseronte

Rhinoscope *n.* rinoskopyo

Rhizocarpous *adj.* risokarpiyo

Rhizome *adj.* risoma

Rhodic *adj.* rodiko

Rhodium *n.* rodyo

Rhododendron *n.* rododendro

Rhodonite *n.* espato

Rhodonite *n.* rodora

Rhombus *n.* rombo

Rhubarb *n.* ruwibarbo

Rhyme *n.* rima, tugma

Rhyme *v.* tumula

Rhythm *n.* ritmo, indayog, ugmaan

Rhythmic *adj.* maindayog, maugma

Rhythmics *n.* agham pang-indayog

Rhythmist *n.* mangin-gindayog

Rib *n.* tadyang, kustilyas

Rib *v.* tadyangan, lokohin, biruin

Ribald *adj.* magaspang, malaswa

Ribaldry *n.* kalaswaan, kahalayan

Ribbon *n.* sintas, laso

Rice *n.* palay, bigas

Rich *adj.* mayaman, sagana, malasa, mataba

Rick *n.* mandala

Rickets *n.* rakitis

Rickety *adj.* giringgiring

Rid *v.* makaibis, maibsan, alisin, makalaya, palisin

Riddle *n.* bugtong, hiwaga, kababalaghan

Riddle *n.* bithay

Riddle *v.* magbithay, magtahip

Ride *n.* sakay, pagsakay

Ride *v.* sumakay, sakyan

Ridge *n.* balakang, tagaytay, tuktok, palupo

Ridicule *n.* kutya, pagkutya, tuya, pagtuya

Ridicule *v.* kutyain, tuyain

Ridiculous *n.* katawa-tawa, kakutya-kutya

Rife *adj.* laganap, palasak, sagana

Riffle *v.* magsuksok ng baraha, magbalasa

Rifle *n.* riple

Rifle *v.* halungkatin, halughugin

Rift *n.* bitak, lahang, hati

Rig *n.* ayos, kalayagan, karwahe

Rigadoon *n.* rigodon

Right *adj.* tumpak, wasto, dapat, kanan

Right *adj.* tuwiran, agad, pakanan

Right *n.* ang tama, ang wasto, katarungan, karapatan

Right *v.* ituwid, iwasto, itayo, ipaghiganti, ayusin, iayos

Righteous *adj.* makatarungan

Rightful *adj.* makatarungan

Rigid *adj.* matibay, maigting, matigas, mahigpit

Rigidity *n.* katibayan, katigasan, kahigpitan

Rigor *n.* kalupitan, kasungitan, paninigas

Rigorous *adj.* mahigpit, malupit, masungit

Rim *n.* gilid, labi, tabihan

Rind *n.* balat, pinagtalupan, upak, talupak

Ring *n.* singsing, ruweda, anilyo, buklod, ring

Ring *v.* tugtugin, tumaginting

Ring *v.* tumunog, tumugtog, patunugin, patugtugin

Ringleader *n.* pasimuno

Ringlet *n.* munting singsing

Ringworm *n.* kulebrilya, kulebrang-tubig

Rink *n.* rink, patinadero

Rinse *n.* magbanlaw, banlawan , anlawan

Riot *n.* kagulo, pagkakagulo

Riot *v.* magkagulo, manggulo, manligalig

Riotous *adj.* magulo, maligalig

Rip *v.* punitin, pilasin

Ripcord *n.* ripkord, kurdong hilahan

Ripe *adj.* magulang, hinog, pinagulang

Ripen *v.* mahinog, pahinugin

Ripeness *n.* kahinugan

Ripple *n.* saluysoy, lagasaw

Rise *v.* umahon, umakyat, mamaga, tumaas, lumaki, sumilang, bumasa, umabot

Risible *adj.* palatawa, nakakatawa

Risk *n.* riyesgo, panganib, sapalaran

Risky *adj.* mapanganib

Rite *n.* rito, seremonya

Ritual *n.* ritwal, seremonya

Rival *adj.* karibal, kaagaw, kaligsa

Rivalry *n.* pagriribalan, pagpapangagawan

Rive *v.* bakbakin, lansagin, biyakin

River *n.* ilog

Riverside *n.* tabing-ilog

Rivet *n.* rematse, silsil

Roach *n* ipis

Road *n.* daan, lansagan, kalye

Roadblock *n.* harang, halang

Roam *v.* gumala, magpagalagala

Roan *adj.* bayo, kastanyo

Roar *n.* atungal, angal, hiyaw, ungol, sigaw

Roar *v.* umatungal

Roast *v.* magbusa, litsunin, iihaw, ibangi, isangag

Roaster *n.* ihawan

Rob *v.* magnakaw, pagnakawan, nakawin

Robber *n.* magnanakaw

Robbery *n.* pagnanakaw

Robe *n.* bata, damit, toga, balabal, manta

Roborant *adj.* pampalakas

Robot *n.* robot

Robust *adj.* malusog, malakas, matipuno

Rock *n.* roka, bato

Rock *v.* iugoy, yanigin, giwangin

Rocket *n.* kuwitis, raket

Rocketry *n.* palarakitan

Rocking *adj.* umuugoy

Rocky *n.* mabato, batuhan

Rod *n.* baras, pamalo

Rodeo *n.* rodeo

Rodomontade *adj.* palalo, hambog

Rogation *n.* litanya, samo, luhog

Rogatory *adj.* sumasamo, lumuluhog

Rogue *n.* bagamundo, hampaslupa, mandaraya

Roguery *n.* kawalang-hiyaan

Roguish *adj.* walang-hiya

Role *n.* papel

Roll *n.* alon, gulong, rolyo, bilot, rodilyo, talaan, balumbon, listahan, lulon

Roll *v.* biluhin, pagulungin, balumbunin, ilulon, umalon

Roman *adj.* romano

Romance *n.* romansa

Romanesque *adj.* romanesko

Romanize *v.* romanisahin

Romantic *adj.* romantiko, romantika

Romanticism *n.* romantisismo

Rompish *adj.* malaro, maharot

Roof *n.* bubong, bubungan

Roofing *n.* atip

Rookie *n.* baguhan, singki, rekluta

Room *n.* kuwarto, silid

Roost *v.* hapunan, dapuan, pahingahan, humapon

Rooster *n.* tandang

Root *n.* ugat, sanhi, pinagmulan

Root *v.* lipulin

Rope *n.* lubid

Rosary *n.* rosaryo

Rose *n.* rosas

Roseate *adj.* rosado

Rosebay *n.* adelpa

Rosebud *n.* buko ng rosas

Rosebush *n.* rosal

Rosemary *n.* romero

Rosette *n.* roseta

Rosewater *n.* agwarosas

Rosewood *n.* palorosas

Rosin *n.* resina, kamanyang

Roster *n.* talaan, listahan

Rosy *adj.* rosado, kulay-rosas

Rot *v.* mabulok, masira

Rotary *adj.* umiinog, painog, rotatoryo, paikit

Rotate *v.* uminog, umikit, umikot

Rotation *n.* ikot, ikit, inog

Rotator *n.* pampainog

Rote *n.* ulit, rutina

Rotor *n.* rotor

Rotund *adj.* bilog, bilugan

Rotunda *n.* rotunda

Rouge *n.* kolorete

Rough *adj.* magaspang, bakubako, magalas, bastos

Rouse *v.* gisingin

Route *n.* daan, ruta

Row *n.* alitan, kagalitan, away, hanay, pila

Row *v.* gumaod, sumaguwan, saguwanan

Rub *v.* kuskusin

Rubber *n.* goma

Rubbish *n.* yagit, basura

Rude *adj.* bastos

Rug *n.* alpombra

Ruin *v.* iguho, wasakin

Rule *n.* tuntunin, alituntunin

Rule *v.* ipasiya, pamahalaan

Ruler *n.* puno, reglador

Rumor *n.* bulung-bulungan

Run *v.* itanan, tumakbo, umikot, magpalakad, mamahala

Rush *v.* madaliin, magmadali

Rust *v.* kalawangin

Rustic *adj* magaspang, simple, rural, pambukid

Rusticate *v.* mamukid

Rustle *n.* agaas, kaluskos

Rustle *v.* umagaas, kumaluskos, magnakaw

Rustle *v.* kumaluskos

Rustproof *adj.* hindi kina

Rusty *adj* maykalawang, kalawangin

Ruthless *adj.* malupit, walang-awa

Rye *n.* senteno, ray

Rythmical *adj.* maindayog, maugma

S s

Sabbath *n.* sabado

Saber *n.* sable

Sabotage *n.* sabotahe, pagpapahamak

Saboteur *n.* sabotyur

Sac *n.* suputan

Saccate *adj.* hugis-supot

Saccharate *n.* sakarato

Saccharine *n.* sakarina

Sachet *n.* satset

Sack *n.* sako, pagtatanggal, kustal, laggotse, sakeo, pagtitiwalang

Sacrament *n.* sakramento

Sacrarium *n.* sagrayo

Sacred *adj.* sagrado, banal, panrelihiyon

Sacrifice *n.* sakripisyo, pagpapakasakit, pagsasakripisyo

Sacrifice *v.* magsakripisyo, magpakasakit

Sacrilege *n.* sakrilehiyo, kalapastanganan

Sacrilegious *adj.* sakilego, mapaglapastangan

Sacristan *n.* sakristan

Sacristy *n.* sakristiya

Sacroliac *adj.* sakroliyako

Sacrosanct *adj.* sakrosanto

Sacrum *n.* sakro

Sad *adj.* nalulungkot, malungkot, malumbay

Sadden *adj.* malungkot

Saddle *n.* siya

Saddle *v.* siyahan

Saddlebag *n.* alporahas, kabalyas

Sadism *n.* sadismo

Sadist *n.* sadista

Sadistic *adj.* sadistika

Safari *n.* sapari

Safe *adj.* walang-panganib, ligtas

Safe *n.* kabang bakal

Safeguard *n.* pangangalaga

Saferon *n.* asapran

Safety *n.* kawalang-panga-nib, kaligtasan sa panganib

Safety belt timbulan, salbabida

Sag *v.* lumaylay, humabyog, lumuyloy, lumawit, lumundo, yumutyot

Saga *n.* saga

Sagacious *adj.* matalas, matalino, maalam

Sagacity *n.* katalasan

Sage *adj.* paham, pantas

Sage *n.* paham

Sagitarious *n.* sahitaryus, mamamana

Sail *n.* layag, bela

Sail *v.* lumayag, maglayag

Sailboat *n.* batel, paraw

Sailor *n.* marino, mandaragat

Saint *n.* santo

Saintly *adj.* banal

Sake *n.* layunin, kapakanan

Salable *adj.* maipagbibili

Salad *n.* insalada, ensalada

Saladious *adj.* mahalay

Salami *n.* salami

Salary *n.* suweldo, sahod, kita, upa

Sale *n.* pagbibili, benta

Salesman *n.* despatsador

Salesmanship *n.* galing magbili

Salient *adj.* nakaungos, nakatungki, lanted

Saline *adj.* may-asin

Saliva *n.* laway

Salivate *v.* maglaway

Salivation *n.* paglalaway

Sallow *adj.* manilaw-nilaw, barak

Sally *n.* pagluwal, pagbitak

Salmon *n.* salmon

Salon *n.* bulwagan, salon

Salt *n.* asin

Salt *v.* asnan

Salted *adj.* inasnan

Salter *n.* salero, asinan

Salutary *adj.* nakapagpapagaling

Salutation *n.* bigay-galang, bati, bating pambungad

Salute *n.* saludo, pagsaludo, pagpupugay

Salute *v.* sumaludo, saluduhan, magpugay, pagpugayan

Salvable *adj.* maisasalba, maililihtas

Salvage *n.* salba, sagip

Salvation *n.* kaligtasan, katubusan, pagkatubos

Salve *n.* ungguwento, pamahid, panlunas, pampaginhawa

Salve *v.* paginhawahan, lunasan

Salver *n.* bandeha

Salvo *n.* pasalba

Samaritan *adj.* samaritano

Same *adj.* kapareho , kapantey, katumbas

Sample *n.* muwestra, pakita, patikim, halimbawa

Sanative *adj.* nakagagamit, nakalulunas

Sanatorium *n.* sanatoryo

Sanctification *n.* santipikasyon

Sanctity *n.* santidad, kasantuhan

Sanctuary *n.* santuwaryo

Sanctus *n.* santos

Sand *n.* buhangin

Sand *v.* lihahin

Sandal *n.* sandalyas

Sandalwood *n.* sandalo

Sandpaper *n.* liha

Sandstone *n.* batubuhangin

Sandwich *n.* sandwich, emparedado, sanwits

Sandy *adj.* mabuhangin

Sane *adj.* matino, maalam

Sanguine *adj.* palaasa, maasahin

Sanitarium *n.* sanatoryo

Sanitary *adj.* sanitaryo, malinis

Sanitary *n.* sanitaryo, malinis

Sanitation *n.* kalinisan

Sanity *n.* katinuan

Sanskrit *n.* sanskrito

Sap *n.* gunggong, uslak, katas

Sap *v.* katasan

Sapling *n.* batang puno, binatilyo

Saponaceous *adj.* malasabon, madulas

Saponification *n.* pagiginsabon

Sapphire *n.* sapiro

Sarcasm *n.* tuya, uyam

Sarcastic *adj.* mapanuya

Sarcastic *n.* nanunuya, nang-uuyam

Sardine *n.* sardinas

Sardonic *adj.* mapanlibak, mapang-aglahi, mapanuya

Sardonyx *n.* sardonise

Sargasso *n.* sargaso

Sarsaparilla *n.* sarsaparilya

Sartorial *adj.* sartoryo

Sash *n.* baskagan, kuwadro, bigkis

Satan *n.* satanas, lusiper

Satchel *n.* maletin

Sate *v.* busugin

Satellite *n.* satelite, kasamang buntala

Satiate *v.* busugin, suyain, bundatin

Satire *n.* tuya, uyam

Satiric *adj.* nanunuya, nanguuyam, satiriko

Satisfaction *n.* kasiyahan

Satisfactory *adj.* kasiya-siya

Satisfied *adj.* nasisiyahan, satispetso

Satisfy *v.* bigyang-kasiyahan

Saturate *v.* mamarin, pagtain, tigmakin, saturahin

Saturated *adj.* mamad, pigta, tigmak, saturado

Saturation *n.* pagkamamad, kapigtaan, katigmakan, saturasyon

Saturday *n.* sabado

Saturn *n.* saturno

Sauce *n.* sarsa, sawsawan

Saucepan *n.* kasirolang munti

Saucer *n.* platito, platilyo

Sauciness *n.* kapangahasan

Saucy *adj.* pangahas

Sausage *n.* longgonisa, salsitsas, embutido, batutay, soriso

Saute *adj.* pritos

Savage *adj.* mabangis, mabalasik

Savage *n.* ligaw, mabangis, labuyo, disibilisado, mabagsik

Savagery *n.* kabarbaruhan, barbarismo, kabagsikan

Savanna *n.* sabana, kapatagan

Savant *n.* pantas, paham

Save *prep.* matangi

Save *v.* ilaan, iligtas, ingatan, itaan, magtipid, sagipin, tubusin, tipirin

Savings *n.* natitipid, naiimpok

Saviour *n.* manliligtas, tagapagligtas, manunubos

Savor *n.* lasa, linamnam, sarap

Savor *v.* bigyang-lasa, sarapan, masarapan

Savory *adj.* malasa, malinamnam, masarap

Saw *n.* kasabihan, sawikain, salawikain

Saw *n.* lagari, lagariin, maglagari

Sawdust *n.* aserin, kusot, pinaglagarian

Sawmill *n.* lagarian

Sawyer *n.* tagalagari

Saxhorn *n.* bombardino

Saxon *n.* sahon

Saxophone *n.* saksopon

Say *n.* sabi

Say *v.* bigkasin, bumigkas, magsabi, sabihin, magpahayag, magsalita ipahayag, salitain

Scab *n.* langib, eskirol

Scab *v.* maglangib, mag-iskirol

Scabbard *n.* kaluban, bayna

Scabbies *n.* galis

Scabby *adj.* malangib

Scabrous *adj.* maligagas, makaliskis, hirap

Scads *n.* salapi, tusak

Scald *n.* banli, paso, paltos

Scald *v.* banlian, mabanlian

Scale *n.* plato, platilyo, balansa, gatla, timbangan, iskala

Scale *v.* antasan, graduhan, kaliskisan, talupan, magtutong, magkulili, sukatin

Scalebeam *n.* astil

Scaleboard *n.* reglador

Scallop *n.* kabibi

Scalp *n.* anit

Scalp *v.* anitan

Scan *v.* siglawan, bigkasin ayon sa

Scandal *n.* iskandalo, alingasngas

Scandalous *adj.* iskandaloso

Scandinavian *n.* eskandinabo

Scant *adj.* kakaunti, di-sapat

Scantiness *n.* kauntian, kakulangan

Scanty *adj.* katiting, kakarampot

Scaper *n.* magtatakbo

Scapula *n.* paypay

Scapular *n.* eskapularyo

Scar *n.* pilat, piklat

Scar *v.* magpilat, magpeklat

Scarce *adj.* makita, kakaunti, bihira, madalang, mahirap

Scarcity *n.* kabihiraan, kadalangan

Scare *n.* takot, sindak

Scare *v.* takutin, sindakin

Scarf *n.* bupanda, bandana

Scarfication *n.* kadlit

Scarlatina *n.* iskarlatina

Scarlet *n.* iskarlata

Scathe *v.* pinsalain, saktan, pasuin, sunugin

Scatter *v.* ipamudmod, isabog, mangalat, manabog, lumaganap, ikalat

Scavenger *n.* basurero

Scenario *n.* isinaryo, dulang pansine

Scene *n.* esena, paysahe, tagpo, tagpuan, tanawin, bista

Scenery *n.* tanawin, bista, paysahe

Scenographer *n.* esenograpo

Scent *n.* amoy, bango

Scepter *n.* setro

Schedule *n.* oraryo, listahan, talaan, talatakdaan

Schedule *v.* itakda

Scheme *n.* plano, balak, intriga, palatuntunan, pamamaraan

Scheme *v.* magbalak, magplano

Scholar *n.* estudyante, magaaral, iskolar

School *n.* kawan ng isda

School *n.* paaralan, eskuwelahan, iskul

School *v.* magkawan-kawan

School *v.* magturo, turuan, turo

Science *n.* siyensiya, agham

Scientfic *adj.* pang-agham, makaagham, maagham, siyentipiko

Scientist *n.* taong-agham, siyentipiko

Scimitar *n.* simitar

Scion *n.* supling, supang

Scirrhus *n.* siro

Scission *n.* paggupit

Scissor *v.* gupitin, guntingin

Scissors *n.* gunting, panggupit

Scissure *n.* pagkaputol

Scleroma *n.* iskleroma

Sclerosis *n.* isklerosis

Sclerotic *adj.* matigas, isklerotiko

Sclerous *adj.* iskleroso, naninigas

Scoff *n.* libak, libakin, aglahiin, aglahi, kutya, kutyain, manlibak

Scold *n.* taong mapagmura

Scold *v.* alimurahin, magmura, murahin, kagalitan, pagsabihan, manisi, sisihin

Sconce *n.* kandelabro, kuta, bubong, multa

Scoop *n.* sandok, pagsandok, labak, iskup, panandok, panghukay, pansirok, pampala

Scoop *v.* sandukin, sirukin, maiskupan

Scoot *v.* sumibad, scoot, alis, layas

Scooter *n.* iskuter, panibad

Scope *n.* abot, lawak, saklaw

Scorch *v.* dangdangin, dagandangin, puksain, lipulin

Score *n.* tanda, puntos, paya, katotohanan, dahilan, iskor

Score *v.* guhitan, itala, kudlitan, makamit, pumaya, payahan

Scorn *n.* panghahamak, panlilibak, upasala

Scorn *v.* manghamak, manlibak, mandusta

Scorpio *n.* eskorpiyon, alakdan

Scorpion *n.* alakdan, pitumbuko

Scot *n.* eskoses, tasa, tasasyon, buwis, multa

Scotch *n.* eskoses, matipid, kuripot

Scoundrel *n.* taong-imbi

Scour *v.* galugarin, gaygayin, kuskusin, kudkurin

Scourage *n.* latiko, palo, parusa

Scourage *v.* latikuhin, parusahan, paluin

Scout *n.* iskaut, pag-iiskaut, pagmamatyag

Scout *v.* maghanap, magsaliksik

Scow *n.* gabara

Scowl *n.* simangot

Scowl *v.* sumimangot

Scrabble *v.* kalmutin, galmusin

Scragy *adj.* payagod, yayang

Scramble *v.* mangunyapit, makipagpangagawan, haluin, ikalatkat

Scrap *adj.* patapon

Scrap *n.* piraso, kapyangot, iskrap

Scrap *v.* itapon, pagpirapirasuhin

Scrape *v.* kaskasin, magkayod, kayurin

Scraper *n.* pangkayod, kayuran

Scratch *n.* kamot, kalmot, galmos

Scratch *v.* kamutin, himasin, kalmutin, galmusin

Scrawl *v.* gumuri, magguri, gurihan

Scrawny *adj.* payagod, payangod, butuhan

Scream *n.* tili, sigaw

Scream *v.* tumili, magtitili

Screech *v.* humiyaw

Screen *n.* tabing, kurtina

Screen *v.* tabingan, kurtinahan, maghirang, mamili

Screw *n.* turnilyo

Screw *v.* turnilyuhan

Screwdriver *n.* disturnilyador

Screwy *adj.* kakatwa, hibang

Scribble *v.* magguguri

Scribe *n.* eskribyente, manunulat, mamamahayag

Scrimmage *n.* labulabo

Scrip *n.* sertipiko, iskrip

Script *n.* iskrip, manuskrito

Scripture *n.* bibliya, biblia

Scroll *n.* sulat

Scrub *v.* kuskusin, kusutin

Scruple *n.* atubili

Scrupulous *adj.* matubili, maulik-ulik

Scrutiny *n.* masusing pagsisiyasat

Scuffle *n.* babagan, panunggaban

Sculptor *n.* eskultor, manlililok

Sculture *n.* eskultura, panlililok

Scum *n.* linab, espuma, halagap, halipawpaw

Scummy *adj.* malinab, mahalagap

Scurf *n.* balayubay

Scurry *v.* magkumamot, magmadali

Scurvy *n.* iskurbuto

Scutch *v.* humagot, maghagot, hagutin

Scuttle *n.* butas, eskutilyon

Scythe *n.* karit, lilik

Sea *n.* dagat

Sea horse *n.* kabayong-dagat

Sea lion *n.* leong-dagat

Seal *n.* poka

Seal *n.* selyador, panatak, tatak, selyo

Seal *v.* takpan, tatakan, selyuhan, sarhan, pasakan

Seam *n.* tutop, hugpong, tahi

Seaman *n.* mandaragat, marinero

Sear *adj.* tuyo, lanta, kuluntoy

Sear *n.* hero, paso

Sear *v.* pasuin, heruhan, malanta, mangalirang, manguluntoy

Search *n.* paghahanap, pagsisiyasat, paghalungkat, saliksik

Search *v.* maghanap, hanapin, siyasatin, halungkatin

Searchlight *n.* prodyektor

Season *n.* panahon, kapanahunan

Season *v.* sarapan, rekaduhan, palabukan

Seasonal *adj.* pana-panahon

Seasoning *n.* rekado, palabok, kahinugan

Seat *n.* upuan

Seat *v.* iupo, iluklok

Seaweed *n.* gulaman

Sebaceous *adj.* masebo

Sebum *n.* sebo

Secco *n.* alseko

Secede *v.* tumiwalag, humiwalay

Seceder *n.* separatista

Secession *n.* sesesyon, pagtiwalag, paghiwalay

Seclude *v.* ibukod, ihiwalay

Secluded *adj.* hiwalay, malayo

Seclusion *n.* seklusyon, pagkabukod

Second *adj.* sigundo, sandali, saglit, pangalawa

Second *v.* pumangalawa, pangalawahan, itaguyod

Secondary *adj.* pampangalawa, sekundaryo

Secondhand *adj.* segunda-mano

Secrecy *n.* pagiging lihim

Secret *adj.* lihim, sekreto, tago

Secretary *n.* kalihim, sekretaryo, sekretarya

Secrete *v.* magsekresyon

Secretion *n.* sekresyon

Secretive *adj.* malihim, mapaglihim

Sect *n.* sekta

Sectarian *adj.* sektaryo

Sectile *adj.* sektil

Section *n.* seksiyon, pangkat, bahagi, tuntunin

Sectionalism *n.* seksiyuna-lismo

Sector *n.* sektor

Secular *adj.* sekular, seglar, sibil

Secularism *n.* sekularismo

Secularist *n.* sekularista

Secularize *v.* sekularisahin

Secure *adj.* panatag, tiwasay, lamikmik, matatag

Secure *v.* kumuha, pangalagaan, iseguro, garantiyahan, tibayan, matamo, tamuhin

Security *n.* katiwasayan, kapanatagan, proteksiyon, panagot

Sedan *n.* sedan

Sedantry *adj.* paupo, nakaupo, nakatigil, nakahimpil

Sedate *adj.* walang-balino, tahimik, mahinahon

Sedative *adj.* sedatibo, pampakalma, pampaginhawa

Sediment *n.* latak, tining

Seditious *adj.* sedisyoso

Sedtion *n.* sedisyon , paglataksil

Seduce *v.* rahuyuin, hibuin

Seduction *n.* panrarahuyo, panghihibo

Seductiveness *n.* pagkana-karararahuyo

Seductress *n.* babaing mapanrahuyo

Sedulous *adj.* masigsa, masigasig

See *n.* sede

See *v.* makita, manood, maunawaan, tingnan, panoorin, tanawin, masdan

See-saw *n.* salabawan, siso

Seed *n.* butil, buto, binhi

Seedling *n.* punla

Seedy *adj.* mabuto

Seek *v.* maghanap, hanapin, dumulog, magtanong

Seem *v.* tila, animo, wari, para

Seep *v.* tumagas, kumayat

Seepage *n.* tagas, saimsim, talaytay

Seer *n.* manghuhula, propeta

Seethe *v.* kumulo, sumulak, sumilakbo

Segment *n.* bahagi, seksiyon, segmento

Segmentation *n.* segmenta-syon

Segregate *v.* ibukod, ihiwalay, piliin, hirangin

Segregated *adj.* nakabukod

Segregation *n.* pagbubukod

Seism *n.* lindol

Seismology *n.* sismolohiya

Seize *v.* agawin, sunggaban, samantalahin, daklutin, samsamin, dakpin

Seldom *adj.* bihira

Select *adj.* pili, hirang, tangi

Select *v.* pumili, humirang, piliin, hirangin

Selection *n.* pagpili, pamimili, paghirang

Selective *adj.* namimili, mapamili

Self *adj.* sarili, pansarili

Selfish *adj.* maramot, sakim, makasarili

Sell *v.* magbili, ipagbili

Semantic *adj.* semantika

Semblance *n.* wangis

Semen *n.* tamud

Semester *n.* semestre, hatingtaon

Semestral *adj.* semestral

Semi *pref.* medyo, hati, mala

Semicircle *n.* hating-bilog

Semicolon *n.* puntukoma, tuldukuwit

Semifinal *adj.* bago magtapos

Seminar *n.* seminar

Seminarian *n.* seminarista

Seminary *n.* seminaryo

Semite *n.* semita

Semitic *adj.* semitiko

Semivowel *n.* malapatinig

Senate *n.* senado

Senator *adj.* senador

Send *v.* magpadala, ipadala

Senile *adj.* ulianin, senil

Senior *adj.* nakatatanda, sinyor, ama

Seniority *n.* kaunahan, karapat-mauna, katandaan

Sensation *n.* pakiramdam

Sensational *adj.* sensasyonal

Sensationalism *n.* sensasyonalismo

Sense *n.* pakiramdam, sintido, pandama, damdam, talino

Sense *v.* makaramdam, maramdaman, mapakiramdaman, maunawaan

Sensibility *n.* talas ng pakiramdam, sensibilidad

Sensitive *adj.* sensitibo, napakamaramdamin

Sensitize *v.* sensitisahin

Sensory *adj.* sensoryo

Senssible *adj.* maramdamin, matalino

Sensual *adj.* makalaman, malibog

Sentence *n.* palagay, kurukuro, pasiya, hatol

Sentence *v.* sentensiyahan

Sententious *adj.* malaman, mapangaral

Sentience *n.* malay, kamalayan

Sentient *adj.* nakadarama

Sentiment *n.* damdamin, sintimyento, palagay, kurukuro

Sentimental *adj.* sentimental

Sentimentalism *n.* sentimentalismo

Sentinel *n.* taliba, tanod, bantay, guwardiya

Sepal *n.* salundahon, seplalo

Separable *adj.* maihihiwalay

Separate *adj.* hiwalay, bukod

Separate *v.* ihiwalay, ibukod, ilayo, pagbukurin

Separation *n.* paghihiwalay, paglalayo

Separatist *n.* separatists

Separator *n.* panghiwalay

Sepsis *n.* sepsis

September *n.* septiyembre, setyembre

Septet *n.* septeto, pituhan

Septic *adj.* septiko

Septicemia *n.* septisemya

Septum *n.* septum

Sepulcher *n.* sepulkro, nitso

Sequacious *adj.* mapanunod, lohikal

Sequel *n.* sekwela, karugtong

Sequence *n.* pagkakasunudsunod, kapanunuran

Sequent *adj.* kasunod, karugtong, bunga

Sequester *v.* ibukod, ihiwalay, paglayuin

Sequin *n.* sekin

Seraglio *n.* harem

Seraph *n.* serapin

Serb *adj.* serbiyo

Serbian *adj.* serbiyo

Serenade *n.* serenata

Serenade *v.* mangharana, haranahin

Serenata *n.* serenata

Serene *adj.* maaliwalas, maliwanag, mahinahon, tiwasay

Serenity *n.* katiwasayan, kahinahunan

Serf *n.* alipin, busabos

Serfdom *n.* kaalipnan

Sergeant *n.* serhento

Serial *adj.* dugtung-dugtong

Sericeous *adj.* sutlain, malasulta, mabulo

Sericulture *n.* pagsusutla, panunutla

Series *n.* serye, kabit-kabit

Serious *adj.* seryo, malubha, mapanganib, pormal, taimtim, mabigat

Sermon *n.* sermon, aral, pangaral

Sermonize *v.* magsermon, pagsermunan, mangaral, pangaralan

Serous *adj.* malabnaw

Serpent *n.* serpiyente, ahas

Serpentine *adj.* malaahas

Serum *n.* suwero

Servant *n.* alila, katulong, utusan

Serve *v.* maglingkod, magsilbi, magamit

Server *n.* serbidor, tagasilbi, bandeha

Service *n.* serbisyo, paglilingkod

Serviceable *adj.* makapag-lilingkod, magagamit, mapakikinabangan, matibay

Serviette *n.* serbilyeta

Servile *adj.* serbil, mapangayupapa

Servitor *n.* serbidor, tagapagsilbi, katulong

Servitude *n.* kaalipnan, kabusabusan

Sesame *n.* sesame, linga

Session *n.* sesyon, pulong

Set *adj.* tiyak, nakatakda, sadya, nakakabit

Set *n.* direksiyon, paninigas, pangkat, lote, terno, tigas, tikas, porma

Set *v.* iupo, ilipat, itakda, paupuin, pahalimhimin, ilagay

Setting *n.* paglubog, esena, tagpo, paghalimhim

Settle *v.* ilagay, mamahay, ipuwesto, patauhan, patirahan

Settlement *n.* kumunidad, kasunduan, pamayanan, panirahan, pagaayos

Seven *adj.* pito

Sevenfold *adj.* makapitong ibayo

Sevenfold *adv.* makapitong ibayo

Seventeen *adj.* labimpito

Seventh *adj.* ikapito

Seventy *adj.* pitumpu

Sever *v.* tagpasin, biyakin, putulin, tanggalin

Several *adj.* iba-iba, ilan

Severe *adj.* mahigpit, malubha, malupit

Severity *n.* kahigpitan, kalubhaan, kasimplihan

Sew *v.* manahi, tahiin

Sewage *n.* dumi ng tuberiyas

Sewer *n.* mananahi

Sewerage *n.* sistema ng tuberiyas

Sewing *n.* pananahi, pagtahi, tinahi, tahiin

Sex *n.* sekso, tauhin, kasarian

Sexless *adj.* walang-sekso

Sexologist *n.* seksologo

Sexology *n.* seksolohiya

Sextant *n.* sektante

Sexton *n.* sakristan mayor

Sexual *adj.* seksuwal, pansekso

Shabby *adj.* nasnas, nisnis, nutnot, gasgas

Shabbyness *n.* panlilimahid

Shack *n.* barungbarong, kubo, dampa

Shackle *n.* posas

Shackle *v.* posasan, tanikalaan, hadlangan, sagkaan

Shade *n.* lilim, silungan

Shade *v.* , liliman, diliman, sombrahan

Shading *n.* sombra

Shadow *n.* anino

Shadow *v.* liliman, dimlan, sombrahan

Shady *adj.* malilim, madilim

Shaft *n.* poste, ehe, sibat, tandos, tikin, tagdan

Shaggy *adj.* buhukan, balahibuhin

Shake *v.* ipagpag, ugain, iuga, yugyugin, umuga, mangatog

Shaker *n.* alugan, kalugan, ig-igan, pikpikan

Shaking *n.* pangangatal, pangangatog

Shaky *adj.* umuuga, nangangatog, mabuway, kalog, umalog

Shale *n.* iskisto

Shallow *adj.* mababaw

Shallowness *n.* kababawan, pagkamababaw

Sham *adj.* palso, di-tunay, paimbabaw

Sham *n.* kunwa, kunwari, imitasyon, huwad

Shamble *n.* , matadero

Shame *n.* hiya, kahihiyan, pagkahiya

Shame *v.* hiyain

Shameful *adj.* nakakahiya, mahalay

Shameless *adj.* walang-hiya

Shamols *n.* gamusa

Shampoo *n.* panggugo, siyampu

Shampoo *v.* magsiyampu, maggugo

Shamrock *n.* tripolyo

Shank *n.* asta, binti, hawakan, lulod, pata, puluhan, manggo

Shanty *n.* dampa, kubo

Shape *n.* hugis, anyo, hubog, tabas

Shape *v.* hugisan, hubugin, kortehan, tabasan

Shapeless *adj.* walang-hugis, walang-porma

Shapely *adj.* mabuting pagkakahugis, timbang-hubog

Share *n.* aksiyon, bahagi, kabahagi, parti, kaparti, sama

Share *v.* bahaginin, makiparti, makisalo, makisama, makibahagi

Shareholder *n.* aksiyunista, kasosyo

Shark *n.* pating

Sharp *adj.* matalim, matalas, matilos, mahayap, nakahihiwa

Sharpen *v.* ihasa, ilagis, itagis, patalimin, taliman, patalasin, talasan

Sharpener *n.* pataliman, patalasan, hasaan, lagisan, tagisan

Sharpnel *n.* granada-metralya

Shatter *v.* durugin, basagin, gibain, manabog, sirain

Shave *n.* ahit, pag-ahit

Shave *v.* mag-ahit, ahitin, ahitan

Shaver *n.* binatilyo, bata

Shaving *adj.* pang-ahit, pag-aahit

Shawl *n.* manton, panyulon

She *pron.* siya

Sheaf *n.* tungkos

Shear *v.* manggupit, gupitin , tabsan

Shears *n.* panggupit

Sheath *n.* kaluban, sapot, saklo, bayna, punda, balok

Sheathe *v.* isalong, isuksok, isuot

Shed *n.* pinaglunuhan

Shed *n.* habong, silungan

Shed *v.* magluno, maghunos, magbuhos, ibuhos

Shedder *n.* ang nagluluno, ang naghuhunos

Sheen *n.* ningning, kintab

Sheep *n.* tupa, karnero, obeha, kordero

Sheepish *adj.* malatupa, maamo

Sheepskin *n.* balat ng tupa

Sheepwalk *n.* pastulan ng tupa

Sheer *adj.* dalisay, puro , matarik

Sheer *n.* pagsinsay, paglihis, tangwa, gilid

Sheer *v.* suminsay, lumihis

Sheet *n.* kumot, oha, pliego, kubrekama, pohas, dahon

Sheeting *n.* balot, pagpipliego, pagpopohas

Sheik *n.* heke

Shelf *n.* istante, pitak, aparador

Shell *n.* kabibi, kontsa

Shell *v.* maghimay, himayin, magtalop, talupan

Shelter *n.* tanggulan, taguan, ampunan, silungan

Shelter *v.* ampunin, kupkupin, sumilong, magkubli

Shelve *v.* bimbinin, itiwalag

Shepherd *n.* pastol

Sheriff *n.* serip

Sherry *n.* alak jerez

Shibboleth *n.* bansag, lema, sabihin, wikain

Shield *n.* eskudo, kalasag, panangga

Shield *v.* ikubli, ikanlong

Shift *n.* pagpupumilit, turno, lipat, punyagi, paraan, pagbibihis

Shift *v.* magbago, pagpalitpalitin, ipasa

Shimmer *n.* andap, diklap, kurap, kisap, kislap

Shin *n.* lulod

Shindig *n.* sayawan

Shine *n.* iluminasyon, kinang, kintab, kislap, ningning

Shine *v.* bantog, sumikat, magliwanag, kuminang, magningning

Shingle *n.* karatula, tahamanil

Shinny *adj.* makintab, makinang

Ship *n.* sasakyangdagat, buke, barko, bapor

Ship *v.* ilulan sa bapor, ipadala

Shirk *v.* umilag, umiwas

Shirt *n.* kamisadentro

Shiver *v.* manginig, mangatal, mangatog, mangaligkig

Shoal *n.* babaw

Shoat *n.* kulig, bulaw, biik

Shock *adj.* buhukan, balahibuhin

Shock *n.* dagok, gulat, pagkagulat, tagupak, bangga, yanig

Shock *v.* mabigla, takutin, matakot, gitlahin, magitla, sindakin

Shocking *adj.* nakasisindak, nakagagalit

Shoddy *adj.* kinanyamaso, bulastog

Shoddy *n.* balindang, kanyamaso, kabulastugan

Shoe *n.* sapatos

Shoemaker *n.* sapatero

Shoemaking *n.* sapateriya

Shoot *n.* tubo, usbong, talbos, buko, suloy, supling, supang

Shoot *v.* bumaril, panain, mamana, mamaril, barilin, tudlain

Shooting *n.* pamamaril, pamamana, panunudla, putok, siyuting

Shop *n.* gawaan, pagawaan, talyer, tindahan

Shop *v.* manindahan, mamili

Shore *n.* baybayin, baybaydagat, pampang

Short *adj.* maikli, maigsi, mababa, pandak

Shortage *n.* kakulangan

Shortcoming *n.* pagkukulang, kapintasan

Shorten *v.* paikliin, paigsiin

Shorthand *n.* takigrapiya, iklilat

Shortness *n.* kaigsian, kaiklian

Shot *n.* punglo, perdigones

Shotgun *n.* eskopeta, riple, baril

Should *v.* dapat, nararapat

Shoulder *n.* balikat, tabihan

Shoulder *v.* balikatin, isabalikat

Shout *v.* sumigaw, humiyaw

Shove *n.* tulak, sulong

Shove *v.* itulak, isulong

Shovel *n.* pala

Shovel *v.* magpala, palahin

Show *n.* ipakita, ipaalam, ipatalos, itanghal, ituro, magpakita, magpamalas

Show *n.* pakita, pamalas, palabas, pagtatanghal

Showcase *n.* mustrador, eskaparate

Showdown *n.* harapan

Shower *n.* ambon , regaluhan

Shower *v.* umanbon, paulanan

Showman *n.* impresaryo

Showroom *n.* silid-mustrador

Shred *n.* pilas, gutay, kapiraso, katiting

Shred *v.* gutayin, pilasin

Shredder *n.* pampilas, pamilas

Shrew *n.* babaing matangas

Shrewd *adj.* maalam, matalas, matalino, tuso

Shrewish *adj.* matangas

Shriek *n.* tili, irit, hiyaw

Shriek *v.* tumili, umirit, humiyaw

Shrift *n.* kumpisal, kompesyon, pagbubunyag

Shrill *adj.* matinis

Shrimp *n.* hipon, taong marawal, kulanta

Shrine *n.* dambana, altar

Shrine *v.* idambana

Shrink *v.* mangayupapa, yumukod, mangurong, umudlot

Shrinkable *adj.* mapangun-gurong

Shrinkage *n.* pangungurong

Shrive *v.* mangumpisal, kumpisalim

Shrivel *v.* mangulubot, manguluntoy

Shroud *n.* sapot

Shroud *v.* saputan, balutan

Shrub *n.* palumpong

Shrug *v.* magkibit, ikibit

Shrunken *adj.* mangurong

Shuck *n.* balat, bunot

Shudder *v.* manginig, mangatog, mangatal

Shuffle *v.* balasahin, magbalasa

Shuffleboard *n.* salisuran, pasalisuran

Shuffler *n.* tagabalasa, pagsuksok, pagsasalisod

Shun *v.* ilagan, iwasan, layuan

Shunt *v.* ilipat, ibaling, ihabi, patayin

Shuot *n.* sigaw, hiway

Shut *adj.* sarado, pinid

Shut *v.* isara, itiklop, sarhan, magsara, ipinid

Shutter *n.* persiyana

Shuttle *n.* lansadera

Shuttlecock *n.* bolang maypakpak

Shy *adj.* mahiyain, kimi

Shyness *n.* pagkamahiyain, kakimian, pagkakimi

Siamese *adj.* siyames

Sibilant *adj.* pahingasing, pasutsot, pasingasing

Sibilate *v.* humingasing, sumingasing, sumutsot

Sibyl *n.* propetisa, manghuhula

Siccative *adj.* sekante, pantuyo

Sick *adj.* mayasakit, maykaramdaman

Sickening *adj.* nakapagbibigay-sakit

Sickle *n.* lilik, karit

Sickly *adj.* masasaktin

Sickness *n.* sakit, karamdaman

Side *n.* ayon, tabi, gilid, tagiliran, panig

Side *v.* pumanig, kumampi, panigan, kampihan, katigan

Sidelong *adj.* patagilid, patago

Sidelong *adv.* patagilid, patago

Sidetrack *n.* sinsayan

Sidewalk *n.* bangketa

Sideways *adv.* patagilid

Siege *n.* pagkubkob

Siege *v.* kubkubin

Sieve *n.* bithay, bistay, salaan, panala

Sieve *v.* magbithay, magbistay

Sigh *n.* buntunghinga, hinagpis

Sigh *v.* magbuntunghininga, maghinagpis

Sight *n.* tanawin, panoorin, paningin, pakita, tanaw

Sight *v.* makita, matingnan, matanaw, masdan

Sightless *adj.* walang paningin, bulag

Sightseeing *n.* paglilibot-panood

Sign *n.* tanda, karatula, sintomas, lagda, marka, hudyat, senyas

Sign *v.* markahan, hudyatan, lumagda, lagdaan, humudyat

Signal *adj.* kapansin-pansin, namumukod

Signal *n.* senyas, hudyat, senyal

Signal *v.* sumenyas, humudyat, sumenyal

Signalman *n.* tagahudyat

Signatory *n.* signatoryo

Signature *n.* lagda, pirma

Signboard *n.* karatula

Signet *n.* selyo, tatak

Significance *n.* kahulugan, kahalagahan, kabuluhan

Significant *adj.* makahulugan, mahalaga

Signify *v.* isenyas, ihudyat, ipaalam, ipahayag

Signpost *n.* posteng palatandaan

Silence *n.* katahimikan

Silence *v.* patahimikin, papamahingahin

Silencer *n.* silensiyador

Silent *adj.* tahimik, walangkibo

Silhoutte *n.* silweta

Silk *n.* seda, sutla

Silken *adj.* malasutla

Silky *adj.* malasutla

Sill *n.* palababahan, pasamano

Silly *adj.* gunggong, hangal, tanga

Silt *n.* burak, labwab

Silver *adj.* pinilakan, plateado

Silver *n.* pilak, plata

Silver *v.* asugihan

Silversmith *n.* platero

Silverware *n.* kubiyertos na pilak

Similar *adj.* katulad, magkatulad, kauri, magkauri, kawangis

Simile *n.* simil, pagtutulad

Simmer *v.* bumulak, sumulak

Simony *n.* simoniya

Simper *v.* ngumisi, ngumisngis

Simple *adj.* simple, magaan, payak, tapat, madali

Simpleton *n.* hangal, maang

Simplicity *n.* kasimplihan, kapayakan

Simplify *v.* simplipikahin, padaliin, gaanan, pagaanin

Simulacrum *n.* simulakro, larawan, wangis

Simulate *v.* magkunwa, magpanggap

Simulation *n.* pagkukunwa, pagpapanggap

Simulcast *n.* simulkas

Simulcast *v.* magsimulkas, isimulkas

Simultaneous *adj.* sabay, magkasabay, panabay, magkapanabay

Sin *n.* sala, kasalanan

Sin *v.* magkasala

Sinapism *n.* sinapismo

Since *adv.* mula

Since *conj.* sapagka't, yayamang, sa gayon, dahil sa

Since *prep.* mula sa

Sincere *adj.* sinsero, tapat, matapat, tunay

Sincerety *n.* katapatan

Sine *n.* sine

Sinecure *n.* sinekura

Sinew *n.* lakas, puwersa, igkal, kaigkalan, tendon

Sinewy *n.* maigkal, malitid, malakas, mapuwersa

Sinful *adj.* makasalanan

Sing *v.* awitin, umawit, kantahin, kumanta, humuni, awitin

Singe *n.* isalab, idangdang, idarang

Singhaless *adj.* singgales

Single *adj.* isa, iisa, bukod, nagiisa, binata, dalaga, walangasawa

Singleness *n.* pagkaiisa, pagkadalaga, pagkabinata, kadalagahan

Singlet *n.* kamiseta

Singly *adv.* isa-isa, nag-iisa

Singular *adj.* katangi-tangi, namumukod, di-karaniwan, kakaiba

Sinister *adj.* kaliwa, lisya, masama, nakapagpapahamak

Sink *v.* lumubog, manghina, ilubog, palubugin, bumaha

Sinker *n.* pabigat, palubog

Sinner *n.* taong makasalanan

Sinus *n.* seno, lugong

Sinusitis *n.* senositis

Sip *n.* higop

Sip *v.* humigop, higupin

Siphon *n.* panghigop, pampahigop

Sir *n.* ginoo

Sire *n.* poon, panginoon, ama

Siren *n.* sirena

Sirup *n.* harabe

Sissy *adj.* biniboy

Sister *n.* kapatid na babae, sor, ermana, mongha

Sister-in-law *n.* hipag

Sisterly *adj.* parang kapatid

Sit *v.* maupo, luminilim, humalimhim

Site *n.* lugar, pook, sityo, kinalalagyan

Sitting *n.* pag-upo, paglimlim, bista, pulong

Situate *v.* bugyang-lugar

Situated *adj.* may kinatatayuan

Situation *n.* katayuan, kalagayan

Six *adj.* anim

Sixfold *adj.* anim na ibayo, makaanim

Sixfold *adv.* anim na ibayo, makaanim

Sixteen *adj.* labing-anim

Sixteenth *adj.* ikalabing-anim

Sixth *adj.* ikaanim

Sixtieth *adj.* ikaanimnapu

Sixty *adj.* animnapu, sesenta

Sizable *adj.* malaki

Size *n.* laki, lawak, sukat, dami

Sizzle *v.* sumirit, sumagitsit

Sizzling *adj.* sumisirit, napakainit

Skate *n.* patin, isket

Skate *v.* magisketing

Skater *n.* patinador, isketer, mag-iisketing

Skating *n.* isketing, pag-iisketing

Skedaddle *v.* sumepa, pumuslit, tumipas, tumalilis

Skein *n.* labay

Skeletal *adj.* pangkalansay

Skeleton *n.* kalansay, balangkas

Skeptic *adj.* eseptiko, mapangila, mapagkila

Skeptical *adj.* eseptiko, nangingila, nagkikila

Skepticism *n.* eseptisismo, pangingila, pagkila

Sketch *n.* disenyo, burador, krokis

Sketch *v.* iguhit

Ski *n.* iski

Skid *v.* dumulas, madulas

Skiff *n.* lunday

Skill *n.* kakayahan, kasanayan, kaalaman, sining

Skilled *adj.* sanay, bihasa, marunong

Skim *v.* hapawin, halagapan, basahing, pahapyaw

Skimpy *adj.* kakauti

Skin *n.* balat, kuwero, katad

Skinner *n.* magbabalat, mambabalat

Skinny *adj.* mabalat, payat, patpatin, butu't-balat

Skip *n.* lundag, ligwin, lukso, laktaw, ligta

Skip *v.* maglulundag, ligwinan, ligtaan, laktawan, lakdawan

Skipper *n.* kapitan ng bapor

Skirmish *n.* iskaramusa, sandaling sagupaan, maikling labanan

Skirt *n.* saya, palda, gilid, tabihan

Skirt *v.* manggilid, manabi

Skit *n.* dulang katatawanan

Skittish *adj.* malikot, kapritsoso, magitlahin

Skulduggery *n.* panlilinlang

Skulk *v.* magtago

Skull *n.* bungo, bao ng ulo

Skullcap *n.* gora

Sky *n.* langit, himpapawid

Skylark *n.* layanglayang

Skylight *n.* bintanilya

Skyscraper *n.* gusaling tukudlangit

Slab *n.* bakbak, kalap, laha

Slack *adj.* pabaya, makupad, mahinay, kulang

Slacken *v.* tagalan, luwagan, hinaan

Slacks *n.* islaks

Slake *v.* bawahan, bawasan, hinaan, lunasan

Slam *n.* kalampag, dagubang, lagapak, tagupak

Slam *v.* pakalampagin, ibagsak

Slang *n.* balbal, islang

Slangily *adv.* pabalbal, paislang

Slant *adj.* gilid, pahilig, sulyap, hilig, pananaw, palagay

Slanting *adj.* hilig, nakahilig

Slantingly *adv.* pahilig

Slap *n.* tampal, sampal, tapik

Slap *v.* tampalin, sampalin, tapikin

Slash *n.* laslas

Slash *v.* laslasin, humiwa, hiwain, hagupitin, lumaslas

Slashed *adj.* laslas, nalaslas

Slat *n.* patpat, bara, tablilya, dahon

Slate *n.* munting pisara

Slaughter *n.* pagkatay, pangangatay, pagpapatay

Slaughter *v.* katayin, kumatay, patayin, pagkatay

Slaughterhouse *n.* matadero

Slave *n.* alipin, busabos, alila

Slave *v.* mag-alipin, alipinin, magpaalipin

Slavery *n.* kaalipnan, kabusabusan, pagkaalipin, pagkabusabos

Slavish *adj.* may ugaling alipin, asal-busabos

Slay *v.* patayin, puksain

Slayer *n.* mamamatay

Sled *n.* paragos, kareta

Sleek *adj.* makinis, makintab

Sleek *v.* pakintabin

Sleep *n.* tulog, idlip, himlay, himbing

Sleep *v.* matulog, umidlip, humimlay, humimbing

Sleeper *n.* ang natutulog

Sleepiness *n.* kaantukan

Sleeping *adj.* natutulog

Sleepwalker *n.* sunambulista

Sleepy *adj.* nag-aantok, nagtutuka, nagtutukatok

Sleet *n.* siliska

Sleeve *n.* manggas, manggito, kulyar

Sleeveless *adj.* walang-manggas

Slender *adj.* balingkinitan, munti, payat, mahina

Slenderizer *n.* pampapayat

Sleuth *n.* detektib, tiktik, sekreta, espiya

Slice *n.* hiwa, lapang, hilis, tahada, piraso

Slice *v.* hiwain

Slick *adj.* makinis, makintab, maalam, mapanlinlang

Slicker *n.* kapote

Slide *n.* pagkadulas, dausdos, guho, portaplaka

Slide *v.* magpadulas, magpakadulas, dumausdos, magpadausdos

Slider *n.* pandausdos

Sliding *adj.* dumadausdos, padausdos, dausdusin

Slight *adj.* balingkinitan, munti't mahina, kakaunti

Slight *v.* walang-halaga, maliitin

Slim *adj.* manipis, kaunti, payat, patpatin, bahagya

Slime *n.* labwab, lahod, burak, pusali, gitata

Slimy *adj.* maburak, mapusali, malahod

Sling *n.* bitinan, sakbat, panakbibi, sakbibi, tirador

Sling *v.* tiradurin, manaltik, tumirador, isakbat, manirador

Slink *v.* sumukot, magpasukut-sukot

Slip *n.* pagkadulas, kamison, pagkahulog, pagkakamali, tali

Slip *v.* magtanan, mapadulas, makatanan, isulot, tumipas, madulas

Slipper *n.* tsinelas, sinelas

Slippery *adj.* madulas

Slit *n.* laslas, gahak, litas, sipak, hiwa, siwang

Slit *v.* hiwain, laslasin, gahakin

Slither *v.* magpadau-dausdos

Sliver *n.* bikig, salugsog, salubsob, tinik, subyang

Slob *n.* kulanta

Slobber *v.* maglaway

Slogan *n.* bansag, islogan

Sloop *n.* salupa, paraw, binta

Slope *n.* gulod, dahilig

Sloppy *adj.* maputik

Slot *n.* siha, siwang, butas, susian

Sloth *n.* kaalisagaan, katamaran

Slouch *n.* kaalisagsagan, paglaylay, pagluyloy

Slough *n.* lusak, pusali, latian

Slovenlines *n.* kaburaraan, kaalisagaan, panlilimahid

Slow *adj.* makupad, marahan, makuyad, mahina, mabagal

Slug *n.* islag, suntok

Slug *v.* bambuhin, suntukin, hambalusin, bumambo

Sluggard *adj.* batugan

Sluggish *adj.* tamad, batugan , mapagpaliban

Slum *n.* islam, pook ng mahihirap

Slumber *n.* tulog, idlip, hipig

Slumber *v.* matulog, umidlip

Slump *v.* masadlak, mapasadlak, mabulid, mapabulid, yumukayok

Slur *v.* siraan, mantsahan

Slush *n.* labwab, putik, lusak

Slut *n.* babaing burara, babaing masama, puta

Sly *adj.* pailalim, maalam, magdaraya, tuso, mapamaraan, palihim

Smack *n.* lasa, palatak, lagutok, lagitik

Smack *v.* sumapak

Small *adj.* munti, maliit, munsik, munsing

Smallpox *n.* bulutong

Smalt *n.* esmaltin

Smart *adj.* bibo, makisig, mahapdi, listo, gising, matalino

Smash *n.* pagkadurog, pagkabasag, pagkawasak, pagkagiba

Smash *v.* durugin, basagin, wasakin, paguhuin

Smattering *n.* kakaunti

Smear *n.* dumi, dungis, kulapol, kapol, bahid, mantsa

Smear *v.* pahiran, dungisan, kulapulin, kapulin, bahiran, mantsahan

Smell *n.* amoy, bango, baho, dumhan

Smell *v.* amuyan

Smelly *adj.* nangangamoy

Smelly *v.* amuyin, maamoy, mangamoy

Smelt *v.* magtugnas, tugnasin, magpundi, pundihin

Smelter *n.* manunugnas, pundidor, pundisyon

Smile *n.* ngiti

Smile *v.* ngumiti, ngitian

Smiling *adj.* nakangiti

Smilingly *adv.* pangiti, nakangiti

Smirch *v.* kulapulan, kapulin, mar. sahan, dumhan, dungisan

Smirk *n.* ngisi

Smite *n.* bugbugin, bambuhin, paluin, hambalusin

Smite *v.* dagukan, hampasin, hambalusin

Smith *n.* panday

Smithy *n.* pandayan

Smock *n.* blusa

Smog *n.* ulap-usok

Smoke *n.* aso, paghitit, paninigarilyo, usok, asbok, singaw

Smoke *v.* manigarilyo, umaso, manabako, humitit, umusok, magtapa, umasbok, sumigaw

Smokehouse *n.* tapahan

Smokeless *adj.* walang-aso, walang-usok

Smokestock *n.* tsiminea, pausukan

Smoky *adj.* maaso, mausok

Smolder *v.* magbaga, magdupong

Smooth *adj.* makinis, mahusay, patag, pantay, mahinahon

Smother *v.* inisin, sugpuin, pigilin, ipagsawala

Smudge *n.* pausok, mantsa, kulapol

Smudge *v.* pausukan

Smug *adj.* magara, makisig, malinis, makinis

Smuggle *v.* magpuslit, magkontrabando

Smuggler *n.* mamumuslit, kontrabandista

Smut *n.* kulili, kahalayan

Snack *n.* sansubo, meryenda, mirindal, minandal

Snag *n.* tuod, buko

Snail *n.* suso

Snake *n.* ahas

Snap *n.* tuklaw, lagitik, sakmal, sikmat, bakli

Snap *v.* tumuklaw, sumunggab, manunggab, mabakli

Snappy *adj.* maliksi, masigla, matalino

Snare *n.* patibong, pang-umang, bitag, silo, panaling

Snatch *v.* saklutin, daklutin, sunggaban, agawin

Sneak *v.* pumuslit

Sneer *n.* tuya, atsoy, uyam

Sneer *v.* manuya, tuyain, mangatsoy, atsuyin

Sneerer *n.* manunuya, mangaatsoy

Sneeze *n.* bahin

Sneeze *v.* bumahin, magbahin, magbabahin

Snicker *n.* alik-ik, halikhik, tawa

Snicker *v.* umalik-ik, humalikhik, tumawa

Sniff *v.* suminghot, makaramdam, makaamoy

Sniffle *v.* humalak, humikbi

Snip *v.* gupitin, guntingin

Snipe *n.* labuyo

Snivel *n.* uhog, singhot, hikbi

Snivel *v.* uhugin, suminghot, humikbi

Snob *n.* taong mapagmalaki, tang mapagmataas

Snobbery *n.* pagmamalaki, pagmamataas

Snobbish *adj.* mapagmalaki, suplado

Snoop *n.* manunubok

Snoop *v.* manubok, mamatyaw

Snooze *n.* idlip, hipig

Snooze *v.* mapaidlip, mapahipig

Snopy *adj.* mapanubok

Snore *n.* hilik, paghihilik

Snore *v.* maghilik

Snort *n.* nguso, ilong, bokilya

Snow *n.* niyebe

Snowball *n.* niyebeng binilo

Snowfall *n.* ulan ng niyebe, nebada

Snowy *adj.* maniyebe

Snub *v.* pagmalakhan, pagmataasan

Snuff *n.* tulo

Snuff *v.* patayin

Snug *adj.* maginhawa, panatag

Snuggle *v.* magsumiksik, kumayungkong, kalungkungin, kayungkungin

So *adv.* pagayon, sa gayon, kaya, upang

Soak *v.* ibabad, tigmakin, babarin

Soap *n.* sabon

Soapbark *n.* gugo

Soapbos *n.* habonera

Soapy *adj.* masabon

Soar *n.* lipad, hilayog, ilanilang, sibad, salimbay

Soar *v.* lumipad, humilayog, tumayog, pamailanlang, sumibad, sumalimbay

Sob *n.* hikbi, iyak

Sob *v.* humikbi, umiyak, humibik

Sober *adj.* seryo, matino, dilasing

Sociable *adj.* palasama. palakaibigan, magiliw, mapagpakilipon

Social *adj.* sosyal, panlipunan

Socialism *n.* sosyalismo

Socialist *adj.* sosyalista

Socialite *n.* taong tanyag sa lipunan

Socialize *v.* sosyalisahin

Society *n.* sosyedad, pagsasama, pagsasamahan, kapisanan, lipunan

Sociology *n.* sosyolohiya

Sock *n.* suntok, medyas, buntal, kalsitin

Socket *n.* suksukan, saket, para sa bombilya

Soda *n.* soda, sosa

Sodality *n.* kopradiya, kapatiran

Sodden *adj.* mamad, babad

Sodium *n.* sosa

Sodomy *n.* sodomiya

Sofa *n.* supa

Soft *adj.* malambot, mayumi, suwabe, mahinay

Soften *v.* palambutin, humina, pahinain, papanghinain, palamlamin

Soggy *adj.* basang-basa, tigmak, mamad

Soil *n.* lupa, abok, gabok

Soil *v.* dumhan, dungisan

Soiree *n.* saraw

Sojourn *n.* panunuluyan

Sojourn *v.* manuluyan

Sol *n.* sol

Solace *n.* aliw, kaaliwan

Solace *v.* aliwin, mag-aliw

Solar *adj.* ng araw, solar

Solarium *n.* solaryum

Solder *n.* panghinang, soldadura

Solderer *n.* manghihinang, tagahinang, soldador

Soldier *n.* kawal, sundalo, mandirigma

Sole *adj.* tangi, mutya, nagiisa

Sole *n.* talampakan, suwelas

Solecism *n.* solesismo

Solemn *adj.* solemne, maringal, taimtim, tapat

Solemnity *n.* solemnidad, dingal, karingalan

Solemnize *v.* magdiwang, ipagdiwang

Solicit *v.* manghingi, hingan, humiling, hilingan

Solicitation *n.* panghihingi, pangangalap, mangingilak, abugado

Solicitous *adj.* maalalahanin, maassikaso, maatindi, sabik, maintindihin

Solid *adj.* solido, nagkakaisa, buo, matatag, matibay

Solidarity *n.* solidaridad, pagkakaisa, kaisahan

Solidify *v.* papamuuin, mamuo, mapikpik

Solidity *n.* solides, pagkabuo

Soliloquy *n.* solilokyo, monologo

Solitaire *n.* solitaryo

Solitary *adj.* nag-iisa, nagso-solo, mapanglaw, tangi

Solitude *n.* pag-iisa, pamamanglaw, pagkabukod

Solo *n.* solo

Soloist *n.* soloista, solista

Solon *n.* mambabatas, lehislador

Solstice *n.* solstisyo

Solubility *n.* pagkamatunawin, katunawin, pagkamakatunaw

Soluble *adj.* matunawin, natutunaw

Solution *n.* kalutasan, solusyon, timplada, pagkatunaw, tugon, sagot

Solve *v.* lutasin, ipaliwanag, lumutas

Solvency *n.* solbensiya

Solvent *n.* solbente

Somber *adj.* malagim, madilim

Some *adj.* ilan, kaunti

Somebody *pron.* isang tao

Somehow *adv.* sa papaanuman

Somersault *n.* balintukis, sirko

Somersault *v.* magbalintukis, magsirko

Sometime *adj.* dati

Sometime *adv.* sa dakong, hindi lamang tiyak

Sometimes *adv.* kung minasan, maminsan-minsan, manakanaka

Somewhat *adv.* mala, tila, wari

Somewhere *adj.* sa kung saan, kung saan sa

Somnifacient *adj.* pampatulog, nakapagpapatulog

Somnolence *n.* antok, kaantukan, pagtutungka

Son *n.* anak na lalaki, iho

Sonance *n.* tunog, tono, himig

Sonant *adj.* pantunog, isinatinig

Song *n.* awit, kanta

Songster *n.* mang-aawit, manganganta

Sonic *adj.* sonik

Sonnet *n.* soneto

Sonority *n.* alalad

Sonorous *adj.* maalalad, matunog

Soon *adj.* agad, dagli, maaga, pagdaka

Sooner *adv.* lalong madali; lalong maaga

Soot *n.* agiw, uling

Soothe *v.* payapain, patahimikin, aliwin, pahinahunin

Soothing *adj.* nakagiginhawa, nakaaaliw

Sop *n.* alpahol

Sophisticated *adj.* masalimuot, makamundo

Sophomore *n.* sopomor

Sophomoric *adj.* sopomoriko

Soporific *adj.* pampatulog

Soprano *n.* soprano

Sorcerer *n.* mangkukulam, manggagaway

Sorceress *n.* bruha, mangkukulam, manggagaway

Sorcery *n.* pangungulam, panggagaway

Sordid *adj.* marumi, karumirumi, imbi, magaspang

Sore *adj.* masakit, yamot, nayayamot, mahapdi, nakalulungkot, nagagalit

Sorites *n.* sorites

Sorrel *n.* alasan

Sorrow *n.* pighati, dalamhati, sakit, kalungkutan

Sorrowful *adj.* namimighati, nagdadalamhati

Sorry *adj.* nagdaramdam, nagsisisi, nalulungkot

Sort *n.* uri, klasa, kalidad, katangian

Sort *v.* uriin, paguri-uriin

Sortie *n.* salida, labas

Sot *n.* lasenggo

Soul *n.* kaluluwa, espiritu, hilagyo

Soulful *adj.* madamdamin

Sound *adj.* malusog, matatag, matipuno, malakas, buo

Sound *n.* tunog

Sound *v.* tumunog, patunugin

Soup *n.* sopas, sabaw

Sour *adj.* maasin

Sour *v.* umasim, asiman

Source *n.* mula, simula, pinagmulan, pinanggalingan

Sourness *n.* kaasiman

Soutance *n.* sutana

South *n.* timog, sur

Southeast *n.* timog-silangan

Southern *n.* dakong timog

Southwest *n.* timog-kanluran

Souvenir *n.* souvenir, alaala

Sovereign *n.* soberano, maykapangyarihan

Soviet *adj.* sobyet

Sow *n.* inahing baboy

Sow *v.* maghasik, ihasik, hasikan

Sower *n.* maghahasik, tagahasik

Soy *n.* toyo, munggo, balatong

Spa *n.* bukal mineral, balong mineral

Space *n.* espasyo, pook, puwang, agwat, pagitan, kalawakan, alangaag, tagal

Spacious *adj.* malawak, maluwag, maaliwalas

Spade *n.* pala, ispada

Spade *v.* palahin

Spaghetti *n.* spagheti

Span *n.* dangkal, agwat, pagitan, layo

Span *v.* dangkalin, sukatin

Spaniard *n.* kastila, espanyol

Spank *n.* palo sa puwit

Spank *v.* paluin sa puwit

Spar *n.* mastil, palo, albor

Spare *adj.* reserba, labis, kuripot, kakaunti

Spare *n.* labis, ekstra, isper

Spare *v.* tipirin, pinsalain, parusahan

Sparib *n.* kostilyas, tadyang

Sparing *adj.* matipid, mapagsimpan, maawain

Spark *n.* kislap, diklap

Spark *v.* kumislap, dumiklap, pukawin, mapukaw

Sparkle *n.* ningning, kinang, kislap, diklap

Sparkle *v.* magningning, kuminang, kumislap, dumiklap

Sparrow *n.* pipit, ibong pipit, maya

Sparse *adj.* madalang, kakaunti, kaunti

Spasm *n.* pulikat, hilab, sintak, sigalbo, silakbo

Spat *n.* away, kagalitan

Spatter *n.* pilansik, tilamsik, tabsak, tabsik

Spatter *v.* mapilansikan, matilamsikan, matabsakan

Spatula *n.* espatula

Spawn *v.* mangitlog

Speak *v.* magsalita, magtalumpati, banggitin, magpahayag

Speaker *n.* espiker, tagapagsalita, mananalumpati

Spear *n.* sibat, suligi, salapang

Special *adj.* espeyal, tangi, sadya, pasadya, itinatangi

Specialist *n.* espesyalista, dalubhasa

Specialize *v.* mag-espesyalista, magpakadal-ubhasa

Specialty *n.* espesyaldad, ang ekinapamumukod, ang ikinatatangi

Species *n.* uri, sari, espesye

Specific *adj.* tiyak, tahas, partikular

Specification *n.* espesipika-syon

Specify *n.* tiyakin

Specimen *n.* espesimen, muwestra, halimbawa, tipo

Specious *adj.* animo, wari

Speck *n.* batik, pekas, mantsa

Spectacle *n.* panoorin, tanghal, eksibisyon

Spectacles *n.* gapas, antiparas

Spectator *n.* ang manonood, ang nanonood, miron

Specter *n.* manlalabas, impakto, multo

Spectrum *n.* espektro

Speculate *v.* magnilay-nilay, nilay-nilayin, maghula-hulo, hulu-huluin

Speculation *n.* espekula-syon, pagsasapalaran, pakikipagsa

Speculative *adj.* espekula-tibo, mayriyesgo

Speculator *n.* espekulador

Speech *n.* pagsasalita, wika, talumpati, pananalita, pahayag, salita

Speechless *adj.* walang-kibo, walang-imik, tahimik

Speed *n.* tulin, bilis, pagpapatulin

Speed *v.* magpatulin, magmadali, magpabilis

Speedometer *n.* kilometrahe

Speedy *adj.* matulin, mabilis

Spell *n.* engkanto, gayuma, pagkagaway, pagkakulam

Spell *v.* magbaybay, baybayin, mangahulugan

Spellbind *v.* engkantuhin, gawayin, kulamin

Spelling *n.* ispeling, pagbabaybay, baybay

Spend *v.* gumasta, gastahin, gumugol, gugulin

Spender *n.* ang gumagasta, gastador

Sperm *n.* tamud, esperma, balyena

Spew *n.* suka

Spew *v.* bumuga, ibuga, sumuka, isuka

Sphere *n.* bilog, espera, globo

Sphinx *n.* espinghe

Spice *n.* rekado, palasa

Spider *n.* gagamba, alalawa

Spiel *n.* diga, salita, sabi

Spigot *n.* pasak, sampal

Spike *n.* espiga, tulos, istako, pako

Spile *v.* maligwak

Spill *n.* ligwak, tapon

Spin *v.* magsulid, uminog, sulirin, lubirin, painugin

Spinach *n.* espinaka

Spinal *adj.* panggulugod, sa gulugod

Spindle *n.* iliran, kidkiran

Spine *n.* gulugod

Spineless *adj.* walang-gulugod

Spinet *n.* espineta

Spinner *n.* manunulid, habihan

Spinning *n.* pagsusulid, paghahabi, inog

Spinster *n.* matandang dalaga

Spiny *adj.* matinik

Spiracle *n.* hingahan

Spiral *adj.* paikid-ikid, espiral

Spirant *n.* pahingasing

Spirit *n.* ispiritu, loob, sigla, kalooban, buhay, kaluluwa, diwa

Spiritism *n.* espiritismo, espiritwalismo

Spiritist *n.* espiritista

Spit *n.* lura, laway

Spit *v.* lumura, dumura, maglaway, ilura

Spittle *n.* lura, laway

Spittoon *n.* luraan

Splash *n.* tilamsik, pilansik

Splash *v.* tumilamsik, pumilansik

Spleen *n.* pali

Splendent *adj.* makinang, makintab, maningning

Splendid *adj.* maluningning, marilag, maringal, napakagaling

Splendor *n.* dingal, ningning, kariktan

Splice *n.* dugsong

Splice *v.* idugsong

Splint *n.* lapat, bangkot, balangkat

Splinter *n.* sipak, tapya, pilas

Split *adj.* baak, biyak, hati, bali

Split *v.* baakin, biyakin, hatiin, punitin

Spoil *v.* masira, sayangin, mabulok, palayawin, aksayahin

Spoke *n.* rayos ng gulong

Spokesman *n.* tagapagsalita

Sponge *n.* espongha

Spongy *adj.* esponghado

Sponsor *n.* padrino, ninong, madrina, ninang

Spontaneous *adj.* kusa, natural, sarili

Spook *n.* impakto, multo, mumo

Spool *n.* karete, ikiran

Spoon *n.* kutsara

Spoon *v.* kutsarahin

Spoor *n.* bakas

Sporadic *adj.* manakanaka, mangisa-ngisa

Spore *n.* tinasik, espora

Sport *n.* isport, laruan, libangan, laro, biro

Sport *v.* maglibang, ipagparangalan, magbiro, maglaro

Sportsman *n.* isportsman, maginoo

Sportsmanship *n.* pagka-maginoo

Spot *n.* mantsa, marka

Spot *n.* pook, lugar

Spot *v.* mantsahan, markahan, mamataan

Spotless *adj.* walang-mantsa

Spotlight *n.* saboy na ilaw, ispatlait

Spotted *adj.* batik-batik

Spouse *n.* asawa, maybahay, esposo, bana, esposa

Spout *n.* labi, bibig, palabasan, tuka

Spout *v.* tumilandoy, tumilaroy, tumaliris

Sprain *n.* pagkapilok

Sprain *v.* mapilok

Sprawl *v.* matimbuwang, mapatimbuwang

Spray *n.* tibalsik, tilamsik, wisik, wilig

Spray *v.* wisikan, wiligan, magwisik

Sprayer *n.* pambomba, atomisador

Spread *v.* ikalat, ilatag, ihasik, isabog, ibudbod

Spree *n.* pagsasaya, lasingan

Spring *n.* bukal, balong, lukso, lundag

Spring *v.* lumundag, lumukso, sumibol, umagos

Sprinkle *v.* magwilig, iwilig, magdilig, diligin

Sprinkler *n.* pandilig, regadera

Sprint *n.* takbong, matulin

Sprite *n.* manlalabas, multo, tianak, ada

Sprout *n.* supang, usbong, supling

Spruce *adj.* makinis, makisig, mabikas

Spry *adj.* maliksi, aktibo

Spume *n.* espuma, bula

Spur *n.* panundot, espuwelas, tari, pasigla

Spurn *v.* tanggihan, sikaran

Spurt *n.* bulwak, silakbo, sidhi, bugalwak, tilandoy, tilaroy

Spurt *v.* bumulwak, bumugalwak, tumilandoy, tumilaroy

Sputum *n.* lura

Spy *n.* espiya, batyaw, tiktik

Spy *v.* espiyahan, batyawan, tiktikan

Squab *n.* pitson

Squabble *n.* babag-away, basag-ulo

Squad *n.* ekuwadra, iskuwad, pulutong

Squalid *adj.* marumi, salaula

Squall *n.* unos, sigwa, bagyo

Squall *v.* umunos, sumigwa, bumagyo

Squander *v.* lustayin, aksasayahin

Squardron *n.* armada, plota, eskuwadron

Square *adj.* tahas, marangal, makatarungan, impas

Square *n.* kuwadrado, parisukat

Square *v.* bayaran , eskuwalahin, pagbayaran

Squaring *n.* kuwadratura, pagpaparisukat

Squash *n.* kalabasa

Squat *adj.* nakatimpuho, nakalupagi, pandak

Squat *v.* tumingkayad, umiskwat, maningkayad, manimpuho, lumupagi

Squawk *n.* piyak, siyak, reklamo, daing

Squeak *n.* tili, irit

Squeak *v.* tumili, umirit, lumangitngit

Squeal *n.* palakat, palahaw

Squeal *v.* pumalakat, pumalahaw, magkanulo, ipagkanulo

Squeamish *adj.* malulain, makiluhin, maselang

Squeeze *v.* pigain, pindutin, isiksik, sumiksik

Squeezer *n.* pigaan

Squid *n.* pusit

Squint *adj.* banlag, pairap, duling

Squire *n.* eskudero, abay

Squirm *v.* mamilipit

Squirrel *n.* ardilya

Squirt *n.* tilandoy

Squirt *v.* patilanduyin

Stab *v.* saksakin, tusukin, tarakan, sundutin, turukin, duruin

Stability *n.* tatag, tibay, kapirmihan

Stabilize *v.* patatagin, ipirmi, tibayan

Stabilizer *n.* pampatag, estabilisador

Stable *adj.* matatag, matibay, panatilihan

Stable *n.* establero, sota, kuwadra

Stack *n.* bunton, salansan

Stadium *n.* istadyum

Staff *n.* tungkod, tukod, pamunuan

Stag *n.* lalaking usa

Stage *n.* panahon, plataporma, intablado, tanghalan, baitang

Stage *v.* magtanghal, magpalabas

Stagecraft *n.* kadalubdulaan, dramaturhiya

Stagger *v.* sumuray, gumiray, kumibang, gumibang, gumiwang

Stagnant *adj.* walang-agos, di-umaagos, tigil, bungkok

Stagnate *n.* mabungkok

Stagy *adj.* maarte

Staid *adj.* matatag, panatilihan, tahimik, seryo

Stain *n.* mantsa

Stainless *adj.* walang-bahid, walang-mantsa

Stair *n.* baitang, eskalon, hagdan

Stairway *n.* akyatan-panaugan

Stake *n.* istaka, tulos, pusta, taya

Stake *v.* pumusta, itaya, tulusan, tumaya

Stale *adj.* lipas, laon, bilasa, luma, gastado, laos

Stalemate *n.* hake, istopel, patas, tabla

Stalk *n.* tangkay, uhay

Stalk *v.* manubok

Stall *n.* kuwadra, tindahan

Stall *v.* patigilin, pigilan, patagalan

Stallion *n.* kabayong bulugan

Stalwart *adj.* matipuno, malakas, matapang

Stamina *n.* tira, lakas

Stammer *n.* mautal

Stamp *n.* tatak, selyo, padyak

Stamp *v.* tatakan, selyuhan, pumadyak

Stamped *adj.* maytatak, mayselyo

Stampede *n.* panakbuhan

Stampede *v.* magpanakbuhan

Stand *n.* puwesto, lagay, pagsalungat, pook, istasyon, posisyon

Stand *v.* tumindig, ibangon, tiisin, manindigan, itindig, itayo

Standard *adj.* normal, panatilihan, tularan, uliran

Standard *n.* sagisag, panukat, watawat, pamautayan, istandard

Standardize *v.* istandardi-sahin

Standing *adj.* nakatindig, pamalagian, patuloy, nakatayo, nakatigil, panatilihan

Standing *n.* tindig, tayo, kalagayan, katayuan

Standpoint *n.* pananaw

Standstill *n.* tigil

Stanza *n.* estropa, saknong, taludturan

Staple *n.* pakong baluktot, istepol

Staple *n.* produktong pangunahin, materya prima

Stapler *n.* istapler

Star *n.* bituin, estrelya

Starch *n.* arina

Starched *adj.* inalmirulan

Stare *n.* titig

Stare *v.* tumitig, titigan

Starfish *n.* isdang-bituin

Stargazer *n.* astrologo, mamimituin

Stark *adj.* lubos, puspos

Starlet *n.* munting bituin

Starry *adj.* mabituin

Start *n.* simula, umpisa

Start *v.* magsimula, mag-umpisa, simulan, umpisahan

Starter *n.* istarter, tagasimula, tagaumpisa

Startle *v.* gitlahin, gulatin, sindakin

Startling *adj.* nakagigitla, nakagugulat, nakasisindak

Starve *v.* mahayak sa gutom, mamatay sa gutom, patayin sa gutom

State *n.* estado, kondisyon, kalagayan, katayuan

State *v.* isalaysay, ipahayag, sabihin

Stately *adj.* kagulat-gulat, kahanga-hanga, makahari, darakila

Statement *n.* pahayag, say-say, kabatiran, mungkahi

Stateroom *n.* kamarote

Statesman *n.* estadista

Static *n.* estatika

Station *n.* kinatatayuan, istasyon, himpilan, distino

Stationary *n.* estasyonaryo, piho, piramihan, di-gumugalaw

Stationer *n.* papelero

Stationery *n.* papeleriya, gamit-panulat

Statistician *n.* estatistiko

Statistics *n.* estatistika

Statuary *n.* estatwaryo

Statue *n.* estatwa, bantayog

Statuesque *adj.* malaistatwa

Statuette *n.* pigurilya, pigurin

Stature *adj.* taas, tayog

Status *n.* kalagayan, katayuan

Statute *n.* estatuto, batas, kautusan

Stave *n.* pamugbog, pambambu, panapal, baras

Stave *v.* butasan, busbusin, umiwas, iwasan

Stay *n.* suhay

Stay *v.* antalahin, tumigil, tumahan, manirahan, tigilan, tumira, bimbinin, matira

Stead *n.* pook, lugar, bentaha, pakinabang

Steadfast *adj.* matatag, matibay, matimtiman, matapat

Steady *adj.* patuloy, matatag, panay

Steak *n.* hiniwang karne

Steal *v.* magnakaw, nakawin

Stealer *n.* magnanakaw

Stealing *n.* pagnanakaw

Stealth *n.* gawang lihim

Stealthily *adv.* palihim

Stealthy *adj.* lihim, sekreto

Steam *n.* singaw

Steam *v.* sumingaw, pasingawan

Steamboat *n.* bapor

Steamroller *n.* pison

Steamy *adj.* masingaw

Steed *n.* kabayo

Steel *n.* asero, patalim

Steelyard *n.* timbangang romana

Steep *adj.* matarik

Steep *v.* ibabad

Steeped *adj.* babad, tigmak

Steeple *n.* espira, tore, kampanaryo

Steer *n.* torong kapon

Steer *v.* manehohin, magmaneho, patnugutan, patnubayan

Steerage *n.* pilotahe, pamamahala, pamamatnugot

Steersman *n.* tagaugit, timonero

Stellar *adj.* pambituin , estelar

Stem *n.* puno, tangkay

Stem *v.* magmula, manggaling

Stench *n.* baho, alingasaw

Stencil *n.* istensil, estarsidor

Stenographer *n.* takigrapo

Stenography *n.* takigrapiya

Stenosis *n.* estenosis

Step *n.* hakbang, paraan, indak, baitang, yabag, yapak

Step *pref.* panguman

Step *v.* humakbang, lumakad, humakbang, tuntungan

Stepladder *n.* hagdan

Stereography *n.* esterogra-piya

Stereophonic *adj.* estereopo-niko

Stereotype *n.* estereotipo, klitse

Sterile *adj.* baog, di-mamunga, tuyo, esteril

Sterility *n.* kabaugan, esterilidad

Sterilization *n.* esterilisasyon

Sterilize *v.* esterilisahin

Sterling *adj.* esterlina, puro, dalisay

Stern *adj.* mahigpit, masungit

Stesmanship *n.* estadismo

Stethoscope *n.* istetoskopyo

Stew *n.* nilaga

Stew *v.* ilaga

Steward *n.* tagapamahala, mayordomo, tagamasid, katiwala, kamarero

Stewardess *n.* istewardes

Stewpan *n.* kasirola

Stick *n.* sanga, tungkod, tangkay, baras, tukod

Stick *v.* idikit, dumikit, kumapit, tuhugin, manatili, sundutin, saksakin, isuksok

Sticker *n.* etiketa

Sticky *adj.* malagkit, nanlalagkit

Stiff *adj.* matigas, naninigas, mahirap, malapot, banat, maganit, pikpik

Stiffen *v.* patigasin, manigas

Stifle *v.* inisin, patayin, pigilan, mainis

Stigma *n.* estigma, marka, dungis

Stile *n.* lakdawan

Stiletto *n.* panusok, punson

Still *adj.* , tahimik

Still *conj.* gayunman, kahit na

Still *n.* alambike, distilador

Still *v.* patahimikin, pahinahunin

Stillborn *adj.* inianak na patay

Stilt *n.* tiyakad

Stilted *adj.* nakatayakad, alsado

Stimulant *adj.* estimulante, pamabuyo, nakapagpapasigla, nakapagpalakas

Stimulate *v.* pasiglahin, pukawin

Stimulus *n.* estimulo, pasigla, pamukaw, buyo

Sting *n.* tibo

Sting *v.* sundutin, saktan, duruin, tuksuhin, kagatin

Stingy *adj.* kuripot, maigot, maramot

Stink *n.* baho

Stink *v.* mamaho, mangamoy, umalingasaw

Stint *n.* gawain, tungkulin, limitasyon, kuwota

Stipend *n.* gantimpagal, upa, sahod, suweldo

Stipple *n.* tulduk-tuldok, butil-butil

Stippling *n.* pagtutulduk-tuldok

Stipulate *v.* makipagkasunduan, makipagkayari, itakda, itaning

Stipulation *n.* kasunduan, kayarian, takda, taning

Stir *n.* ibo, galaw, gulo, kuriri

Stir *v.* umibo, gisingin, haluin, pagalawin, pukawin, magpaibo, magpagalaw

Stirring *adj.* nakapukaw, mapamukaw, makapukawsigla

Stirrup *n.* estribo

Stitch *n.* tahi, hilbana, sulsi

Stitch *v.* tahiin, hilbanahan, sulsihan

Stitcher *n.* tagatahi, tagahilbana, tagasulsi

Stock *n.* kalakal, sosyo, pinagmulan, hawakan, poste, tinda, istak, puhunan

Stock *v.* mag-istak, mag-imbak, ipangaw

Stockade *n.* estakada, kuta

Stockbroker *n.* bolsista, kambista

Stockholder *n.* aksiyonista, kasapi

Stocking *n.* medyas

Stockpile *n.* tipon, ipon

Stocky *adj.* balisaksak, matipuno

Stockyard *n.* kural, kulungan

Stoke *v.* magparubdob

Stoker *n.* pugunero

Stole *n.* estola

Stolid *adj.* dungo, duko

Stomach *n.* sikmura, tiyan, gana

Stone *n.* bato

Stony *adj.* mabato

Stool *n.* bangkito, dumi, tuod, pangati

Stoop *n.* yumuko, yumukod, nagpakababa, sumuko

Stoop *v.* yumuko, yumukod

Stop *n.* tigil, wakas, pasak, pagtigil, hinto, paghinto

Stop *v.* takpan, pahintuin, ihinto, patahanin, pigilin, pasakan, harangan, patigilin, itigil

Stopcock *n.* liyabe

Stopper *n.* pasak, tapon

Storage *n.* almasenahe, pagtitinggal

Store *n.* tipon, reserba, tindahan, bodega

Store *v.* itago, magtago, magtipon, ideposito

Storekeeper *n.* maytinda

Storied *adj.* makasaysayan

Stork *n.* sigwenya, tagak

Storm *n.* bagyo, sigwa

Storm *v.* bumagyo

Stormy *adj.* mabagyo

Story *n.* palapag, piso, kuwento, salaysay

Stout *adj.* matipuno, mataba, matatag, malakas, matapang

Stove *n.* kalan, hurno

Stow *v.* iligit, pagpatas-patasin, isalansan

Straddle *v.* bumukaka, kumaang, sumaklang

Straggle *v.* maligaw, mawala

Straggler *n.* ligaw

Straight *adj.* tuwid, matuwid, makatarungan, lantay

Straighten *v.* ituwid, tumuwid

Straightforward *adj.* tapat, matapat

Straightforward *adv.* tapat, matapat

Straightway *adv.* kagyat

Strain *n.* lipi, lahi, himig

Strain *n.* panghapit, pagpapahigpit, pagpupumilit, pagpupunyagi

Strain *v.* mabanat, hapitin, salain, higpitan, pagpumilitan, pagpunyagian

Strainer *n.* salaan

Strait *n.* kipot

Straiten *n.* kiputan

Suckle *v.* magpasuso, pasusuhin

Sucrose *n.* sukrosa

Suction *n.* supsop, pagsupsop, sipsip, pagsipsip

Sudden *adj.* bigla, kagyat

Suddenly *adv.* pabigla, kaginsaginsa

Sue *v.* magdemanda, lingan, idemanda, maghabla, ihabla

Suet *n.* sebo

Suffer *v.* alintanahin, bayaan, magtiis, dumanas, pagtiisan, maghirap, magdusa

Suffice *v.* sumapat, magkasiya

Sufficient *adj.* kainaman, sapat

Suffix *n.* panghuling lapi, hulapi

Suffix *v.* ihulapi, hulapian

Suffocate *v.* sakalin, manakal, inisin

Suffrage *n.* suprahiyo, prangkisya, karapatang, bumoto

Suffuse *v.* matigmak, makulayan, malipos

Sugar *n.* asukal, matamis

Suggest *v.* magmungkahi, imungkahi, magpahiwatig, ipahiwatig

Suggestion *n.* suhestiyon, mungkahi

Suicide *n.* pagpapakamatay, pagpapatiwakal, pagbibigti

Suit *n.* terno, sakdal, pagsasakdal, pamanhik, demanda, pagdedemanda, habla

Suit *v.* iangkop, bumagay, makibagay, bagayan, ibagay, mabagay, maakma

Suitable *adj.* bagay, angkop, tumpak, akma

Suitcase *n.* maleta

Suite *n.* tauhang abay, mga kahuwego, mga katerno, mga kasangkap

Suiting *n.* teternuhin

Suitor *n.* manliligaw, mangingibig

Sulk *n.* pagtatampo

Sulk *v.* magtampo

Sulking *adj.* nagtatampo

Sulky *adj.* matampuhin

Sullen *adj.* namamanglaw, galit, yamot, mapanglaw

Sully *v.* dungisan, mantsahan, magkadungis, madungisan

Sultan *n.* sultan

Sultanate *n.* kasutanan, sultanato

Sultry *adj.* mabanas, maalinsangan, mainit, nagngangalit

Sum *n.* kabuuan, suma, kalahatan, total

Sum *v.* sumahin, magsuma

Summarize *v.* buurin, lagumin

Summary *n.* buod, lagom

Summer *n.* tag-araw

Summit *n.* tuktok, taluktok, karurukan, kasukdulan

Summon *v.* tawagin, ipatawag, tipunin, paharapin

Summons *n.* sitasyon, tawag, patawag

Sumptuous *adj.* marangya, sagana, masagana

Sun *n.* araw

Sunbeam *n.* sinag ng araw

Sunburn *n.* paso ng araw

Sunburst *n.* silahis

Sunday *n.* Linggo, Domingo

Sundries *n.* miselanea, sarisari

Sundry *adj.* sarisari, ibaiba, iba't iba

Sunflower *n.* hirasol, mirasol

Sunny *adj.* maaraw

Sunrise *n.* liwayway, silang ng araw

Sunset *n.* lubog ng araw, takipsilim, dapit-hapon

Sup *v.* maghapunan

Superb *adj.* superyor, napakahusay, napakagaling, dakila, marilag

Supercilious *adj.* mapagmataas, mapagmalaki, palalo

Superficial *adj.* superpisyal, paimbabaw

Superfluous *adj.* surplus, labis, sobra, kalabisan

Superimpose *v.* ipatong

Superintend *v.* pamanihalaan

Superintendent *n.* superintendente, tagapamanihala

Superior *adj.* nakatataas, puno

Superiority *n.* superyoridad, kahigtan

Superlative *adj.* superlatibo, panukdol, pasukdol

Superman *n.* superman

Supermarket *n.* supermarket

Supernal *adj.* panlangit, pangkalangitan

Supernatural *adj.* sobrenatural, kahima-himala

Supernormal *adj.* sobrenormal

Supersede *v.* palitan, halinhan

Superstition *n.* pamahiin

Supervise *v.* superbisahin, pangasiwaan, pamanihalaan

Supervision *n.* superbisyon, tagapangasiwa, tagapamanihala

Supper *n.* hapunan

Supplant *v.* palitan, halinhan

Supple *adj.* malambot, mayumi, masunurin

Supplement *n.* suplemento, dagdag, karagdagan

Supply *n.* tustos, panustos, kagamitan

Supply *v.* tustusan

Support *n.* alalay, taguyod, tangkilik

Support *v.* alalayan, madala, itaguyod, patunayan

Supporter *n.* suporter, tagataguyod, tagatangkilik

Suppose *v.* ipagpalagay, magsapantaha, akalain

Supposition *n.* palagay, sapantaha, akala

Suppository *n.* supositoryo

Suppress *v.* supilin, ampatin, sugpuin, ipaglihim, ipagbawal

Supremacy *n.* pananaig, supremasya

Supreme *adj.* pinakamataas

Sure *adj.* sigurado, tiyak, nakatitiyak

Surety *n.* katiyakan, piyador, kasiguruhan, garantiya, piyansa

Surf *n.* alimbukay

Surface *n.* ibabaw, pangibabaw, labas, kalatagan

Surface *v.* katamin, pakinisin, bulihin

Surfeit *n.* pagbubultak, pagbubundat, sawa, suya

Surfeit *v.* bultakin

Surge *n.* daluyong, alimbukay, alon

Surge *v.* dumaluyong, umalon

Surgeon *n.* siruhano, maninistis

Surgery *n.* siruhiya, paninistis

Surgical *adj.* kirurhiko

Surly *adj.* masungit, galit, bastos, magaspang

Surmise *n.* sapantaha, hula

Surmise *v.* sapantahain, hinalain, hulaan

Surmount *v.* pangibabawan, pagtagumpayan

Surname *n.* apelyido

Surpass *v.* lampasan, daigin, madaig, mahigtan, higtan

Surplus *adj.* surplus, labis

Surprise *v.* biglain, mabigla, mamangha, gulatin, manghain, magulat

Surrender *n.* pagsuko

Surrender *v.* sumuko

Surround *v.* paligiran, palibutan, kulungin

Surroundings *n.* paligid, palibot, kaligiran

Survey *n.* pagsusuri, inspeksiyon, pagsukat

Survey *v.* suriin, siyasatin, sukatin

Surveyor *n.* agrimensor

Survival *n.* pananatiling buhay, pananatili

Survive *v.* manatili, manatiling buhay

Susceptible *adj.* suseptible, maramdamin

Suspect *v.* maghinala, paghinalaan, magsospetsa, pagsospetsahan

Suspend *v.* ibitin

Suspense *n.* pag-salinlangan, kapanabikan

Suspension *n.* suspensiyon, pagkabitin , pagtigil

Suspicion *n.* hinala, sapantaha bintang, hiwatig

Suspicious *adj.* naghihinala, mapaghinala, mahinalain

Sustain *v.* sustinihin, panindigan, umalalay, pagtiisan

Sustenance *n.* sustento, pakain, manutensiyon

Suzerain *n.* soberano, panginoon

Swab *n.* suwab, paniampaso, lampaso

Swaddle *v.* balutan ng lampin, pahahan

Swag *n.* botin, dinambong, ninakaw

Swage *n.* hugisan, molde, estampador

Swallow *n.* langay-langayan

Swallow *v.* lumunok, lumangga, lunukin, lulunin, lumulon

Swamp *n.* latian

Swan *n.* sisne

Swank *n.* rangya

Swanky *adj.* marangya

Swap *n.* palitan, baligyaan

Swap *v.* magpalitan, makipagpalitan, magbaligyaan

Swarm *n.* pagkakalibumbon

Swarm *v.* mamunini, mamutiktik, pagkulupunan, pagkalibumbunan

Swarthy *adj.* maitim-itim, kayumanggi, moreno

Swash *n.* sagwak, ligwak, bulwak, sagalwak

Swat *v.* hampasin

Sway *v.* umugoy, gumiwang, madala, lumiko, bumaling, ibaling, humilig

Swear *v.* sumumpa, mangako

Sweat *n.* pawis, sikap, pagpapakapagod

Sweat *v.* pawisan, pumawistayon, magpapawis, magsikap

Sweater *n.* suweter

Swede *n.* Suweko

Swedish *adj.* Suweko

Sweep *v.* magwalis, walisin, walisan

Sweeper *n.* tagapagwalis

Sweet *adj.* matamis

Sweet *n.* dulse

Sweeten *n.* patamisin

Sweetening *n.* pampatamis

Sweetheart *n.* kasintahan, katipan

Sweetmeat *n.* kendi

Sweetness *n.* katamisan, pagkamatamis

Swell *n.* bukol, umbok, alon, daluyong

Swell *v.* lumaki, bumintog, mamaga, magpalalo

Swift *adj.* matulin, mabilis, maliksi, maagap

Swig *n.* higop, lunok

Swim *v.* lumangoy, languyin

Swimmer *n.* manlalangoy

Swimming *n.* paglangoy

Swindle *v.* manuba, mananso, mangantso, mandaya

Swindler *n.* manunuba, manenekas, balasubas

Swine *n.* baboy

Swing *n.* tayon, suwing, ugoy, pagtayon, indayog, duyan

Swing *v.* iwasiwas, itayon, iugoy

Swipe *n.* sapok

Swipe *v.* magnakaw, nakawin

Swirl *v.* uminog, mag-ininog, painugin

Swiss *adj.* Suwisa, Suwiso

Switch *n.* latiko, liyabe, suwits, kumpas, pagbabago, paglilipat

Switch *v.* ilipat

Swivel *n.* paikutan

Swoon *v.* maghimatay, himatayin

Swoop *n.* pagdagit, pagdaragit

Swoop *v.* maudagit, dagitin

Sword *n.* ispada, sable

Swordfish *n.* isdang, ispada

Sycophant *n.* manghihibo, mamumuri

Syllabicate *v.* magpantig, pantigin

Syllabary *n.* silabaryo, pantigan

Syllabic *adj.* silabika, papantig, pamantig

Syndicate *n.* sindikato, kompaniya, samahan, korporasyon

Synesthesia *n.* sinestesya

Synod *n.* sinodo

Synonym *n.* sinonimo, kasingkahulugan

Synonymous *adj.* sinonimo, magkasingkahulugan

Synopsis *n.* sinopsis, buod, lagom

Syntax *n.* sintaksis, palaugnayan

Synthesis *n.* sintesis, pagbubuo, pagyayari

Synthetic *adj.* sintetiko, binuo, niyari, ginawa

Syphilis *n.* sipilis

Syringe *n.* heringga, heringilya

Syrup *n.* harabe, pulot, arnibal

System *n.* sistema, kaayusan, paraan, pamamaraan, kaparaanan

Systematic *adj.* sistematiko, metodiko, mapamaraan

T t

Tab *n.* ungos, pardilya, tagetiketa

Table *n.* mesa, tabulasyon, tabla, manghad

Tableau *n.* tableau, kuwadrong buhay

Tablespoon *n.* kutsara

Tablet *n.* tablet, pad, tabletas, lapida

Tableware *n.* kubyertos

Tabloid *adj.* tabloid

Taboo *adj.* tabu, bawal

Tabor *n.* tamburil

Taboret *n.* taborete, bangkito

Taborin *n.* pandereta

Tabular *adj.* tabular, tabulado

Tabulator *n.* tabulador

Tacit *adj.* di-sinabi, tahimik, pahiwatig

Tack *n.* tamtak

Tack *v.* ipako, itamtak

Tackle *n.* ekipo, aparato, kasangkapan

Tackle *v.* sunggaban, isagawa, tuparin, tupdin

Tacky *adj.* malagkit

Tact *n.* takto, pakikitungo, pakikiharap

Tactic *n.* taktika, pamamaraan

Tactical *adj.* mataktika, mapamaraan

Tactician *n.* taktiko, tagapamaraan

Tactile *adj.* nahihipo, mahihipo, madarama, nadarama

Tadpole *n.* uluulo, kikinsot

Taffy *n.* bagkat

Tag *n.* tag

Tahitian *n.* Tahityano

Tail *n.* buntot, hulihan

Tailless *adj.* walang buntot, punggi

Tailor *n.* sastre, mananahi

Tailoring *n.* pananahi

Tailpiece *n.* apendise, panghulihan, pambuntot

Taint *n.* lalin, hawa, dungis

Taint *v.* lalinan, hawahan, dungisan

Take *n.* huli

Take *v.* alisin, awasin, bawasin, hulihin, ihatid, dalhin, uminom, tanggapin, kunin

Talc *n.* talko

Tale *n.* kuwento, salaysay

Talent *n.* talino, kakayahan

Talisman *n.* agimat

Talk *n.* pagsasalita, daldalan, ulat

Talk *v.* magsalita, talakayin, mag-usap, magdaldalan, magpulong

Talkative *adj.* masalita, madaldal, matabil

Talking *adj.* nagsasalita, nakapagsasalita, masalita

Tall *adj.* matangkad, mahagway, matayog, mataas

Tallness *n.* katangkaran, kataasan, kahagwayan

Tally *n.* paya, tara, taha

Tally *v.* tayahin, payahan, tarahan, magpaya

Tamale *n.* tamales

Tamarind *n.* tamarindo, sampalok

Tambour *n.* tambol

Tambourine *n.* pandereta, tamburin

Tame *adj.* amak, maamo, mabait

Tame *v.* amakin, paamuin, supilin

Tamer *n.* domador, tagapagpaamo

Tamp *v.* bayuhin, pukpukin, tabunan, tambakan

Tamper *n.* pambayo, pamikpik

Tamper *v.* pakialaman, makialam

Tamperature *n.* temperatura, init

Tamperer *n.* taong pakilalam, pakialamero

Tamtamount *adj.* katumbas, katulad

Tan *adj.* abelyana, kayumanggi

Tan *v.* magkulti, kultihin, abelyanahin

Tandem *adj.* magkasunod, tandem

Tang *n.* tulos, taka, ngipin

Tangent *adj.* sapyaw, pasapyaw, daplis, padaplis

Tangent *n.* tanhente

Tangerine *adj.* tangherina

Tangible *adj.* nahihipo, nadarama, nasasalat

Tango *n.* tanggo

Tank *n.* tangke

Tanker *n.* barko-tangke

Tanner *n.* mangungulti, magkukulti, kurtidor

Tannery *n.* kultihan

Tanning *n.* pagkukulti, pangungulti

Tantalize *v.* takawin, takamin, papanabikin

Tantalizing *adj.* nakapagpapatakam

Tantrum *n.* alboroto, pagliligalig

Taoism *n.* Taoismo

Taoist *n.* Taoista

Tap *v.* tumapik, tapikin, kumatok, tumuktok

Tape *n.* sintas, plaster

Taper *n.* kandila

Tapestry *n.* tapiseriya

Tapeworm *n.* tenya, solitarya

Tapioca *n.* balinghoy, kasaba, tapyoka

Tar *n.* alkitran

Tarantella *n.* tarantela

Tardy *adj.* mabagal, huli

Tare *n.* tara

Target *n.* target, tudlaan

Tariff *n.* taripa, buwis

Tarnish *v.* kumupas, kupasan, madumhan, madungisan

Taro *n.* gabi

Tarpaulin *n.* trapal

Tarry *v.* magtagal, tumigil, tumahan, maghintay

Tart *adj.* maaskad, makahat

Tartan *n.* tartan

Task *n.* gawain, tungkulin, trabaho

Tassel *n.* borlas, palawit

Taste *n.* pagtikim, panlasa, hilig, sarap

Taste *v.* tumikim, tikman, maglasa, magkalasa

Tasteless *adj.* walang-lasa

Taster *n.* tagatikim

Tasty *adj.* malasa, masarap

Tatter *n.* pilas, punit

Tattoo *n.* tatu

Tattoo *v.* magtatu, tatuhan

Taunt *v.* laitin, aglahiin

Taurus *n.* taurus, toro

Taut *adj.* banat, mahigpit, hatak

Tavern *n.* taberna

Tawdry *adj.* maringal, marangya

Tax *n.* buwis, pataw

Tax *v.* magpabuwis, pabuwisin, patawan, pagurin

Taxable *adj.* malalapatan ng buwis

Taxation *n.* pagpapabuwis

Taxi *n.* taksi

Taxidermy *n.* taksidermiya

Taximeter *n.* taksimetro

Taxonomy *n.* taksonomiya

Tea *n.* tsa, tsaa, saa

Teach *v.* magturo, ituro, turuan, edukahin

Teacher *n.* guro, titser, maestro, tagapagturo

Teaching *adj.* pagtuturo, turo, panuto, doktrina

Teacup *n.* tasa ng tsa

Teak *n.* teka

Team *n.* tim, koponan

Teammate *n.* kakopon, katim

Teapot *n.* tsarera

Tear *n.* luha

Tear *v.* pumilas, pilasin, punitin, pumunit

Tearful *adj.* mayluha, lumuluha

Tease *v.* suklayin, tuksuhin, tisin

Teaser *n.* tagatis, manunukso

Teaspoon *n.* kutsarita

Teat *n.* utong

Technical *adj.* tekniko, teknolohiko

Technicality *n.* teknikalidad

Technician *n.* tekniko, dalubhasa

Technics *n.* teknika, teknisismo

Technique *n.* pamamaraan, sining, paggawa, teknik

Technologist *n.* teknologo

Technology *n.* teknolohiya

Tedious *adj.* nakaiinip, nakapapagod

Tedium *n.* inip, pagkainip

Teem *v.* magdumami, managana, mamutiktik, mamunini

Teeming *adj.* masagana, namumutiktik, namumunini

Teenager *n.* tinedyer, teenager

Teeth *n.* mga ngipin

Teething *n.* pagngingipin

Telecast *n.* telekast

Telecast *v.* matelekast

Telecommunication *n.* telekumunikasyon

Telegram *n.* telegrama, pahatid-kawad

Telegraph *n.* telegrapo, pahatirang-kawad

Telegraph *v.* tumelegrama, telegramahan

Telegraphy *n.* telegrapiya

Telepathy *n.* telepatiya

Telephone *n.* telepono

Telephone *v.* teleponohan, tumelepono

Teleprinter *n.* telemakinilya

Telescope *n.* teleskopyo

Teleview *v.* manood ng telebisyon

Television *n.* telebisyon

Tell *v.* sabihin, magkuwento, ikuwento, ipahayag

Teller *n.* kuwentista, batyaw, pagador, teler

Temper *n.* timpla, pagpipigil, hinahon

Temperament *n.* tempera-mento

Temperamental *adj.* temperamental, tangkilin, maramdamin

Temperate *adj.* timplado, katamtaman, pigil

Tempest *n.* unos, bagyo, sigwa

Template *n.* suleras

Temple *n.* templo, pilipisan, sintido, simbahan

Tempo *n.* tempo, bilis, takbo, lakad

Temporal *adj.* pampilipisan, panilupa, sekular, panandalian

Temporary *adj.* pansamantala

Tempt *v.* tuksuhin, akitin, halinahin, maakit

Temptation *n.* tentasyon, hibo, tukso

Tempting *adj.* nakatutukso

Ten *adj.* sampu

Tenable *adj.* maipagtatanggol

Tenacious *adj.* makapit, makunat, maganit

Tenaculum *n.* pansuit, tenakulo

Tenancy *n.* pamumusesyon

Tenant *n.* inkilino, kasama, nangungupahan

Tend *v.* bantayan, mamahala, kumiling, alagaan, magbantay, pamahalaan

Tendency *n.* hilig, kiling, ugali

Tender *adj.* malambot, mura, mahinay, magiliw, mapagmahal

Tender *n.* pambayad, pangupa

Tender *v.* iharap, magharap, ihandog, handugan

Tenderfoot *n.* baguhan, bagito

Tenderloin *n.* solomilyo

Tendon *n.* litid

Tenement *n.* tenement

Tenesmus *n.* tibi, balisawsaw

Tenet *n.* simulain, paniwala

Tenfold *adj.* sampung ibayo

Tennis *n.* tenis

Tenon *n.* mitsa, dila

Tenor *n.* hilig, katangian, tenor

Tense *adj.* hapit, malubha, mahigpit, banat, maigting

Tense *gram.* panahon, panahunan

Tensile *adj.* makunat, maganit

Tension *n.* hapit, higpit, igting, kabalisanhan

Tent *n.* tent, tolda

Tentative *adj.* pansamantala

Tenth *adj.* ikasampu, pansampu

Tenuous *n.* manipis, balingkinitan, malabnaw

Tenure *n.* pagmamay-ari

Tepid *adj.* malahininga, maligamgam

Tequila *n.* tekila

Term *n.* taning, katawagan, tagal, takda, tadhana

Termagant *n.* birago

Terminal *adj.* terminal, pangwakas

Terminal *n.* hanggahan, terminal, duluhan

Terminate *v.* hangganan, magwakas, tapusin, wakasan, matapos

Termination *n.* pagtatapos, pangwakas, hangganan, katapusan, pagwawakas, wakas

Terminology *n.* terminolohiya, katawagan

Termite *n.* anay

Terrace *n.* terasa, pilapil, asotea

Terrain *n.* lupain, kampo

Terrible *adj.* terible, hilakbot, nakatatakot, nakasisindak, labis

Terrify *v.* takutin, sindakin, masindak

Terror *n.* sindak, hilakbot, kilabot

Terrorism *n.* terorismo, paninindak

Terrorist *n.* terorista, maninindak

Terrorize *v.* manindak, sumindak, sindakin

Tertiary *adj.* tersyaryo

Test *n.* test, pagsubok, iksamen, pagtitikim

Testament *n.* testamento, huling habilin

Tested *adj.* probado

Testicle *n.* bayag

Testify *v.* sumaksi, magpatunay, patunayan

Testimonial *n.* katibayan

Testimony *n.* testimonyo, pahayag, salasay, patunay, patotoo

Tetanus *n.* tetano

Tether *n.* suga, panuga

Tether *v.* isuga, itali

Teuton *n.* teuton

Text *n.* teksto, aklat, testo, nilalaman, letra

Textile *n.* tela

Textual *adj.* tekstuwal, testuwal, literal

Texture *n.* habi, pagkakahabi, kayarian

Than *conj.* kaysa, sa

Thanatopsis *n.* tanatopsis

Thank *v.* magpasalamat, pasalamatan

Thankful *adj.* nagpapasalamat, grato

Thankless *adj.* walang utangna-loob, ingrato

Thanksgiving *n.* pagpapasalamat

That *pron.* iyan, yaon, iyon

Thatch *n.* atip, pawid, kugon

The *art.* si, sina, ang

Theater *n.* teatro, dulaan

Theft *n.* pagnanakaw, angninakaw

Their *pron.* kanila, nila

Theism *n.* teismo

Them *pron.* kanila, nila

Theme *n.* tema, paksa

Themselves *pron.* kanilang sarili, sila na rin

Then *adj.* noon

Then *adv.* pagkatapos

Then *conj.* samakatuwid

Theology *n.* teolohiya

Theorem *n.* teorema, simulain, batas

Theory *n.* teoriya

Theosophy *n.* teosopiya

Therapeutics *n.* terapeutika

There *adv.* diyan, doon, roon

Thereabouts *adv.* malapit, doon

Thereafter *adv.* pagkatapos noon, pagkaraan noon, mula noon

Therefore *adv.* dahil doon, kaya, samakatuwid

Therefrom *adv.* mula roon, riyan

Therein *adv.* doon, roon

Thereinafter *adv.* sa susunod

Thermal *adj.* mainit

Thermodynamics *n.* termo-dinamika

Thermometer *n.* termometro

Thermos *n.* termos

Thermostat *n.* termostat

Thesaurus *n.* tesauro

These *pron.* ang mga ito

Thesis *n.* tesis

They *pron.* sila

Thick *adj.* makapal, malapot, masinsin

Thicken *v.* kumapal, kapalan, laputan, sinsinan

Thickening *n.* pangangapal

Thief *n.* magnanakaw

Thievery *n.* pagnanakaw

Thigh *n.* hita

Thimble *n.* dedal, didal

Thin *adj.* manipis, malabnaw, payat, madalang, manipis

Thin *v.* pumayat, numipis, panipisin

Thing *n.* bagay, bagay-bagay, kagamitan

Think *v.* umisip, mag-isip, isipin, akalain

Thinkable *adj.* maiisip

Thinker *n.* taong palaisip

Third *adj.* ikatlo, pangatlo

Thirst *n.* uhaw, pagkauhaw

Thirst *v.* mauhaw

Thirsty *adj.* uhaw, nauuhaw

Thirteen *adj.* labintatlo

Thirteenth *adj.* kalabintatlo

Thirty *adj.* tatlumpu

This *pron.* ito, iri

Thither *adv.* doon, paroon

Thorax *n.* toraks, karibdiban, tinadyangan

Thorn *n.* tinik, subyang, dawag

Thorny *adj.* matinik

Thorough *adj.* ganap, lubos, puspos

Thoroughfare *n.* daanan, liwasan

Those *pron.* ang mga iyon

Thou *pron.* kayo, ikaw, sila

Though *conj.* kahit na bagaman

Thought *n.* isip, idea, diwa, layunin, isipan, kaisipan, pagmumuni

Thoughtful *adj.* maalala-hanin, maasikaso

Thoughtless *adj.* walan-gingat, sagasa, pabaya

Thousand *adj.* libo

Thrash *v.* gumiik, manggiik, hampasin, magpagulunggulong

Thrashing *n.* palo, bugbog

Thread *n.* sinulid

Threadbare *adj.* nutnot, nisnis, gasgas

Threat *n.* banta, pagbabanta

Threaten *v.* magbanta, pagbantaan

Three *adj.* tatlo

Thresher *n.* tagagiik, panggiik

Threshold *n.* pasukin, simula

Thrice *adv.* tatlong, beses, tatlong ulit, maikatlo

Thrift *n.* pagtitipid, katipiran, pag-iimpok

Thrifty *adj.* matipid, mapagimpok

Thrill *n.* kilig, pangingilig

Thrill *v.* , mangilig, pangilligan

Thrive *v.* mabuhay, umunlad, tumubo, lumakas

Throat *n.* lalamunan

Throb *n.* tibok, hibok, pintig

Throb *v.* tumibok, humibok

Throe *n.* kirot, hirap, paghihingalo

Throne *n.* trono

Throng *n.* libumbon

Throng *v.* dagsaan, dumagsa, magkalibumbon

Throttle *n.* gasulinador, aselerador

Through *adj.* lagos

Through *adj.* tapos na

Throughout *adv.*. saanman, kahit saan

Throw *v.* iitsa, ibato, ipukol, itsa, ihagis, ipukol, ihalibas

Thrust *v.* isaksak, saksakin, tuhugin, lulos, itulak, ulusin

Thryoiditis *n.* tiroyditis

Thud *n.* hampas, kalabog

Thud *v.* kumalabog

Thug *n.* butangero, mambubutang

Thumb *n.* hinlalaki

Thump *n.* bugbog, kalabog

Thunder *n.* kulog

Thunderbolt *n.* lintik, kidlat

Thundering *adj.* duma-dagundong

Thunderous *adj.* madagun-dong, maragunlong

Thursday *n.* Huwebes

Thus *adv.* dahil dito, ganito, gayong

Thwart *v.* hadlangan, biguin

Thy *pron.* iyo, mo, sa iyo, ng iyo

Thyroid *adj.* throydeo

Thyself *pron.* ikaw rin

Tibetan *n.* Tibetano
Tibia *n.* tibya, sapi-lulod
Tick *n.* garapata, pulgas
Ticket *n.* tiket, bilyete, talaan
Tickle *v.* mangiliti, kilitiin, kalamkaman
Ticklish *adj.* makilitiin, maramdamin, maselan
Tide *n.* agos
Tidings *n.* balita
Tidy *adj.* makinis, malinis, maayos
Tie *n.* tali, patas, gapos, suga, bigkis
Tie *v.* talian, magpatas, itali, magbuhol, ibuhol
Tier *n.* hanay, pila, saray, suson
Tiff *n.* kagalitan, away
Tiffany *v.* sutlang pino, muslin
Tiger *n.* tigre
Tight *adj.* mahigpit, pitis, hapit, makipot, masikip
Tighten *v.* higpitan, humigpit
Tilde *n.* tilde, kilay
Tile *n.* tisa, baldosa
Till *n.* kaha
Till *prep.* hanggang, hanggang sa
Till *v.* bungkalin, sakahin
Tilt *n.* torneo, labanan, paligsahan
Tilt *v.* itikwas, makilaban
Timber *n.* kahoy, tabla
Timbre *n.* tono, taginting
Time *n.* panahon, beses, pagkakataon, oras, ulit
Timely *adv* napapanahon
Timepiece *n.* orasan, relos, relo
Timesaving *adj.* pampadali
Timetable *n.* itiniraryo
Timid *adj.* matakutin, mahiyain
Timing *n.* kumpas, pagkumpas, tayming
Timorous *adj.* matakutin
Tin *n.* lata
Tincture *n.* tintura
Tingle *v.* manguliting, pangulitingan, mamiltik, pamiltikan
Tinker *n.* latonero
Tinkle *n.* kulling, kililing
Tinkle *v.* kulilingin, pakulilingin, kalansingin
Tinsel *n.* urupel, tinsel
Tint *n.* bahid, kulay
Tint *v.* bahiran, kulayan
Tinware *n.* lateriya
Tinwork *n.* ohalateriya
Tiny *adj.* munsing, munsik
Tip *n.* dulo, tip, pabuya, tapik, tulis, tuktok, pabatid
Tip *v.* itaob, tapikin, itagilid, tikwasin, kantiin
Tiptop *n.* karurukan, taluktok
Tira *n.* tiyara
Tirade *n.* tuligsa, atake
Tire *n.* goma

Tire *v.* pagurin, pagalin, hapuin

Tired *adj.* pagod, napapagod

Tireless *adj.* walang-pagod

Tissue *n.* tisu, nilala, tisyu, habi, lala

Tit *n.* ganting suntok

Titbit *n.* kakanin

Tithe *n.* diyesmo

Title *n.* titulo, pamagat, kampeonato, karapatan

Title *v.* pamagatan

Titrate *v.* titiin

Titular *adj.* titular

To *prep.* sa, kay

Toad *n.* palaka

Toadstool *n.* pandong-ahas, kabuting-lason

Toast *n.* brindis, tagay

Toast *v.* iihaw, tustahin

Toaster *n.* ihawan, tustahan, tustador, tagabrindis

Toastmaster *n.* toastmaster, tagapagpakilala

Tobacco *n.* tabako, sigaro, upaop

Tobacconist *n.* tabakero

Tobogan *n.* tobogan

Today *adv.* ngayon, sa kasalukuyan

Toddle *v.* mangulabat

Toe *n.* daliri, kuko

Toenail *n.* kuko ng paa

Tog *n.* kasuutan, pananamit

Toga *n.* toga

Together *adv.* magkasama, sama-sama

Toggle *n.* tarugo, kasunete, kodilyo

Toil *n.* gawa, trabaho, pagpupumilit

Toil *v.* gumawa, magtrabaho, magpakasakit

Toilet *n.* tokador, pagbibihis, palikuran, banyo

Token *n.* tanda, sagisag, alaala, tiket

Tolerable *adj.* matitiis, mapararaan, kainaman

Tolerance *n.* toleransiya, pagpaparaanan

Tolerant *adj.* mapagparaya

Tolerate *v.* tiisin, ipahin-tulot, tulutan, ipaubaya

Toll *n.* buwis, bayad, upa, singil

Tomahawk *n.* tomahok, puthaw

Tomato *n.* kamatis

Tomb *n.* nitso, libingan, puntod

Tomboy *n.* tomboy, binalaki

Tome *n.* tomo

Tomorrow *adv.* bukas

Tomtom *n.* tomtom, kalatong, ton

Tone *n.* tono, tunog, himig

Tongs *n.* sipit

Tongue *n.* dila, wika

Tonic *adj.* toniko, pampalakas

Tonight *adv.* ngayong gabi, mamayang gabi

Tonnage *n.* tonelahe

Tonsil *n.* tonsil

Tonsillectomy *n.* tonsilotomiya

Tonsillitis *n.* tonsiliis

Too *adv.* din, lubha, rin, labis, masyado

Tool *n.* kasangkapan

Toolmaker *n.* manggagawa ng kasangkapan

Toot *v.* magbusina, bumusina

Tooth *n.* ngipin

Toothache *n.* sakit ng ngipin

Toothbrush *n.* sepilyo sa ngipin, panghiso

Toothed *adj.* mayngipin

Toothless *adj.* walang-ngipin, bungal, bungi

Toothpick *n.* palito sa ngipin

Toothsome *adj.* malinamnam, masarap

Top *n.* ibabaw, ulo, dulo, tuktok, karurukan

Top *v.* talbusan, tumaas

Topaz *n.* topasyo

Topflight *adj.* pangunahin

Topfull *adj.* bumabalawbaw

Topic *n.* paksa, tema

Topmast *n.* mastero

Topmost *adj.* pinakamatayog, kataas-taasan

Topnot *n.* pusod

Topographer *n.* topograpo

Topography *n.* topograpiya

Toponym *n.* ngalang-pook

Topple *v.* matumba, gumuho

Topsail *n.* gabya

Topsoil *n.* abok, alabok

Topsy-turvy *adv.* balintuwad, gulo

Torch *n.* sulo, sigsig

Torment *n.* hirap, pighati

Tormentor *n.* ang nagpapahirap

Tornado *n.* buhawl

Torpedo *n.* torpedo

Torpedo *v.* torpeduhin

Torpid *adj.* matamlay, tulog, manhid

Torpor *n.* tamlay, katamlayan

Torrent *n.* baha, sagalwak

Torrential *adj.* bumabaha, nagbabaha

Torrid *adj.* tuyot, tigang, nakapapaso

Torsion *n.* pamamaluktot, tursiyon

Torso *n.* katawan

Torticollis *n.* tortikoli, pagbabangkiling

Tortoise *n.* pagong, pawikan

Torture *n.* pagpapahirap

Torture *v.* pahirapan

Toss *v.* ipagpahagis-hagis

Tosspot *n.* maglalasing, lasenggo

Tot *n.* batang munti

Total *n.* total, kabuuan

Total *v.* buuin, pagsamahin

Totalitarian *adj.* totalitaryo

Totalize *v.* totalsahin, buuin

Totem *n.* totem

Totlizer *n.* totalisador

Totter *v.* gumiray, magpagiray-giray, sumuray

Tottering *adj.* pagiray-giray, pasuray-suray

Touch *n.* hipo, kalabit, tatak, sira, bahid

Touch *v.* humipo, kalabitin, hipuin, dumait, dumaiti

Touchy *adj.* maramdamin, magagalitin, tangkilin

Tough *adj.* makunat, maganit, matatag, mahirap

Toughen *v.* paganitin, patigasin

Toupee *n.* tupe

Tour *n.* biyahe, paglilibot, paglalakbay

Tour *v.* magbiyahe, maglibot, maglakbay, libutin

Tourism *n.* turismo

Tourist *n.* turista

Tournament *n.* torneo, paligsahan

Tourniquet *n.* tornikete

Tousled *adj.* lugay, gusot

Tow *n.* rimolke, hila, arastre

Towage *n.* pagririmolke

Toward *prep.* sa patungo sa, sa dakong, palapit sa, hinggil sa

Towel *n.* tuwalya

Tower *n.* tore

Towering *adj.* nanghihilayog, matayog

Town *n.* bayan, munisipyo

Townsfolk *n.* taong-bayan

Toxic *adj.* nakalalason, toksiko

Toxicology *n.* toksikolohiya

Toxin *n.* toksin, lason

Toy *n.* laruan

Toy *v.* maglaro, paglaruan

Trace *n.* dasto, marka, bakas, landas

Trace *v.* dibuhuhin, iguhit, bakasin, tuklasin

Tracer *n.* trasador, sinagan

Trachea *n.* lalaugan

Trachoma *n.* trakoma

Tracing *n.* guhit sa sinag, traso

Track *n.* bakas, riles, daanan, landas, patakbuhan

Track *v.* sundan, sunsunin, daanan

Tract *n.* lawak, lagay, lote

Traction *n.* traksiyon

Tractor *n.* traktora

Trade *n.* negosyo, hanapbuhay, pangangalakal

Trade *v.* magnegosyo, magkalakal

Trader *n.* negosyante, mangangalakal

Tradition *n.* tradisyon, salinsabi, salindunong

Traditional *adj.* tradisyunal

Traduce *v.* siaang-puri, alipustain

Traffic *n.* trapiko, sasakyan

Trafficker *n.* trapikante

Tragedy *n.* trahedya, kapahamakan

Tragic *adj.* trahiko

Tragicomedy *n.* trahiko-medya

Trail *v.* kaladkrin, subaybayan, bakasin

Trailer *n.* treyler

Train *n.* tren

Train *v.* itunton, magsanay, turuan, sanayin, papagsanayin

Trainer *n.* tagasanay, tagapagsanay

Training *n.* pagsasanay, pagkapagsanay, pansanay

Trainman *n.* taong-perokaril

Traitor *n.* traidor, taksil

Traitorous *adj.* taksil, traidor

Traject *v.* sumibad, magpahagibis

Trajection *n.* pagsibad, paggibis

Trajectory *n.* trayektorya

Tramcar *n.* trambiya

Tramp *n.* hampaslupa, lagalag, yabag

Tramp *v.* maglakad, maglalagalag, yapakan

Trample *v.* yapakan, yurakan, pagmalupitan

Trampoline *n.* tampolin

Trance *n.* kalingmingan

Tranquil *adj.* tiwasay, tahimik, panatag

Tranquility *n.* katiwasayan, katahimkan

Tranquilize *v.* patiwasyin, patahimikin

Tranquilizer *n.* transgkilisador, pampatiwasay

Transact *v.* magnegosyo, makipagnegosyo, makipagtransaksiyon, gawin

Transcend *v.* lumamapas, makalampas, humigit, manaig

Transcendent *adj.* transendente, nananaig

Transcribe *v.* kopyahin, sipiin

Transcript *n.* transkrip, kopya

Transcription *n.* trnaskripsiyon, kopya

Transfer *n.* lipat, paglilipat

Transfer *v.* lumipat, maglipat, ilipat

Transferable *adj.* maililipat

Transfiguration *n.* pagbabagong-anyo

Transfix *v.* tuhugin, tindagin

Transform *v.* baguhin, ibahin

Transformation *n.* transpormasyon, pag-iibang-hugis, pagbabanyuhay

Transformer *n.* transpormador, transpormer

Transfuse *v.* magsalin, patalaytayin, isalin, palusutin, palampasin

Transfusion *n.* transpusyon, pagsasalin

Transgress *v.* lumabag, magkasala, lumabis, sumuway

Transgression *n.* paglabag, pagkakasala, paglabis, pagmamalabis

Transient *adj.* pansamantala

Transistor *n.* transistor

Transit *n.* pagdaraan, pagdadala, transit

Transitive *adj.* nagdaraan, palipat, transitibo

Transitory *adj.* di-nagtatagal, pansamantala

Translate *v.* ilipat, magsalin, isalin, maglipat

Transliterate *v.* isatitik

Transliteration *n.* pagsasatitik, transilterasyon

Translucent *adj.* nanganganinag

Transmigration *n.* transmigrasyon

Transmission *n.* transmisyon, pagtatrasmiti, pagbobrodkas

Transmit *v.* ipadala, ilipat, ibrodkas, itrasmiti

Transmitter *n.* transmiter, tagatrasmiti, pantrasmiti

Transmutation *n.* transmutasyon, pagpapabagu-bago

Transmute *v.* magbago, magiba, baguhin, ibahin

Transom *n.* tranbinsanyo

Transparent *adj.* aninag, nanganganinag

Transpire *v.* ihinga, ipapawis, mangyari, maganap

Transplant *v.* maglipat ng tanim

Transport *n.* transportasyon, sasakyan

Transport *v.* isakay at ihatid, dalhin

Transpose *v.* baligtarin

Transude *v.* pumawis, mamawis

Transverse *adj.* halang, nakahalang

Trap *n.* patibong, panghuli, umang, bitag, silo

Trap *v.* patibungan, pikutin, umangan, siluin

Trapeze *n.* trapesyo

Trappings *n.* pinagtalupan, pinagkayasan

Trash *n.* yagit, basura, kahangalan

Trauma *n.* lesyon, sugat, pagkalingaw

Travail *n.* sakit, pagsasakit, paghilab, pagdaramdam

Travail *v.* hilaban, magdamdam

Travel *n.* biyahe, paglilibot

Travel *v.* maglakbay, maglibot, magbiyahe

Traveller *n.* manlalakbay, biyahero

Traverse *v.* magdaan, tumawid, daanan, tawiran, bagtasin, bumagtas

Travesty *n.* imitasyon, panggagagad, parodya

Tray *n.* trey, bandeha

Treacherous *adj.* mapagkanulo, taksil

Treachery *n.* pagkakanulo, pagsusukab, kataksilan, kaliluhan

Treacle *n.* pulot

Tread *n.* tapak, bakas, tuntong, yapak

Tread *v.* tapakan, lumakad, yapakan, lakaran, tuntungan

Treadle *n.* pedal

Treadmill *n.* gilingang pinepedalan

Treason *n.* traisyon

Treasure *n.* tesoro, yaman, kayamanan, salapi

Treasure *v.* pagyamanin, mahalagahin, mahalin

Treasurer *n.* tesorero, ingatyaman

Treasury *n.* tesoreriya

Treat *n.* handog, kainan

Treat *v.* makipagtrato, gamutin, anyayahan, makipagnegosyo, tumalakay, talakayin

Treatise *n.* akda, tratado

Treatment *n.* trato, pakikitungo

Treaty *n.* kasunduan, tratado, kayarian

Tree *n.* punungkahoy, puno

Trek *v.* maglakbay

Trellis *n.* balag, enrehado

Tremble *v.* manginig, mangatal, mangatog, mangaligkig

Trembling *adj.* nanginginig, nangangatal, nangangatog

Tremendous *adj.* nakapanghihilakbot, napakalaki, kamanghamangha

Tremor *n.* panginginig, pangangatal, pag-uga, lindol

Tremulous *adj.* nangangatal, nanginginig

Trench *n.* trintsera, kanal

Trenchant *adj.* matilos, matalas

Trend *n.* hilig, takbo, lakad, agos

Trespass *n.* pakikialam, pagkakasala

Trespass *v.* makialam, pakialaman, mangamkam, magkasala

Trespasser *n.* makasalanan

Trestle *n.* kabalyete, tukod

Trial *n.* pagsubok, hirap, paglilitis

Triangle *n.* trianggulo, tatsulok

Triangular *adj.* trianggular

Triangulation *n.* trianggulasyon

Tribal *adj.* pantribu, panlipi, pang-angkan

Tribe *n.* tribu, lipi

Tribesman *n.* katribu, kalipi, kaangkan

Tribulation *n.* pagtitiis, pagkaapi

Tribunal *n.* tribuna, hukuman

Tribune *n.* tribuno, mahistrado, manananggol

Tributary *adj.* namumuwis, sakop, umambag, umaagos

Tribute *n.* tributo, alay, handog, paglilingkod

Trick *n.* lalang, linlang, kasanayan, galing

Trickery *n.* panlilinlang, panlalansi

Trickle *n.* patak, tagas, tulo

Trickle *v.* tumagas, pumatak, umagos

Tricky *adj.* mapanlinlang, mapanlansi

Tricolor *n.* trikolor, tatlongkulay

Tricycle *n.* trisiklo

Tried *adj.* natikman na, subok na

Trifle *n.* munting bagay, munting halaga

Trifle *v.* magbiro, paglaruan

Trigger *n.* gatilyo, kalabitan

Trigon *n.* trigono, trianggulo

Trigonemetry *n.* trigonometriya

Trill *n.* pakatal ng tinig

Trillion *adj.* trilyon, sang-angaw na angaw

Trilogy *n.* trilohiya, tatlong akda

Trim *adj.* maayos, makinis, pantay

Trim *n.* ayusin, gupitan, palamutihan, katamin

Trim *v.* pakinisin, pantayin, gupitan

Trimester *n.* trimestre, tatlong-buwan

Trinitarian *adj.* trinitaryo

Trinitarianism *n.* trinitaryanismo

Trinitrololuebe *n.* trinitrotolwen

Trinity *n.* trinidad, tatlongisa

Trinket *n.* tringket, alahas, palamuti

Trio *n.* trio, tatluhan

Triode *n.* triodo

Trip *n.* biyahe, paglalakbay, patid, kamalian

Trip *v.* matisod, biguin, patriin, magkandirit, umindak

Tripartite *adj.* nababahagi sa tatlo, pinagtatlo

Tripe *n.* tripa

Triplet *n.* tatlong magkakambal

Triplicate *adj.* triplikado, pinagtatlong-sipi

Tripod *n.* tripode, tatlong-paa

Triptych *n.* triptiko

Trisect *v.* pagtatluhin

Trite *adj.* bulgar, karaniwan, luma, dati

Triturate *v.* dikdikin, ligisin, pulbusin

Triumph *n.* pagwawagi, tagumpay

Triumphant *adj.* mapagwagi, mapanagumpay

Trivial *adj.* di-mahalaga

Trnasceiver *n.* transibo

Trochaic *adj.* trokayko

Troche *n.* tablilya, pastilyas

Trochee *n.* trokeo

Trochlea *n.* troklea

Trojan. *n* Troyano

Trolley *n.* trole

Trombone *n.* trumbon

Troop *n.* tropa

Troop *v.* magkalibumbon

Trophy *n.* tropeo

Tropic *n.* tropiko

Tropical *adj.* tropikal

Trot *n.* trote, yagyag

Trot *v.* tumrote, yumagyag

Troth *n.* pananalig, katapatan

Trouble *n.* ligalig, gulo, pagkabahala

Trouble *v.* gambalain, guluhin, mabahala

Troublesome *adj.* mapanligalig, mapanggulo, pampabigat

Troublous *adj.* maligalig, magulo

Trough *n.* sabsaban, labangan, alulod

Troupe *n.* tropa

Trouseau *n.* trusu

Trousers *n.* pantalon

Trowel *n.* dulus

Truant *adj.* bulakbol, lakwatsero

Truant *v.* magbulakbol, maglakwatsa

Truce *n.* tregwa, armistisyo

Truck *n.* trak

Truculent *adj.* mabilasik, malupit

Trudge *v.* maglakad

True *adj.* tapat, totoo, autentiko, tumpak, eksakto, wasto, tama

Trump *n.* mananaig

Trump *v.* manaig

Trumpet *n.* trompeta

Trumpeter *n.* trompetero

Truncate *v.* pungusan, padparan

Truncheon *n.* batuta

Trunk *n.* puno, kalson, katawan, trompa, baul

Truss *n.* balutan, pakete, tali, bragero

Truss *v.* balutin, paketehin, talian, tukuran

Trust *n.* kompiyansa, tiwala, pagtitiwala, pag-asa

Trust *v.* magtiwala, asahan, umasa, ipagkatiwala

Trustee *n.* katiwala, kabahala

Trusteeship *n.* pagkakatiwala, pagkakabahala

Trustful *adj.* mapagtiwala

Trustworthy *adj.* mapagtitiwalaan

Truth *n.* katotohanan

Truthful *adj.* makatotoo, mapagaabi ng totoo

Try *v.* umato, litisin, tikman, atuhin, magsubok, subukin

Tryout *n.* pagsubok

Tryst *n.* tipanan

Tsar *n.* sar

Tsarina *n.* sarina

Tub *n.* taong

Tube *n.* tubo, tunel

Tubercle *n.* bukol, umbok, buko, tuberkulo

Tubercular *adj.* tuberkular

Tuberculosis *n.* tuberkulosis, tisis

Tuck *v.* isukbit, isalukbit, isuksok

Tuesday *n.* Martes

Tuft *n.* borlas, lamuymoy

Tug *n.* hila, batak, hatak, arastre

Tug *v.* batakin, bumatak, humila, hilahin

Tulip *n.* tulipan

Tulle *n.* tul

Tumble *v.* magsirko, mabulid, mapabulid, bumalintong

Tumbler *n.* sirkero, baso

Tumbrel *n.* kareta

Tumefaction *n.* pamumukol, pamamaga

Tumid *adj.* namamaga, paga, maga, mabintog

Tumor *n.* tumor, bukol

Tumult *n.* kagulo, pagkakagulo, linggal, linggaw

Tumultuous *adj.* magulo, malinggal

Tuna *n.* atun

Tune *n.* tono, himig

Tune *v.* magapina, apinahin

Tuneful *adj.* mahimig

Tuneless *adj.* disintunado

Tuner *n.* apinador, pangapina

Tungsten *n.* tungsten

Tunic *n.* tunika, blusa

Tuning *n.* apinasyon, sinkronisasyon

Tunnel *n.* tunel, jaang-yungib

Tupentine *n.* turpentina, agwaras

Turban *n.* turbante

Turbid *adj.* labusaw, malabo

Turbine *n.* turbina

Turbulence *n.* gulo, ligalig

Turbulent *adj.* magulo, maligalig

Turean *n.* sopera

Turf *n.* lupang-damuhan, lupang-pikpik

Turgid *adj.* mabintog, paga, maga

Turk *n.* Turko

Turkey *n.* pabo

Turkey (country) *n.* Turkiya

Turkish *adj.* Turko

Turmeric *n.* dilaw

Turmoil *n.* pagkakagulo, kaligaligan

Turn *n.* ikit, ikot, inog, pihit

Turn *v.* paikutin, baligtarin, ilihis, paikitin, pihitin, ibaling

Turncoat *n.* traidor, taksil

Turner *n.* tornero, manlililok

Turnip *n.* turnip, singkamas

Turnkey *n.* liyabero, ingatsusi

Turnout *n.* paglabas, aklasan, produkto

Turnstile *n.* tornikete

Turntable *n.* paikutan

Turquoise *n.* turkesa

Turret *n.* toresilya

Turtle *n.* pagong

Turtledove *n.* kalapati, batubato

Tusk *n.* pangil

Tusker *n.* pangilan

Tussis *n.* ubo

Tussle *n.* panunggaban, pagpapambuno

Tutelage *n.* tutela, pagtuturo

Tution *n.* tutela, pagtuturo

Tutor *n.* tutor, guro

Tutorial *adj.* tutoryal

Tuxedo *n.* tuksedo

Twaddle *v.* magsalitang palamya

Twain *adj.* dalawa

Twang *n.* tainting, tunoghumal

Tweed *n.* lana

Tweet *n.* tiririt, huni

Tweezers *n.* tiyani

Twelfth *adj.* ikalabindalawa

Twelve *adj.* labindalawa

Twentieth *adj.* ikadalawampu

Twenty *adj.* dalawampu

Twice *adj.* dalawang beses, makalawa, doblado

Twiddle *v.* paglaruan, kalantariin

Twig *n.* pilpil, yagit

Twilight *n.* agaw-ilwanag, pamimitak, takipsilim

Twin *n.* kambal

Twine *n.* pisi, pulupot

Twine *v.* pilutin, pagpuluputin

Twinge *n.* kirot

Twinge *v.* kumirot

Twinkle *v.* kumurap, kumislap

Twirl *n.* ikit, ikot, inog

Twirl *v.* mag-inikot, paikutin, paikitin, painugin

Twist *v.* pilipitin, pilutin, baluktutin, tursihin

Twitch *n.* haltak, baltak

Twitch *v.* baltakin, haltakin

Two *adj.* dalawa

Twofold *adj.* doble, doblado

Tycoon *n.* kaske

Type *n.* tipo, uri, huwaran

Type *v.* makinilyahin

Typescript *n.* orihinal makinilyado

Typewriter *n.* makinilya

Typewriting *n.* pagmamakinilya

Typhoid *adj.* tipus

Typhoon *n.* unos, sigwa, bagyo

Typical *adj.* tipiko

Typify *v.* mangatawan, maglarawan

Typographic *adj.* tipgrapika

Typography *n.* tipograpiya

Tyrannical *adj.* malupit, mapaniil

Tyranny *n.* tiraniya, paniniil, kalupitan

Tyrant *n.* tirano, panginoong malupit, mang-aapi

Tyro *n.* nobato, baguhan

U u

U-boat *n.* submarinong Aleman

Ubiquitous *adj.* ubikwo

Ubiquity *n.* ubikwidad

Udder *n.* lawit ng suso

Ugliness *n.* kapangitan, pagkapangit

Ugly *adj.* pangit

Ukase *n.* ukase, kautusang, opisyal

Ukranian *adj.* Ukranyo

Ulcer *n.* ulsera

Ulcerate *v.* mag-ulser

Ulterior *adj.* tago, nalilingid, nakatago, lihim, lingid

Ultima *n.* huling pantig, ultima

Ultimate *adj.* pinakamalayo, pinakadulo, panghuli

Ultimatum *n.* ultimatum, huling-sabi

Ultraviolet *adj.* ultrabyolado, ultrabyoleta

Ululate *v.* umangal, tumambaw, dumaing

Umbilicus *n.* pusod

Umbra *n.* sombra, lilim

Umbrella *n.* payong

Umpire *n.* reperi, tagahatol

Unaccompanied *adj.* walang kasam

Unanimity *n.* unanimidad, buong pagkakaisa

Unanimous *adj.* buong pagkakaisa

T t

Unarmed *adj.* walang armas, walang sandata

Unavailing *adj.* walang-bisa, di-magkabisa

Unavoidable *adj.* di-maiwasan, di-mailagan

Unaware *adj.* walang-kamalayan

Unbecoming *adj.* di-bagay

Unborn *adj.* di pa isinisilang

Uncanny *adj.* mahiwaga

Unceremonious *adj.* pabig-labigla

Uncertain *adj.* di-tiyak, dinakatitiyak

Uncircumcised *adj.* supot

Uncle *n.* tiyo, amain

Uncomfortable *adj.* di-maalwan

Uncommon *adj.* di-karaniwan, bihira, pambihira

Unconcern *n.* kawalang-bahala

Unconditional *adj.* lubos, ganap, puspusan

Unconscious *adj.* di-namamalayan, walang-malay

Unconsitutional *adj.* labag sa Konstitusyon

Uncounted *adj.* di-binilang, di-mabilang

Uncouth *adj.* kakaiba, kakatwa

Uncover *v.* ihantad, ihayag, buksan, magpugay

Uncovered *adj.* walang-takip, walang piyansa

Uncultivated *adj.* di-linang

Undaunted *adj.* walang-gulat, walang-takot

Undemonstrative *adj.* masinop, matimpi

Undeniable *adj.* di-maitatanggi, di-matatanggihan

Under *adj.* pangilalim, kulang, kontrolado, supil

Under *adv.* sa ilalim

Under *prep.* sa ilalim, ayon sa

Underage *adj.* kulang sa edad

Underbid *v.* tumawad, tawaran

Underclothes *n.* damit pangilalim

Undercover *adj.* lihim

Undercurrent *n.* agos na pangilalim, agos na tago

Underdog *n.* taong-hamak, taong-api

Underdone *adj.* malasado

Underestimate *v.* meno-spresyuhin

Underestimation *n.* meno-spresyo

Underfeed *v.* gutumin

Underfoot *v.* sa paanan

Undergo *v.* dumanas, dumaan, magbata, magdanas, tumikim

Undergraduate *n.* kasalu-kuyang mag-aaral

Underground *adj.* lihim

Underground *adv.* palihim

Underhanded *adj.* pakubli, panakaw

Underline *v.* salungguhitan

Undermine *v.* magpaguho, paguhuin, papanghinain

Underneath *prep* sa ilalim ng

Underpass *n.* daang pangilalim

Underprivileged *adj.* kulang-karapatan

Underrate *v.* matahin, paliitin, siguruhin, maliitin

Undersell *v.* magmura, ipagmura

Undershirt *n.* kamiseta

Undersign *v.* lumagda, lagdaan

Undersized *adj.* maliit kaysa karaniwan

Understand *v.* maunawaan, maintindihan, mabatid

Understanding *n.* kauna-waan, pang-unawa, unawaan, kasunduan

Undertake *v.* magasagawa, isagawa, gumawa

Undertaker *n.* taong-punerarya

Undertaking *n.* empresa, pagsasagawa

Undertone *n.* kabilang sintido

Undervalue *v.* uriing mababa, maliitin

Underwear n. kasuutang, pangilalim

Underwear *n.* kasuutang, pangilalim

Underweight *adj.* bigat na kulang, kulang na bigat

Underworld *n.* lipunang mababa

Underwrite *v.* iseguro

Undesirable *adj.* di-kanaisnais

Undo *v.* kalagin, tastahin, kalasin, buksan, tanggalin

Undress *v.* maghubad, hubuan, hubarin, hubaran, maghubo

Undressed *adj.* hubad, hubo

Undulate *v.* umalimbukay, umalon

Unduly *adj.* labag sa batas, di-wasto

Undying *adj.* di-mamatay, di-magtatapos

Unearth *v.* matuklasan, mahukay

Uneasy *adj.* balisa, di-mapakali

Unemployed *adj.* disempleado

Unemployment *n.* pagka-desempleado

Unequal *adj.* di-pareho, dipantay

Unequaled *adj.* di-map-antayan, dalang-kapantay

Unequivocal *adj.* tiyak sa kahulugan, malinaw

Unerring *adj.* di-nagka-kamali, walang mali

Uneven *adj.* baku-bako, dipantay, di-makinis

Uneventful *adj.* tahimik

Unexpected *adj.* di-inaasahan, di-akalain

Unfair *adj.* di-makatarungan, di-tapat

Unfaithful *adj.* di-matapat, di-marangal

Unfamiliar *adj.* kinami-hasnan, di-alam

Unfathomable *adj.* di-maarok, di-matarok

Unfavorable *adj.* di-paborable, pasalungat

Unfinished *adj.* di-tapos, diganap

Unfit *adj.* di-husto, di-bagay

Unfold *v.* iladlad, ikadkad, ibuka, ihayag

Unforgettable *adj.* di-malilimutan

Unfortunate *adj.* sawi, kapos-palad, kulang-pala

Unfriendly *adj.* galit, mailap

Unfruitful *adj.* di-mabunga, di-nagbubunga, baog, esteril

Unfurl *v.* iladlad, iwagayway, pawagaywayin

Ungainly *adj.* lampa

Ungrateful *adj.* ingrato

Unhand *v.* bitiwan

Unhappy *adj.* malungkot, sawi

Unhealthy *adj.* salaula, maysakit

Unhitch *v.* disingantsahin

Unhurried *adj.* di-padalusdalos

Unicameral *adj.* unikameral

Unicellular *adj.* uniselular

Unicorn *n.* kabayong may sungay

Unification *n.* unipikasyon, pagsasang-isahan

Uniform *n.* uniporme

Unify *v.* pag-isahin, papagkaisahin

Union *n.* unyon, hugpong, pagkakaisa, samahan

Unique *adj.* tangi, kakaiba, pambihira

Unison *n.* katunog, ugma

Unit *n.* yunit, bahagi, pangkat, isa

Unite *v.* pag-isahin, papagkaisahin, magkaisa, pagsamahin

United *adj.* pinagsama

Unity *n.* kaisahan, pagkakaisa

Universal *adj.* unibersal, panlahat, pandaigdig

Universe *n.* uniberso, sansinukuban

University *n.* unibersidad, pamantasan

Unjust *adj.* di-makatarungan

Unkempt *adj.* di-suklay, magaspang

Unkind *adj.* malupit, marahas

Unknown *adj.* di-kilala, dialam

Unlawful *adj.* labag sa batas, ilegal

Unleash *v.* alpasan

Unless *conj.* maliban kung

Unlike *adj.* di-katulad, magkaiba

Unlikely *adj.* walang-kasiguruhan, walang-katiyakan

Unlimited *adj.* walang hanggan, walang hangganan

Unload *v.* magdiskarga, diskargahin, mag-ibis, ibsan

Unlucky *adj.* walang-suwerte, sawi

Unman *v.* papanghinain

Unmindful *adj.* malimutin

Unmistakable *adj.* di-mapapapagkamalan

Unnatural *adj.* di-likas, dikatutubo, artipisyal

Unnecessary *adj.* di-kailangan

Unoccupied *adj.* di-okupado

Unpack *v.* magdisimpake, disimpakihin

Unpacked *adj.* disimapakado

Unpaid *adj.* di-bayad

Unpardonable *adj.* di-mapatatawad

Unpleasant *adj.* di-magiliw, nakayayamot

Unreasonable *adj.* wala sa katwiran, di-makatuwiran

Unrelenting *adj.* patuloy, walang-tigil

Unroll *v.* ikadkad, iladlad, ilatag

Unruly *adj.* di-masupil, magulo

Unsafe *adj.* mapanganib, piligroso

Unsanitary *adj.* salaula

Unscientific *adj.* walang-siyensiya, walang-agham

Unseat *v.* alisin sa pagkakaupo

Unseen *adj.* di-kita, lingid tago

Unselfish *adj.* di-maimbot, di-mapag-imbot

Unsettle *v.* silsin sa lugar, manggulo, guluhin

Unsightly *adj.* pangit

Unskilled *adj.* di-sanay, dibihasa

Unsophisticated *adj.* simple, di-mapagkunwari

Unstable *adj.* di-matatag, dimatibay

Unsuitable *adj.* di-bagay

Unsung *adj.* di-napapurihan, di-naparangalan

Untidy *adj.* limahid, marumi

Untie *v.* kalagin, kalasin

Until *prep.* hanggang sa

Untimely *adj.* wala sa panahon, maaga

Untold *adj.* di-masayod, dimaulatan

Untouchable *adj.* di-mahipo, di-masalat

Untoward *adj.* pampahirap, di-mabuti, masama

Untrue *adj.* di-totoo, di-tunay

Untruth *n.* kasinungalingan, kabulaanan

Untruthful *adj.* sinungaling, bulaan

Untutored *adj.* di-naturuan, mangmang

Unused *adj.* di-gamit, di-ginagamit, di-bihasa

Unusual *adj.* di-karaniwan

Unutterable *adj.* di-mabigkas, di-maipahayag

Unveil *v.* alisan ng kulubong

Unwary *adj.* di-maingat

Unwilling *adj.* di-gusto, ayaw

Unwind *adj.* ituwid

Unwitting *adj.* di-alam, walang-malay

Unworthy *adj.* di-karapatdapat, di-bagay

Unwrap *v.* alisan ng balot

Unwritten *adj.* di-nakasulat, di-nasusulat

Up *adv.* pataas, paitaas

Upbringing *n.* pag-aalaga, pagpapalaki

Upgrade *n.* paakyat, pataas

Upgrade *v.* itaas, iasenso

Upheaval *n.* transtorno, lindol

Uphill *adv.* paakyat, pabarangka

Uphold *v.* tabanan, itaas, tukuran, ayunan, itaguyod

Upholstery *n.* tapisero, tapiseriya

Upkeep *n.* pangangalaga

Upland *n.* ilaya

Uplift *n.* pag-aangat, pagtataas, pagpapabuti

Uplift *v.* buhatin, langat, pataasin, patayugin

Upon *prep.* sa, sa ibabaw ng

Upper *adj.* higit na mataas, higit na pataas, nakatataas

Uppercut *n.* aperkat, sapok

Uppermost *adj.* pinakamataas, pinakamatayog, ituktok

Uppish *adj.* hambog, palalo

Upright *adj.* tuwid, nakatayo, marangal, makatarungan

Uprising *n.* ribulusyon, pagbabangon, paghihimaksik

Uproar *n.* kagulo, kaingay, linggal

Uproot *v.* bunutin, ganutin, labnutin, lipulin

Upset *v.* itaob, guluhin, itumba, mabalisa

Upside *n.* ibabaw

Upstairs *adv.* sa itaas

Upswing *n.* pagtaas, pagtayog

Upward *adv.* pataas, paitaas

Uranium *n.* uranyo

Uranus *n.* Urano

Urban *adj.* panlungsod, urbano

Urbanity *n.* urbanidad, pagkamagalang

Urchin *n.* batang malikot, batang pilyo

Urea *n.* urea

Uremia *n.* uremya

Ureter *n.* daang-ihi, ureter

Urge *n.* panghihikayat, silakbo, pagluhog, pagsamo, simbuyo

Urge *v.* manghikayat, itagubilin, hikayatin, lumuhog, iluhog

Urgent *adj.* urhente, apurahan, mahigpit

Urinal *n.* ihian, urinal

Urinary *adj.* ukol, sa ihi

Urinate *v.* umihi

Urination *n.* pag-ihi

Urine *n.* ihi

Urn *n.* urna

Ursa *n.* osa

Urticaria *n.* urtikarya, tagulabay

Us *pron.* tayo, amin, atin, natin, kami

Usable *adj.* magagamit, gamitin

Usage *n.* gamit, paggamit, ugali, kaugalian

Use *n.* paggamit, pagpapagamit, kagamitan

Use *v.* gumamit, gamitin

Useful *adj.* gamitin , mapakikinabangan

Useless *adj.* walang kagamitan, walang-kuwenta, inutil

User *n.* ang gumagamit

Usher *n.* tagahatid

Usher *v.* ihatid, samahan

Usherette *n.* tagahatid

Usual *adj.* karaniwan, kinaugalian

Usufruct *n.* usuprukto

Usurer *n.* usurero, mapagpatubo

Usurious *adj.* usuraryo

Usurp *v.* magamkam, kamkamin

Usurpation *n.* pangan-gamkam

Usurper *n.* mangangamkam

Usury *n.* usurya

Utensil *n.* kasangkapan

Uterus *n.* matris, bahay-bata

Utilitarian *adj.* utilitaryo

Utility *n.* kagamitan, utilidad

Utilize *v.* gamitin, utilisahin

Utmost *adj.* kalayu-layuan

Utopia *n.* Utopya

Utter *adj.* ganap, lubos

Utter *v.* bumigkas, ipahayag, bigkasin, magsalita, salitain

Utterance *n.* pagbigkas, pamumutawi

Utterly *adv.* ganap

Uxorious *adj.* talusaya

V v

Vacancy *n.* bakante

Vacant *adj.* bakante

Vacate *v.* bakantihin, iwan, umalis

Vacation *n.* bakasyon, pahinga, tigil

Vacationist *n.* bakasyunista

Vaccinate *v.* magbakuna, bakunahan

Vaccination *n.* pagbabakuna

Vaccine *n.* bakuna

Vaccum *n.* alangaang

Vacuity *n.* tahaw, hawan, kabasiyuhan

Vacuole *n.* ligata

Vacuum *adj.* bakuum, weko

Vagabond *n.* bagamundo, hampaslupa

Vagary *n.* ikot, kalibutan, sumpang, kapritso

Vagina *n.* bayna, talusok, kauban

Vagrancy *n.* bagansiya, paghahampaslupa

Vagrant *adj.* lagalag, palaboy

Vagrant *n.* hampaslupa

Vague *adj.* malabo, di-tiyak

Vain *adj.* marangya, hambog

Vainglorous *adj.* balunlugurin, hambog

Vainglory *n.* balunlugod, kakahambugan

Valance *n.* senepa, palawit

Valediction *n.* baledikasiyon, pamamaalam

Valedictorian *n.* bale-diktoryan

Valedictory *adj.* nama-maalam

Valence *n.* balensiya, bagsiksama

Valentine *n.* kasuyo, kasintahan

Valet *n.* balet, kamarero

Valhalia *n.* balhala

Valiant *adj.* matapang, magiting

Valid *adj.* balido

Validate *v.* baluduhin, bigyang-bisa, patotohanan

Validity *n.* balides, kabisaan, kairalan

Valise *n.* maleta, maletin

Valkyrie *n.* balkirya

Valley *n.* lambak

Valor *n.* giting, kagitingan

Valuable *adj.* mahalaga, mamahalin

Valuation *n.* tasa, tasasyon

Valuator *n.* tasador

Value *n.* balor, halaga, kahalagahan, kagamitan

Valve *n.* balbula

Vampire *n.* bampiro

Van *n.* pangunahin, taliba

Van *n.* ban, wegon

Vandal *adj.* bandalo, maninira

Vandalism *n.* bandalismo, paninira

Vane *n.* pabiling, girimpula, dahon, talim

Vanguard *n.* taliba, pangunahin

Vanilla *n.* banilya, banila

Vanish *v.* mawala, maparam, pumanaw, mamatay

Vanity *n.* banidad

Vanquish *v.* malupig, manlulupig, lupigin

Vantage *n.* bentaha, kahigtan

Vapor *n.* singaw

Vaporize *v.* pasingawin

Vaporizer *v.* pampasingaw, baporisador

Vaporous *adj.* masingaw

Variable *adj.* pabagu-bago, paiba-iba, salawahan

Variance *n.* pagkapabagu-bago

Variant *adj.* iba

Variant *n.* ibang

Variation *n.* baryasyon, pagiibang-anyo

Varicose *adj.* maga-maga, bukul-bukol

Varied *adj.* pabagu-bago, iba-iba, sarisari

Variety *n.* pagkaiba-iba, sarisari, uri

Various *adj.* iba, iba't iba, sarisari

Varlet *n.* lakayo, pahe

Varnish *n.* barnis

Varnish *v.* barnisan

Varnisher *n.* barnisador, tagabarnis

Varsity *n.* barsiti

Vary *v.* mag-iba-iba, magbagu-bago

Vascular *adj.* baskular

Vase *n.* plorera, paso

Vaseline *n.* baselina

Vassal *n.* basalyo

Vast *adj.* malawak

Vastness *n.* kalawakan, kalakhan

Vat *n.* tangke, bariles, kawa

Vatican *n.* batikano

Vaudeville *n.* bodabil

Vault *n.* balantok, arko, lundag, lukso

Vaulted *adj.* binalantukan, inarkuhan

Vaunt *v.* maghambog, magpalalo

Vection *n.* pagkahawa, pagkalalin

Vector *n.* hakot-mikrobyo, bektor

Vegetable *n.* gulay

Vegetal *adj.* behetal, panggulay

Vegetarian *n.* kaing-gugulay

Vegetate *v.* kumain-tumubo

Vegetation *n.* pananim, halaman

Vehemence *n.* pagngangalit, silakbo, kapusukan

Vehement *adj.* nagngangalit, masilakbo, mapusok

Vehicle *n.* sasakyan, bihikulo

Vehicular *adj.* pansasakyan, bihikular

Veil *n.* belo, tabing, takip

Veil *v.* beluhan

Vein *n.* giha, bena, ugat, lahang, lamat, lahid

Velar *adj.* ng ngalangala

Velocity *n.* liksi, dali, bilis, tulin

Velum *n.* ngalangala

Velvet *n.* tersiyupelo

Venalty *n.* karawalan, kabalakyutan

Vend *v.* magbili, magtinda

Vendee *n.* ang pinabilihan, ang mamimili

Vendetta *n.* bendeta, higanti

Vendor *n.* magbibili

Veneer *n.* kapa, pangibabaw

Venerable *adj.* kapintu-pintuho, kapita-pitagan

Venerate *v.* pintuhuin, pagpitaganan

Veneration *n.* pamimintuho, pamimitagan

Venereal *adj.* benereo

Venetian *n.* Benesyano

Vengeance *n.* higanti, benggatibo

Venial *adj.* benyal, mapatatawad

Venison *n.* karning-usa

Venom *n.* kamandag, lason

Venomous *adj.* makamandag, nakalalason

Vent *n.* butas, labasan

Ventilate *v.* bentilahan, pahanginan

Ventilator *n.* bentilador

Ventral *adj.* bentral, abdominal, pantiyan

Ventricle *n.* bentrikulo

Ventriloquism *n.* bentrilokiya

Ventriloquist *n.* bentrilokwo

Venture *n.* bentura, pakasam, pakikipagsapalaran

Venture *v.* magbentura, magpakasam, makipag-sapalaran

Venturesome *adj.* mapag-pakipagsapalaran

Venturous *adj.* pangahas

Venue *n.* pook na nakakasasaklaw

Venus *n.* Benus

Veracious *adj.* makatotoo

Veracity *n.* pagkamakatotoo, pagkatotoo

Verb *n.* pandiwa, berbo

Verbal *adj.* pandiwari

Verbena *n.* berbena

Verbiage *n.* kaliguyan

Verbose *adj.* masalita, maligoy

Verdant *adj.* lungtian, berde, sariwa

Verdict *n.* beredikto, palyo, pasiya

Verdure *n.* kalungtian, kaberdehan

Verge *n.* gilid, tabihan, hanggan

Veridical *adj.* beridiko, totoo, tunay

Verify *v.* hanapin ang patotoo, beripikahan

Vermicelli *n.* pideos

Vermicular *adj.* parang bulati

Vermiform *adj.* anyong bulati

Vermillion *n.* bermelyon

Vermin *n.* mga mumunsik na hayop

Vermouth *v.* bermut

Vernacular *adj.* bernakular, katutubo, lokal

Vernacular *n.* inangwika

Vernal *adj.* primabernal, bernal

Versatile *adj.* bersatil

Versatility *n.* bersatilidad

Verse *n.* berso, tula

Versicle *n.* bersikulo

Versification *n.* bersipikasyon, pagtula

Versify *v.* magberso, bumerso, tumula

Version *n.* bersiyon, salin

Versus *prep.* laban sa, kontra

Vertebra *n.* bertebra

Vertebrate *n.* , maygulugod

Vertex *n.* taluktok, ituktok

Vertical *adj.* bertikal, patayo

Vertigo *n.* hilo, liyo

Verve *n.* talino, sigla, buhay

Very *adv.* napaka

Vesical *adj.* besikal, ukol sa pantog

Vesicle *n.* orasyon

Vessel *n.* sisidlan, lalagyan

Vest *n.* tsaleko

Vested *adj.* ganap, lubos

Vestibule *n.* bestibulo, pasilyo

Vestige *n.* bakas, dasto, palatandaan

Vestment *n.* kasuutan, karamtan

Vestry *n.* sakristiya, bestuwaryo

Veteran *n.* beterano

Veto *n.* beto

Veto *v.* betuhan

Vex *v.* mangyamot, yamutin, inisin

Vexation *n.* yamot, pagkayamot, pagkainis

Viadict *n.* tulay

Vial *n.* munting bote, ampolyas

Viand *n.* biyanda, ulam

Viaticum *n.* biyatiko

Vibrant *adj.* tumitibok, masidha, mataginting

Vibrate *v.* mangatal, manginig, tumibok

Vicar *n.* bikaryo

Vice *n.* bisyo

Vice *pref.* bise

Vice *prep.* sa halip ng, sa lugar ng

Viceroy *n.* birey

Vicinity *n.* kapitbahayan

Vicious *adj.* bisyoso, mabisyo

Victim *n.* biktima

Victimize *v.* biktimahin

Victor *n.* ang nagwagi, angnagtagumpay

Victorious *adj.* mapagwagi, mapanagumpay

Victory *n.* biktorya, pagwawagi, tagumpay

Victuals *n.* pagkain

Video *n.* bideo

Vie *v.* makipagpaligsahan, makipaglaban

Vietnamese *adj.* Biyetnames

View *n.* tingin, patingin, pagmamasid, tanaw

View *v.* tanawin, tingnan, malasin, masdan

Viewpoint *n.* paningin, pananaw, palagay

Vigil *n.* bantay, pagbabantay, lamay, paglalamay

Vigilance *n.* bihilansiya

Vigilant *adj.* mapagbantay, mapangalaga

Vignette *n.* binyeta

Vignettist *n.* binyetista

Vigor *n.* lakas, kalakasan, kakayahan

Vigorous *adj.* malakas, masigya, malusog

Vile *adj.* mababa, hamak, imbi

Villa *n.* bilya

Village *n.* nayon, baryo

Villager *n.* taganayon, tagabaryo

Villain *n.* buhong, kontrabida

Villify *v.* hamakin

Vindicate *v.* patbayan ang katwiran, ipagtanggol

Vindictive *adj.* mapa-ghiganti, benggatibo

Vine *n.* baging, ubas

Vinegar *n.* suka

Vineyard *n.* binya

Vintage *n.* gulang ng alak

Violate *v.* lumabag, labagin, lumapastangan

Violation *n.* paglabag, pagispastangan, paghalay

Violence *n.* dahas, pagdara

Violent *adj.* marahas, mapusok

Violet *n.* , biyuleta

Violin *n.* biyulin

Violinist *n.* biyulinista

Viper *n.* bibora

Virago *n.* birago, amason

Virgin *n.* birhen, dalaga

Virile *adj.* maypagkalalaki, biril, lalaki

Virility *n.* pagkalalaki, birilidad

Virtue *n.* birtud, kalinisangbudhi, bisa

Virtuoso *n.* birtuwoso

Virulent *adj.* makamandag

Virus *n.* birus, lason, kamandag

Visa *n.* bisa, tulot-pasok

Visage *n.* pagmumukha, itsura

Viscera *n.* binubong

Viscid *adj.* malagkit

Viscosity *n.* lagkit, kalagkitan

Viscount *n.* biskonde

Vise *n.* ipitan

Visibility *n.* linaw ng tanaw

Visible *adj.* kita, halata, hayag

Vision *n.* bisyon, malikmata, malas, tingin

Visit *n.* dumalaw, bumisita

Visitor *n.* bisita, dalaw, panauhin

Vista *n.* bista

Visual *adj.* biswal, paningin

Visualize *v.* larawanin , biswalisahin

Vital *adj.* mahalaga sa buhay

Vitality *n.* bitaliad, buhay, tatag, sigla, lakas

Vitamin *n.* bitamina

Vitiate *v.* ialinan, hawahan, sirain, iligaw

Vitrescent *adj.* mabububog

Vitrify *v.* gawing bubog

Vituperate *v.* mang-alimura, alimurahin, laitin, tungayawin

Vivacious *adj.* bibo, masigla, masaya

Vivacity *n.* kabibuhan, kasiglahan, pagkamasaya

Vivid *adj.* buhay , matingkad

Viviparous *adj.* bibiparo, manganganakbuhay

Vixen *n.* sora

Vocabulary *n.* bokabularyo, talasalitaan

Vocal *adj.* pantinig, maytinig, matinig, pasalita

Vocalist *n.* manganganta, mang-aawit

Vocalization *n.* bokalisasyon

Vocation *n.* bokasyon

Vocational *adj.* bokasyonal, panghanabuhay

Vocative *adj.* bokatibo, patawag

Vodka *n.* bodka

Vogue *n.* moda, uso, istilo

Voice *n.* tinig, boses, boto

Void *adj.* walang-laman, nulo

Void *v.* nuluhin

Volatile *adj.* bolatil, madaling sumingaw

Volcano *n.* bulkan

Volcanologist *n.* bulkanologo

Volcanology *n.* bulkanolohiya

Volition *n.* kalooban, pagloloob, pasiya

Volley *n.* sibad, putok, bulya

Volleyball *n.* bolibol

Volt *n.* boltiyo, bolt

Voltage *n.* boltahe

Voluble *adj.* masalita, madaldal

Volume *n.* aklat, tomo, bulumen, bulto

Voluminous *adj.* makapal

Voluntary *adj.* kusa, kusangloob

Volunteer *n.* boluntaryo, taong prisintado

Volunteer *v.* magprisinta

Vomit *v.* sumuka, magsuka, isuka

Voodoo *n.* budu, mangkukulam

Voodooism *n.* pangkukulam

Voracious *adj.* masiba, matakaw

Vortex *n.* ipuipo, uliuli

Votary *n.* deboto

Vote *n.* boto, halal

Vouch *v.* sumaksi, saksihan, magpatunay

Vote *v.* bumoto, iboto, ihalal

Votive *adj.* pamanata

Voucher *n.* bautser, komprobante

Vow *n.* panata, pangako, debosyon

Vowel *n.* patinig, bokal

Voyage *n.* paglalayag, paglalakbay

Vulcanization *n.* bulkani-sasyon

Vulgar *adj.* bulgar, magaspang, mahalay, mababa

Vulnerable *adj.* pangkarani-wan, mababa, hamak, matattalban

Vulnerable *adj.* bulnerable

Vulnerary *adj.* pampabahaw

Vulture *n.* buwitre

Vying *adj.* ang nag-aagawan

W w

Wabble *v.* gumiray-giray, sumuray-suray

Wacky *adj.* nahihibang

Wad *n.* piraso, bilot, bugal

Wad *v.* bilutin

Wadding *n.* wading, pading

Waddle *v.* kumampang-kampang

Wade *v.* tumawid, magpansaw, maglunoy

Wafer *n.* apa, biskuwit-apa

Waff *n.* samyo, kaway, wasiwas

Waffle *n.* waffle

Waft *n.* dapyo, iwasiwas, dapyo, simoy

Waft *v.* palutangin, paliparin, iwasiwas

Wag *n.* ikawag, paypay

Wag *v.* ikawag

Wage *n.* sahod, bayad, upa

Wage *v.* mandigma, digmain

Wager *n.* pusta, taya, pagbabakasakali

Waggle *v.* sumuray, gumiray, gumiwang, KUMAWAG

Wagon *n.* karo, bagon

Wagoner *n.* karetero

Wagonette *n.* baguneta

Waif *n.* napulot, naligaw

Wail *n.* taghoy, daing, himutok

Wail *v.* managhoy, manambitan, mamighati, dumaing

Waist *n.* baywang

Wait *n.* paghihintay

Wait *v.* maghintay, hintayin, ipaghintay

Waiter *n.* serbidor, serbiyente, serbidora

Waive *v.* ipalamang, iwaksi, ipaubaya, talikdan, itakwil

Waiver *n.* renunsiya

Wake *n.* agwahe, alimbukay, daanan, landas

Wake *n.* pagpupuyat, paglalamay

Wake *v.* magising, gisingin, magpuyat, maglamay

Wakeful *adj.* di-makatulog

Waken *v.* magising, pukawin, gisingin

Wale *n.* latay

Walk *n.* lakad, hakbang, uri

Walk *v.* lumakad, maglakad, lakarin

Walkaway *n.* magaang pananalo

Walker *n.* tagalakad

Walkie-talkie wokotoki, walkie-talkie

Walkout *n.* aklasan, welga

Wall *n.* pader, harang, kuta, dingding, tabike

Wall *v.* bakuran, tabikihan, paderan

Wallboard *n.* pohas, pandingding

Wallet *n.* kartera, pitaka

Wallflower *n.* pamutas-silya

Wallop *n.* malakas na suntok

Wallow *v.* maglublob, maglunoy

Walnut *n.* nugales

Walrus *n.* seacow, bakangdagat, walrus

Waltz *n.* balse

Waltz *v.* magbalse

Wampum *n.* wampum, abaloryo

Wan *adj.* malabo, malamlam

Wand *n.* baras, barita

Wander *v.* maglagalag, gumala, magpagala-gala

Wanderer *n.* taong-libot, taong-gala

Wanderlust *n.* kati ng paa

Wane *v.* lumiit, umunti, manghina, magtapos

Wangle *v.* makalusot, makaligtas

Want *n.* kakulangan, pangangailangan

Want *v.* magkulang, mangailangan, naisin

Wanton *adj.* walang-taros, mahalay

War *n.* digma, labanan, pagbabaka

War *v.* digmain, magdigmaan, mandigma

Warble *v.* magpatremulo, yumodel

Ward *n.* , sangay, purok

Ward *v.* magbantay, bantayan, magtanggol

Warden *n.* warden, karselero, alkayde

Wardrobe *n.* guwardaropa, aparador

Ware *n.* kalakal, tinda, kagamitan

Warehouse *n.* bodega, pintungan

Warfare *n.* pagdirigmaan, paglalabanan

Warlike *adj.* mahilig sa digmaan, mapandigma

Warlock *n.* mangkukulam

Warm *adj.* mainit, magiliw, taos-puso

Warm *v.* uminit, painitin, mainitan

Warmonger *n.* manunul-soldigma

Warmth *n.* init, kainitan

Warn *v.* papag-ingatin, paalalahanan, babalaan

Warning *n.* babala

Warp *n.* kibal, hibla, kiwal, kibang, sulid

Warp *v.* kumibal, kumiwal, mamilipit, ilisya

Warrant *n.* utos, garantiya, mandamiyento

Warrant *v.* garantiyahan, tiyakin, hingin

Warren *n.* kulungan ng kuneho

Warrener *n.* kunehero

Warrior *n.* mandirigma

Warship *n.* sasakyang-dagat na pandigma

Wart *n.* kulugo, butig

Wary *adj.* maingat, maalaga

Wash *v.* maghugas, hugasan, maglaba, labhan

Wash-out *n.* agnas, pagkaagnas

Washable *adj.* malalabhan

Washboard *n.* kaskusang panlaba

Washbowl *n.* palanggana

Washcloth *n.* bimpo, panyudimano, basahan

Washer *n.* tagahugas, anilyo, kitse

Washerman *n.* labandero

Washing *n.* paghuhugas

Washroom *n.* labatoryo

Washstand *n.* patungan ng palanggana

Wasp *n.* putakti

Waste *adj.* tapon, itinapon, di-ginagamit

Waste *n.* tapon, dumi, pagtatapon, basura

Waste *v.* magtapon, mag-aksaya, aksayahin

Wastebasket *n.* basurahang basket

Wasteful *adj.* aksaya, mapag-aksaya

Wastrel *n.* taong mapag-aksaya, gastador

Watch *n.* kronometro, relos, orasan

Watch *n.* pagbabantay,. pagmamasid, bantay

Watch *v.* magbantay, bantayan, umabang, abangan

Watchful *adj.* mapagbantay, maalaga, maingat

Watchmaker *n.* riluhero

Watchman *n.* bantay, tanod

Watchower *n.* banayaban, bantayan

Watchword *n.* kontrasenyas

Watchwork *n.* mekanismo ng rilos

Water *n.* tubig

Water *v.* basain, magdilig, diligin

Watercourse *n.* daan ng tubig, agusan

Watercraft *n.* sasakyang, pantubig

Waterfall *n.* talong

Wateriness *n.* pagkamatubig

Watermark *n.* guhit ng lubog sa tubig, tatak-tubig

Watermelon *n.* pakwan

Watery *adj.* malabnaw

Watt *n.* batyo

Wattage *n.* batiahe, batyaho

Wave *n.* alon, daluyong, kulot

Wave *v.* wumagayway, pumagaspas, kumaway, iwasiwas

Waver *v.* manginig, mag-atubili, sumuray

Wavy *adj.* maalon, alun-alon, kulot

Wax *n.* waks, sera

Wax *v.* lumaki, dumami, lumakas, sumibol

Waxen *adj.* desera, plastik

Waxwork *adj.* pigurang desera

Way *n.* direksiyon, dako, ruta, daan

Waybill *n.* papel na ruta

Wayfarer *n.* manlalakbay

Waylay *n.* , mangharang, harangan

Waylayer *n.* mang-aabat, manghaharang

Wayside *n.* tabing-daan

Wayward *adj.* layaw, suwail

We *pron.* tayo, kami, kata

Weak *adj.* mahina, mahuna

Weaken *v.* pahinain, manghina, humina

Weakling *n.* taong may mahinang katawan

Weal *n.* kabutihan, kagalingan

Wealth *n.* yaman, kayamanan

Wealthy *adj.* mayaman

Wean *v.* awatin, iwalay

Weaning *n.* pag-awat, pagwawalay

Weapon *n.* sandata, armas

Wear *n.* pagsusuot, pagkakapagsuot

Wear *v.* magsuot, isuot, magastado

Wearisome *adj.* nakapapagod, nakakainip

Weary *adj.* pagal, suya, napapagal, inip, naiinip

Weather *n.* panahon, klima

Weather *v.* pahanginan, malusutan, maligtasan

Weatherboard *n.* tabla-sulapa

Weathercock *adj.* kupas sa panahon

Weathercock *n.* pabiling, girimpula

Weathering *n.* agnas, pagkaagnas

Weatherman *n.* meteorologo

Weatherproof *adj.* may-kontra-panahon

Weave *n.* habi, lala, wanla

Weave *v.* humabi, habihin, lumala, maglala

Weaver *n.* manghahabi, tagahabi, manlalala, tagalala

Web *n.* tela, kayo, bahayalalawa

Wed *v.* mag-asawa, pakasal

Wedding *n.* kasal, pagkakasal, kasalan

Wedge *n.* kalang, kalso

Wedlock *n.* matrimonyo, pagaasawa, pagkakasal

Wednesday *n.* Miyerkules

Wee *adj.* munti, munsik

Weed *n.* damo, damong gamasin

Weed *v.* maggamas, gamasan

Weedy *adj.* madamo

Week *n.* linggo

Weekly *adj.* lingguhan

Weep *v.* umiyak, lumuha, tumangis, manangis

Weevil *n.* bukbok

Weigh *v.* magtimbang, timbangin

Weight *n.* bigat, timbang, halaga, kahalagahan

Weight *v.* pabigatin

Weighty *adj.* mabigat, mahalaga

Weird *adj.* nakasisindak, mahiwaga

Welcome *adj.* nakalulugod

Welcome *intr.* maligayang, pagdating

Welcome *n.* magiliw na pagtanggap

Weld *v.* manghinang, iwelding, ihinang, magwelding, weldingin

Weldor *n.* manghihinang, tagahinang, magwewelding, tagawelding

Welfare *n.* kagalingan, kabutihan

Well *adj.* mabuti, malusog, magaling, bagay, dapat

Well *adv.* mahusay, magaling

Well *n.* balon, balong, bukal

Welt *n.* tupi

Welter *n.* gulo, ligalig

Welter *v.* maglublob, gumumon, magpakagumon

Wen *n.* butlig

Wench *n.* dalagita, dalaga

Wend *v.* tumungo

West *n.* kanluran, oeste

Westerly *adv.* pakanluran, kanluranin

Westward *adj.* pakanluran

Wet *adj.* basa

Wetness *n.* pagkabasa

Whack *n.* bugbog, tagupak

Whale *n.* balyena

Wharf *n.* pantalan, piyer

What *adj.* ano

Whatever *pron.* anuman

Whatsoever *pron.* anuman, kahit ano

Wheat *n.* trigo

Wheel *n.* gulong, ruweda

Wheelbarrow *n.* karetilya

Wheeze *v.* humingasing, sumingasing

Whelp *n.* tuta, kuwa

When *adj.* kailan

When *adv.* kailan

When *pron.* kailan

Whenever *adv.* kailanman

Wherat *adj.* tungo sa, sa dahilang

Where *adv.* saan

Where *conj.* kung saan

Where *pron.* saan

Whereabouts *n.* kinalalagyan, kinatatayuan

Whereas *conj.* yayamang, sapagkat, sa gayon, gayong ang totoo'y

Whereby *adv.* sa pamamagitan ng

Wherefore *adj.* sa anong dahilan

Wherein *adv.* pook na kakikitaan noon

Wherever *adj.* saanman

Whet *v.* maghasa, patalasin, patalimin

Whether *conj.* kung

Whether *pron.* alinman

Whethertone *n.* batong basaan

Whey *n.* suwero

Which *conj.* na

Which *pron.* alin

Whichever *adv.* alinman, kahit alin

Whiff *n.* buga, simoy, singaw

While *conj.* samantala, habang

While *n.* sandali

While *v.* magparaan ng oras

Whim *n.* kapritso, sumpong

Whimper *v.* umingit, humikbi

Whimsical *adj.* makapritso, sumpungin

Whine *v.* humaluyhoy, haluyhoy

Whinny *v.* humalinghing

Whip *n.* latiko, pamalo, latikuhin, paluin

Whir *n.* haging

Whir *v.* humaging

Whirl *n.* ikit, liyo, ikot, inog, hilo

Whirl *v.* uminog, mahilo, maliyo

Whirlpool *n.* puyo sa dagat

Whirlwind *n.* ipu-ipo, buhawi

Whisk *n.* pagwawalis, palis

Whisk *v.* walisin, palisin

Whisker *n.* balbas, patilya, bigote

Whiskey *n.* wisky

Whisper *n.* bulong

Whisper *v.* bumulong

Whisperer *n.* ang bumubulong

Whispering *adj.* bumubulong

Whistle *n.* sipol, silbato, pitada

Whistle *v.* sumipol, sumilbato, pumitada

White *adj.* maputi, blangko

White *n.* puti, blangko

Whiten *v.* magpaputi, paputiin, pumuti, mamuti

Whitener *n.* pampaputi

Whiteness *n.* kaputian

Whitewash *n.* pintang puti

Whitewash *v.* pintahan ng puti

Whither *adv.* pasaan

Whiting *n.* tisa, yeso

Whittle *n.* magkayas, kayasin, kayasan

Who *pron.* sino

Whoever *pron.* sinuman

Whole *adj.* buo, ganap, kompleto, lahat

Wholehearted *adj.* buong-puso

Wholesale *n.* pakyaw, pakyawan, aap

Wholesome *adj.* nakabubuti, nakapagpapabanal, matino

Wholly *adj.* buung-buo, lubos, lahatan

Whoop *n.* sigaw, hiyaw

Whoop *v.* sumigaw, humiyaw

Whore *n.* puta

Whorl *n.* likaw

Whose *pron.* kanino

Whosoever *pron.* kaninuman

Why *adv.* bakit, sa anong dahilan

Why *intr.* aba!

Wick *n.* mitsa

Wicked *adj.* masama, buhong, buktot, nakaaani

Wickedness *n.* kasamaan, kabalayutan

Wicker *n.* uway, yantok

Wickerwork *n.* yaring-uway, yaring-yantok

Wicket *n.* munting pinto, munting tarangkahan

Wide *adj.* malawak, malapad, maluwang

Widen *v.* paluwangin, palaparin, lumuwang, lumapad

Widow *n.* biyuda, balong babae

Width *n.* luwang, lapad

Wield *v.* humawak, hawakan, gumamit

Wife *n.* esposa, asawa

Wig *n.* peluka

Wiggle *v.* mamaluktot, mamilipit, pumayupoy, ipayupoy

Wiggler *n.* kitikiti

Wigwag *v.* iwagayway, iwasiwas

Wigwam *n.* wigwam

Wild *adj.* ligaw, ilang, labuyo, mailap

Wildcat *n.* musang
Wilderness *n.* desyerto, ilang
Wildfire *n.* malaking sunog
Wile *n.* linlang, lalang, daya
Will *n.* kalooban, habilin, nais, hangad, utos
Will *v.* iutos, ipamana, nasain, naisin
Willful *adj.* sinadya, kusa, matigas ang ulo
Willing *adj.* payag, pumayag, kusa
Wilt *v.* malanta, maluoy
Wilted *adj.* lanta, luoy, laing, unsiyami
Wily *adj.* malinlang, malalang, madaya
Wimble *n.* pambutas
Wimple *n.* pandong, talukbong
Win *v.* magwagi, manalo, matagumpay, magtamo
Wince *v.* umudlot, umigtad, umurong, umilag
Winch *n.* malakate
Wind *n.* hangin
Wind *v.* pilipitin, iikid, ipulupot, ilikaw, ikirin
Windbag *n.* bululusan
Winded *adj.* nahahanginan, hingal, humihingal
Windfall *n.* laglag ng hangin
Windlass *n.* muton
Windmill *n.* mulino
Window *n.* bintana, durungawan
Windower *n.* biyudo, balo
Windpipe *n.* trakea, lalaugan
Windshield *n.* parahangin
Windstorm *n.* bagyong hangin
Windward *adj.* dakong mahangin
Windy *adj.* mahangin
Wine *n.* alak
Wineglass *n.* kopa ng alak
Winery *n.* alakan
Wing *n.* pakpak, bagwis, ala
Wing *v.* lumipad
Winged *adj.* maypakpak, matayog, matulin
Wingless *adj.* walang-pakpak
Winglet *n.* munting-pakpak
Wingspread *n.* dipa ng pakpak
Wink *n.* kisapmata, pikit, saglit, kisap, idlip
Wink *v.* kumisap, kumurap, kumindat
Winner *n.* ang nanalo
Winnow *v.* magtahip, maghungkoy
Winsome *adj.* kalugud-lugod, masaya, kaakit-akit
Winter *n.* taglamig, winter
Wipe *n.* magpunas, kuskusin, punasan, pahirin, punasin
Wiper *n.* panlinis, wayper, pamunas, pamawi
Wire *n.* kawad, telegrama, alambre, kable, kuwerdas
Wiring *n.* instalasyon ng mga kawad
Wiry *adj.* maigkal, malitid, matibay, matatag

Wisdom *n.* alam, dunong, katalasan, bait

Wise *adj.* maalam, marunong

Wish *n.* nais, nasa

Wish *v.* magnais, naisin

Wishbone *n.* buto ng pitso

Wisp *n.* tingting, piraso, pilas, dayami

Wistful *adj.* maasahin

Wistfulness *n.* pagka-maasahin

Wit *n.* talino, katalinuhan, katalasan, pagka-mapagpatawa

Witch *n.* bruha, mangkukulam

Witchery *n.* pangkukulam, panggagaway

With *prep.* kasama ng, kapantay ng

Withdraw *v.* bawiin, babalikin, iurong

Wither *v.* malanta, matuyo, maluoy

Withhold *v.* pigilin, bimbinin

Within *prep.* sa loob, sa loob ng

Withstand *v.* malabanan, mapaglabanan, matagalan, matiis

Witness *n.* saksi, testigo

Witness *v.* sumaksi, tumestigo, saksihan

Witticism *n.* kasistihan, paniniste

Witty *adj.* matalinong magsalita, matalas, masiste

Wizard *n.* mangkukulam, mago, pantas

Wizardry *n.* pangkukulam, pangungulam

Wizened *adj.* hukluban, tuyot

Wobble *v.* sumuray, gumiray, umuga

Wobbly *adj.* sumusuray

Woe *n.* hirap, dusa, pighati

Woeful *adj.* lipos-dusa, mahirap

Wolf *n.* lobo, palikero

Wolfish *adj.* asal-lobo

Woman *n.* babae

Womanish *adj.* malababae, binabae

Womanly *adj.* mayumi, maamo

Womb *n.* uterus, bahay-bata

Wonder *n.* pagtataka, pagkamangha

Wonder *v.* mamangha, mabaghan

Wonderful *adj.* kahanga-hanga

Wont *n.* ugali, kaugalian, gawi, kinagawian

Woo *v.* manligaw, ligawan, manuyo, suyuin

Wood *n.* kahoy, tabla, panggatong

Wood craft *n.* karpinteriya

Wood craftsman *n.* kar-pintero, alwagi

Wood cut *n.* grado ng kahoy

Woodland *n.* kakahuyan

Woodman *n.* mangangahoy, manggugubat

Woodpecker *n.* ibong manunuktok

Woodpile *n.* talaksan

Woodwork *n.* karpinteriya

Wooing *n.* panliligaw, suyo, panunuyo

Wooing *n.* pagligaw, panliligaw

Wooing *v.* pagligaw

Wool *n.* lana

Woolen *adj.* delana

Word *n.* salita, sabi, pahayag, sermon

Wordy *adj.* masalita, maligoy

Work *n.* gawain, trabaho, tungkulin

Work *v.* gumawa, magtrabaho, magpaandar

Workbench *n.* kabalyete

Workbook *n.* aklat

Worker *n.* manggagawa

Workmanship *n.* kabutihang gumawa

Workshop *n.* gawaan

World *n.* daigdig, mundo

Worldly *adj.* makamundo, makalupa

Worm *n.* bulati

Wormwood *n.* ahenho

Worn-out *adj.* gasgas, gastado

Worry *n.* balisa, kabalisanhan, balino, tigatig

Worry *v.* mabalisa, mabagabag, matigatig

Worse *adj.* lalong masama

Worship *n.* pagsamba, pintuho, pamimintuho

Worst *adj.* pinakamasama

Worsted *n.* estambre

Worth *adj.* karapat-dapat, nagkakahalagang

Worth *n.* halaga, presyo, katumbas

Worthless *adj.* inutil

Worthwhilee *adj.* kapakipakinabang

Worthy *adj.* marapat, karapat-dapat

Wound *n.* sugat

Wound *v.* manugat, sugatan

Wow *intr.* wow!

Wrangle *v.* magtaltalan, magbangayan

Wrap *v.* magbangayan

Wrath *n.* galit, poot

Wrathful *adj.* galit na galit, nagngangalit

Wreath *n.* likaw, bilog, girnalda

Wreathe *v.* mamulupot, mangulubot

Wreck *n.* pagkabagbag, paglubog

Wreck *v.* mamulupot, mangulubot

Wreck *v.* gibain, igiba, wasakin, lansagin

Wrecker *n.* tagagiba, tagalansag

Wrench *n.* pagpilipit, pagwail, liyabe, tuwerka

Wrench *v.* pilipitin, wailin

Wrest *v.* mangagaw, agawin

Wrestle *v.* magbuno, makipagbuno, bunuin

Wrestler *n.* mambubuno

Wrestling *n.* buno, pagbubuno

Wretch *n.* taong imbi, taong marumal

Wriggle *v.* magpapili-pilipit, magpabalu-baluktot

Wriggler *n.* kitikiti

Wring *v.* pigain, pilipitin

Wringer *n.* tagapiga, pampisuklam

Wringer *n.* tagapiga, pampiga, pigaan

Wrinkle *n.* kulubot, kunot

Wrinkle *v.* mangulubot, mangunot

Wrist *n.* pupulsuhan, galanggalangan

Write *v.* sumulat, magsulat, sulatin, manulat

Writer *n.* manunulat

Writhe *v.* magkalikaw-likaw

Writing *n.* sulat, katha, titik, sinulat, akda

Written *adj.* nakasulat, nakalimbag

Wrong *adj.* mali, nakalimbag

Wrong *adj.* mali, sala

Wrong *n.* gawang-mali, gawang masama, apihin, usigin

Wrought *adj.* nilabra, pinalamutihan, hinugisan, pinanday

Wry *adj.* ngiwi, nakangibit, baluktot

Wryneck *n.* paling

X x Y y

X-ray *v.* eks ray, kunan ng larawan sa rayos ekis

Xylograph *n.* ukit sa kahoy

Xyloid *adj.* parang kahoy

Xylophone *n.* silopon

Xyster *n.* pangayod

Yacht *n.* yate

Yacht *v.* magyate

Yachting *n.* pagyayate

Yachtsman *n.* manyayate

Yachtsmanship *n.* panyayate

Yam *n.* tugi, lami

Yawn *n.* hikab , puwang

Yawn *v.* humikab, maghihikab

Yaws *n.* prambesya

Year *n.* taon

Yearbook *n.* taunang-aklat, anwal

Yank *v.* labnutin, halbutin

Yankee *n.* yangki

Yap *n.* tahol, kahol, yapyap

Yap *v.* tumahol, kumahol, yumapyap

Yard *n.* yarda

Yarn *n.* sulid, kuwento

Yield *v.* magbunga, mamunga, sumuko, isuko

Yodel *n.* yodel

Yodel *v.* yumodel, magyodel

Yoga *n.* yoga

Yogi *n.* yogi

Yearling *adj.* , sasantaunin
Yearly *adj.* santaunan
Yearn *n.* magnais, maghangad
Yeast *n.* lebadura, pampaalsa
Yell *n.* sigaw, hiyaw
Yell *v.* humiyaw, sigawan
Yellow *n.* dilaw, marilaw, amarilyo
Yellowish *adj.* madilaw-dilaw
Yelp *n.* kahol, tahol, takin
Yelp *v.* kumahol, tumahol, tumakin
Yen *n.* hangad, pananabik
Yen *v.* maghangad, hangarin
Yeoman *n.* taong malaya, katulong
Yes *adv.* oo, opo, oho
Yesterday *adj.* kahapon, ang nakaraan
Yet *adv.* pa, muna
Yet *conj.* gayunpaman
Yield *n.* produkto, pakinabang, tubo, ani, yari
Yogurt *n.* ginatan
Yoke *n.* pamatok , kabusabusan
Yolk *n.* pula
Yonder *adv.* iyon, yaon
Yore *n.* dating panahon
You *pron.* ikaw, kayo, ka
Young *adj.* bata, mura
Young *n.* kabataan
Youngster *n.* bata
Your *pron.* iyo, mo, inyo, ninyo
Yours *pron.* iyo, inyo
Yourself *pron.* iyong sarili, sarili mo
Youth *n.* kabataan
Youthful *adj.* bata, maykabataan, mura, sariwa
Yowl *n.* tambaw
Yuan *n.* yuan
Yugoslav *adj.* Hugoslab
Yule *n.* pasko, kapaskuhan
Yuletide *n.* pasko

Z z

Zeal *n.* sigasig, punyagi, sigsa
Zealot *n.* panatiko, partidaryo
Zealotry *n.* panatismo
Zenith *n.* kaitaasan, taluktok, kataluktukan
Zero *n.* sero, wala
Zest *n.* pagtatamasa, pagkalugod, linamnam, lasap
Zigzag *adj.* paesease
Zigzag *n.* sigsag
Zinc *n.* sink
Zingiberaceous *adj.* malaluya
Zinnia *n.* sinya
Zealous *adj.* masigasig, magpagpunyagi, masigsa
Zebra *n.* sebra
Zip *n.* haging, hagibis, haginit
Zip *v.* humaging, humagibis, humaginit
Zipper *n.* siper
Zither *n.* sitara
Zodiac *n.* sodyako, sirkuwito, libot, ligid
Zone *n.* sopa
Zoo *n.* palahyupan
Zoology /*n.* soolohiya
Zoom *v.* sumibad

Part II

Tagalog - English

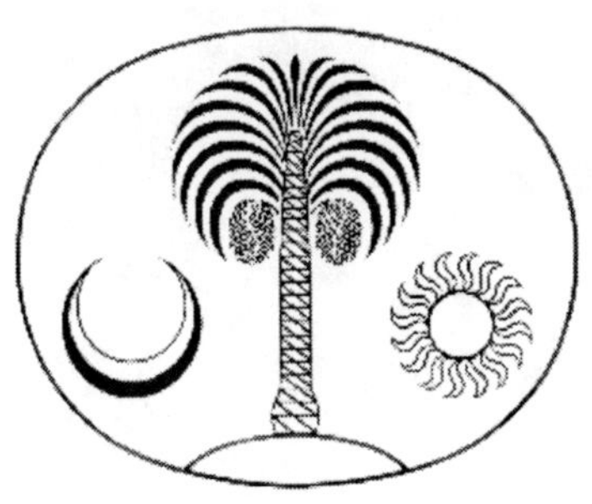

Index to this Section :

ALPHABETS IN TAGALOG

The Tagalog alphabets are composed of twenty letters; five vowels (patinig) and fifteen consonants (katinig).

They are the following:

vowels (patining) a, ė, i, o, u.

consonants — pronounceed as

b—ba	ng—nga
k—ka	p—pa
d—da	r—ra
g—ga	s—sa
h—ha	t—ta
l—la	w—wa
m—ma	y—ya
n—na	

Centuries of contact with western culture necessitated the use by the Tagalogs and other Filipinos of certain letters not originally in the old alphabet. Being of Spanish origin, names of persons adopted by the Filipinos, and the names of many places in the Philippines, are spelled as they are in the original language.

❑❑❑

LIST OF ABBREVIATIONS

N — noun

Pron. pronoun

V. — verb

Adj. — adjective

Adv. — adverb

Prep. — preposition

Conj. — conjunction

Interj. — pangkasalukuyan

Pangnagda. — pangnagdaán

Panghi. — panghináharáp

Ind. — indicative

Imp. — imperative.

Inf. — infinitive

GRAMMAR (TAGALOG)– MGA TULONG SA BALARILA

Nouns – Mga Pangngalan

A noun is the name of anything. ang pangngalan ay pangalan ng kahit anóng bagay.

Nouns are divided into two classes: common and proper; Ang pangngalan ay nahahatias dalawáng uri: pambálaná at Pantangì:

Common; pambálaná - tao, pusó, babae, hayop, aso-**Proper; pantangì** José, Pablo, Juan, Dios, Ana-

In tagalog, noun have three numbers, not like in English where there are only two. Sa Tagalog ang mga pangngalan ay may tatlóng kabilangan (number) hindî tulad sa Inglés na may dálawa lamang.

In English there are only two number, singular and plural;

Ang tatlóng kabilangan ay;

1. **Ísahan** (singular) - aklÿt (book), batà (child), aso (dog),
2. **Dálawahan** (dual) fslseánh sklát, dalawáng batà, dalawáng aso
3. **Máramihan,** (Plural) mga aklát (book) (chldren) mga batà

Nouns have four genders in English, but in Tagalog there are only three:

1. **Panlalaki**–masculine (amá–mother); ninang (godmothe)
2. **Pambabae**–feminine (iná–mother); ninang (godmothe)
3. **Pambalaki**–common (pinsan–cousin); biyenán (in-law)
4. **Waláng kasarián**– neter (bahy–house); aklát–book

Nouns have three cases (kaukulán). Ang pangngalan ay may tatlóng kaukulán

1. **Palagy (nominative)** – Ang lapis ay matulis; The *pencil* is sharp.
2. **Paarî (possessive)**–Ang aking iná ay si Tessie *My mother* is Tessie..

   Ang *pangalan ng aking ina* ay Tersa. My *mother's name* is Teresa
3. **Palayón (objective)** – Ang aking aklát ay nasa *ibabaw ng mesa.* My book is *on the table*

In English nouns are generally made plural by adding s to the

singular, like dog – dogs; bpu – boys; pencil – pencils

Sa Tagalog, ang pangngalan ay ginagawáng maramihan (plural) sa pamamagitan ng pagdaragdag ng *mya sa* isahan-(singular)

1. mesa –. *mga* mesa; 2. papél – *mga* papel; table – tables; paper – papers; 3. bahay – *mga* bahay; 4. pugad – *mga* pugad; nest – nests;

PRONOUNS – MGA PANGHALÍ

A pronoun is a word used instead of noun; Ang panghalip ay-isang salitâ na ginagamit sa halip ng isang pangngalan;

One class of pronouns is the personal (panghalip na panao). Isang uri ng panghalip ay ang *panghalip na panao.*

Pronouns have three persons. Ang mga panghalip ay may tatlóng panauhan (person):

1. Unang panauhan (first person) – tanog nagsásalitâ (person speaking) – akó (I); we (kamí o tayo)
2. Pangalawáng panauhan (second person) – ikáw (you); kayo (you) (person spoken to – ang taong kausap)
3. Pangatlong panauhan (third person) – siya (he or she); (sila – they) – taong pinag-uusapan (person spoken of.)

Pronouns generally have to numbers: singular and plural; Angmga panghalip karaniwan ay may dalawang bilang o kabilangan, nguni't kung minsan ay nagagamit na pandálawahan ang kita, ta, at nita na gaya ng sumusunod;

1. ***Katá* ay magsayáw.** (atá is used before the verb.) You and I dance.
2. **Magsayáw *kitá*** (Kitá is used after the verb.) Ltet us (you and I) dance.
3. **Ang bahay *ta* ay bago.** (*Ta* in the *possessive* case, is used after the noun bahay. *Our* house (yours and mine) is new Ang bahay nitá ay bago. (***Nitá*** in this sentence, has the same use as *ta* in the previous; it is used after the noun also.

There are two numbers in English:

1. Singular (isahan)
2. Plural (máramihan)

3. Dálawahan (no English equivalent) (kitá, katá, ta, nitá, only.)

1. Nominative case – paturól

2. Possessive case – paarî

3. Objective – palayón

Declension of pronouns showing persons, number, and case: Ayos ng mga panghalip sang-ayon sa panauhan, Kabilangan at kaukulán:

Ísahan – Singular

Kaukulán – Kabilangan – Panauhan

Kaukulán (case) – Panauhang una – Panauhang ikalawá – Panauhang ikatló

Paturól (nom.) – akó (I) -- ikáw (you) – siyá (he or she)

Paarî (pos.) – akin, ko (my or mine – iyó, mo) – kaniya your or yours) niya

Palayón (obj.) – sa akin (me) – sa iyó (to you) – sa kaniyá (to him or to her.)

Máramihan – Plural

Kaukulán (case)

Paturól – (nom.) – kami, tayo (we) – silá (they)

Paarî (pos.) – amin, atin (our or ours) – kanilá (their)

Paukól (obj.) – sa amin, sa atin (us) – sa kanilá (to them) examples – mga halimbawá

Paturól – Akó ay isáng gurò. I am a teacher

Ikáw ay isáng mánanayaw. You are dancer.

Siyá ay isáng karpintero. He is a carpenter.

Siyá ay isá isáng dalaga. She is lady.

Silá ay kumakain. They are eating.

Paarî (pos.) – Ang aking payong ay lumà. My umbrella is old.

Ang bulakläk na iyán ay akin. That flower is mine.

Basahin mo ang iyong aklat. Read your book.

Ibinigá ni Jose ang kaniyáng sulat kay Juan. José gave his letter to Juán.

Ang aming bahay ay may pintá. Our house is painted.

Nasirà ang kaniyáng ay sa Lunes. Their departure is on Monday.

Pilipinas ang ating bayan. The Philippines is our country.

Ang bahay na iyán ay amin. That house is ours.

Paukól (obj.) – Ibigáy mo sa akin ang iyóng bard. Give me your dress.

Sabihin mo sa kaniyá na pumuntá sa palengke. Tell her to go to market.

Hihingî siyá as iyó ng kuwalta. He will ask you for some money.

Bibigyán to siyá ng aginaldo. Iwill give her a Christmas gift.

Sa kanilá ibibigáy ang premyo. To them the prize will be given.

Other pronouns – Ibá pang mga panghalíp

Demonstrative pronouns (panghalíp na pamatlíg) :

1. itó (malapit sa nagsásalitâ) – this (close to the speaker)
2. iré, yari (malapit na malapit sa nagsásalitâ) (this) (still closer to the speaker)
3. iyán (malapit sa kausap) – that (close to the person spoken to)
4. iyón, yaón (malayò sa dalawá) – that (far from both)
5. ayún o hayún (malaymalayo sa dalawa). – there (far from both)

Examples – Mga halimbawà

1. Itó ay aking bola. This is my ball. (close to the speaker)
2. Iréng o iríng pusod ko ay malakí. My queue or this queue of mine is big. (still closer to the speaker).
3. Iyán ang katulad ng payong ko. That is the umbrella similar to mine. (close to the person spoken to)
4. Iyón o yaón ang manggagamot nilá. That is their doctor. (far from both).
5. Ayûn o hayún ang bahay ni José as ituktók ng bundók. There is Jose's house on top of the mountain

Interrogative pronouns – Panghalíp na Pananóng

Ísahan – Máramihan – Pangungusap

Sino (whó) sinu-sino – Sino akó? Sinu-sino ang magsisialis?

Anó (what) – anu- anó – Ano ang pangalan mo'?

Saán (where) saan, saan-saán – nároón ang inyóng papel? Where is your paper? Saán-saán nároón ang inyóng mga papél? Where are your papers?

Magkano (how much) – magka-magkano – Magkano ang kita mo isáng arw? How much do you earn daily? Magka-magkáno ang mga ambág? How much are you contributions

Gaano (how much) – gaa-gaano – Gaano ang inanic mong palay? How much rice did you place? How much did your tenants harvest?

Kailán (when) – kai-kailán – Kailán ang pistá sa inyó? When is the fiesta at your place? Kai-kailan ang mga alis ninyó? When do you all leave?

Kanino (whose) – kani-kanino – Kanino ang lapis na ito? Whose pencil is this? Kani-kanino ang mga aklát na ito? Whose books are these?

Alin (which) – alin-alin – Alin ang mga payong ninyo? Which are you umbrellas?

Articles – Mga tulong sa Pantukoy

Articles used in common nouns (pangngalang pambálaná) Isahan Máramihan Mga pangungusap – sentences ang – ang mga - - Ang batà ay natutulog. The child is sleeping. Ang mga batà ay natutulog. The children are sleeping. nh – nh mhs – Ang bote ng batà ay nabasag. The bottle of the child is broken. Ang mga bote ng mga batà ay nangadurog. The bottles of the children got broken. Sa – sa mga – ligay mo sa batang lalaki ang atis. Give the atis to the boy. Ibigay mo sa mga batang lalaki ang mga prutas. Give the fruits to the boys.

Articles used with proper nouns – (panghalip panao)

Isahan Maramihan – Mga pangungusap – Sentences si – siná – Si Juan ay masunurin. Juan is obedient. Siná Juan at Pablo ay masisipag. Juan and Pablo are industrious.

Ni – niná – Ang barò niná Ana at Rità ay bago. kay – kiná – Sabihin mo kay Pablo na pumarito. Tell Pablo to come here. Sabihin mo kiná Pablo at José na pumarito. Tell Pablo and José to come here.

Verbs – Mga Pandiwà

A verb is a word which gives meaning or thought to a phrase or word group so that it may have significance or express action.

Ang pandiwà ay salitáng pinakakáluluwa ng pangungusap sapagka't nagbibigay diwà sa parirala o mga salitâ nang ang mga ito'y magkadiwà, mabuhay, kumilos o gumanáp.

Some verbs may be conjugated and some may not. Ay in Tagalog which is the equivalent of the verb to be in English is the first among the verbs that cannot be cojjugated. May and mayroon are the others that are commonly used.

All the verbs may be grouped under seven ways of conjugation. Ang lahat ng pandiwà ay mapagsasama-sama sa pitóng paraán ng pagbabangháy ng gaya ng sumúsunód:

Bangháy sa UM – isáng paraán

Conjugation in Um – one way

Bangháy sa MA, MAG MANG – tatlóng paraán

Conjugation in MA, MAG MANG – three ways

Banghay sa PA – isang paraan

Conjugation in PA – one way

Banghay sa IN O HIN. – dalawang paraan

Conjugation in IN or HIN – two ways

Mga Halimbawà – Examples

1. SiRita ay matalino at masipag na dalaga. Rita is an intelligent and industrious lady.
2. Siyá ay nagsisimbá araw-araw. She goes to church every day.
3. Si Rizal ay pángunahíng bayani ng Pilipinas. Rizal is a national hero of the Philippines.

Ang **may** ayginagamit king ang kasunod ay pangngalan, pang-urí, pandiwà, pantukoy na **mga**, pang-ukol na sa at panghalíp na paarî.

May is used if it is followed by a noun, an adjective, a verb, the article mga, the preposition sa; and possessive pronouns.

May taosa loób ng páaralán. There **is** a man inside the school building.

May magandáng anák si Idad. **Idad has** a prettydaughter. **May**

ibibigáy kaba sa akin? Are you going to give me something?

May mga Kumakain sa kanilá na pumapasok sa págawaan. There are people working in the factory, who are eating with them.

Maysa-darating na panauhin nang ako'y kakain na. There is an unexpected visitor that arrivved when I was about to eat.

May akin akó kayâhindi ko na gagamitin iyan. I have my own so I will not use that;

Ang *mayroon* ay ginagamit kung may katagáng nasisingit sa pagitan ng salitáng itó at ng pangngalan, pang-uri, o pandiwang kasunód; kung panagót sa tanong; kung ginagamit na patalinghagà; kung pagtútumbasán ng mayroon at walâ; at kung ang sumusunod ay panghalip na palagy

Mga halimbawà:

Mayroóm paláng tao sa loob ng bakuran. So there is a man in the yard.

May bagong barò ka ba? Mayroón. Have you a new dress? Yes.

Ang angkán niná Luisa mayroón sa aming bayan.

We have some relatives of Luisa in our town.

Lahat ba kayo'y may mga aklát? Mayroóng wala, at mayroong mayroom. Do you all have books? Some have, some have none.

Kahulugán ng mga panlapi. Meaning of prefixes

panlapi — prefix

unlapi — affix

gitlapi — infix

hulapi — suffix

Ang mga panagano (mood) ng pandiwà ay :

pawatás – infinitive   pasakali – subjunctive

pautós — imperative

Paturól — indicative

Bangháy sa UM

Conjugation in UM   umasa (hope)   Kumain (eat)

Paturól – indicative – pangkasalukuyan-present

umasa – kumain – pangnagdaan – umasa – kumain

Rules of the conjugation in UM

Present tense

Take the first two sylables of the infinitive and add the root word: umasa (to hope) umaasa (UMA-ASA)

If the second wyllable of ehe infinitive has a final consonant, it should not be included.

tumakbó (to run) – tumátakbó (TUMA-TAKBO)

kumain (to eat) – kumakain (KUMA-KAIN)

Past tense – of the same form as in the infinitive

Future tense

Remove the UM and reduplicate or double the first syllable of the root word.

umsà–Asa

.umakbó–TATAKBÓ

Rules of the conjugation in MA, MAG, MANG

Present tense

Change the M of the infinitive into N and reduplicate the first syllable of the root word.

mabuhy (to live) nabubuhay

magbayad (to pay) nagbabayad

manghingî (to ask) nanghihingî

Past tense

Change the M of the infinitive into N

Magbayad–nagbayad

mabuhay–nabuhay

manghingi–nanghingî

Future tense

Reduplicate the first sylable of the root word.

mabuhay–mabubuhay

magbayad–magbabayad

manghingî–manghihingî

We use IN or NI in the past or present tenses. The IN and NI mentioned here, therefore, are affixed for conjugation purposes and not affixes for the infinitive. ibigáy (to give)

Present tense – ibinibigáy

Past tense – ibinigáy

All IN or NI verbs which end in the suffixes IN, HIN or NIN lose their suffixes in the present and past tenses. Si Rita ang pinakamagandá sa tatlóng batang babae. Rita is the most beautiful of the three girls.

Mga kahululugan – Word meaning

lipon o lupon .... group

any .... form

pakiusap .... request

uri .... kind

utos .... command

sugnáy .... clause

apat .... four

salitâ .... word

panagano .... mood

The suffixes are restored in the future tenses.

Present – sagutin (to answer) sinasagot – inaagaw

Past – sinagot (answered), sinagot – inagaw

Future – sasagutin (will answer) sasagutin – aagawin

Adjective – Ang mga pang-uri

Ang pang-uri ay salitang umuri sa isang pangngalan o panghalip. An adjective is a word used to describe or modify a noun or pronoun.

Ilan sa mga pang-uri ay ang mga sumusunod:

Some adjectives are the following:

pula (red) white (puti) pino (fine) matayog (tall) mataas (high) itim (black) mababa (low) magaspang (coarse) dilaw (yellow) madulas (slippery) mahal (dear, expensive)

Paghahambing ng mga pang-uri – Comparison of adjectives

Positive – panulád – Pahambing – Comparative

pasukdól — superlative

Positive — Comparative — Superlative

Panulád — Pahambíng — Pasukdól

mataás (high), nataas-taás (Higher, taller), nataas ba nataás (tallest)

magandá (magandá-gandá) (magandáng-magandá) most beautiful (lalong magandá) (ubod ng ganda) beautiful most beautiful (pinakamaganda)

Mga halimbawa-examples

Si Juan ay mataas — Juan is tall.

Si Pedro ay lalong mataas kay Juan. Pedro is taller than Juan.

Kiná José Pedro at Juan, si José ang pinakamataas.

Of the three José Pedro and Juan, Josée is the tallest.

Si Sofia ay higit na maganda kay Laura. Sofia is more beautiful than Laura.

Rita is the most beautiful of the three girls.

Sa tatlong batang babae, pinakamaganda si Rita.

Ang mga pang-abay-adverbs

Ang pang-abay ay isang salitang umaabay sa isang pandiwa, isang pang-uri, o kapwa pang-abay.

An adverb is a word that modifies a verb, an adjective, or another adverb.

Ang mga sumusunod na pang-abay ay lagíng ginagamit:

The following adverbs are often used:

matulin — fast marahn-slowly

totoong-totoo-very truly

mabuti-well

1. Matuling tumakbó si Julio — Julio runs fast.
2. Totoóng matalino si Ana — Ana is truly intellgent.
3. Tuwang-tuwang dumating ang mag-ina — Mother and son came happily.
4. Marahang umakyát sa itaás ang batà. The child went upstairs slowly.

Ang mga pang-ukol-prepositions

Mga pang-ukol na laging ginagamit: Prepositions often used:

sa hapág—*on* the table – *tungkól kay* Juan – *about* Juan

Sa ilalim – under – adverb *ukol kay* Rita

sa ilalim ng mesa-*under* the table

sa pagitan ng dalawáng batà – *between* the two children

sa harapán ng bahay – *in front* of the house

sa gitnâ ng ilog – *at the middle* of the river

sa loób ng kahon – *inside* the box

sa halip ng – instead of

sa likod ni Pedro – *at the back* of Pedro

sa pugad – *in* the nest

tungkól sa – according to

Ang pang-ukol ay isáng katagâ o salitáng ginagamit upang ipakita ang kaugnayán ng isang pangngalan o panghalip sa ibang salitâ sa pangungusap.

The preposition is a particle or word used to show the relation of a noun or pronun to another word in the sentence.

Mga pangatinig–Conjunctions

Ang pangatnig ay isáng salitâ parirla, o ng isáng sugnáy sa kapwà salitâ, isáng parirals sa kapwà parirala, o ng isáng sugnáy sa kapwà sugnáv.

A conjunction is a word used to join a word to another word, a phrase to another phrase, or a clause to another clause.

May dalawang uri ng pangatnig:

1. Panimbáng – coordinate – at (and); anunit (but)
2. Pantulong – subordinate – kung (if); bagi (before)

Mga halimbawà – examples:

1. Si Julio at si Pedro ay magkapatid. Julio *and* Pedro are brothers.
2. Si Ana ay mayaman ngunit si Lina av mahirap. Ana is wealthy but Lina is poor.
3. Kung sasama si Juan ay sasama si Pablo. If Juan is going,

Pablo is going.

4. Bago Ka umalis, sabihin mo sa adin. Let me know before you leave.

Mga pandamdám-Interjections

Ang mga salitáng nagpáng ng isáng matinding damdamin ng isang tao na gaya ng pagkatuwâ, pagkaulungkót, pagkagulat ay tinatawg na pandamdám. Words that show a strong feeling of a person like joy, sorrow, surprise, fear hate and others are called interjections

Mga halimbawà – examples

naku – oh! a–ah! a;os!–get out! go away!

aba–abah! e..e–oh yes! mabuhay! long live!

Mga pangungusap0: Seentences

Nakú! nasusunog ang bahay. Oh! the house is burning.

A. .ayokò ngâ! ah, I don't like it!

Alis! hindî katá ibig makita. Go away! I don't want to see you.

Aruy, kay sakit ng paá ko! Oh, how painful my foot is! mabuhay ang ating bayan! Long live our country, the Philippenes!

Mga pangungusap – Sentences

Ang pangungusap ay isáng lipon ng mga salitâ na nagbibigáy ng isang buong diwà. A sentence is a group of words expressing a complete thought.

Kaniong aklát iyán? Whose book is that?

Ang mga pangungusap ay payák, tambalan, at hugnayan o langkapan ayon sa any . There are three kinds fo sentences according to form: simple, compound and complex.

1. Payák – simple. Si ina ay pupunta sa bayan. Mother goes to town.
2. Tambalan –compound. Akô ay sisimba at si Lilia ay papasok sa paaralán. I will go to curch and Lilia will go to school.
3. Langkapan — complex. Samantalang kumakain si Nena,naglulutò namán si Rosa. While Nena is eating, rosa is cooking.

May apat na urì ang pangungusap ayon sa gamit:

There are four kinds of sentences according to use:

1. Paturól – declarative. Si Luis ay masunuring batà. Luis is an obedient child.
2. Pautós – imperative.
   a. utos (command). Kunin mo ang aklát, Lula. Get the book, Lula.
   b. pakiusap (request). Ipakikuha mo ang aklát Lula. Please get the book, Lula. Maaari bang kunin mo ang aklát, Lula? Can you get the book, Lula?
3. Patanóg – interrogative. Sino ang iyóng amá? Who is your father? Whose book is that? Kaninong aklat iyan? Ano ang pangalan mo? What is your name? Kailan ka aalis? When are you leaving?
4. Padamdán – exclamatory. Pshe, hitsura lang! Oh, how ugly! A..., wala kang pakialam!. Ah,it is none of your business!

GRAMMATIAL TERMS

abstract noun	Pangalang makadiwa
active voice	táhasang tinig
adjective	pang-uri
adjective clause	pang-uring sugnáy
adverb	pang-abay
adverb of affirmation	pang-abay panang-ayon
adverb of comparison	pang-abay panulád
adverb of doubt	pang-abay pang-agam
adverb of manner	pang-abay pamaraán
adverb of place	pang-abay panlunán
adverb of quantity	pang-abaypanggaano
adverb of quality	pang-abay pang-uri
adverb of time	pang-abaypamanahón
adverbial clause	pang-abayna sugnáy
adverbial phrase	pang-abay na parirala
apostrophe	kudlit
article	pantukoy
case	kaukulán
nominative case	kaukulang palagy
possessive case	kaukulang paari
objective case	kaukulang palayón
class	uri
clause	sugnáy
collective noun	pangagalang palansák
colon	tutuldók
comma	kuwit
common noun	pangngalang pambalana
comparative degree	panularang antás
complex sentence	hugnayang pangungusap
compound sentence	tambalang pangungusap
compound subject	tambalang simunò

compound predicate	tambalang panaguri
conjugation	pagbabangháy, palábangha yan
contraction	pang-angkóp, may angkóp
declension	pag-uukol, páukulán
definition	pakatuturán
dedmonstrative	panghalip pamatlig
direct objec..........................	tuwirang layon
exclamation mark	tandáng pamanghâ
feminine gender	kasaráng pambabae
first person	unang panauhan
future tense	unang panauhan
future tense	panahong pandarating
grammar	balarilà
hypen	gitling
imperative mood	panaganong pautós
indefinite pronoun	panghalip na di-tiyák
indicative mood	panaganong paturól
indirect object	layong di-tiyák
infinitive mood	panaganong pawatás
interjection	pandamdám
interrogative pronoun	panghalip pananóng
intransitve verb	pandiwang káraniwan
Irregular verb	pandiwang di-karaniwar
masculine gender	kasariáng panlalaki
noun	pangngalan
noun clause	pangngalang sugnáy
noun in apposition	pangngalang pantiyák
number	kailanán
numeral adjective	pang-uring pambilang
object of the sentence	layon ng pangungusap
participle	pandiwari
particle	katagâ

passive voice	balintiyák na tinig
past tense	panahunang pangnagdaán
period	tuldók
person	panauhan
personal pronoun	panghalip pantao
plural	pangmarami
possessive pronoun	panghalip pantao
predicate nominative	panaguring palagy
preposition	pang-ukol
present tense	panahong pangkasalukuyan
principal verb	pandiwang nambadyá
pronoun	panghalip
proper noun	pangngalang pantngi
punctuation	bantasan, palábantasan
question	tanóng
question mark	tandáng pananóng
quotation mark	tandáng pambanggit
regular verb	pandiwang karaniwan
relative pronoun	panghalip pamanggit
rule	panuto
second person	likalawáng pangungusap
semi-colon	tuldukwit
simple sentence	páyakang pangungusap
simple predicate	payakang taguri
singular	isahan
subject of a sentence	simunó ng pangungusap
subjunctive mood	panaganong pasakall
superlative degree	kaantasáng pánukdulan
syntax	paláugnayan
tense	panahunan
third person	ikatlóng panauhan
transitive verb	pandiwang palipát

Language and Reading

antonym	kasalungát na kahulugan
articulate, to	bumigkás, bigkasín, umusál, usalín
capitalize	malakintitik
card	tarheta
character	tauhan
command	utos
to command	mag-utos, utusan
composition	saysayin
copy	sipi
to copy	sipiin,
criticize	punahin, pumun
dash	guhit
declarative (sentence)	pasalaysáy (na pangungusap)
define	pakahuluganán
degee of comparison	kaantasán (sa hambingan)
dicate, to	taláng itambis, tambisán,
dramatize, to	dulaín, isadulà
enunciate, to	bumigkás, bigkasín
expression	pahayag
table	pábulá
fairy tale	kuwento
formal note	liham pormál
idiom	kawikaán
illustrate, to	uliranmán
incident	pagkakataón pangyayari
indention	paglulugi
inflection	pagbabadling
margin	gilid
mechanics	pagkakaakmá-akmâ, pagka-kaugnáy-ugnáy

memorize, to	isaulo, sauluhin
modulate, to	inaluyan
oposite	kasalungát
pantomine	mustrahan
perfecte tense	panahóng pangnagdaán, panahóng nakaraán
phonics	palatinigan
progressive tense	panahóng pangkasalukuyan
pronounce, to	bigkasín, bumigkás
pronunciation	bigkás, pagbigkás, pagbibigkás
postscript	pahabol, habol
recite, to	bigkasín, bumigkás
reproduce, to	ihulog
request, to	humilíng, hilingín
review, to	magmulíng-aral, magrepaso
rough draft	boradór
sandtable	hapág-búhanginán
sense	kahulugán
series	sunuran
silent, (reading)	di bigkás (na pagbasa)
stick to the point, to	manatili sa pinag-úusapan
suggest, to	ipalagáy, imungkahi
synonym	singkahulugán
topic	paksâ
topic sentence	paksaing pangungusap
written composition	saysaying sulát; saysaying nakasulat

❑❑❑

COMMONLY-USED TERMS IN SCHOOL

athletic goods	gamit pampálarun
audience reading	pagbasang patalastas
closing exercises	palatúntunang pangkatapusan
commencement	palatuntunang pansjmula
course of study	takdang aralin
diagnostic test	pagsubok na pantiyak-kaalaman
dictate, to	bumigkas upang isulat
division circular	palibot-kalatas ng dibisyon
division memorandum	paalaala ng dibisyon
first year high school	unang taon, mataas na paaralan
form 178	huwarang 178
grade five	ikalimang baytang
inventory test	pagsubok na pantiyak-uri
lesson plan	banghay sa pagtuturo
lunch counter	dulutang hapag
mastery test	pagsubok na pantiyak kasanayan
narrative report	ulat na pasalaysay
percentage of attendance	kasandaan ng dalo
remedial teaching	pagtuturong pangwasto
rural high school	mataas na paaralang ukol sa pagsasaka
school administration	pangasiwaan ng paaralan
school clinic	pasurian (klinika) ng paaralan
school organization	kabuuan ng paaralan
supevisory bulletin	lathalaang pantagamsid
supervision of classes	pagmamasid sa mga klase
sylabus	buod (salaysay)

GYMNASTIC COMMANDS :

ARMS FORWARD – BEND – bisig paharáp – baluktót!

ARMS FORWARD – **THRUST** – bisig paharáp – sulong (tuwid)

ARMS HALF-FORWARD – BEND – bisig kalahating-paharáp – baluktót!

ARMS IN REVERSE T POSITION – PLACE – bisig ayos t ng baligtád – lagay (huwit)

ARMS IN T POSITION – Place – bisig ayos T – lagay (huwit)

ARMS OBLIQUEL DOWNWARD – RAISE – bisig hilis paibabâ – taá (huwit)

ARMS OBLIQUELY UPWARD – RAISE – bisig hilis paitaás – taás (hiwit)

ARMS SIDEWARD – THRUST bisig patagilid – sulong (tuwid)

ARMS TO THRUST – THRUST – PLACE – bisig pasuntók baluktót – lagáy (huwit)

ARMS UPWARD – BEND bisig paitaás – baluktót!

ARMS UPWARD – THRUST – bisig paitaás – sulong (tuwid)

CLASS – ATTENTION – klase makinig'

CROOK SITTING POSITION – PLLACE – upóng pabaluktót – lagáy (huwit)

CROSS SISTTING POSITION – PLACE – upóng pasabát. – lagáy (huwit)

FALL – IN – ha...nay!

FOLDED POSITION – BEND – payukód – yuk !

FOURS BASE POSITION – Place – paa't kamáy patuhód – lagáy (huwit)

FULL KNEE REST POSITION – PLACE –buong tuhod ayos pahingá – lagáy (huwit)

FULL KNEES – BEND – buóng tuhod – baluktót !

PHYSICAL EDUCATION TERMS :

about face	pabalík
arms downward	bisig paibabâ
at ease	pahingá
crook sitting	upóng yakap-tuhod
cross sitting	upóng magkakurús ang paá
foot touching	pagditit ng paá
fours base	paá't kamáy patukód
half kneel standing position .	kaliwáng (kanang) paá paluhód
knee stride	luhód pabuká
leg raising	pagtaá ng paá
long sitting	upóng pahabâ
long sitting rest	upóng pahabâ ayos pahingá
prone leaning rest	dapáng nakasandál ayos pahingá
prone lying	higáng padapâ
side leaning rest	patagilid na nakasandál ayos pahingá
prone lying	higáng padapâ
side leaning rest	patgilid na nakasandál ayos pahingá
stride backward	hakbáng pauróng
stride forward	hakbáng paharáp
stride kneel sitting	luhód-buká paá"y sa ilalim
stride sideward	hakbáng patagilíd
supine	higáng patihayâ

DANCE TERMS :

arms in revers "T"	bisig ayos "T" ng baligtád
arms in "T" position	bisig ayos "T"
brush	pagaspás
clockwise	ikot pakanán
counterclockwise	ikot pakaliwâ

cut	palít
flap	pasapyáw
free foot (hand)	malayang paa (kamáy)
outside foot (hand)	paáng (kamáy) na palabás
partners	magkasayáw, magkakasayáw
place	lagáy
point	tutok
slide or glide	dausdós
stamp	padyák
star right (left)	ayos-bituwíng pakanán (pakaliwâ)
step	hakbáng
sway	indák
swing	indayog
tap	tuktók
tiptoes	patiyád
touch	diít
vis-avis or opposites	katapát
arms in lateral position	mga bisig magkapanig
Change step or two step	palit hakbáng, sunód-hakbáng, tuwistep
change, step, turn	palit-hakbáng-pihit
close or follow step	hakbáng na masinsín o pasunód
cross step	hakbáng-pasabát
cross step turn	hakbáng-pasabát-pihit
crosswaltz	balseng-pasabát
crossed arms	bisig pasalaunting
cut step	palit-hakbíng
double sway balance steps	mga hakbáng na may dala wáng indák timbáng
gallop step	hakbáng-palundág

glide or slide polka	polkang padagusdós
glide or slide step	hakbáng-padagusdós
heel and toe polka	polkang sakong at tiyád
hop polka	polkang padirit
hop step	kalahating-dirit
inside foot	paáng paloób
inside hand	kamáy paloób
mincing step	tiyád-dirit
outside foot	paáng palabás
ouside hand	kamáy na palabbás
habJwrutubg scake	panukatan sa pagsulatkamáy
indirect oval	di-tuwirang biluhabâ
legibly	nabábasa
loop	balikò, habyóg
medium slant style	pangkaraniwang anyóng pahilís
muscle pad	kalamnán ng bisig
oval	biluhabâ
project	balak, panukalà, handáng gawin
push and pull	hila't batak, tulak at kabig
slant	pahilis
standard	pamantayan
stroke	guhit
visualization	pagkikintál

ART EDUCATION :

angular	sinulukan, sinulok
appreciation	pagpapahalagá; pagbibigáy -halagá
applique (work)	idinikit; ipinatong
art	sining
background	lunas, duyo, pondo
bookmarks	mga panandâ sa aklát

brushes	mga pinsél
character	tauhan
circle	sabilóg
circular	pasabilóg
clear cut lines	malilinaw na guhit
correlate	pag-uyunin, pagbanusin pagtakinin
craftwork	yari ng bihasá
cream	diláw na mapusyáw; burok, binurok.
creative	likhain
cylinders	mga bumbóng
design	budlis
designing	pagbubudlís
dominate	umiral; makapangibabaw, mangibabaw
drawing freehand	pagguhit ng malayang kamáy
enamel paint	hibong esmalte
fabrics	mga habi
gemetric	hineometriya
gray (color)	abuhin
horizon lines	pamantayan ng paningig
horizontal	pahaláng, pahigâ
intermediate color	pagitanang kulay
landscape	tanawin, pangitain
loom	habihán
medium of expression	parán ng pagpapahayag, paraán ng pagsisiwalat
motif	diwà
mounting picture	pagdidikit ng larawan
netrals (colors)	mga alinlangang kullay
oblong	tagibilog

optional	.sáibigan; sápilián
orange color	diláw dalandán
paralleel	paagapáy
perspective	patuntóng-tanáw
pictorial representation	pagsasalarawan
pliable	sunúd-sunuran
portrayal	pagbabadhâ
poster	dikit
primary color	pangunahimg li;au
sculpture	lilok, pagliloj
seascape	tánawing dagat
secondary color	pangalawahing kulaly
slogan	sambitin
square	parisukát
statuette	munting bantayog
stencil	istensil
symbolic	naglalarawan
symmetry	pagkakatimbáng
tones (color)	mga kakulayan
triangle	tatlvnsulok
vanishin point	tuldók ng pagkahiwaláy
vertical	patindig, patay
warp	pahanay
wax crayons	krayola
woof	pahilig

❑❑❑

PROMINENT FRUITS

Abukado o avodado, *n.* geen or reddish, fleshy fruit, pear-shaped but smooth skin; can be eaten with sugar or made into ice cream or salad.

Anunas, n. rounded fleshy fruit, reddish or yellowish in color, smooth-skin, and size smaller than a grapefruit; can be eaten as is.

Atis, *n.* green, weet and delicious fruit with brocaded like skin; eaten as is and can be made into delicious ice cream.

Balimbing, *n.* green or yellowish, juicy fruit with angular form or shape; can be eaten as is or made into preserves.

Blubad or kasóy, *n.* yellow or reddish fuit, smooth skin shaped like a jar and has a big seed at the end; seed which produces kasóy nuts made into candies.

bayabas or guava, *n.* seedy fruit, either green or yellow-ish, about the size of a lemon; can be eaten as is or made into preserves or jelly or used for flavoring.

Kaimito, *n.* green or reddish fleshy fruit, with seeds in side; can be eaten as is or made into ice cream.

Kalamansè, *n.* green segmented fruit like the size of native lemon; made into preserves or used for flavoring or lemonade.

Kamias, *n.* greeen; juicy, elongated fruit used for flavoring, made into pickles, or preserves.

Dalandán, *n.* big, juicy, segmented gruit, like the size of an orange and eaten like the yellos orange imported from abroad.

Dalánghita, *n.* segmented juicy fruit like dalandán but with loose skin which can easily be peeeled;

Dayap, *n.* green juicy fruit used for flavoring or made into lemonade.

Duhat, *n.* black, smooth-skin fruit like the size of a smallplum; has a big seed inside which grows easily.

Bungulan, *n.* a kind of banana which is green when ripe, however it turns yellow sometime and is soft.

butuan, *n.* a kind of banana which has plenty of seeds that do not grow; green in color but ripe; the leaves and flowers of this banana are more useful than the fruit.

Guwebano, *n.* green, fleslhy fruit with rough needle-like skin like that of a breadfruit; the size is like the size of a papaya fruit.

Lakatán, *n.* the best kind of banana; sweet and yellow in color when ripe, the most expensive kind of banana.

Langkâ, *n.* or nangka or breadfruit in English, has a big, sharp skinny fruit with thread-like. flesh surrounded with sticky and sappy material; can be eaten as is or made into preserves or ice cream.

Manggá, *n.* green when unripe and yellow when ripe; sweet and delicious fruit with a flat seed inside; fruit larger than a pear, oblong shape smooth skin fruit which can be eaten as is; made into ice cream, and into pickles when unripe.

Pinña, *n.* rough-skinned fruit like the size of a papaya, but with plenty of eyes which need to be scooped before it is sliced, and eaten; can be made into preserves also or jam.

Sabá, *n.* a kind of banana, a little flat shaped fruit usually boiled, fried or made into fritters.

Sampalok, *n.* poddy fruit, dark brown in color, used for flavoring when unripe and made into candies when ripel

Santól, *n.* round fruit with 3 or 4 seeds inside; has a yellow color and is about the size of an orange.

Siniguwelas, *n.* plumlike fruit with a big seed inside; has reddish or yellow color; eaten as is, no cooking necessary.

Suhà, *n.* big, yellowish fruit, with thick skin; juicy and segmented, larger than a grapefruit.

Tindulán or tordán, *n.* a kind of banana, common in the market; green when unripe and yellow when ripe.

Tsiko or chico, *n.* roundish, dark brown fruit with hairy seeds which do not grow as this is propagated by cuttings; fruit is sweet and delicious generally eaten as is.

Tiyesa, *n.* fruit like the size of a pear, yellow and fleshy, the flesh of which is like that of a sweet potato when boiled. It is eaten without cooking. The skin and flesh stay yellow.

Aa

Aagam-agam, *adv.* doubt: hesitating; suspicion;

Aalipinin, *v.* to make a slave of;

Aandáp-andáp, *adj.* flickering

Aanim, *adj.* only six

Abâ, *adj.* humble; poor;

Abá, *interj.* an expression of strong feeling; .

Abahín, *v.* to remind; to make one know;

Abaín, *v.* to make miserable; to mistreat;

Abakada, *n.* alphabet;

Abalá, *adj.* busy; occupied;

Abala, *n.* delay; nuisance; one who tarries; disturbance;

Abalahin, *v.* to bother; to trouble;

abangán, *v.* to wait for; to watch for; to waylay;

Abay, *n* bridesmaid; attendant; companion;

Abayan, *v* to accompany; to attend to;

Abó, *n.* ashes; what is left over after burning;

Abóg, *n.* notice; sign;

Abót, *v.* arrived; comprehend; reached;

Abt-Tanáw, *n.* horizon;

Abubot, *n.* article; thing;

Abubot, *n.* knick-knacks;

Abugado *n.* lawyer; attorney;

Abuhín *adj.* gray;

Abuhín *v.* to clean with ashes;

Abuloy *n.* contribution; help;

Abuluyan, *v.* to help; to contribute;

Abután, *v.* to hand to; to give;

Abutan, *v.* to overtake;

Abutin *v.* to take hold of; to receive

Adhikâ, *n.* ambition; intention; wish;

Adobo, *n.* pork or chicken seasoned with vinegar, salt garlic, and pepper;

Adyós, *v.* to say farewell; to say good-bye;

Aga, *adv.* early;

Agád, *adv.* immediately;

Agad-agád, *adv.* at once; right away;

Agahan, *n.* breakfast;

Agam-Agam, *n.* doubt

Agap, *n.* alertness, punctuality;

Agaw-buhay, *adj.* between life and death;

Agawán *n.* stuggle

Agawan, *v.* to get things from another by force

Aghám, *n.* science;

Aghan, *n.* breakfast

Agiw, *n.* cob-web; soot;

Aglahi, *n.* mockery; jest;

Agnás, *adj.* decayed; rotten;

Agos, *n.* flow; current of water;

Agpáng, *adj.* fitted; adjusted;

Agrabiyado, *adj.* offended; at a disadvantage;

Agridulse, *n.* agridulse;

Agridulse, *n.* sauce made of oil; flour; vinegar; sugar; garlic; onion; pepper;

Agunyás, *n.* funeral; dirge; music for the dead;

Agwát, *n.* distance;

Ahas, *n.* snake; serpent;

Ahit, *n.* shave;

Ahon, *n.* ascent; going up; disembarking form the ship;

Akalà, *n.* belief; opinion; idea; estimate;

Akalain, *v.* to believe; to think; to make an estimate of;

Akay, *n.* a person guided by the hand;

Akayin *v.* to direct; to guide; to conduct;

Akbayàn, *v.* to put one's arm over one's shoulder;

Akdâ, *n.* works; writings;

Akin, *pron.* my or mine;

Akitin, *v.* to attract; to persuade;

Aklás, *n.* strike; trouble;

Aklát, *n.* book;

Aklatan, *n.* library;

Akó, *pron.* I;

Aksayá, *adj.* wasteful;

Aksayahin, *v.* to squander; to waste;

Akuwariyum, *n.* aquarium

Akyát, *v.* to climb; to ascend; to go up;

Alaala, *n.* remembrance; souvenir;

Alab, *n.* blaze;

Alabók, *n.* dust;

Alakdan, *n.* scorpion;

Alalahanin, *v.* to remember; to recolect;

Alam, *v.* to know;

Alamm *n.* what one knows;

Alampáy, *n.* shawl; neckerchief;

Alang-Alang, *n.* consideration; respect;

Alangán, *adj.* improper; doubtful;

Alanganin, *adj.* hesitating; doubtful;

Alapaáp, *n.* cloud;

Alat, *n.* legend; folklore;

Alay, *n.* offering; dedication;

Aldaba, *n.* door latch;

Ali, *n.* aunt; auntie; a term used in addressing a woman

Alibadbád, *n.* nausea; dizziness;

Aliburghâ *adj.* dishonest; irresponsible; unfaithful;

Alilà, *n.* servant; maid; slave;

Alimango, *n.* crab;

Alimbukáy *n.* surging of water when rowing due to strong current.

Alimpuyó *n.* whirl; dense smoke or dust in a whirl;

Alimuon *n.* vapor rising from the ground;

Alín, *pron.* which;

Alingasaw, *n.* effustion of strong and offensive odor;

Alingasngás, *n.* scandal; confusion

Alingawngáw, *n.* indecision; rumor; echo; news;

Alinlangan, *n.* doubt; hesitancy;

Alinsunod sa or kay, *prep.* according to;

Alipato, *n.* flying ember;

Alipato, *n.* sparks;

Alipin, *n.* slave, servant;

Alipungá, *n.* athlete's foot;

Alipustaín, *v.* to insult; to despise;

Alis, *n.* departure;

Alis, *v.* to remove; to take away; to go away;

Alkaide, *n.* warden;

Alkalde, *n.* mayor; president;

Alligi, *n.* ovary of crustaceans;

Almusál, *n.* breakfast;

Alóg, *n.* shake; jumble; .

Alsahin, *v.* to raise; to lift;

Alumana *v.* to pay attention to; to mind;

Am, *n.* broth of boiling rice;

Amâ, *adj.* fitted; applicable;

Amag, *n.* mildew; mold;

Amain *n.* uncle; mother or father's brother;

Ambâ *v.* to threaten; when one raises his hand to strike;

Ambâg *n.* contribution; help;

Ambil, repetition of a word or a story many times;

Ambón, *n.* drizzle; shower; gentle pattering of rain;

Amihan, *n.* northeast wind;

Amis, *adj.* persecuted; oppressed;

Amò, *n.* caress;

Amóy, *n.* smell; odor;

Ampalayá, *n.* amargoso;

Ampát, *v.* to check the flow of blood in a hemorrhage;

Ampáw *n.* sweetened popcorn;

Ampunan, *n.* asylum;

Amukiin, *v.* to persuade; to induce;

Anahaw, *n.* a kind of palm

Anák *n.* son or daughter;

Anás *n.* whisper

Andamyo *n.* gangplank;

Andukhain *v.* to take care of to raise;

Ang particle used before a common noun;

Ang, *n.* article;

Angkák *n.* a specially treated cereal used for seasoning fish;

Angkák *n.* to buy goods in anticipation on credit or cash for the pupose of reselling;

Angkák, *n.* a kind of coloring used in buring isdâ;

Angkán *n.* family;

Angkás *n.* to ride with somebody;

Angkát, *v.* goods gotten on credit with the promise of paying it agter it is sold;

Ani, *n.* harvest;

Anib *v.* to join an organization: to unite:

Anib, *v.* joined:

Anim, *adj.* six:

Aninag, *adj.* t ansluecnt: transparent:

Aninag, *v.* can be traced:

Anino, *n.* shadow:

Anito, *n.* deity:

Anito, *n.* god or goddess worshipped by some wild people. or pagans:

Anó, *pron.* what:

Antaia, *n.* delay: native delicaty:

Antala, *n.* late arrival: Boiled rice with cocoanut milk:

Antók, *n.* sleepiness:

Anunas, *n.* a kind of fruirt: brown and larger than an orange: or atis:

Apat, *adj.* four:

Apoy, *n.* fire

Apuyan *n.* hearth: fireplace:

Aral *v.* to study: to learn: to teach:

Aralín *n.* assignment:

Araw, *n.* sun: day:

Araw-Araw, *adv.* every day:

Ari, *n.* property: belonging:

Arí-Arían, *n.* tumble as in a circus:

Aringkin, *n.* somersault by tripping over something:

Arugà *v.* to take care of: to raise:

Aruga, *n.* care:

Asal, *n.* habit: custom:

Asaról, *n.* hoe:

Asawa, *n.* wife or husband:

Asín, *n.* salt:

Aso, *n.* dog:

Asó, *n.* smoke:

Asuhos, *n.* a kind of very fine fish:

Asukal *n.* sugar:

Asúl, *adj.* blue:

Asusena, *n.* an herb with white sweet flowers:

Asuwág, *n.* an injurious and evil character believed to be capable of assuming various forms like a dog etc:

At, *conj.* and:

Ataúl, *n.* bier: coffin:

Atáy, *n.* liver:

Atáy-atay, *adv.* cook in slow fire:

Atíp, *n.* roofing;

Atis, *n.* a tree that bears very sweet furit;

Atsuwete, *n.* a common shrub used for medicinal and coloring purposes;

Atubili, *v.* to act with doubt;

Awá, *n.* pity;

Awáng, *n.* crevice; crack;

Awás, *n.* discount;

Awat, *n.* weaning of a baby; separating and pacifying quarreling persons;

Away *n.* quarrel; fight;

Awit, *n.* song;

Ay, *v.* equivalent of linking verb to be;

Ayán, *interj.* there!

Ayaw, *n.* expression of negation; dislike;

Ayáw-awáy, *n.* distribution; proportion;

Ayò, *v.* to favor partially;

Ayon, *v.* to agree; to conform;

Ayop, *v.* to offend; to humiliate;

Ayos, *n.* form; appearance;

Ayungin, *n.* a species of theraponids called lukaok;

Aywan, *n.* ignorance; denial of knowledge;

Bb

Baák *v.* split into halves;

Babà *n.* chin;

Babâ, *v.* to go down;

Babád *adj.* soaked;

Babae, *n.* woman; female;

Babág, *n.* clash; quarrel; fight;

Babalâ, *n.* notice; warning;

Badya, *n.* what one expresses or says;

Badyá, *v.* to express; to say;

Bagabag, *n.* trouble; restlessness;

Bagamán, *conj.* althogh; notwithstanding; nevertheless; however;

Baging, *n.* vine;

Bago, *adj.* new;

Bagsák, *n.* fall;

Baguhan, *n.* novice;

Bagwis, *n.* tender and delicate wing of fowls;

Bagyó, *n.* typhoon;

Bahág ang buntót; fearful;

Bahalà, *n.* trust; custody;

Bahay, *n.* house;

Bahay-batà, *n.* uterus;

Bahín, *n.* sneezs;

Bahò, *n.* repulsive, foul odor.

Baít *n.* prudence; virtue; judgment; understanding;

Baitang, *n.* step of a stairway; grade;

Bakâ, *n.* a particle used in expressing doubt or uncertainty;

Baka, *n.* cow; bull;

Bakal, *n.* iron;

Bakál, *v.* using sharp pointed sticks.

Bakás, *n.* footprints;

Bakasyón, *n.* vacation;

Bakbák, *adj.* unglued; detached;

Bakit, *pron.* Why;

Bakod, *n.* fence;

Bakyà, *n.* wooden shoes;

Bala *n.* bullet;

Balabà, *n.* whole leaf of banana;

Balagat, *n.* clavicle;

Bálagtasan, *n.* a modern poetical joust named after Francisco Balagtas;

Balak, *n.* plan; intention; project;

Balakang, *n.* hip;

Balakíd, *n.* obstacle;

Balakubak, *n.* dandruff;

Balakyót, *adj.* mean; willful; vile, irascible, and without word of honor;

Balangáw, *n.* rainbow;

Balangkás, *n.* outline; plot;

Balás, *adj.* syrup solidified particles of sugar;

Balasubas, *adj. n.* one who does not fulfill his obligations promptly;

Balatay, *n.* a whip on the back of an animal;

Balátkayô, *n.* disguise; transfiguration;

Balawís,. *adj.* fierce;

Baldá, *n.* abasence; failure; cripple;

Balibol, *n.* auger;

Baligtád, *v.* fall backwards with force; upside down;

Balík *n.* return; restoration; coming and going back;

Balik-aral, *n.* review.

Balikán, *v.* to return for something or someone.

Balikat, *n.* shoulder;

Balikutsá, *n.* molasses candy; taffy;

Balikuwás, *v.* to jump to one's feet especially when one is in bed and is frightened by something;

Balimbíng, *n.* a tree which produces acid edible fruit

Balingkinitan, *adj.* slender; slim;

Balinguyngóy, *n.* nasal hemorrhage;

Balinsusô, *n.* a kind of the woman's hair knot;

Balintatáw, *n.* pupil of the eye;

Balintawak, *n.* native dress of Filipino women with dress and skirt woven of local fibers and kerchief and apron to match;

Balintunà *adj.* unnatural; apparent not real; pretend what one is not; contrary to what one expects;

Balisungsóng, *n.* funnel made of plant leaves or paper;

Balità, *n.* news;

Balíw, *adj.* demented; mentally deranged; crazy;

Balo, *n.* widow or widower;

Balok, *n.* thin pellicle of peanuts; skin of fruits or shell of egg;

Balón, *n.* well;

Balong, *n.* oozing of water;

Balót, *n.* duck's egg with grown-up embryo;

Balot, *n.* wrap; cover;

Balsá, *n.* raft;

Balumbalunan, *n.* gizzard;

Balutan, *n.* bundle; package;

Balutì *n.* breastplate; thighguards; armor;

Banâ, *n.* lowland; pool;.

Banaag, *n.* glimmering rays; soft and faint light;

Banabá, *n.* a kind of tree with purple flowers;

Banakal, *n.* the rind of trees.

Banál, *adj.* virtuous; pious;

Banát, *v.* tight; stretched;

Bandilà, *n.* flag;

Bangál, *v.* to tear off branches;

Bangán *n.* granary;

Banggâ, *n.* collision; clash; encounter;

Banggit, *n.* mention; citation; allusion;

Bangin, *n.* ravine;

Bangis, *n.* ferocity; brutality;

Bangkô, *n.* bench;

Bangó, *n.* aroma; fragrance;

Bangós, *n.* milkfish;

Bangungot, *n.* nightmare accompanied by moaning and groaning;

Baníg, *n.* mat;

Banláw, *n.* rinse;

Banli, *v.* to scald;

Bansá, *n.* country or nation;

Banság, *n.* motto; nickname; surname;

Bansot, *adj.* aborted; arrested development;

Bantâ, *n.* menace; threat; threaten;

Bantáy, *n.* guard;

Bantód, *n.* diameter;

Banyagà, *n.* stranger; foreigner;

Baóg, *n.* sterile woman;

Baon, *n.* provisions and necessities taken by a person who goes away for a time, like food, money etc.

Bara, *n.* a measure equivalent to 2.78 ft.;

Baraha, *n.* playing cards;

Baraka, *n.* market place;

Barandilya, *n.* ballustrade;

Barát, *n.* one given to bargaining;

Bareta, *n.* small iron bar;

Barò, *n.* dress;

Basa, *adj.* wet;

Basa, *v.* & *n.* read;

Baság, *adj.* cracked; broken; fractured;

Basag-ulo, *n.* altercation; trouble; fight;

Basahan, *v.* read

Basahin, bumasa, magbasá, *v.* read;

Bastós, *adj.* indecent; rustic;

Batà, *adj.* young;

Batà, *n.* child;

Bata, *n.* gown;

Batá, *v.* to suffer; to bear:

Batás, *n.* law;

Bataw, *n.* a kind of bean;

Batayán, *n.* basis; foundation;

Bathalá, *n.* God;

Batid, *v.* to know; to understand;

Batingáw, *n.* a large bell;

Batis, *n.* spring; rivulet; brook;

Bató, *n.* stone; kidney;

Batok, *n.* nape;

Batugan, *adj.* lazy; indolent;

Batutáy, *n.* pork sausage;

Batyâ, *n.* shallow wooden tube for laundry;

Bawal, *v.* to prohibit; to forbid;

Bawang, *n.* garlie;

Bayad, *n.* payment;

Bayan, *n.* twon;

Bayaní, *n.* hero; patriot;

Bayáwm *n.* brother-in-law;

Baywáng, *n.* waist;

Bibi, *n.* young duck;

Bibig, *n.* mouth;

Bigás, *n.* husked rice;

Bígasan, *n.* rice mill;

Bigát, *n.* weight;

Bigáy, *n.* gift;

Bigay-kaya, *n.* dowry;

Bigay-loob, *n.* granting of request;

Bígayan, *n.* granting each other's request; reciprocal giving;

Bigkás, *n.* pronunciation;

Bigkís, *n.* bundle; pack; abdominal band;

Bigô, *adj.* frustrated; disappointed;

Bilanggô, *n.* prisoner;

Bilasâ, *adj.* spolied;

Bilin, *n.* order requisition;

Bilóg, *adj.* round; circular;

Biloy, *n.* dimple;

Binat, *n.* relapse;

Binatà, *n.* young man; unmarried man; bachelor;

Bingi, *adj.* deaf;

Bingí, *adj.* incapable of bearing children;

Bingit, *n.* edge; border;

Binibini, *n.* young lady; unmarried woman;

Binidíd, *n.* bandaged;

Binilog ang ulo, made to believe in foolishness; fooled;

Binitay ng kasugál, *(dinayà ng-kasugàl)*, fooled by the other gamblers;

Binitháy ang kagubatan, looked at every corner of the forest;

Bintanà, *n.* window;

Bintang, *n.* false suspicion;

Binuksán, *v.* opened:

Biró, *rw.* joke;

Bitukang-manók, *adj.* winding; zigzag;

Biyayà, *n.* favor; gift; grace;

Biyernes, *n.* friday;

Bola, *n.* ball;

Btil, *n.* grain of cereal;

Bubog, *n.* piece of glass;

Bubót, *adj.* unripe;

Bubuwit, *n.* small rat or mouse;

Budhî, *n.* conscience;

Bugaw, *n.* go between;

Bugaw, *v.* to drive away;

Bugawan, *v.* to drive away as to flies;

Bugawin *v.* to protect from destruction or distrubance;

Bugtóng, *n.* riddles;

Buhat, *prep.* from; since;

Buhatin, *v.* to raise; to lift up;

Buhawi, *n.* whirlwind;

Buháy, *adj.* alive; living; growing;

Buhay, *n.* life; life story;

Buhay-alamáng, *adj.* short-lived; dies easily; with a short life;

Buhayin *v.* to grow; to raise.

Buhók, *n.* hair;

Bukál *adj.* inborn; voluntary;

Bukáng-bibig, always talking about it;

Bukás *adj.* open;

Bukas, *adj.* tomorrow;

Bukás-palad, *adj.* gallant; helpful;

Bukid, *n.* farm; field;

Buklód *n.* tie; binding,

Buko *n.* bud of a flower; young coconut;

Buksán *v.* to open;

Bulâ, *n.* bubble; sud;

Bulaan, *adj.* false; not true;

Bulagtâ *adj.* fallen on one's back

Bulak, *n.* cotton:

Bulaklák *n.* flower:

Bulo *n.* young carabao:

Bulo, *n.* hairs (of fruit or leaves):

Bulóng, *n.* whispers:

Bulwagan, *n.* sala: living room:

Bumabalong, *v.* springing from:

Bumalik,. *v.* to return: to go back:

Bumaling, *v.* to turn to one side:

Bumangon, *v.* to get up:

Bumilang, *v.* to count:

Bumilí, *v.* buy:

Bumuwís, *v.* pay taxe:

Bunga, *n.* fruit:

Bungad, *n.* front: beginning:

Bungál, *adj.* incissors missing:

Bungang-araw, *n*, prickly heat:

Bungang-isip, *n.* works: writings:

Bungang-tulog, *n.* dreams

Bungangá, *n.* gullet of large animals:

Bunggô, *n.* impact: collosion:

Bunggo, *v.* bump: bumping:

Bungí, *adj.* hare-lip:

Bungì, *n.* jag in the edge of the tools:

Bungisngia, *v.* always laughing:

Bungisngís, *n.* giggling: one who giggles at the slightest provocation:

Bungô, *n.* skull:

Bunso, *n.* youngest or pet child:

Buntón, *n.* mound: heap:

Buntong-hiningá, *n.* sigh:

Buntót, *n.* tail: rear:

Buo, *n.* whole:

Buòd, gist: quintessence:

Buód, *n.* brief summary:

Burá, *n.* erasure:

Buradól; *n.* kite:

Busabos, slave:

Busál, (ng kabayo): cover of the month:

Busal, *n.* corn cob :

Busisí, *adj.* meticulous:

Busisi, *adj.* overnice; scrupulous; fastidious;

Busóg, *adj.* very much satisfied;

Busog, *n.* arrow;

Busog, *n.* spear;

Butas, *n.* hole;

Butas, *n.* hole; butás arj; with a hole;

Butó *n.* bone;

Butones, bitones, *n.* buttons;

Butsè *n.* crop;

Butsé, *n.* place where grains eaten by the chicken are temporarily stored before digestion;

Buwâ *n.* a woman's disease

Buwál, *adj.* torn down; demolishe;

Buwál, down;

Buwán, *n.* moon; month;

Buwí *n.* bunch; cluster;

Buwí *n.* tax; tribute;

Buwíg, *n.* bunch as of bananas;

Buwís, *n.* pay taxes;

Buwisan, *adj.* rented leased;

Buwisit, *adj.* ill luck;

Buwisit, *adj.* one who brings bad luck;

Buyón, *n.* big stomach;

Byradól, *n.* kite.

Kk

Ka, *pron.* the personal pronoun;

Ka, *pron.* you;

Kaakí-Akibat, *n.* constant companion; supporter;

Kaáng, *n.* earthen jar for holdig drinking water;

Kaanib, *adj.* affiliated;

Kaanib, *n.* member of an organization;

Kaapihá, *n.* oppression;

Kaasál, *n.* marriage;

Kaawa-Awa, *adj.* pitiful;

Kabá, *n.* premonition; fear;

Kabá, *n.* pulse palpitation; restlessness; premonition;

Kababalagháb, *n.* miracle;

Kababalaghán, *n.* something unusual or obscure; mystery;

Kababayan, *n.* townmate;

Kabag, *n.* flatulence;

Kabag, *n.* flatulence; gas pain; windiness;

kabágkabág, *n.* aspecies of fruit-bat;

Kabaitan, *n.* virtue; prudence;

Kabaka, *n.* enemy;

Kabaka, *n.* opponent:

kabalitaan, *adj.* famous; renown;

Kabalitaan, *adj.* well-known;

Kabán, *n.* chest; trunk;

Kabán, *n.* trunk; (for clothes);

Kabanalan, *n.* religious practices;

Kabanatà, *n.* chapter;

Kabaong, *n.* a place where the body of a dead person is placed before burial;

kabaong, *n.* coffin;

Kabataan, *n.* youth; childhood;

kabayo, *n.* horse;

Kabbayan. *n.* townmate; countryman;

Kabihasnán, *n.* civilization;

Kabila, *n.* neighbor or next house; next door;

kabilâ, *n.* other side;

Kabilán, *adj.* not even;

Kabilán, *adj.* unsymmetrical; unequal;

Kabít, *adj:* joined together;

Kabít, *n.* unite; fasten; stick; adhere;

Kabiyawan, *n.* sugar mill;

Kabiyawan, *n.* uncle;

Kabuhayan, *n.* livelihood;

Kabuluhán, *n.* importance; value; worth;

Kabuluhán, *n.* usefulness;

Kabutí, *n.* mushroom;

Kagabi', *adv.* last night;

Kagabi, *adv.* last night;

Kagalang-Galang, *adv.* respectful;

Kagalingan, *n.* welfare;

Kagát, *n.* bite;

Kagatín, *v.* bite;

Kagawad, *n.* Member;

Kágawarán, *n.* department;

Kaginsá-ginsá *adv.* all of a sudden; suddenly;

Kagipitan, *n.* hardship; difficulty;

Kagitingan, *n.* heroism;

Kagyát, *adv.* at once: immediately;

Kahahantungán, *n.* destiny; end;

Kahalili, *n.* substitute; successor;

Kahapon, *adv.* yesterday;

Kahati, *n.* partner;

Kahati, *n.* shareholder;

Kahimanawarì *interj.* may God will it!

Kahirapan, *n.* poverty; hardship;

Kahit, *conj.* although; even if;

Kahón, *n.* box;

Kahoy, lumber; wood;

Kahulugán, *n.* meaning;

Kaibigan, *n.* friend;

Kaibiganin, *v.* to make a friend of him;

Kailan, *adv.* when;

Kailan, *pron.* when?

Kailangan, *n.* necessary; necessity;

Kailangan, *n.* smething necessary; needs;

Kailanman, *adv.* nevermore;

Kain *nv.* eat;

Kainaman, *adj.* about right.

Kainin O Kanin, *v.* to eat;

Kakà, *n.* elder brother, sister, or cousin;

Kaka, *n.* uncle;

Kaka, *n.* uncle; aunt;

Kaká, older brother;

Kakak, *n.* cackling of chickens;

Kakak, *n.* cackling of hens;

Kakanán, *n.* dining room;

Kakanán, *n.* place where animals like pigs are fed;

Kakauntí, *adj.* very little;

Kakilala, *n.* acquaintance;

Kalabasa, *n.* squash;

Kalabáw, *n.* buffalo; water buffalo; carabao;

Kalabáw, *n.* carabao;

Kalãgayan, *n.* condition state;

Kalagim-lagim, *adj.* terrible; horrible;

Kalahati, *n.* half;

Kalahati, *n.* one half;

Kalakal, *n.* merchandise;

Kalakalin, *v.* to sell; to make business of or on;

Kalán, *n.* a native stove made of earth;

Kalaníng, *n.* letter; epistle;

Kalánm *n.* cooking stove;

Kalapati, *n.* dove; pigeon;

Kalatas, *n.* letter;

Kalatís O Kilatís, *n.* noise made by footsteps;

Kalatís, *n.* extremely soft noise;

Kalawang, *n.* rust;

Kalayaan, *n.* liberty; freedom;

Kalaykáy, *n.* rake;

Kalbó, *adj.* bald headed;

Kalesa, *n.* two-wheeed vehicle pulled by a horse;

Kaligtasan, *n.* safety; liberation;

Kalihim, *n.* secretary;

Kalikasan, *n.* nature;

Kaliktián, *n.* crookedness;

Kaliluhan, *n.* crueltly;

Kaliluhan, *n.* treachery;

Kalimutan, *v.* to forget;

Kalingà *n.* act of taking care of;

Kalinga, *n.* care;

Kalinisan, *n.* federation;

Kaliwa, *adj.* left-handed;

Kaliwâ, *n. and adj.* left;

Kalo, *n.* pulley;

Kalupì, *n.* pocket book; hand bag;

Kaluwalhatian, *n.* glory;

Kalye, *n.* street;

Kalye, *n.* street; road;

Kamag-Anak, *n.* relative;

Kamalig, *n.* barn; storehouse;

Kamandág, *n.* poison;

Kamangmangán, *n.* ignorance;

Kamátayan, death;

Kamátayan, *n.* death;

Kamatis, *n.* tomato;

Kamay, *n.* hand;

Kambál, twin;

Kami, *pron.* we (including the person speaking)

Kamí, *pron.* we;

Kamiseta, *n.* undershirt;

Kamot, *n.* scratch

Kamote, *n.* sweet potato;

Kampit, *n.* kitchen knife;

Kampon, *n.* follower;

Kampon, *n.* follower; disciple;

Kamunduhán, *n.* worldliness;

Kamusmusán, *n.* childhood;

Kamusmusán, *n.* innocence; childhood;

Kanan, *n.* right hand;

Kanan, *n.* right;

Kandila, *n.* candle;

Kandugan, *n.* lap;

Kanilá, *pron.* their or theirs;

Kanin, *n.* boiled rice;

Kanina, *adv.* a little while ago; a moment ago;

Kanina, *adv.* a while ago;

Kanino, *pron.* whose;

Kanino, *pron.* whose;

Kaniyá O Kanyá, *pron.* her or hers; his;

Kaniya, to her or to him;

Kanluran, *n.* west;

Kanluran, *n.* west; occdent;

Kantá O Awit, *n.* song;

Kanya O Kaniya, *pron.* his or her;

Kapabayaán, *n.* neglect;

Kapahamakán, *n.* danger;

Kapahamakán, *n.* misfortune; tragedy;

Kapahintulután, *n.* misfortune; tragedy;

Kapahintulután, *n.* permission;

Kapangyarihan, *n.* power; authority;

Kapangyarihan, *n.* right;

Kapansanan, *n.* obstacle;

Kapatid o Kápatiran, brother or sister; brotherhood;

Kapayakán, *n.* simplicity;

Kapayapaan, *n.* peace;

Kapé *n.* coffee; I take cofee every morning;

Kapé, *n.* coffeee;

Kapighatian, *n.* sorrow

Kapighatian, *n.* sorrow; grief;

Kapiraso, *n.* a little bit; a small piece;

Kapiraso, *n.* piece;

Kapisanan, *n.* society;

Kapit-Bahay, *n.* neighbor;

Kapita-APitagan, *adj.* respectful;

Kapita-Pitagan, *adj.* deserving respect or honor;

Kapós, *adj.* insufficient;

Kapote, *n.* raincoat;

Kapuluán, *n.* archipelago;

Kapuná-Puná, *adj.* calling attention;

Kapuná-Puná, *adj.* noticeable; censurable;

Kapusukán, *n.* state of beng vehement;

Kapuwá, *pron.* both;

Karampatan, *adj.* adequate;

Karaniwan, *adj.* ordinary;

Karaniwan, ordinary; nearly always;

Karapatán, *n.* right;

Karayom, *n.* needle;

Karimlán, *n.* darkness;

Karit, *n.* sickle;

Karitela, *n.* two-wheeled vehicle larger than a calesa also pulled by a horse;

Karitón, *n.* cart;

Karné *n.* meet;

Karneng baboy, pork;

Karneng baka, beef

Karneng usá, venison

Karpintero, *n.* carpenter;

Karugtóng, *n.* additional;

Karugtóng, *n.* continuation;

Karunungan, *n.* knowledge; wisdom;

Kasalanan, *n.* sin;

Kasalo, *n.* messmate;

Kasalukuyan, *adv.* presently; at present;

Kasalungát, *adj.* opposite;

Kasalungát, *n.* adversary; opponent;

Kasama, *n.* companion;

Kasamá, *n.* tenent;

Kasamaán, *n.* something bad;

Kasamaán, *n.* state of being bad or evil;

Kasangkapan, *n.* household belongings;

Kasangkót, *n.* accomplice;

Kasapi, *n.* member;

Kasarinlan, *n.* independence;

Kasarinlán, *n.* liberty;

Kasáyahan, *n.* celebation; festivity;

Kasaysayan, *n.* history;

Kasi, *n.* sweetheart; darling;

Kasibulan, *n.* spring time; prime of life;

Kasibulan, *n.* youth;

Kasing, a prefix denoting similarity or equivalence;

Kasing, *n.* prefix;

Kasinlaki, *adj.* as big as;

Kasinlaki, *adj.* having the same size;

Kasulatan, *n.* document;

Kasunód, *n.* next; following;

Katá, *pron.* you and I;

Katabilán, *n.* talkativeness;

Katad, *n.* carabao hide;

Katad, *n.* leather;

Katahimikan, *n.* silence; peace;

Katám, *n.* plane;

Katámaran, *n.* laziness;

Katampatan, *n.* sufficient;

Katangian, *n.* characteristic; quality;

Katapatan, *n.* loyalty;

Katapatan, *n.* sincerity;

Katarungan, *n.* justice;

Katawán, *n.* body;

Katawán, *n.* body;

Katayin, *v.* butcher ad in pigs;

Katayin, *v.* slaughter for food;

Kathâ, *n.* literary work;

Katha, *n.* writings;

Kathân, *n.* body;

Katibayan, *n.* proof;

Katimpian, *n.* restraint;

Katitikan, *n.* minutes (as of a meeting);

Katiwala, *n.* one in charge;

Katiwalá, *n.* Overseer; manager

Katiyakán, *n.* definiteness;

Katotohanan, *n.* truth;

Katre, *n.* bed;

Katre, *n.* bed; kama;

Katulong, *n.* helper; maid;

Katumbás, *n.* equivalent;

Katungkulan, *n.* duty; occupation;

Katungkulan, *n.* duty; position;

Katuwaan, *n.* Happiness;

Katuwaan, *n.* Merriment;

Kaugalian, *n.* custom;

Kaugalian, *n.* custom; habit;

Kaugnayán, *n.* relationship;

Kaunlarán, *n.* success;

Kauntî, *adj.* little;

Kaunti, *n.* a little; a bit;

Kausap, *n.* person spoken to;

Kawad, *n.* wire;

Kawal, *n.* soldier;

Kawali *n.* frying pan;

Kawan, *n.* group;

Kawan, *n.* school of fish or of birds;

Kawanggawá, *n.* charity; mercy;

Kawangki, *adj.* similar;

Kawaní, *n.* employee;

Kawawà *n.* somebody to be pitied; one who is pitiful;

Kawayan, *n.* bamboo·

Kawikaán, *n.* sayingss; proverbs;

Kay, *prep.* to; for; of;

Kayâ *conj.* for this or that reason; therefore; that is why;

Kaya, *n.* ability; aptitude; wealth;

Kayamanan, *n.* riches;

Kayamután, *v.* be angry with; annoyed with;

Kayó, *pron.* Plural or used with respect in the singular number;

Kayumanggi, *adj.* brown;

Keso, *n.* cheese;

Kibd, *n.* motion; movement;

Kidlát, *n.* lightning;

Kilatis-pinggan, easily invited; popular;

Kilay, *n.* eyebrow;

Kimî, *adj.* shy: timid;

Kinamayan, *v.* shook hands with;

Kinamot, *v.* scratched;

Kinapál, *n.* creation;

Kináratnán, *v.* fate; esestiny; result;

Kinke, *n.* kerosine lamp;

Kinupkóp, *v.* sheltered;protcted; took care of;

Kisápmatá, *n.* in a wink

Kita, *n.* earning; salary;

Kitá, *pron.* you and I (used after the verb);

Kita, *rw.* see;

Kiwal, *n.* wriggle (like a snake);

Klase, *n.* class;

Ko, *pron.* (used after the verb);

Komedór, *n.* dining room;

Kubo, *n.* small hut;

Kudkuran, *n.* grater;

Kudyapî, *n.* old Philippine guitar;

Kuha, *rw.* get; take;

Kukuti-Kutitap, *v.* flickering;

Kulang, *adj.* not enough; not sufficient;

Kulang, *adj.* short; lacking;

Kulay, *n.* color;

Kulilíg, *n.* small bell;

Kulungin, *v.* enclose;

Kumain, *v.* to eat;

Kumalansáng *v.* tinle; jingle;

Kumantá, *v.* to sing;

Kumatóg O Kumatók, knock (as at the door);

Kumatók, *v.* to knock;

Kumot, *n.* bedsheet; blanket;

Kumubkób, *v.* surround;

Kumuha O Kunin, *v.* take, get;

Kumupit, *v.* pifeered; stole;

Kumutób, *v.* to have a premonition;

Kung, *conj.* if; when;

Kurukuro, *n.* opinion; observation;

Kusinà, *n.* kitchen;

Kutsara, *n.* spoon;

Kutsarahin, *v.* use a spoon;

Kutsero, *n.* driver;

Kutsilyo, *n.* knife;

Kutya, *n.* ridicule; sarcasm

Kuwadro, *n.* frame;

Kuwako, *n.* pipe;

Kuwenta, *n.* account;

Kuwento, *n.* story;

Dd

Daán *n.* way; street; road;

Daán, *n.* hundred; sandaanone hundre;

Daáng-Bakal, *n.* railroad track;

Dagâ, *n.* rat; mouse;

Dagán *v.* lie on something or somebody; press weight;

Dagat, *n.* sea;

Dagat, *n.* sea; ocean;

Dagdá *n.* increase; addition;

Dagok, *n.* blow; dagukan;

Dagok, *n.* strike with the fist;

Dagtâ, *n.* juice; sap;

Dagukan, *v.* give a blow;

Dahák, *v.* to expectorate phlegm;

Dahil, *pref.* because of;

Dahilán, *n.* motive; cause;excuse;

Dahon, *n.* leaf;

Dahóp, *adj.* not enough

Dahóp, *adj.* scarce; needy;

Daigdí *n.* universe; world;

Daigdig, *n.* world;

Daigin, *v.* to surpass; to be better than;

Daing, *n.* fish sliced open;

Daing *n.* leamentation; moaning;

Dakila, *adj.* great;

Dako, *n.* spot;

Dakpin, *v.* to capture;

Dalá *v.* to carry; bring; take;

Dalâ, *adj.* taught by painful experience or punishment;

Dala, *n.* net;

Dalahirà *n.* gossiper;

Dalamhati, *n.* extreme sorrow; affliction;

Dalaw, *n.* visitor; visit;

Dalawá, *adj.* two;

Dali *n.* one finger width;

Dalî, *n.* quickness; promptness;

Daliri *n.* finger;

Daló, *n.* Succor;help;

Dalubhasà, *n.* specialist;

Daluṛò *n.* cork tree;

Daluyong, *n.* big wave; swell of the sea;

Damák, *n.* breadth of the hand;

Damay, *n.* help; aid;

Dambanà *n.* altar;

Dambuhalà, *n.* a big monster; a whale;

Damdám, *n.* feeling sensation; resentment;

Damhiín, *v.* to feel;

Dami, *n.* quantity; great amount or number;

Damít, *n.* cloth; clothes;

Dampâ, *n.* hut;

Dampt. *n.* stinginess; selfishness;

Dangál, *n.* honor; reputation;

Dangkál, *n.* span from the tip of the thumb to tip of middle finger extended;

Dapdáp, *n.* a kind of tree which is leafless or partly leafless at the time of flowering;

Dapò, *n.* orchid;

Dapóg, *n.* hearth; cooking; place;

Dapt, *v.* must; ought;

Darák, *n.* rice bran;

Daráng, *v.* exposed to the fire or live embers to dry or heat;

Dasál, *n.* group prayer;

Dasál, *n.* prayer;

Daskól, *adj.* hastily and carelessly done;

Dátapuwâ, *conj.* but; notwithstanding;

Dawag, *n.* thorny path; jungle;

Daya, *n.* deceit; fraud;

Dayami, *n.* straw; dried rice stalks;

Dayukdok *adj.* starved; hungry;

Dentista, *n.* dentist;

Di-Hindî, *adv.* no; not;

Dibdib, *n.* breast;

Digmá, *n.* revolution; war;

Diilím, *n.* darkness;

Dilág, *n.* beauty; splendor;

Dilidili, *n.* meditation;

Diligin, *v.* to sprinkle; to water;

Din (rin), *adv.* also; still;

Dinamtán, *v.* clothed;

Dingdig, *n.* wall; partition;

Dini, *adv.* here;

Dito, *adv.* here;

Diwà, *n.* spirit; soul; consciousness;

Diyan, *adv.* there; (far from the speaker but close to the person addressed);

Doon, *adv.* there ;

Dukha, *adj.* poor; destitute;

Dukláy, *n.* hanging or drooping branches;

Duktor, *n.* physician; doctor;

Dula, *n.* drama;

Dulang, *n.* low dining table;

Dulig, *adj.* cross-eyed;

Dulo, *n.* end;

Dumaan *v.* pass by; drop in;

Dumadaloy, *v.* flowing (as of tears);

Dumalaw, *v.* visit;

Dumambót, *v.* to pick up;

Dumí, *n.* dirt;

Dumí, *n.* dirt; filth;

Dumog, *adj.* absorbed;

Dumumi *v.* to become dirty;

Dungd, *adj.* bashful; timid; shy;

Dungo, *adj.* timid;

Dunong, *n.* knowledge;

dunong, *n.* wisdom; knowlede;

Dupiká *n.* ringing of the bells;

Dupilas *v.* to slip or slide accidentally;

Dupók, *n.* weakness; brittleness; fragility;

Duróh. *sdj.* pulverized;

Dúrungawan, *n.* window;

Dusa, *n.* Suffering; affliction; grief;

Dusdós, *n.* sarna on the head;

Dustâ, *n.* insult; abuse;

Duwág, *adj.* coward; not brave;

Duyan, *n.* cradle;

Ee

Ebidensiya, *n.* proof; evidence;

Edad, *n.* age; era;

Eklipse, *n.* eclipse;

Eksportadór, *n.* exporter;

Embahador, *n.* ambassador; representative of a nation in another country;

Enkanto, *n.* enchantment;

Eskabetse, *n.* onekind fo dish; one way of cooking fish;

Eskala, *n.* scale in music;

Eskandalo, *n.* trouble; noise that distructs;

Eskape, *n.* the rush and fast running of a horse;

Eskina, *n.* corners of streets;

Eskirol *n.* laborers taking the place of strikers;

Eskoba, *n.* brushes for clothes;

Eskopeta, *n.* a kind of gun used in hunting birds;

Eskribano, *n.* an official who keeps the records of the court; sheriff;

Eskultor, *n.* engraver; sculptor;

Eskupidor, *n.* container or dish where one spits in a public place;

Eskuwela, *n.* school; student;

Eskuwelahan, *n.* school house;

Esmeralds, *n.* green stone called emerald;

Espada, *n.* sword; a kind of fish in the form of a sword;

Espanya, *n.* Spain;

Espasol, *n.* a kind of native cake;

Esperma, *n.* candles made from the fat of whales.

Espiker, *n.* speaker (of the house);

Espiritu, *n.* soul; spirit;

Espiya, *n.* spy;

Espongha, *n.* sponge; a product of the sea;

Estados Unidos, *n.* United States;

Estagparti, *n.* stage party; a party for boys only;

Estampa, *n.* a framed picture of the saint;

Estante, *n.* cabinet for books or things for sale;

Estasyon, *n.* station (rail road);

Estatuwa, *n.* statue;

Estima, *n.* good entertainment;

Estraik, *n.* strike;

Estrelya, *n.* stars;

Estrelyado, *n.* fried egg;

Estribo, *n.* the part on which one steps when he gets on on a horse or a vehicle;

Estudiyante, *n.* student;

Eto O Heto, *adv.* here it is;

Ewan O Aywan, don't know;

Gg

Gaán, *rw.* easiness; lightness;

Gaanás, *v.* to make easy; to make light;

Gaano, *pron.* how much?

Gabáy, *n.* guide; support;

Gabayán *v.* to support; to make a support of;

Gabayán, *v.* put railings on

Gabi *n.* night; evening;

Gabi, *n.* night; gabi, n. tuber;

Gabi, *n.* tuber; yam;

Gabihin, *v.* to be caught by night time; benighted;

Gadgarin, *v.* grate;

Gagá *v.* to usurp; to appropriate;

Gaga, *adj.* fool; simpleton;

Gagád, *n.* imitation;

Gagambá *n.* spider;

Gagarín, *v.* to imitate;

Gahasà, *n.* force; recklessness;

Gahasain, *v.* to force to submit;

Gahì, *n.* rupture; rip;

Gahisín, *v.* subdue;

Gahố *adj.* short of time; to be short of;

Gahulím, *v.* to be short of time;

Galâ, *n.* traveller;

Galák *n.* joy;

Galamáy, *n.* helpers; sppendages;

Galáng, *n.* bracelet;

Galang, *n.* respect;

Galás, *n.* roughness;

Galáw *n.* movement;

Galawín, *v.* to move;

Galíng *n.* charm; excellence;

Galís, *n.* itch;

Galisin, *adj.* full of itches;

Galit, *n.* anger;

Galitin *v.* to make angry;

Galos, *n.* scratch; mark;

Galusan, *v.* to scratch;

Gambalà *n.* dustyrbabcel;

Gambala, *n.* trouble; bother;

Gambalain *v.* to disturb;

Gamit, *n.* use; utility;

Gamitin, *v.* to use;to utilize; wear;

Gamót, *n.* medicine;

Gampanán *v.* to fulfill on's duty;

Gamutan *n.* treatment;

Gamutín, *v.* to cure; to apply medicine;

Gana, *n.* appetite; profit;

Ganá, *n.* salary; earnings;

Ganahan, *v.* to wet one's appetite;

Ganáp, *adj.* complete;

Gandá, *n.* beauty;

Gandahán, *v.* to make beautiful;

Ganît, *n.* toughness, state of being tough;

Ganitó, *pron.* like this;

Ganiyán, *pron.* like that;

Gansâ, *n.* goose;

Gansál *adj.* odd number;

Gansál, *adj.* not even; odd number;

Ganti, *n.* retaliation; reply;

Gantihán, *v.* to reciprocate;

Gantimpalà *n.* Prize; reward;

Gantimpalaan, *v.* to reward;

Gaod, *n.* row;

Gapák, **gabák**, *adj.* ripped;

Gapangin, *v.* to creep; to crawl; to climb;

Gápasan, *n.* harvest;

Gapî *adj.* subdued; over-powered;

Gapiin, *v.* to overpower;

Gapos, *n.* binding; tie;

Gapsin, *v.* to harvest;

Gapusin *v.* to tie; to bind;

Garà *n.* pomposity; style; brilliance;

Garaan, *v.* to make stylish or pompous;

Garantiya *n.* pledge; guaranty;

Gargantilya *n.* necklace;

Garíl, *adj.* defective; faulty pronunciation;

Garing, *n.* ivory;

Garing, *n.* work;

Gasláw, *n.* vulgarity; inhibition;

Gaspás, *adj.* scrached;

Gaspàs, *n.* scratches;

Gata, *n.* coconut milk;

Gatâ, *n.* pure juice;

Gatang, *n.* chupa;

Gatas, *n.* milk;

Gatlâ, *n.* marks; pointer;

Gatól, *n.* sudden stops; interruptions;

Gatong, *n.* fuel;

Gatungan, *v.* to increase the fuel of;

Gawa *n.* work

Gawâ, *n.* cccupation; ork;

Gáwaan, *n.* place of work; factory;

Gawagáw, *n.* starch;

Gaway, *n.* withchcraft;

Gawayin, *v.* topractice sorcery;

Gawî. *n.* habit; custom;

Gaya, *n.* imitation;

Gayahin, *v.* to imitate;

Gayák *n.* decoration;

Gayatin, *v.* slice into pieces;

Gayuma, *n.* charm;

Gayunman, *adv.* however;

Gibâ, *adj.* ruined, demolished;

Giba, *v.* wrecked; torn down;

Gibík, *n.* shout for help;

Gigil, *n.* gritting of the teeth;

Giikan, *n.* threshing machine;

Giikín *v.* to thresh;

Gilagid, *n.* gum;

Gilalás, *n.* wonder; suprse;

Gilas, *n.* galant action;

Gilid, *n.* edge; rim;

Gilingan, *n.* grinder;

Gilingin, *v.* grind;

Giliw, *n.* a term of affection or love;

Gimbalín, *v.* to disturb peace; to surprise;

Ginalugad, *v.* sarched thoroughly;

Ginang, *n.* Mrs.; Madam;

Gináw *n.* coldness;

Ginintuán *v.* to make golden;

Ginoó, *n.* Mr; Mister; Sir;

Gintd *n.* gold;

Gisá, *v.* stew;

Gisado, *adj.* stewed;

Gisíg, *adj.* pawake;

Gitara, *n.* guitar;

Gitgit, *n.* marks made by a tight rope or twine;

Giting, *n.* herosim excellence;

Gitlá, *n.* shock; fright;

Gitlain, *n.* to frighten to shock;

Gitnâ, *n.* middle; midst;

Giwang, *n.* rocking of the boat;

Guagol, *n.* expenses;

Gubat, *n.* forest; woods;

Gugo *n.* gogo;

Guguan *v.* (to clean hair with) will be removed;

Gugulan, *v.* to finance; to invest money;

Guhit, *n.* line; sketch;

Guhitan, *v.* to make lines on; to sketch;

Guhò *n.* crumbling; collapse; demolition;

Gulang, *n.* maturity; age;

Gulanít, *v.* tattered; worn out;

Gulapáy, *adj.* overworked; weak;

Gulat, *n.* fright; shock;

Gulatin, *v.* to frighten; to shock;

Gulay, *n.* vegetables;

Gulilát, *adj.* panicky;

Gulò, *n.* confusion; disorderliness; riot;

Gulod *n.* hill top;

Gulok, *n.* bolo;

Gulóng, *n.* wheel; turn;

Gulugód *n.* backbone;

Gulujhin, *v.* to bring on disorder; to confuse;

Gulungan, *v.* to turn; to run over;

Gumaán, *v.* to become light in weight;

Gumanáp, *v.* perfrom;

Gumawâ, *v.* to make; to do;

Gumising O Gising, *v.* to wake up;

Gumuhit, *v.* to draw;

Gunam-gunam, *n.* recolection; meditation;

Guniguni *n.* memory; remembrance;

Guniguni, *n.* Imaginstion; meditation;

Gunitain, *v.* to recall; to remember;

Gunting *n.* scissors;

Guntingin, *v.* to cut with scissors;

Gupitán, *v.* to trim; to cut hair;

Guró. *n.* teacher;

Gusai, *n.* building;

Gusgusin, *adj.* dirty; in rags;

Gusót, *adj.* crumpled; confused;

Gustin, *v.* to crumpl; to confuse;

Gusto, *n.* liking; desire;

Gutóm *adj.* hungry;

Gutom, *n.* hunger;

Guumin *v.* to make hungry;

Guwáng, *n.* crevice;

Guya, *n.* calf of cow or carabao;

Hh

Haás *adj.* thin;

Habâ, *adj.* long; elongated;

Habà, *n.* length;

Habaan, *v.* to make long; to lenghen;

Habág, *n.* pity;

Habagat, *n.* wind from thewest monsoon;

Habangbuhay, *n.* lifetime;

Habas, *n.* discretion;

Habì, *interj.* let me pass;

Habi, *n.* weave;

Habihán *n.* loom; weaving instrument;

Habihin, *v.* to weave;

Habilin, *n.* will; instructions;

Hablá, *n.* suit;

Habol, *n.* postscrpt; hurry to overtake somebody;

Habong, *n.* temporary roofing; shelter;

Habulin, *v.* run after; chase;

Hadláng *n.* barrier; obatacle;

Hadlangán, *v.* to stop; to cause and obstacle;

Hagad, *n.* cop; speed cop;

Hagarin, *v.* to overtake; to follow;

Hagdán, *n.* stairway; ladder;

Hagdanán *v.* to build a ladder;

Hagibis, *n.* fast runner;

Hagilapin, *v.* to look for; to search for;to gather;

Haging, *n.* buzz; hiss;

Hagis, *n.* throw;

Hagod, *n.* caress;

Hagok *n.* gasping;

Hagpós *adj.* loose;

Hagulhól, *n.* loud cry; weeping;

Hagurin *v.* to rub; to caress;

Hakà, *n.* idea; suspicion

Haka-hakà, *n.* supposition;

Hakbáng, *n.* step;

Hakbáng, *n.* steps; measure;

Hakot,, *n.* load; baggage;

Hakutin, *v.* to deliver; to take;

Halaán *n.* edible clam;

Halabósw, *adj.* boiled and dried;

Halagá, *n.* price: cost; value;

Halagȟág *adj.* full fo neglect;

Halakhak, *n.* laughter;

Halakhakán, *v.* to laugh at;

Halál *n.* vote:

Hálalan, *n.* election;

Halaman, *n.* plants; vegetation;

Halamanan, *n.* garden;

Halatâ *adj.* noticed; can be seen or felt; detected;

Halatáng-Halatâ, *adj.* very noticeable;

Haláw, *n.* translation; translation from and original;

Halawin,, *v.* to condense; to translate; to pick out;

Halayin, *v.* to embarrass;

Haligi *n.* post; pillar;

Haligihan *v.* to put posts; to place support;

Halika, *v.* coma;

Halikán, *v.* kiss;

Halimaw, *adj.* greedy;

Halimbawa, *n.* example;

Halimhimán *v.* to hatch;

Halimuyak *n.* fragrance;

Halíng, *adj.* fool; mad;

Halinghíng, *n.* moaning;

Halò *n.* mixture;

Halo, *adj.* mixed or mixture;

Halo, *n.* pestle;

Halos, *adv.* almost;

Halu-Halò, *n.* refreshments;

Halughugín *v.* to ransack;

Haluin *v.* to stir; to mix;

Halukayin, *v.* to lok carefully or examine throroughly;

Halukipkip, *v.* to cross arms across the breast;

Halumigmig *adj.* moist; damp;

Halungkatin *v.* to search roughly;

Hamak, *adj.* humble;

Hamakin, *v.* to belittle;

Hambalso, *n.* beating; blow;

Hambalusin, *v.* to beat;

Hambóg, *adj.* boastful;

Hamóg, *n.* dew;

Hamon, *n.* challenge;

Hamón, *n.* ham; smoked pork;

Hampás, *n.* blow; strike;

Hampasin *v.* to strike; to beat;

Hampaslupà, *n.* vagabond;

Hamunin, *v.* to challenge;

Hanap, *n.* object of search;

Hanapbuhay, *n.* occupation; ·profession; work;

Hanapin, *v.* look for;

Hanay *n.* row; line;

Handâ, *n.* food; menu;

Handaan, *n.* place where the party is held; party;

Handaán, *v.* have ready;

Handóg, *n.* gift; offering;

Handugán, *v.* to render a gift; to celebrate;

Handusáy, *adj.* fatigued; weary; tired;

Hangád, *n.* wish; desire;

Hangál *adj.* stupidp;

Hanggá, *v.* till; until;

Hangganan, *n.* border; end of;

Hangin, *n.* wind;

Hangò, *adj.* derive; adapted;

Hangos, *adj.* out of breath;

Hanón, *n.* Japanese;

Hantungan, *n.* end; destination;

Hapág, *n.* table;

Hapáy, *adj.* bankrupt; defeated;

Hapd, *adj.* tired; weary;

Hapdì, *n.* smarting pain;

Hapìs *adj.* afflicted; sorrowful;

Hapis, *n.* sorrow; anguish;

hapít *v.* fittingly close;

Haplit *v.* quicken;

Haplitin, *v.* to eat voraciously; to lash;

Haplós *n.* caress;

Haplusín *v.* to massage; to caress;

Hapò, *n.* tiredness, weariness;

Hapon, *n.* afternoon;

Hapunan, *n.* dinner or supper;

Hapunán, *n.* roosting place of chickens;

Harà, *n.* king;

Harang, *n.* obstruction;

Harangán, *n.* hold up;

Harangin, *v.* to waylay; to stop;

Haráp, *n.* front;

Hari-Harian, a man acting like a king;

Harót *adj.* prankish;

Hasâ, *adj.* Sharpened; experienced;

Hasang, *n.* gills of fishes;

Hasík, *n.* seedling;

Hatinggabí, *n.* midnight;

Hatol, *n.* decision;

Hatulan, *v.* to judge'

Haula, *n.* cage;

Hawa, *v.* contaminate;

Hawak, *n.* hold; grasp;

Hawakan, *v.* to take hold of;

Hawig, *adj.* similar to;

Hayaán *v.* allow; permit;

Hayág, *adj.* open: obvious; known;

Háyagan, *adj.* open not a secret;

Hayán, *adv.* there it is;

Hayók *adj.* greedy; hungry;

Hayop, *n.* animal;

Hero, *n.* brand of cow or carabao or horse:

Heto o eto, *adv.* here it is;

Hibáng, *adj.* delirious;

Hibík, *n.* leamentation; love proposales;

Hiblá, *n.* thread; fiber;

Hibò *n.* seduction;

Hidhíd, *adj.* stingy;

Hidwâ, *adj.* wrong; astray· mistaken;

Higâ, *v.* lie down;

Higad, *n.* catterpillar;worm;

Higante, *n.* giant;

Higing, *n.* cue of musical piece; rumor;

Hihip, *n.*.blow; blower;

Hikà *n.* asthma;

Hikahós *adj.* needy; poor;

Hikain, *adj.* asthmatic;

Hikaw, *n.* earrings;

Hikawan, *v.* to wear earrings;

Hikayatin *v.* to persuade; to convince;

Hikbí, *n.* sobbing,

Hilà, *n.* envy; dependence;

Hilaga, *n.* north;

Hilahil, *n.* hardishp; suffering;

Hilam, *n.* eye pain due to soap or lie or gogo;

Hilamusan, *v.* to wsh the face:

Hilat, *interj.* good for you!

Hiláw, *adj.* uncooked; not ripe;

Hilbana, *n.* baste stitch;

Hilera, *n.* row; file;

Hilig, *n.* tendency; inclination; liking;

Hiliin, *v.* to adk somebody to do the work for him;

Hilík, *n.* snore;

Hiling, *n.* request;

Hilo, *n.* dizziness; nausea;

Hilód, *n.* scrubbing;

Hilom, *n.* closing or healing of wound;

Hilot, *n.* midwife;

Himagas, *n.* dessert; sweets;

Himagsikan, *n.* revolution;

Himakás, *n.* parting;

Himbin, *n.* profound sleep;

Himig, *n.* tune; melody;

Himpapawid, *n.* space; air;

Himutók, *n.* expression of resentment; disappointment; sorrow;

Hinagpis, *n.* sorrow; affliction;

Hinahon, *n.* serenity; prudence;

Hinaing, *n.* lamentation;

Hinanakit, *n.* grudge; ill feeling;

Hinay, *n.* slowness; lightness;

Hindi, *adv.* not; no; huwag; don't;

Hinete,. *n.* horseman; jockey;

Hinirang, *v.* picked out; selected;

Hinkin, *n.* modesty;

Hinlalatò, *n.* middle finger·

Hinlóg, *n.* relatives;

Hinóg, *adj.* ripe;

Hintáy, *rw.* to wait for

Hinugot, *v.* pulled out;

Hipag, *n.* sister-in-law;

Hipò, *n.* touch;

Hipon, *n.* shrimps;

Hipuin, *v.* to touch;

Hirám, *adj.* borrowed;

Hirám, *n.* something borrowed or lent;

Hiraman, *n.* act of borrowing;

Hirang, *n.* one chosen;

Hirangin, *v.* to choose; to appoint;

Hirangin-humirang, *v.* to select;

Hirap, *n.* hardship; poverty;

Hirati, *adj.* accustomed; good at;

Hirmín, *v.* to borrow;

Hità, *n.* thigh;

Hitik, *adj.* bent due to weight; full; heavy;

Hititin, *v.* to smoke;

Hitsura, *n.* figure; form; looks;

Hiwà, *n.* slice; cut;

Hiwagà, *n.* mystery;

Hiwaláy, *adj.* separate; aprt;

Hiyâ, *n.* shame;

Hiyág, *adj.* good; agreeable;

Hiyain, *v.* to put to shame;

Hiyasán, *v.* to adorn; to put jewelry on;

Hiyáw, *n.* shout;

Hiyawan, *v.* to shout at;

Hubád, *adj.* naked;

Hubd, *adj.* naked from the waist;

Hubog, *n.* form; shape;

Hugas, *n.* rice water;

Hukáy, *adj.* excavated;

Hukay, *n.* grave;

Hukayin, *v.* to dig;

Hukbó, *n.* army;

Hukóm, *n.* judge;

Hukuman, *n.* court;

Hukumán, *v.* to render justice;

Hulà, *n.* guess; prediction;

Hulaan, *v.* to predict; to guess;

Huli, *adj.* caught; captured;

Huli, *adj.* late;

Hulihán, *n.* back; rear;

Hulmahan, *n.* molding; casting;

Hulog, *n.* installment; fall;

Humabá *v.* to become long;

Humál, *adj.* speaking through the nose;

Humanap, *v.* to look for; to search;

Humangà, *n.* to admire;

Humantóng, *v.* to end; to terminate;

Humiga, *v.* lie down;

Humigit-kumulang, *adv.* more or less;

Humigop, *v.* to sip;

Humila, *v.* to pull;

Humilig, to recline to incline;

Humimlay, Recline for a while;

'Humingi, *v.* to petition; to ask;

Humintd, *v.* stop;

Humpák, *adj.* hollow

Humpáy, *n.* rest;

Humuli manghuli *v.* to catch; to capture;

Humupâ, *v.* to subside;

Huni, *n.* chirp of birds;

Hurno, *n.* oven

Hustó, *adj.* fitted; right; sufficient;

Hustuhán, *v.* to complete payments;

Huthutín, *v.* suck; to sip;

Hutukin, *v.* to discipline; to mold;

Huwád, *adj.* reproduction fake; copied;

Huwág, *adv.* no; don't;

Húwaran, *n.* model; sample;

Hwebes, *n.* Thursday;

Hyás, *n.* jewellery;

Ii

Ibá, *pron.* other; another;

Iaáng-Gugulin, *n.* budget;

Iabanan, *v.* to fight; to oppose;

Ibabâ, *v.* to put down; to lower;

Ibabad, *v.* to soak; to imerse in;

Ibabaw, *n.* top; on top of ;

Ibatay, *v.* to base on;

Ibayo, *n.* other side; opposite side;

Ibayó, *v.* to pound;

Ibig, *rw.* to wish; desire; like; love;

Ibitin, *v.* to hang up;

Ibon, *n.* bird;

Ibubd, *v.* to spill; to shed;

Ibunsód, *v.* to launch;

Idaos, *v.* to hold as a meeting;

Igíb, *rw.* to fetch water;

Igláp, *n.* moment; instant;

Igtád, *n.* suddden jump or move;

Ihagis, to throw;

Ihanay, *v.* to place in a row; to relate;

Iharáp, *v.* to bring forward; to face;

Ihaw, *rw.* to roast;

Ika-3, *ng.* Yesterday was March 3.

Ika-5, *ng.* at five o'clock tomorrow morning;

Ikabubuti, *n.* welfare; goodness;

Ikagiginhawa, *n.* cause of one's comfort; ease;

Ikalat, *v.* spread; scatter;

Ikaliligtás, *n.* for one's safety;

Ikatitiwasay, *n.* cause of being at peace;

Ikáw, *pron.* you; thou;

Ikid, *n.* fcoil; roll;

Ikinaluluóy, *n.* cause of bing wilted;

Iklî, *rw.* shortness;

Iladlád, to unfurl; to bring out;

Ilagan, *v.* to avoid;

Ilagáy, **maglagay**, *v.* to put; to place;

Ilak, *n.* contribution;

Ilalim, *adv.* under;

Ilán, *pron.* how many?

Ilan-Ilán, *adj.* very few;

Ilandang, *n.* flying as under;

Iláng, *n.* wildernes; out of the way;

Ilang-Ilang, *n.* a tree bearing fragrant flowers;

Ilap, *n.* act of being wild or untamed;

Ilapat, *v.* to make even; close or compact;

Ilathalà, *n.* to publish; to make public;

Ilaw, *n.* light;

Ilawán, *n.* lamp;

Ilawan, *n.* to light;

Ilipat, *v.* to transfer; to move;

Ilog, *n.* river;

Ilóng, *n.* nose;

Imbák, *n.* preserves; stocks;

Imbakín, *v.* to preserve; to stock;

Imbáy, *n.* swing of the arms; in motion;

Imbí, *adj.* miserable;

Imbót, *n.* greed;

Imík, *n.* talk; speaking;

Imikan, *n.* talking with each other;

Imot, *n.* extreme economy;

Impit, *n.* pressure; tightness;

Impitin, *v.* to tighten;

Impó, *n.* grandmother;

Impók, *n.* savings;

Impukín, *v.* ot save;

Imulat, *v.* to open one's eye; to teach;

Iná, *n.* mother;

Inaglahí, *v.* removed;

Inakáy, *n.* brood;

Inamin, *v.* to admit;

Inamó, *v.* caressed;

Inampalán, *n.* judges;

Indák, *n.* movement in rhythm;

Indayog, *n.* rhythm;

Ingat, *n.* care; protection;

Ingat-Yaman, *n.* treasurer;

Ingay, *n.* noise;

Inggit, *n.* envy;

Iniatas, *v.* ordered;

Inihasík, *v.* planted;

Iniisip, *v.* is thinking of ;

Inilagpák, *v.* to fall;

Inip, *n.* impatience;

Inís, *adj.* impatient;

Inisín, *v.* irritae; to suffocate;

Init, *n.* heat;

Inog, *n.* revolution;

Inóm, *v.* to drink;

Insó, *n.* term used in calling

Insusig, *v.* investigate; persecute;

Inulit-ulit, *v.* do repeatedly;

Inumin, *n.* something to drink;

Inumín, *v.* to take notice of;

Inusig, *v.* was stolen;

Inut-inutin, *v.* to go slowly by degrees; little by little;

Inutusan, *v.* was sent onan errand;

Inuusig, *n.* one in trouble;

Inuutusan, one being ordered or commanded;

Inyó, *pron.* your or your;

Ipakain, *v.* to feed;

Ipakí, prefix to form verbs that denote requests;

Ipalimbág, prnt; to have it printed;

Ipamahagi, *v.* to be boastful of;

Ipanlinláng, *v.* to deceive;

Ipaubayà, *v.* to divide; to distribute;

Ipikit, *v.* close (as of the eyes);

Ipinadpád, *v.* cast by the wind;

Ipinugal, *v.* tied; fastened;

Ipis, *n.* cockroaches;

Ipit, *n.* pincher; pressure;

Ipitin, *v.* to pinch; to press;

Ipod, *v.* to move over while sitting;

Ipon, *n.* pile; heap

Ipu-Ipo, *n.* cyclone; whirlwind;

Ipunin, *v.* to gather; to pile;

Irap, *n.* sullen look;

Irapan, *v.* to glare at;

Irog, *n.* darling;

Isá, *pron. & adj.* one;

Isangguni, *v.* to consult about;

Isaulì, *v.* to return;

Isaw, *n.* large intestine;

Isdâ, *n.* fish;

Isinalok, *v.* dipped;

Isinalok, *v.* scattered;

Isinamâ, *n.* something that made one wrong or bad;

Isinama, *v.* taken along put together;

Isinambulat, *v.* scattered;

Isinauî, *v.* returned;

Isip, *n.* thought;

Isip-Isipin, *v.* to think about;

Isipin, *v.* to think to reflect;

Iskursiyon, *n.* excursion picnic;

Ismád, *v.* to sneer;

Ismirán, *v.* to declare to reveal;

Ispeling, *n.* spelling;

Isuót, *v.* to wear; put on;

Ita, *n.* Negrito;

Itaás, *n.* upstairs;

Itaás, *v.* raise;

Iták, *n.* bag bolo;

Itapon, *v.* to throw away;

Itatuwâ, *v.* to deny;

Iti, *n.* dysentery;

Itik, *n.* duck;

Itím, *adj.* black;

Itimán, *adj.* with predomnant black color;

Itimín, *v.* to blacken; to make black;

Itinago, *v.* hid;

Itinakwíl, *v.* denied; turned one's back on;

Itinatalagá, *v.* to place one self at the mercy of fate;

Itlóg, *n.* egg;

Itó, *pron.* this;

Itudlâ, *v.* to aim at;

Itulak, *to.* push;

Itulak-Kabigin, *n.* difference; distinction;

Itumbás, *v.* to compare with to substitute for something;

Iwasak, *v.* to destroy; to demolish,

Iwasan, *v.* to eavade;

Iyák, *n.* sob; cry;

Iyakán, *v.* to cry over;

Iyakin, *n.* cry baby; inclined to cry;

Iyán, *pron.* that (near the person addressed);

Iyó, *pron.* your or yours (second person, singular, possessive);

Iyón O Yaón, *pron.* that;

Ibasan, *n.* outdoor; doorway;

Ll

Laba, *n.* wash day;

Labág, *adj.* against; in violation of;

Labaha, *n.* razor;

Lábahan, *n.* place for washing;

Labák, *n.* mockery; humiliation;

Laban, *n.* game; fight;

Labanán, *n.* contest; fight;

Labangán, *n.* feeding trough for pigs and horses;

Labanos, *n.* radishes;

Labás, *adv.* outside;

Labasán, *v.* to issue forth; to show;

Labatiba, *n.* enema;

Labatibahin, *v.* to give enema;

Labí, *n.* remnants; surplus: remains; left over;

Labian, *v.* to scorn;

Labindalawá, *adj.* twelve;

Labing-Isá, *pron.* eleven;

Labinsiyám, *adj.* nineteen;

Labintadór, *n.* firecrackers;

Labis, *n.* surplus; left-over;

Labis-Labis, *adj.* sufficient; excessive;

Labisan, *v.* to make more than sufficient;

Labnutín, *v.* snatch;

Labò, *n.* dimness; turbidity;

Labuin, *v.* to dim; to make turbid;

Labuyò, *n.* wild fowl;

Lagabláb, *n.* blaze;

Lagak, *n.* bail; deposit;

Lagak, *n.* deposit; bail;

Lagalág, *adj.* wandering; roving;

Laganap, *adj.* widespread;

Lagarì, *n.* saw;

Lagariin, *v.* saw;

Lagás, *adj.* fallen (as of leaves);

Lagasin, *n.* to destroy;

Lagaslás, *n.* noise made by a brook;

Lagáy, *n.* place; put;

Lagdâ, *n.* signatùre;

Lagdaán, *v.* to sign;

Lagì, *adv.* always;

Lagím, *n.* extreme terror, sorrow;

Lagitík, *n.* lash or creak of a whip;

Lagkiít, *adj.* starchy;

Lagląg, *n.* failure;

Lagnát, *n.* fever;

Lagpak, *n.* failures;

Lagpákán, *v.* to cause to fall;

Lagunlóng, *n.* sound of falling water;

Lagusan, *n.* passage;

Lahà, *n.* segment as of an orange;

Lahad, *n.* narration; statement;

Lahát, *pron.* all; everybody;

Lahì, *n.* race;

Lahiin, *v.* to find out the parentage;

Laitin, *v.* insult; vilify;

Lakad, *v.* to walk;

Lakambini, *n.* muse;

Lakan, *n.* lord; chieftain; lakarin, v. to walk;

Lakandiwà, *n.* judge in a poetic joust;

Lakás, *n.* strength;

Lakasán Mo, *v.* to make loudder;

Lakò, *n.* things to sell;

Laksâ, *n.* ten-thousand;

Laks-Laksâ, *n.* hundreds of thousands;

Lalâ, *adj.* serious;

Lala, *n.* weave;

Lalagyán, *n.* container;

Lalaki, *n.* male; man;

Lalamunan, *n.* throat;

Laláng, *n.* creation;

Lálanggamín, *v.* to render accesible to ants;

Lalawig, *v.* to be continuous;

Lalawigan, *n.* province;

Lalim, *n.* depth; seriousness;

Laliman, *n.* to deepen; to make deep;

Lalngis, *n.* oil;

Lalo, *adv.* ,pre; excessive;

Lamad, *n.* membrane;

Lamág, *n.* coldness;

Lamán, *n.* meat;

Lamang, *adv.* only;

Lamang, *adv.* only; merely;

Lambat, *n.* net;

Lambingan, *n.* affectionate tete-a-tete;

Lambitinan, *v.* to hang on;

Lambóng, *n.* mantel for mourning;

Lambót, *n.* tenderness;

Lamigán, *v.* to control one self; to soften;

Lamlám, *n.* flickering;

Lamóg, *adj.* over-handled;

Lamól, *n.* mosquito;

Lamon, *n.* voracious eating;

Lampá, *adj.* weak; feeble;

Lampá, *n.* light; lamp;

Lampás, *adj.* beyod; peetrating;

Lampasán, *v.* to go over or beyond;

Lamugin, *v.* to manhandle till soft and battered;

Lamukot, *n.* edible part of nangka;

Lamunin, *v.* to eat voraciously;

Lamuyutin, *v.* to overpower; to render easy; to convince;

Lamyós, *n.* caress;

Lana, *n.* wool;

Landá, *n.* path; road; way

Langgám, *n.* ant;

Langis, *n.* oil;

Lángisan, *n.* oil factory;

Langisán, *v.* to oil;

Langóy, *n.* swo,;

Languyan, *n.* swimming contest;

Lansá, *n.* fashy odor;

Lanság, *adj.* dissolved; destryed;

Lansangan, *n.* street;

Lansihan, *n.* a game of tricks;

Lantá, *adj.* withered;

Lantád, *adj.* wide open; exposed;

Lantahin, *v.* to wither;

Laot, *n.* midsea; highsea;

Lapastangan, *adj.* disrespectful; discourteous;

Lapastanganin, *v.* to act with out due respect;

Lapát, *n.* fine strips of bamboo;

Lapatan, *v.* to render treatment of punishment;

Lapián, *n.* party politics;

Lapis, *n.* pencil;

Lapit, *n.* nearness;

Lapitan, *v.* to come near to or for; to approach;

Larangan, *n.* in the field of;

Larawan, *n.* picture; image;

Larawang-diwà, *n.* imaginary picture;

Laro, *n.* game; play;

Laruan, *n.* playground;

Laruín, *v.* to play with;

Lasa, *n.* taste;

Lasapin, *v.* taste;

Lasingan, *n.* bar; drinking place;

Laslás, *n.* rip;

Lason, *n.* poison;

Lasunin, *v.* to poison;

Laswâ, *adj.* indecent;

Latâ, *n.* weariness;

Latag, *n.* spread;

Latak, *n.* residue;

Latayan, *v.* to mark; to produce welt;

Lathalà, *n.* publication;

Latian, *n.* swamps;

Latiko, *n.* whip;

Latikuhin, *v.* to whip;

Lawà, *n.* lake; a wetplace full of water;

Lawak, *n.* area; extent;

Lawakan, *v.* to spread out; to think further;

Laway, *n.* saliva;

Lawig, *n.* duration;

Lawin, *n.* hawk;

Lawít, *n.* something suspended on; hanging;

Lawitán, *v.* to give a favor; to give attention;

Layà, *n.* liberty; freedom;

Layag, *n.* sail;

Layak, *n.* rubbish;

Layás, *n.* wagabond;

Layaw, *n.* ostentation; too much favor;

Layò, *n.* distance;

Layon, *n.* aim;

Layuán, *v.* to move away from;

Letra, *n.* letter; mark;

Letrahán. *v.* to letter; to mark;

Liagw, *n.* suitor;

Libág, *n.* body dirt;

Liban, *v.* to postpone;

Libangan, *n.* recreation; amusement;

Libangin, *v.* to amuse;

Libíng, *n.* burial; funeral;

Libingan, *n.* cemetery;

Libís, *n.* slope;

Liblib, *n.* unfrequented place;

Ligalig, *n.* trouble; restlessness; uneasiness

Ligaligin, *v.* to make trouble;

Ligáw, *adj.* stray;

Ligawan, *v.* to court;

Ligaya, *n.* happiness;

Ligò, *n.* bath;

Ligpitín, *v.* to keep away;

Ligtás, *adj.* free; escape;

Liha, *n.* sandpaper;

Lihahin, *v.* to sandpaper;

Liham, *n.* sulat; letter;

Lihaman, *v.* to write a letter;

Lihí, *v.* conception;

Lihimin, *v.* to talk secretly;

Lihiya, *n.* lye; shampoo made out of burnt straw;

Liig, *n.* neck;

Liip, *n.* hemtitch;

Liit, *adj.* small; tiny;

Liitán, *v.* to make smaller; to decrease;

Likás, *adj.* natural;

Likd, *n.* curve;

Likhâ, *adj.* created;

Likhain, *v.* created;

Likód, *n.* back;

Likót, *n.* restleslsness;

Liku-Likd, *adj.* winding;.

Likutí, *n.* fasness; agility;

Lilim, *n.* shade;

Liliman, *v.* to put shade;

Lilipin, *v.* hemstitch;

Lilís, *n.* rol of sleeves or trousers;

Lilisán, *v.* to rooll up;

Lilukin, *v.* to curve;

Limá, *adj.* five;

Limahang-gilid, *n.* pentagon;

Limampû, *adj.* fifty;

Limasin, *v.* to ladle out;

Limatic, *n.* leech; sucker;

Limayón, *v.* to while away time uselelssly;

Limbág, *n.* publication;

Limbas, *n.* bird of prey;

Limlimán, *v.* to hatch;

Limós, *n.* alms;

Limot, *n.* forgetfulness;

Limpák, *n.* lump;

Limusán, *v.* to give alms; to give contribution;

Limutin, *v.* to forget;

Lináb, *n.* fatty scum;

Linamnám, *n.* savor; taste;

Linangím, *v.* cultivate; till;

Linaw, *n.* clearness;

Linawin, *v.* to make clear;

Lindól, *n.* earthquake;

Linggó, *n.* Sunday;

Linggu-Linggo, *adv.* every week; weekly;

Lingguhan, *adv.* weekly; every weelk;

Lingid, *adj.* unknown;

Lingkod, *n.* service; one ready to serve;

Lingunin, *v.* to look back;

Liningin, *v.* to think over: to meditate;

Linisin, *v.* clean;

Linlangín, *v.* to mislead;

Linsád, *n.*, *adj.* dislocation;

Lintâ, *n.* thunder;

Lintikán, *v.* to be in trouble;

Lipád, *n.* fight;

Lipanà, *adj.* all around; in plenty;

Liparin, *v.* fly;

Lipás, *adj.* out of season;

Lipì, *n.* lineage; ancestry;

Lipunan, *n.* society;

Lira, *n.* lyre;

Lisyà, *adj.* mistaken: erroneous;

Lisyaín, *v.* to commit errors; to commit mistakes;

Litis, *n.* trial in court;

Liwalíw, *n.* vacation; rest;

Liwanag, *n.* light;

Loób, *n.* inside; within; one's will or volition;

Looban, *n.* yard;

Loobin, *v.* to make one feel;

Loók, *n.* bay;

Loro, *n.* parrot;

Losa, *n.* porcelain;

Lubagin, *v.* to calm oneself lubagin mo ang loob niya;

Lubák, *n.* low place;

Lubak-Lubak, *adj.* uneven; rough;

Lubáy, *n.* stop; cessation;

Lubayán, *v.* to stop; to cease;

Lubhâ, *adj.* serious; grave

Lubirin, *v.* to make rope of;

Lublób, *n.* wallow;

Lubóg, *adj.* under water; submerged;

Lubós, *adv.* completely;

Lugá, *n.* puss in the ear;

Lugál, *n.* place;

Lugamî, *adj.* wallow in a degraded condition;

Lugás, *adj.* falling off;

Lugaw, *n.* gruel rice gruel; rice soup;

Lugáy, *adj.* hanging loose;

Luglugín, *v.* to shake;

Lugmók, *adj.* weary; frustrated

Lugó, *adj.* weak;

Lugód, *v.* happy; joy;

Lui, *n.* loss;

Luibid, *n.* rope;

Lukbutan, *n.* pocket;

Luklók, *n.* to be seated;

Luklukan, *n.* seat;

Luko, *adj.* insane;

Luksâ, *adj.* black in mourn;

Luksó, *v.* jump;

Luksuhín, *v.* to hurdle;

Luktón, *n.* grasshopper;

Lukuban, *v.* to protect to be under one's discipline;

Lulan, *n.* cargo; load;

Lumabág, *v.* to violate;

Lumagd, *v.* to become luxurious in growth;

Lumagom, *v.* to amass; to gather; to collect;

Lumakad, *v.* to walk;

Lumalâ, *v.* to become worse;

Lumangóy, *v.* to swim;

Lumapit, *v.* to get near;

Lumawig, *v.* to become prolonged; to take a long time;

Lumigaw, *v.* to court; to make love with;

Lumpó, *adj.* totally or partly paralized;

Lumuksó, *n.* lame;

Lumulan, *v.* to ride in a boat;

Lumulón, *v.* to swallow;

Lumundág, *v.* to jump;

Lumusong, *v.* to come down; to descend;

Lumuwás-Sumubá, *v.* to go to and fro;

Lundáy, *n.* boat;

Lunes, *n.* Monday;

Lunggâ, *n.* hole; burrow;

Lunggatî, *n.* desire; wish;

Luningning, *n.* glitter; brilliance;

Lunó, *adj.* boneless; soft;

Lunos, *n.* compassion;

Lunsód, *n.* city;

Luntaian, *adj.* green;

Luóy, *adj.* faded;

Lupá, *n.* ground; earth;

Lupalop, *n.* sphere; kingdom;

Lupaypáy, *adj.* weakened; frustrated;

Lupî, *n.* fold; hem;

Lupig, *adj.* vanquished; oppressed;

Lupít, *n.* cruelty;

Lupon, *n.* group; committee;

Lurâ, *n.* saliva;

Lusk, *n.* mire; mud;

Luság, *n.* mortal;

Lusót, *adj.* pass through;

Lustayín, *v.* to spend money foolishly;

Lúsutan, *n.* passage;

Lutò, *adj.* cooked;

Luwád, *n.* clay;

Luwalhati, *n.* ecstasy; happiness; glory;

Luwalhatiin, to celebrate; to glorify;

Luwát, *n.* tardiness;

Luwís, *v.* to go to town or city;

Luya, *n.* ginger;

Mm

Maaarí, *v.* cam be; possible:

Maaga, *adv.* early;

Maagap, *adj.* punctual; over ready;

Maagnás, *v.* to be worn out (as by flowing water);

Maagos, *adj.* with swift running water;

Maalab, *adj.* heated; warmed;

Maalam, *adj.* wise;

Maalat, *adj.* salty;

Maalinsangan, *adj.* sultry; hot;

Maalwán, *adj.* rich in legends;

Maamò, *adj.* tame; domesticated;

Maang-Maangan, *n.* ignorance;

Maanggó, *adj.* sour (as of milk;

Maanghít, *adj.* having a bad odor;

Maantá, *adj.* rancid;

Maapóy, *adj.* fiery;

Maapulá, *v.* to srtop; to check;

Maasim, *adj.* merciful;

Maasim, *adj.* sosur;

Mababà, *adj.* low; humble;

Mababaw, *adj.* shallow;

Mabagal, *adj.* slow;

Mabagót, *v.* to be bored;

Mabagsik, *adj.* fierce;

Mabahò, *adj.* having bad smell; stinks;

Mabaít, *adj.* virtuous;

Mabalasik, *adj.* ferocious;

Mabanaagan, *v.* to see in dim light;

Mabanás, *adj.* sultry;

Mabangis, *adj.* wild;

Mabangó, *adj.* fragrant; aromatic;

Mabibig, *adj.* having a wide mouth; talkative;

Mabigát, *adv.* heavy; difficult;

Mabiglâ, *v.* taken by surprisep

Mabilí, *adj.* salable;

Mabilis, *adj.* swift;

Mabilog, *adj.* round; spherical;

Mabinat, *v.* to have a relapse;

Mabini, *adj.* modest; gentle;

Mabisà, *adj.* effective;

Mabuhay, *n.* long life;

Mabulaklák, *adj.* maraming bulakläk of having plenty of flowers;

Mabulo, *adj.* full of prickly hairs;

Mabunyi, *adj.* famous; known;

Mabuti, *adj.* good;

Mabuwáy, *adj.* unbalanced;

Madagtâ, *adj.* full of resin;

Madalang, *adj.* sparse; infrequent;

Madalás, *adj.* often; frequent;

Madali, *adj.* easy; quick;

Madasalin, *adj.* prone ot praying often; religious;

Madiláw, *adj.* yellowish;

Madilim, *adj.* dark; obscure;

Madlâ, *n.* public;

Madulás, *adj.* elusive; slippery;

Maestra, *n.* female teacher;

Maestro, *n.* male teacher; instructor;

Mag-Aamá, father and children;

Mag-Aarál, *n.* pupil; student;

Mag-Alaala, *v.* to be anzxious;

Mag-Alaga, *v.* to take care of;

Mag-Anak, *n.* family;

Mag-Apuháp, *v.* grop; Julic

Mag-Aral, *v.* to study;

Mag-Asawa, *n.* couple; husband and wife;

Mag-Atubili, *n.* to hesitate;

Mag-Atublí, *v.* hesitate;

Mag-Impók, *v.* to save

Mag-Iná, *n.* mother and child;

Mag-ingat, *v.* to take care of;

Mag-Ulat, *v.* to account for;

Mag-Ulayaw, *v.* to converse intimately;

Maga, *adj.* swolen;

Magaán, *adj.* easy; light;

Magalang, *adj.* courteous; respectful;

Magaling, *adj.* good; excellent;

Magandá, *adj.* beautiful; goodlooking;

Magará, *adj.* pompous; splendid;

Magasin, *n.* magazine;

Magasláw, *adj.* rough: uncouth;

Magasó, *adj.* naughty; mischievous;

Magaspáng, *adj.* coarse: rough;

Magatd, *v.* to be worn out;

Mágayuma, *v.* to be charmed to be enchanted;

Magayuót, *adj.* tough;

Magbasa, *n.* to read;

Magbatá, *v.* to bear; to carry through;

Magbayad, *v.* to pay for;

Magbigáy, *v.* to give;

Magbigtí, *v* to hang oneself;

Magbihis, *v.* to change on's clothes;

Magbubó, *v.* to spill;

Magdamág, *n.* all night long;

Magdarayá, *adj.* dishonest;

Maggugó, *v.* to shampoo;

Maghain, *v.* set the table;

Maghampás-Lupà, *v.* to be a vagabond; to roam around;

Maghapon, *n.* all day;

Maghapon, *v.* to keep chickens in a coop;

Maghapon, whole day;

maghiganti, *v.* to revenge; avenge oneself;

Maghilom, *v.* to heal;

Maghintáy, *v.* to wait for; await;

Magigi, *adj.* slow;

Magiging, *v.* will become;

Magináw, *adj.* cold;

Máginoó, *n.* gentleman;

Mágising, *v.* to be awakened;

Magiting, *adj.* heroic;

Magkabilâ, *n.* both sides;

Magkagurlis, *v.* to be

Magkanlóng, *v.* to hide;

Magkano, *pron.* how much;

Magkapatid, *n.* brother and sister;

Magkapé, *v.* have coffee cr take coffe;;

Magkapote, *v.* to wear raincoat;

Magkita, *n.* to see each other;

Magkulang, *v.* to be lacking;

Magkumot, *v.* to put a blanket on;

Magkuwento, *v.* to tell a story;

Maglagalág, *v*. to travel aimlessly;

Maglahó, *v*. to disappear; be eclipsed;

Maglard, *n*. to play;

Magligtás, *v*. to save;

Maglingkód, *v*. to serve;

Maglinis, *v*. clean up;

Maglugaw, *v*. to cook gruel;

Magluto, *v*. to cook;

Magmaáng-Maangan, *v*. to pretebd nót to know;

Magmalasakit, *v*. to put interest in; to care for;

Magmaliw, *v*. to be lost; to be transferred; to disapear;

Magmanmán, *n*. to watch to be on guard;

Magnagalit, *n*. to be enraged;

Magnily, *v*. tc reflect to meditate;

Magpaalam, *v*. to bid good bye;

Magpailanláng, *v*. to go up in the air;

Magpalusóg, *v*. to be healthy;

Magparangál, *v*. honor one self; to fete another;

Magparangalan, *v*. to show off;

Magpasyál, *v*. to take a walk;

Magpatiwakál, *v*. to commit suicide;

Magpaumat-Umat, *v*. to delay; to procrastinate;

Magpaunlák , *v*. to accede; tp give in ; to give favor;

Magpugay, *v*. to make a bow; to salute;

Magsaing, *v*. to cook rice;

Magsaka, *n*. to cultivate soil; to farm;

Magsikap, *v*. towork diligently;

Magsipag, *v*. to be busy; to be industrious;

Magsisi, *v*. to regreat; to repent;

Magsiwalat, *v*. to expose to explain;

Magsulsí, *v*. to darn; to mend;

Magtagál, *v*. stay long

Magtahán, *v*. to stop crying;

Magtahí-Tahî, to fabricate;

Magtamó, *v*. to get; to win a prize;

Magtampisáw, *v*. to walk barefooted in a muddy place;

Magtanan, *v.* to escape; to run away;

Magtanggál, *v.* to cut off; to disconnect; to lay off; to remove;

Magtanggól, *v.* to defend;

Magtanghál, *v.* to turna traitor;

Magtapon, *v.* to throw away;

Magtatág, *v.* found; establish;

Magtugot, *v.* to yield; to stop; to cease;

Magtulóg, *v.* to sleep repeatedly;

Magtulot, *v.* to let by

Mágulangan, *v.* to be taken advantage of;

Maguló, *adj.* full of troubles;

Magulumihanan, *v.* tobe taken aback;

Magutom *v.* to be hungry;

Mahagwáy, *adj.* tall & wel proportioned;

Mahál, *adj.* expensive; dear;

Mahalagá, *adj.* important; valuable

Mahalay, *adj.* vulgar;

Mahalin, *v.* to love; to be infatuated;

Mahapdì, *adj.* painful;

Mahayap, *adj.* piercing;

Mahigpit, *adj.* strict; tight;

Mahilig, *adj.* inclined to;

Máhimláy, *v.* to fall asleep;

Mahiná, *adj.* weak;

Mahinahon, *adj.* orderly;

Mahirap, *adj.* difficult poor;

Mahiwagá, *adj.* mysterious; wonderful;

Máidlíp, *v.* to fall asleep;

Maidulot, *v.* to offer; to give;

Maigaya, *adj.* charming; delightful;

Maiklî, *adj.* short;

Maikling kathâ, short story;

Mailap, *adj.* wild; untame; elusive;

Maimbót, *adj.* greedy; stingy;

Maimpók, *adj.* thrifty; economical;

Maingat, *adj.* careful;

Maingay, *adj.* noisy;

Mainip, *v.* to feel impatient;

Mainit, *adj.* hot;

Mainit, *adj.* hot; fiery;

Maipagbíbilí, *v.* can be sold;

Maipagsanggaláng, *v.* toprotect;

Maipagtitirik, *v.* can light candles as offering;

Makabago, *adj.* modern;

Makabayan, *adj.* patriotic;

Makagitaw, .*v.* to be able to stand out; to excell;

Makalág, *n.* to be untied;

Makalawá, *adj.* day after tomorrow;

Makálawá, *adj.* twice;

Mákaligtaán, *v.* to forgetten; to be left out;

Makalimot, *v.* to forget;

Makálulón, *v.* to swallow accidentally;

Makalumá, *adj.* old fashioned;

Makalupà, *adj.* materialistic; earthly;

Makapaglalatang, *v.* to be the cause of kindling;

Makati, *adj.* itchy; scratchy;

Makisig, *adj.* elegant; lively;

Malagkit, *adj.* sticky;

Malagkit, *n.* glutinous rice;

Malakás, *adj.* influential; strong; mighty;

Malaki, *adj.* large; big;

Malambót, *adj.* soft;

Malamig, *adj.* cold; cool;

Malamlám, *adj.* dim;

Malanság, *v.* to dissolve;

Malantá, *v.* to be wilted;

Malapit, *adv.* near; hindi malayò;

Malawak, *adj.* wide; great;

Malay, *n.* knowledge; information;

Malay-Tao, *n.* consciousness;

Malayó, *adj.* far; distant;

Malî, *adj.* wrong; erroneous;

Mali, *n.* error; oversight;

Máligáw, *v.* astrary;

Maligaya, *adj.* full of happiness;

Maligò, *v.* to take a bath;

Maligoy, *adj.* long; roundabout;

Malihim, *adj.* secretive;

Maliit, *adj.* small; little;

Malikmatá, *n.* vision; apparition;

Malikót, *adj.* Mischievous;

Maliksi, *adj.* quick; agile;

Malinaw, *adj.* clear;

Malinis, *adj.* clean;

Malipol, *v.* to be destroyed; to be annihilated (as an army);

Malitó, *adj.* confused;

Maliwanag, *adj.* brilliant; lighted;

Maliwanagan, *v.* to understand; to be cleared of;

Maliyab, *adj.* full of blaze;

Malubhâ, *adj.* serious;

Malukóng, *adj.* deep; concave;

Malumanay, *adj.* soft; slow;

Malungkót, *adj.* sad; sorrowful;

Malungkutin, *adj.* always or frequently sad;

Malupit, *adj.* cruel; stern;

Maluráy, *v.* to be destroyed in small pieces;

Malusóg, *adj.* strong; healthy;

Maluwág, *adj.* wide; roomy;

Maluwát, *adj.* long delayed; tardy;

Mamá, *n.* an adress used in addressing;

Mama, *n.* mother,

Mamád, *adj.* without feeling;

Mamáy, *n.* nurse;

Mámayâ, *adv.* by and by;

Mamintás, *v.* to criticize and versely; to find fault with;

Mamirinsá, *v.* to iron clothes;

Mamuhay, *v.* to live;

Mamutawí, *v.* to utter; to speak;

Mana, *n.* inheritance;

Manâ, *n.* peanuts;

Manadyer, *n.* manager;

Managano, *v.* to predominate;

Manakop, *v.* to conquer;

Manalig, *v.* to believe in;

Manaliksík, *v.* to make a research;

Manatili, *v.* to stay; reside;

Manaw, *v.* to die;

Maneho, *v.* to manage; to run;

Manggá, *n.* mango;

Manggagawá, *n.* worker; laborer;

Manggagaway, *n.* witch;

Manggubat, *v.* to go to the forest;

Manghuhuthót, *n.* profiteer;

Manghuthót, *v.* to keep asking for money; to atake advantage;

Mangisdâ, *v.* to fish; to catch fish;

Mangisdâ, *v.* tocatch fish;

Mangmáng, *adj.* ignorant;

Mangulila, *adj.* to be lonely;

Mangulila, *n.* to become and orphan;

Mangulubót, *v.* to shrivel;

Mangumpisál, *v.* to confess;

Mangyari, *v.* to occur; to take place;

Manhíd, *n.* numbness;

Mánibaláng, *adj.* mature;

Manikà, *n.* doll;

Manikain, *v.* to make a doll of;

Maniwalà, *v.* to believe in;

Manlikom, *v.* to collect; to hoard;

Manók, *n.* chicken;

Manté, *n.* tablecloth;

Mantiká, *n.* lard; fat;

Mantikilya, *n.* butter;

Mantsá, *n.* stain;

Manugang, *n.* son or daughter-in-law;

Mánunubos, *n.* redeemer;

Mapag-Unawà, *adj.* under standing;

Mapagkandili, *v.* solicitous; protective; thoghtful;

Mapagmataás, *adj.* proud;

Mapágpaimbabáw, *adj.* hypocritical; deceitful;

Mapanaghilíin, *adj.* envious; Mapanaghiliínsi Luis;

Mapanatili, *v.* to maintain;

Mapang-Uyám, *adj.* satirical; sarcastic;

Mapangailangan, *adj.* always in need; needy;

Mapangamkám, *adj.* greedy;

Mapangláw, *adj.* sad; glomy;

Mapanudyó, *adj.* inclined to tease;

Mapapaknit, *v.* will be detached or remove;

Maparam, *n.* to erase; to cause to disappear;

Mapariwarà, *v.* to be misled;

Mápatanyág, *v.* made famous;

Mapawì, *v.* to vanish;

Mapayapà, *adj.* peaceful;

Mapusók, *adj.* furious; vehement;

Marumí, *adj.* dirty;

Marunong, *adj.* wise; bright;

Masagabal, *adj.* full of obstacles;

Masahol, *adj.* worse than

Masaksihán, *v.* to witness;

Masamaín, *v.* to feel bad;

Másangkót, *v.* to be involved in;

Másanlâ, *v.* to be pawned;

Masansalà, to be stopped;

Masaráp, *adj.* delicious; tasty;

Masawî, *v.* to meet misfortune; to have bad luck;

Masayá, *adj.* cheerful:

Masidhî, *adj.* intense; acute;

Masigasig, *adj.* diligent: industrious;

Masikap, *adj.* active; deligent

Masilaw, *v.* to be dazzled;

Masinop, *adj.* industrious; practical; economical;

Masinsín, *adj.* very close;

Masinsinan, *adj.* serious; hearty;

Masiyado, *adj.* selfishl; excesive;

Masiyasatin, *adj.* inquisitive; full of curiousity;

Masungit, *adj.* irritated; morose;

Masunurin, *adj.* obedient;

Masurì, *adj.* critical; analytic;

Masuyó, *adj.* full of affection; obliging;

Matá, *n.* eye;

Mataás, *adj.* high; tall; well-known;

Matigás na ang butó, can stand alone;

Matupok, *v.* to be burned;

Matuwâ, *v.* to be glad;

Matuwíd, *adj.* straight; right;

Mauhaw, *n.* to be thirsty;

Maulán, *adj.* rainy; plenty of rain;

Máulinigan, *v.* to hear;

Maulit, *adj.* repetitious;

Maunlád, *adj.* progressive;

Mawalâ, *v.* to be lost;,

May magandáng hináharáp, somthing good coming;

May, *n.* possessing; denoting possession or authorship;

May-akdâ, *n.* author;

May-arí, *n.* owner;

May-kabuluhán, *adj.* important; of significance;

May-kalokohan, *adj.* humorous; playful; jesting;

Maya, *n.* sparrow;

Mayabang, *adj.* boastful;

Mayabong, *adj.* luxuriant; thriving;

Mayapá, *adj.* insipid;

Maypasak, *adj.* clogged;

Maysakát, *n.* patient;

Mayumi, *adj.* modest; demure;

Mediko, *n.* doctor; physician;

Medyas, *n.* socks; stockings;

Mesa, *n.* table;

Meselang, *adj.* meticulous; fastidious,

Mestiza, *n.* female half breed;

Mga, particle used before a noum to denote plurality;

Mina, *n.* mines;

Minámahál, *v.* beloved;

Minandál, *n.* minute;

Mistulá, *adj.* similar to; likened to;

Mithî, *n.* wish; objective;

Mithiín, *n.* aspiration;

Miting, *n.* meeting; gathering;

Miyerkoles, *n.* Wednesday;

Mo, *pron.* your (possessive case);

Modo, *n.* manners;

Moóg, *n.* fort;

Mukhâ, *adj.* irritated;

Mulâ, *adv.* since; sincé then; since that time;

Mulâ, *prep.* from;

Mulî, *adv.* once more; again;

Multó, *n.* ghost;

Mumo, *n.* left-over;

Muna, *adv.* first move;

Mundó, *n.* world;

Mungkahí, *n.* suggestion;

Muni, *n.* sensible thought; v. think sensibly;

Muntî, *adj.* small;

Muntík, *adv.* almost; nearly;

Munukalá, *n.* idea; plan;

Mura, *adj.* cheap; not costly;

Murá, *adj.* young; not matured;

Murahin, *v.* to condemn;

Musiko, *n.* a band of musicians;

Musmós, *adj.* innocent; young;

Mutà, *n.* secretion of the eyes;

Mutain a, *adj.* full of secretion of the eyes;

Mutyâ, *n.* pearl; loved one;

Muwáng, *n.* knowledge;

Nn

Na, used as prefix to form verbs that express being in ths state;

Na-a, particle used to connect the modifier with the modified;

Naaanod, *v.* to be carried by the current;

Naalaala, *v.* remembered;

Naamis, *v.* to be persecuted; oppressed; disappointed;

Naawás, *v.* was removed; taken away from;

Nabagabag, *v.* to be filled with compassion;

Nabagbág, *v.* demolished broken up;

Nabalták, *v.* to be pulled;

Nabihag, *v.* imprisoned; charme;

Nábihag, *v.*. was taken prisoner;

Nábukó, *v.* disappointed;

Nádaganán, *v.* buried; placed under;

Nádampî, *v.* was touched lightly and gently;

Nadidimlan, *v.* in darkness;

Nag-aalsa, *v.* to strike; to talk loudly;

Nag-áantáy, *v.* waiting for;

Nag-áaral, studying; learning;

Nag-áararo, *v.* to plow the fiedl;

Nag-áatubili, *v.* hesitating;

Nag-ibá, *v.* to change ; to be different;

Nag-inda-indayog, *v.* are swaying;

Nag-ulat, *v.* accounted for;

Nag-unat, *v.* straightened;

Nag-úusap, *v.* conversing;

Nagagalit, is angry with;

Nagalusan, *n.* to be bruised;

Nagantihan, *v.* to be able to reciprocate;

Nagbabadhâ, *n.* foretelling;

Nagbabaguwis, *v.* developing wings;

Nagbabalak, *v.* planning; thinking;

Nagbabaták ng butó, *v.* working hard;

Nagbantáy, *v.* guarded; watched;

Nagbíbird, *v.* to be in joking mood;

Nagbíbiruán, *v.* joking with each other;

Nagbúbuhát ng sariling bangkd, *v.* blowing his horn;

Nagbubuhat, *v.* coming from; issuing from;

Nagbubunót, *v.* husking (as in cleaning the floor;)

Nagbukás mg, dibdib- proposed marriage;

Nagbunsód, made to do;

Nagbuntóng-Hiningá, *v.* sighed;

Nagdaóp, *v.* clasped both hands together;

Naggagapáng, *v.* crawling around;

Naghagikgikan, *v.* giggled;

Naghahamok, *v.* fighting; raging a battle;

Nagháhampasan, *v.* beating or striking eacn other;

Naghalikan, *v.* kissed each other;

Naghanáp, *v.* searched or looked for;

Naghanay, *v.* lined up; placed a row;

Naghíhingald, *v.* dying; about to die;

Naghíhintayan, *v.* waiting for each other;

Naghilamos, *v.* washed the face;

Naghintd, *v.* stopped;

Naghugas, *u.* washe (as of hands);

Nágibâ, *v.* destroyed;

Nágising, *v.* awakened;

Nagkaguló, *v.* to become disorderly;

Nagkatinginan, *n.* looked at each other;

Nagkautang, *v.* was in debt;

Nagkiskis, as a match struck the match;

Nagkuráp, *v.* closed the eyes;

Naglagi-Lagitík, *v.* cresking;

Naglíd ng buhangin, *v.* telling falsehood;

Naglíliparan, *v.* flying about;

Naglílipatán, *v.* moving out;

Naglipaná, *v.* speread; scattered around;

Nagpagibík, *v.* asked for help;

Nagpápasalamat, *v.* thanking;

Nagpúputók ang butse, in terfering in somebody's affair;

Nagsasabog, *v.* sowing seeds;

Nagsasabong, *v.* fighting in the way of roosters;

Nagsasaing, *v.* cooking rice;

Nagsísibák, *v.* splitting wood;

Nagtagál, *v.* lasted a long time;

Nagtagó, *v.* hid oneself;

Nagtatamasa, *v.* enjoying;

Nagtiláḋ, *v.* broke up into small pieces;

Nagtípanan, *v.* made a date; agreed;

Naguas, *n.* underskirt;

Nagulat, *v.* taken by surprise; was surprised;

Nagyakap, *v.* embraced each other;

Nagyayakág, *v.* persuading someone to come along;

Nahapis, *v.* was saddened;

Nahatí, *v.* was divided;

Nahihibáng, *v.* to be in delirium;

Nahulaan, *v.* guessed;

Nahuli, *n.* arrive late;

Nahuli, *v.* was caught;

Naiintindihán, *v.* can understand;

Naikulá, *v.* was bleached;

Nailapat, *v.* was closed tightly;

Nailigtás, *v.* was envious;

Naipit, *v.* sandwiched;

Nais, *n.* desire; wish;

Naisin, *v.* to desire;

Naisipan, *v.* thought of;

Nakaalís, *v.* able to get away;

Nakaambâ, *v.* threatening; in suspended motion;

Nakakatarók, *v.* conceive; glimpse;

Nakakíkilitî, *adj.* ticklish;

Nakakita ng bituwín, hit on the eye;

Nakaladlád, *v.* seen conspicuously;

Nákalimutan, *v.* forgotten;

Nakalúlumbáy, *adj.* sorrowful:

Nakalulunos, *adj.* pityful;

Nakamumuhî, *adj.* disgusting;

Nakapagitan, *adv.* in between:

Nakapanghíhila, *adj.* to feellazy;

Nakapanghíhilakbót, *adj.* frightful; frightening;

Nakapanghíhinayang, *adj.* regrettable;

Nakasakáy, *v.* is riding;

Nakasalalay, *v.* placed on a shelf or any protruding base;

Nakasalampák, *v.* sitting down carelessly on the floor;

• **Nakasalig**, *v.* based on; pat terned after;

Nakasísiguro, *adj.* sure of Nakasísiguro na si Juan;

Nakasisindák, *adj.* frightful;

Nakatanghod, *v.* always looking;

Nakatatandâ, *v.* is able to remember; being older than the rest;

Nakatatarók, *adj.* with full knowledge of;

Nakatawa, *v.* smiling;

Nakatigháw, *v.* was able to recover;

Nakatirá, *v.* is living;

Nakatitiyák, *v.* to be sure of;

Nákatulog, *v.* fell asleep;

Nakatulóy, *v.* was able to get away;

Nakawug, *v.* to oprolong; to take a long time;

Nakíkimatyág, *v.* to observe;

Nakíkisalamuhá, *v.* mixing with others;

Nakikiugali, *v.* to adopt the custom of the locality;

Naku, *enterj.* expressing surprise;

Nalalabî, *n.* remainder;

Nalalaman, *v.* know;

Nalalamangán, *v.* to be at a disadvantage of;

Nalalarawan, *v.* pictured; illustrated;

Nalapitan, *v.* managed to get near;

Naligid, *v.* surrounded;

Nalulugás, *v.* in state of falling;

Nalulumá, *v.* instate of being out of date;

Nalulungkót, *v.* in state of sadness;

Namalas, *v.* saw; observed;

Naman, *adv.* in like manner; similar; again;

Namatáy, *v.* died;

Namin, *pron.* our or ours;

Namnamin, *v.* enjoy pleasent tast tast;

Naná, *n.* pus;

Nanaog, *v.* went down the house;

Nanay, *n.* mother;

Nang, *adv.* Wala nang bigás;

Nang, *conj.* Nang dumating si suan;

Nangambá, *v.* doubted; feared;

Nangasera, *v.* boarded with; lived with;

Nangilag, *v.* avoided;

Nangingilag, *v.* avoiding;

Nanguha, *v.* gathered; collected;

Nangunyapit, *v.* aheld on; clung to;

Nangyari, *v.* happened;

Naniningaláng, *v.* becoing adolescent;

Naninіniіg, *v.* conversed intimately;

Naniwlá, *v.* belived in:

Napaamin, *v.* was made to admít;

Napahinuhod, *v.* was persuaded;

Naparito, *v.* came here;

Napariyán, *v.* went there (close to person spoken to):

Naparoon, *v.* went over there far from speaker and person spoken to:

Nápayukayok, *v.* lowered one's head in drowsiness;

Napulpól, *v.* became dull;

Napulupot, *v.* tied around;

Naputol, *v.* cut off;

Náritó, *pron.* it is here;

Nasaan, *pron.* where;

Nasalantâ, *v.* damaged;

Násalubong, *v.* met ont the way;

Nasipá, *v.* was kicked; kicked out;

Nasok, *v.* entered;

Násulyapán, *v.* seen accidentally;

Nasungo, *v.* got burned;

Natagò, *v.* was hidden;

Natarók, *v.* to know; understand; to comprehend;

Natibág, *v.* crumbled;

Natin, *pron.* our;

Natinag, *v.* has been moved or shaken;

Nátirá, *v.* was left; had lived;

Nátiwalág, *v.* fired; dismissed; separated;

Natuksó, *v.* tempted;

Natunaw, *v.* melted; dissolved;

Natutulog, *v.* is asleep;

Natuwâ, *v.* was glad:

Naunsiyamì, *v.* stunted; delayed in growth;

Nauuhaw, *v.* is thirsty;

Nayon, *n.* town;

Nene, *n.* common term used for a baby girl;

Ng, abbreviated form of nang;

Nga, emphatic particle meaning please;

Ngala-Ngala, *n.* numbness;

Ngalan, *n.* name;

Ngalay, *n.* numbness;

Ngalót, *n.* mastication;

Ngalumatá, *n.* deepened eyes with marks around due to illness or lack of sleep;

Nganga, ang sabi ni susana batà;

Ngangá, *n.* opening of the mouth;

Ngangasab-ngasáb, *v.* opening and closssing of the mouth in anticipation of something pleasant to eat;

Ngani-Ngani, *n.* faltering;

Ngasáb, *n.* movement of the mouth and making noise while eating;

Ngasngás, noise; superflous talk;

Ngatál, *n.* trembling;

Ngawit, *adj.* fatigued;

Ngayón, *adv.* now;

Ngiki, *n.* chill;

Ngiló, *n.* painful feeling due to the setting of the teeth on edges;

Nginsngis-Ngitî, *n.* smile;

Ngipin, *n.* teeth;

Ngisi, *n.* giggle; giggling;

Ngitî, *n.* smile;

Ngitngit, *adj.* irritated;

Ngìwî, *n. adj.* twisted; with a mouth out of place;

Ngiwían, *v.* to move the mouth out of place;

Ngiyán, *n.* mewing of cats;

Ngongó, *n.* one who talks in twang due to nasal disoder;

Ngunit, *conj.* but;

Ngusò, *n.* upper lip;

Nguyâ, *n.* chewing;

Ngwâ, *n.* howling of children;

Ngyaín, *v.* masticate;

Nilá, *pron.* their;

Nilaláng, *n.* creature;

Nilalik, *v.* curved;

Nilapatan, *v.* was fitted with;

Nilikhâ, *v.* created;

Niluko, *v.* fooled;

Niná, plural of ni;

Ninang, *n.* godmother;

Ningas, *n.* flame; blaze;

Nino, *pron.* whose;

Ninong, *n.* godfather;

Ninyó, *pron.* your;

Nipís, *n.* thinness;

Nitó, *pron.* of this;

Niyá, *pron.* his or her;

Niyog, *n.* cocount;

Niyón, *pron.* of that;

Nmayani, *n.* became popular; reigned;

Noón, *adv.* at that time;

Nsnhslsy, *b.* became tired; fatigued;

Nunò, *n.* ancestor; grandparents;

Nunukal, *v.* spring forth;

Nuynuyín, *v.* to think over; to reflect;

Oo

Oatáng-Patâ, *adj.* terribly exhausted;

Obispo, *n.* bishop;

Okoy, *n.* native delicacy;

Oktubre, *n.* October;

Opisyal, *n.* official;

Oras, *n.* hour;

Orasán, *n.* watch;

Orasan, *v.* to time;

Orasyon, *n.* angelus;

Orihinal, *n.* original;

Ougsá, *n.* noil;

Ourubgan, *n.* to cover the eyes;

Oy, *interj.* Oh! halika. Hey come here;

Oyayí, *n.* lulaby;

Pp

Paá, *n.* foot;

Paahin, *v.* to kick; use of a foot;

Páalaman, *n.* act of bidding good-bye;

Paanan, *n.* at the foot;

Paano, *pron.* how;

Páaralán, *n.* school;

Pabahay, *n.* house allowance;

Pabalat-Bunga, *adj.* insincere invitation;

Pabangó, *n.* perfume;

Pabanguhán, *v.* to put perfume;

Pabay, *adj.* negligent;

Pabayaán, *v.* let alone; neglect;

Pabuyà, *n.* payment; tip;

Padaplís, *adv.* indirect; at a tangent;

Padaplisín, *v.* to hit indirectly;

Padér, *n.* wall;

Padparin, *v.* to be carried away by wind or water;

Pag-Aari, *n.* property;

Pag-aarugâ, *n.* act of rearing or taking care of;

Pag-Asa, *n.* hope;

Pagál, *adj.* tired; fatigued;

Pagbaa, *n.* act of fighting against;

Pagbubulay-Bulay, *n.* reflection;

Pagbubunyî, *n.* celebration; exaltation;

Pagbulay-Bulayin, *v.* to reflect on: to think about;

Pagbuntuhán, *v.* to bereceiver of something accumulated (as anger, reproach, etc);

Pagdadahóp, *n.* want; poverty;

Paghati-Hatiin, *v.* divide among;

Pagitan, *prep.* between;

Pagkabinat, *n.* state of having a relapse;

Pagkabuhay, *n.* livelihood; food;

Pagkadayukdók, *n.* hunger;

Pagkain, *n.* food;

Pagkakakilanlán, *n.* identity; means of identification;

Pagkakanuló, *n.* act of being a traitor. treachery;

Pagkakataon, *n.* chance; opportunity;

Pagkakatiklóp, *n.* state of being folded;

Pagkakawangis, *n.* similarity; likeness;

Pagkalingà, *n.* care; protection; adoption;

Pagkampáy, *n.* act of moving (as of wings);

Pagkasi, *n.* act of loving; affection;

Pagkatao, *n.* human nature; human being;

Pagkatapos, *adv.* afterwards;

Pagkit, *n.* wax;

Pagkuru-Kuruin, *v.* think over and over;

Paglalahad, *n.* presentation;

Paglalakbáy, *n.* journey; voyage;

Paglalambitin, *n.* hanging;

Paglalarawan, *n.* description;

Paglambitinan, *v.* to hang on.

Paglilibáng, *v.* recreation;

Paglilibíng, *n.* burial;

Paglilimás, *n.* drying; letlting the water flow out of a ditch or a small stream;

Paglilitis, *n.* trial; hearing;

Pagluhà, *n.* tearful supplication;

Paglunók, *n.* act of swallowing;

Paglusob, *n.* agression;

Pagod, *n.* fatigue; tire;

Pagpagin, *v.* to shake off;

Pagpapakasakit, *n.* sacrifice;

Pagpapalakí, *v.* bringing up; act of making large;

Pagpapalayaw, *n.* act of indulgence;

Pagpapalistá, *n.* registration;

Pagpapalitang-kuro, *n.* discussion; open forum;

Pagsasagupì, *n.* encounter; meeting (as in combat);

Pagsasaulî, *n.* return;

Pagsaulang-Loob, *v.* to regain consciousness;

Pagtalikuwás, *n.* retraction;

Pagtalunan, *v.* argue about;

Pagtataká, *n.* wonder; surprise;

Pagtatamà, *n.* coordination;

Pagtatamasa, *n.* productivity; enjoyment;

Pagtatampók, *n.* act of making it popular;

Pagtatangkilik, *n.* act of supporting;

Pagtatapunan, *n.* dumping place of refuse;

Pagtuligsâ, *n.* an act of criticizing;

Pagtunggâ, *n.* act of dirnking;

Pagtutungayáw, *n.* act of uttering bad words; anger;

Pagurin, *v.* to tire;

Pahám, *adj.* wise; sage;

Pahát, *adj.* meagre; small;

Pahayag, *n.* article;

Páhayagán, *n.* newspaper;

Pahilís, *n.* triangle;

Pahimakás, *n.* farewell;

Pahingá, *n.* rest;

Pahingá;

Pahingahan, *n.* resting place;

Pahingahán, *v.* to stop; to suit, Pahingahín;

Pahintulot, *n.* permission;

Pahintulutan, *v.* to allow; to permit;

Pahinuhod, *n.* acquiescence;

Pahirin, *v.* to wipe off;

Pahirin, *v.* wipe off;

Paikliin, *v.* tooffer; to give;

Pain, *n.* bait;

Pait, *n.* bitterness;

Pakamahalin, *v.* to love dearly;

Pakay, *n.* objective; aim;

Pakikibaka, *n.* struggle; fight;

Pakikihamok, *n.* battle; strife;

Pakikipágkapuwà, *n.* social intercourse;

Pakimkím, *n.* gift in money;

Pakinabang, *n.* project benefit;

Pakinabangan, *v.* to make profitable;

Pakinabangin, *v.* to benefit Hindi pa namin pakinabangin ang aming kinakain sa pagtitindá;

Pakitng-Tao, *n.* hypocrisy;

Pakiusap, *n.* request; entreaty;

Pakiusapan, *v.* to request; to entreat;

Paklí, *n.* reply; answer;

Pakó, *n.* nail;

Pakpák, *n.* wing;

Paksa, *n.* subject matter; theme; topic;

Paksâ, *n.* subject;

Paksáng-Aralín, *n.* subject;

Paksíw, *n.* a native dishcooked with vinegar and ginger and salt;

Pakumbabâ, *n.* humility; submission;

Pakundangan, *n.* respect;

Pakuwán, *n.* watermelon;

Pakyáw, *n.* wholesale;

Pakyawin, *v.* to buy whole sale;

Palá, interjectional article used to express surprise;

Pala, *n.* shovel;

Palababahán, *n.* window sill;

Palabok, *n.* spice; flowery expression (as in one's speech or writing; flattery;)

Palabukan, *v.* to spice;

Palad, *n.* fortune; fate;

Palad, *n.* palm of the and; fate;

Palág, *n.* convulsion; spasm;

Palaganapin, *v.* to propagate;

Palágarián, *n.* saw mill;

Palagáy, *n.* idea; opinion;

Pálagayan, *n.* comardeship; friendship;

Paláisdaan, *n.* fish pond; fishery;

Palakâ, *n.* frog;

Palakhín, *v.* to let grow; to increase;

Palakól, *n.* ax

Palakpák, *n.* applause; clapping of hands;

Palaló, *adj.* proud; bombastic;

Palam, *n.* good-bey; farewell;

Palamán, *n.* stuffing;

Palamara, *adj.* ungrateful, unfaithful;

Palamuti, *n.* decoration;

Palanggana, *n.* wash basin;

Palapag, *n.* floor; story (as of building);

Palarâ, *n.* tinfoil;

Palarin, *v.* to have good luck to be lucky;

Palás, *adj.* even; clipped;

Palasd, *n.* arrow;

Palaták, *n.* clacking noise from the tongue to express admiration;

Palátuntunan, *n.* program;

Palay, *n.* rice;

Palayaw, *n.* nickname;

Palayók, *n.* earthen pot for cooking;

Palengke, *n.* market;

Paligid, *n.* surroundings; environment;

Paligó, *n.* bath;

Páligsahan, *n.* contest;

Paliguan, *v.* to bathe;

Palihís, *adj.* deviating form the right path: erroneous;

Palíng, *adj.* tilted;

Palisán, *v.* to sweep;

Palitán, *v.* to change;

Paló, *n.* strike; beating;

Paltík, *n.* native gun;

Paltós, *n.* blister; miss;

Palugit, *n.* extension of time;

Paluin, *v.* to whip; to peat;

Palumpóng, *n.* plants;

Palupo, *n.* ridge of a roof;

Pamagát, *n.* title; caption;

Pamahayn, *v.* to turn into a dwelling;

Pamahiín, *n.* superstition;

Pamamahay, *n.* shome; house;

Pamamanás *v.* swelling of the body due to beri-beri;

Pamangkín, *n.* nephew or niece;

Pamanhik, *n.* entreaty; request;

Pamanhikán, *v.* to entreat; to request;

Pamantasan, *n.* university;

Páminggalan, *n.* cupboard;

Pamintá, *n.* pepper;

Pampáng, *n.* bank; shore;

Pampu nitik n, *n.* literary;

Pamutas-Silya, usualy ladies that go to dances but do not dance;

Pamutat, *n.* side dish for regular menu like atsarang papaya;

Panà, *n.* bow and arrow;

Panaghilian, *v.* to envy;

Panaghóy, *n.* weeping;

Panaginip, *n.* dream;

Panahón, *n.* season;

Panahón, *n.* time;

Panain, *v.* to shoot with bow and arrow;

Panakíp-Butes, *n.* substitute;

Panalangin, *n.* prayer;

Panambít, *n.* ejaculation;

Panambitan, *n.* wailing; lamentation;

Pananabík, *n.* eagerness; desire;

Pananalig, *n.* belief;

Pananamít, *n.* dress; clothes;

Pananampalataya, *n.* faith;

Panarili, *adj.* private;

Panata, *n.* pledge; vow;

Panatag, *adj.* peaceful; quiet;

Panatilihin, *v.* to make permanent;

Panawan, *v.* to leave;

Panáy, *adj.* all; mostly;

Panayám, *n.* conference;

Panayám, *n.* lecture;

Pandák, *adj.* short; small;

Pandakót, *n.* dust pan;

Pandáy, *n.* blacksmith;

Pangakuan, *v.* to promise;

Pangambá, *n.* worry; anxiety;

Pangangalakal, *n.* business transaction;

Panganib, *n.* danger;

Panganorin, *n.* atmosphere;

Pangarap, *n.* dream;

Panggagagá, *n.* act of appropriating for oneself; usurpation;

Panggaganyák, *n.* motivation;

Panggatong, *n.* firewood;

Panghili, *n.* envy;

Panghimasukan, *v.* interfere with;

Pangimbulo, *n.* jealousy;

Pangingilin, *n.* abstinence;

Panginoon, *n.* master;

Pangit, *adj.* ugly;

Pangitain, vision;

Pangkuhín, *v.* carry a person on the shoulder;

Pangláw, *n.* solitude;

Pangnán, *n.* basket;

Pangulo, *n.* prsident;

Pangungulila, *n.* loneliness; state of being an orphan;

Pangyayari, *n.* happenings; event;

Panig, *n.* side;

Panigan, *v.* side with;

Panikì, *n.* bat;

Panimdím, *n.* profound sorrow;

Panimulâ, *n.* elementary; beginning;

Panís, *adj.* spoiled by fermentation (as foold);

Panisin, *v.* to render spoiled;

Pánitikán, *n.* literature;

Paniwalaan, *n.* to belive;

Paniwalain, *v.* to make belive;

Panlasa, *n.* teaste;

Panót, *adj.* bald;

Pansimba, for chuch wear;

Pansín, *n.* attention; notice;

Pansít, *n.* noodles;

Pantas, *adj.* sage; scholar;

Pantás, *n.* wise; sage;

Pantiyón, *n.* cemetery;

Pantóg, *n.* bladder;

Panunumbalik, *n.* return; coming back;

Panunurí, *n.* criticism;

Panunuyò, *n.* act of showing gratefulness;

Panyd, *n.* handkerchief;

Pap-Part, or prefix to express manner;

Papag, *n.* low bamboo bed;

Papasukin, *v.* to be allowed to enter;

Para sa Kaniya, for her or for him;

Para, *adj.* like; similarl to;

Paraán, *n.* ways & means;

Parang Tinalupang̃ bunga, defeated in gambling; a great loss in gambling;

Parang, *n.* forest; mounatinous region;

Parangalán, to honor;

Paratang, *n.* false accusation or incrimination;

Paratangan, *v.* to accuse;

Parati, *adj.* from time to time;

Paratingin, *n.* to extend;

Parè, *n.* priest;

Pareha, *n.* pair;

Pareho, *adj.* alike; similar;

Pariníg, *n.* insinuation;

Parirala, *n.* phrase;

Parisukat, *n.* square;

Paról, *n.* lantern; lamp;

Paroroon, *v.* will go there;

Parunggit, *n.* derogatory remarks;

Paruparo, *n.* butterfly;

Parusa, *n.* punishment;

Parusahan, *v.* to punish

Pasaring, *n.* insinuation;

Pasd, *n.* flower pot;

Pasimulâ, *n.* beginning;

Pasimunò, *n.* head; one who leads;

Pasinayà, *n.* inauguration;

Pasiya, *n.* decision;

Pasiyók, *n.* whistle;

Paskil, *n.* poster;

Pasko, *n.* Christmas;

Paslit, *n.* young;

Pasó, *n.* burn; scald;

Pasok, *n.* entrance;

Pasok, *v.* enter;

Paspasan, *n.* fight; free for all;

Paspasán, *v.* to dust off;

Pasubali, *n.* disenting action;

Pasuin, *n.* to burn;

Pasukan, *n.* school days; door way;

Pasukin, *v.* to break into;

Pasunod, *n.* discpline;

Pasyalan, *n.* park;

Pataan, *n.* reserve; allowance;

Paták-Paták, *adv.* by drops;

Pátakarán, *n.* policy;

Patalim, *n.* pointedweapon;

Patatas, *n.* potato:

Pataw, *n.* weight;

Patáy, *adj.* dead; not living patáy na ang ama ko nang ako ay dumating;

Patay-Gutom, *adj.* ravenous;

Pati, *adv.* also;

Patibong, *n.* trap; decoy;

Patig, *n.* shark;

Patihayâ, *adj.* lying on one's back;

Patirin, *n.* to trip; to cut;

Patis, *n.* brine;

Patiwarik, *adj.* head down; feet up;

Patláng, *n.* blank;

Patnubay, *n.* guide;

Patnugot, *n.* dirctor;

Pato, *n.* duck;

Patong, *n.* interest;

patpát, *n.* split of bamboo;

Patpatin, *adj.* weak; thin;

Patubig, *n.* irrigation;

Patuloy, *adj.* continuous;

Patulugin, *v.* to cause tro sleep;

Patuyuan, *n.* drying place;

Paunawà, *n.* notice;

Pauns, *n.* Advance; Warning;

Payo, *n.* counsel;

Pekas, *n.* freckles; spots;

Peste, *n.* epidemic;

Pigaín, *v.* to press;

Pigî, *n.* buttock;

Pigil, *adj.* controlled;

Pigilin, *v.* to detain; to stop;

Piging, *n.* banquet;

Pigipitin, *v.* to put pressure on;

Piglás, *n.* struggle;

Pigtás, *adj.* ripped;

Pihitin, *v.* to turn;

Piitan, *n.* cell; prison;

Pikî, *adj.* knock-kneed;

Pikit, closed;

Pila, *n.* file;

Pilak, *n.* silver;

Pilantik, *n.* jerky whip;

Piláy, *adj.* lame;

Pilay, *n.* lemeness;

Pili, *adj.* seleclted;

Piliin, *v.* to select;

Piling, *n.* bunch or cluster;

Pilipit, *adj.* twisted;

Pilit, *adj.* forced;

Pinag-usig, *v.* persecuted;

Pinagsanib, *v.* joined; united;

Pinainom, *v.* given a drink;

Pinakamatalik, *adj.* the most intimate;

Pinalalabò, *v.* caused to be come dim or muddy;

Pinalayas, *v.* ordered to leave;

Pinalitán, *v.* changed;

Pinapangalisag, *v.* caused one's hair to stand on ends;

Pinatuyd, *v.* dried;

Pinawalán, *v.* released; able to get away;

Pinggá, *n.* a pole used to balance two weights;

Pinggán, *n.* plate;

Pingkian, *n.* friction;

Pingkit, *adj.* semi-closed eyes;

Pinopoon, *v.* worshipped;

Pinsan, *n.* cousin;

Pintá, *n.* paint;

Pintahán, *v.* to paint;

Pintd, *n.* door;

Pinulot, *v.* picked up;

Pinund, *v.* filled;

Pipi, *adj.* dumb;

Pipí, *n.* string;

Pipino, *n.* cucumber;

Pipís, *adj.* compressed; flat;

Piraso, *n.* piece;

Pirasuhin, *v.* to cut a piece of;

Piring, *n.* blindfold;

Pirma, *n.* signature;

pirmahan, to sign;

Pisaín, *v.* to hatch;

Pisanin, *v.* to put together;

Pisil, *n.* hold; press;

Piskal, *n.* fiscal; judge;

Pisngí, *n.* cheek

Piso, *n.* peso;

Pisón, *n.* roller;

Pistí, *n.* fiesta;

Pita, *n.* desire; whise;

Pitahin, *v.* to desire; to whsh;

Pitak, *n.* column;

Pitís, *adj.* tight;

Pitó, *adj.* seven;

Pitsel, *n.* pitcher n;

Pituhan, *v.* to press; to poound; to make flat;

Pitumpû, *adj.* seventy;

Pluma, *n.* pen; walâ siyang pluma;

Prusisyón, *n.* procession;p

Psagkamuhî, *n.* state of being disgusted;

Psaniwalá, *n.* belief;

Pthayá, *n.* ambition; desire;

Pulá, *adj.* red;

Pulót-Gatâ, *n.* honey moon;

Pulpito, *n.* church pulpit;

Pumaling, *v.* to incline;

Pumalit, *v.* to change;

Pumanaw, *v.* died; lost

Pumanhik, *v.* to ascend; to go up

Pumaroon, *v.* to go there;

Pumustá, *v.* to bet on;

Pumusyáw, *v.* to fade; to become pale;

Pumuták, *v.* to make an irritating noise;

Pumutok, *n.* to burst;

Puná, *n.* remark;

Punahín, *v.* to make a remark; to notice;

Punasan, *v.* to wipe away;

Pungos, *n.* cut;

Punit-Punit, *adj.* torn;

Punong bayan, *n.* town head· president;

Punong-salitâ, *n.* foreword;

Punsó, *n.* ant hill;

Puntó, *n.* period;

Puntód, *n.* mound;

Punung-Gurò, *n.* principal;

Punyós, *n.* cuff;

Puri, *n.* honor;

Purihin, *v.* appreciate; flatter; praise;

Purók, *n.* district;

Puról, *adj.* blunt;

Pusà, *n.* cat;

Pusá-pusaan, *n.* one who serves wilv· to attain his selfish ends;

Pusali, *n.* mire;

Pusikit, *adj.* dark;

Puslít, *n.* gate crasher;

Pusò, *n.* heart;

Pusod, *n.* navel;

Pusók, *n.* aggressiveness;

Puspós, *adj.* complate; full of;

Putá-Putakî, *adj.* sporadic;

Putahe, *n* servings; menu;

Puták, *n.* cackle;

Puti, *adj.* white;

Putíng-Tainga, *adj.* stingy; tight;

Putlain, *adj.* pale;

Putók, *n.* explosion;

Putól, *adj.* cut off;

Putong, *n.* head gear;

Putót, *n.* short pants;

Putulin, *v.* to cut; to discontinue;

Puwáng, *n.* crack space;

Puwít, *n.* anus;

Puyát, *adj.* sleepless;

Puyó, *n.* cowlick on the head;

Rr

Radyo, *n.* radio;

Raha, *n.* rajah;

Rahuyò, *n.* attraction; charm;

Raketa, *n.* racket;

Raso, *n.* silky fiber of fabric; or clothing material;

Rasyón, *n.* ration;

Raw (Drw), it is said;

Rayos, *n.* wheel spokes;

Rayuma, *n.* rheumatism;

Rebentador, *n.* firecracker;

Rebolber, *n.* rovolver;

Regla, *n.* rule; menstruation; regulation;

Reglahan, *v.* to rule; to regulate;

Renda, *n.* rein;

Rendahan, *v.* to rein; to let loose;

Reto, *n.* challenge; bet;

Reyna, *n.* queen;

Ribulusyón, *n.* revolution;

Rigalo, *n.* gift; offering;

Rikargo, *n.* penalty;

Rikarguhan, *n.* to penalize Rirkarguhán;

Rikisa, *n.* search;

Rikisahin, *v.* to search;

Rilihyón, *n.* disgust;

Rilos, *n.* watch;

Rimas, *n.* a native breadfruit;

Rimatse, *n.* riveting;

Rin (Din), also;

Ripa, *n.* lottery;

Ripaso, *n.* review;

Ripeke, *n.* pealing of the bells;

Ripinado, *n.* refined sugar;

Ripolyo, *n.* cabbage;

Riserbasyon, *n.* reservation;

Rises, *n.* recess;

Riseta, *n.* prescription;

Risibo, *n.* receipt;

Ritaso, *n.* remnants;

Ritirado, *n.* retired;

Ritoke, *n.* retouch;

Riwasá, *n.* riches;

Ronda, *n.* night patrol;

Rosaryo, *n.* rosary;

Rumaragasâ, *v.* tobe plentiful;

Rurok, *n.* highest point;

Ruweda, *n.* wheel;

Ss

Sa, *prep.* to; from; in; on;

Saan, *pron.* where;

Sabado, *n.* Saturday;

Sabáw, *n.* broth;

Sabáy, *adv.* at the same time;

Sabayán, *v.* to do at the same time;

Sabi, *v.* say;

Sabihin, *v.* say; tell;

Sabík, *adj.* eager; ankious;

Sabón, *n.* soap;

Sabong, *n.* cockfigth;

Sadyaín, *v.* to do intentionally;

Saganà, *adj.* abundant; plenty; prosperous;

Saging, *n.* banana;

Sagisag, *n.* symbol; emblem;

Saglit, *n.* in very short time;

Sagot, *n.* answer; reply; response;

Sagupaan, *n.* mutual meeting as in combat;

Sagutín, *v.* to answer or be answered;

Sagwil, *n.* obstacle;

Sahol, *adj.* wanting; lacking;

Sakali, *prep.* in case truction;

Sakalín, *v.* to choke;

Sakáy, *n.* ride; sumakay; sakyán to ride;

Sakdál, *adv.* extremely;

Sakdál, *n.* suit;

Sakím, *adj.* greedy;

Sakít, *n.* sickness; pain;

Saklolohan, *v.* to help; to give adi

Sakmalín, *v.* too snatch with the mouth;

Saknóng, *n.* stanza;

Saktan, *v.* to strike; to whip

Salakay, *n.* invasion; assault;

Salamat, *n.* thanks;

Salapî, *n.* meoney in general;

Salapi, *n.* money;

Salas, *n.* living room;

Salát, *adj.* lacking; inadequate;

Salát, *adj.* scanty;

Salawál, *n.* trousers;

Saláwikain, *n.* proverb;

Saligán, *n.* basis;

Saligáng-Batás, *n.* constitution;

Salità, *n.* word;

Saliw, *n.* accompaniment;

Salot, *n.* pestilence;

Salu-Salo, *n.* party; banquet; gathering;

Salungát, *adj.* go against; contradict;

Sama, *rw.* be with; accompany;

Sama, *v.* go along;

Samahan, *v.* to accomapny;

Samaiing-Palad, *v.* to be unfortunate;

Sambalilo, *n.* hat;

Sambilatin, *v.* to grab; to clutch;

Sambít, *n.* to mention in passing;

Sambulat, *v.* scatter;

Sampalok, *n.* a kind of pod fruit used for flavoring fish when green and eaten as is when ripe or made into candies;

Sampû, *adj.* ten;

Samsamín, *v.* to confiscate; to commandeer;

Sanaysáy, *n.* essay;

Sandaán, one hundred;

Sandalî, *n.* moment;

Sandatahin, *v.* armed;

Sandók, *n.* ladel;

Sanggunián, *n.* consultant; advise;

Sangmaliwanag, *n.* the world;

Sanlâ, *n.* mortgage;

Sanlibo, *n.* one thousand;

Sansalain, *v.* to interrupt;

Sansalapî, *n.* fifty centavos;

Sansinukob, *n.* the world;

Sapantahà, *n.* suspicions; presumption, guess;

Sapát, *adj.* enough; sufficient;

Sapatos, *n.* shoes;

Saplót, *n.* clothes; covering for the body'

Saráp, *n.* savor; taste;

Sarhan, *v.* close; shut;

Sari-Sarì, *adj.* various; mixed; diverse

Sarili, *n.* one's own;

Sárilinán, *adv.* in private;

Sariling Lupà, *n.* native country;

Sariling Wikà, *n.* native tongue;

Sasama, *v.* will go with;

Sastre, *n.* tailor;

Sayaw, *n.* dance;

Silahis, *n.* ray;

Silangan, *n.* east;

Silát, *n.* slits on flooring;

Siláw, *adj.* dazzled;

Silayan, *v.* to visit; to look over;

Silíd, *n.* compartment; room;

Silíd-Aralÿn, *n.* classroom;

Silipin, *v.* to peep; to look through a crevice;

Silò, *n.* noose;

Silong, *n.* rain or sun shade;

Silya, *n.* chair;

Simbahan, *n.* church;

Simoy, *n.* breeze;

Simsimín, *v.* to suck;

Simulâ, *n.* beginning;

Simulain, *n.* principle;

Simutin, *v.* to pick up everything;

Simyento, *n.* cement;

Sinabayán, *v.* to do at the same time;

Sinalakay, *n.* attacked; assaulted;

Sinaluhan, *v.* partook;

Sinamsám, *v.* confiscated; gathereo;

Sinapupunan, *n.* lap;

Sindák, *n.* fright;

Sinelas, *n.* slippers;

Sing-Ibig, *n.* sweetheats;

Singáw, *n.* vapor;

Singkamás, *n.* turnips;

Singkawán, *v.* to put a harness

Sinikap, *v.* tried;

Sining, *n.* art:

Siniyasat, *v.* examined closely;

Sino, *pron.* who;

Sintá, *n.* loved one;

Sintahan, *n.* love affair;

Sintahín, *v.* to love or make love to;

Sintido, *n.* sense; feeling;

Sinuhin, *v.* to ask for identity;

Sinulid, *n.* thread;

Sinungaling, *n.* liar;

Sinusuri, *v.* examining closely;

Sipag, *n.* industry;

Sipatin, *v.* to look carfully;

Sipi, *n.* copy;

Sipiin, *v.* to take a copy of;

Sipilyo, *n.* brush;

Sipilyuhín, *v.* to brush;

Sipón, *n.* cold;

Sipsipin, *v.* to suck;

Sipunin, *adj.* easily afflicted with cold;

Sirâ, *adj.* defective; torn;

Sir[illegible], *n.* tear; defect;

Sisi, *n.* reproach; regret;

Sisid, *n.* dive;

Sisihin, *v.* to reproach;

Sisirin, *v.* to dive;

Sitaw, *n.* pod-bearing vegetable;

Sitsít, *n.* gossip; backbiting;

Siwang, *n.* a small opening;

Siyá, *pron.* third person singular, she or he;

Siyám, *pron.* nine;

Siyámnapú, *pron.* ninety;

Siyáp, *n.* chirp of chickens;

Siyudad, *n.* city;

Sopas, *n.* soup;

Suangót, *adj.* sour or distorted face;

Subain, *v.* to swindle; to cheat;

Subali't, *conj.* but;

Subasob, *adj.* facing downward;

Subaybayán, *v.* to follow secretly; to observe carefuly;

Subd, *adj.* cannot back out;

Subó, *n.* boiling (as of rice being cooked);

Subò, *n.* mouthful;

Subok, *n.* test;

Subuan, *v.* v place food into one's mouth;

Subukan, *v.* to test;

Subyán, *n.* thorn: obstruction;

Súgalan, *n.* a gambling house;

Sugalán, *v.* to gamble with;

Sugat, *n.* wound;

Sugò, *n.* ambassador; representative;

Suhay, *n.* support;

Sukà, *n.* vinegar;

Suka, *n.* vomit;

Súkaban; *adj.* treacherous; dishonest;

Sukát ang bulsá, knowledge of one's ability to pay;

Sukat, *n.* meter; measurement;

Sukatan, *v.* to measure;

Sukdulan, *adj.* zenith; height of developmetn;

Suklám, *n.* loath; loathing;

Sukláy, *n.* comb;

Suklób, *n.* cover;

Sukuban, *v.* to spread over;

Sulat, *n.* letter;

Sulatin, *v.* to write;

Suld, *n.* torch;

Sûliranin, *n.* problem; trouble;

Sulitin, *v.* to examine; to account for;

Sulok, *n.* corner;

Sulong, *v.* to advance;

Sulsí, *n.* mend;

Sulyáp, *n.* glance;

Sumakit, *v.* to become painful;

Sumalok, *v.* to fetch water or draw water from a well;

Sumalungát, *v.* go against; contradict;

Sumama, *v.* to go with;

Sumamó, *v.* approach;

Suman, *n.* glutinous rice;

Sumandál, *v.* to lean on;

Sumansala, *v.* to cause to stop; cease or interrupt;

Sumasaráp, *v.* becoming delicious;

Sumasayáw, *v.* is dancing;

Sumbón, *n.* complaint;

Sumbóńg, *n.* report; complaint;

Sumigáw, *v.* to shout;

Sumingaw, *v.* to evaporate;

Sumingaw, *v.* to overcome;

Sumirà, *v.* to tear;

Sumisid, *v.* to dive;

Sumisidhî, *v.* becoming more intense;

Sumuko, *v.* surrendeer; give up;

Sumuláк, *v.* to boil;

Sumulat, *n.* to write;

Sumumpâ, *v.* to swear;

Sundalo, *n.* soldier;

Sundín, *v.* to follow;

Sunóg, *adj.* burned;

Sunog, *n.* fire; conflagration;

Sunong, *v.* something on the head;

Suntók, *n.* blow with a fist;

Suób, *n.* smoke; fumigation;

Suót na pamburol, wearing the best clothes;

Suót, *n.* something worn;

Suplíng, *n.* Sprout; shoot;

Supot, *n.* bag;

Suriin, *v.* look into; examine;

Surot, *n.* bedbug;

Susd, *n.* snail;

Susi, *n.* key;

Susian, *v.* to open with a key;

Susog, *n.* amendment;

Sustansiya, *n.* substane;

Susuhan, *v.* to set fire;

Sutlâ, *n.* silk;

Sutsót, *n.* whistle;

Sutsután, *v.* to whistle at;

Suubin, *v.* to fumigate;

Suwaayín, *v.* to disobey;

Suwagin, *v.* to horn;

Suwaíl, *adj.* insolent;

Suwelas, *n.* soles;

Suweldo, *n.* salary;

Suwelduhán, *v.* to give pay;

Suwerte, *n.* luck;

Suyà, *n.* disgust;

Suyáng-Suyâ, *adj.* disgusted;

Suyod, *n.* fine comb;

Suyuin, *v.* to make or render one self into the favor orf another;

Suyurin, *v.* to comb firnely; to harrow;

Switik, *adj.* artful;

Tt

Taal, *adj.* native of;

Taás, *n.* height;

Taasán, *v.* make high; raise;

Tabâ, *n.* fat;

Tabako, *n.* tobacco;

Taban, *n.* hold;

Tabanan, *v.* hold;

Tabáng, *n.* ilog; not salty; tastelass;

Tabas, *n.* cut; style;

Tabì, *v.* paraán;

Tabigin, *v.* to push aside;

Tabihán, *v.* sit beside;

Tabíl, *adj.* talkative;

Tabíng-Dagat, *n.* seashore;

Tabingan, *v.* put a screen;

Tabingî, *adj.* no symmetry;

Tablá, *n.* woodboard;

Tadtád, *adj.* chopped;

Tadtarín, *v.* to chop;

Tadyakán, *v.* to kick forcefully;

Tadyáng, *n.* rib;

Tag-Gutom, *n.* famine;

Tag-Ulán, *n.* rainy season;

Tagaayos, *n.* sergeant-at-arms;

Tagaingat-Yamān, htreasurer;

Tagak, *n.* heron;

Tagál, *n.* duration; prolongation of time;

Taganás, *pron.* all; everythingf;

Tagapag-Alagà, care-taker; one who takes care of;

Tagasulit, *n.* examiner;

Tagasuri, *n.* auditor;

Tagausig, *n.* prosecutor;

Tagd, *v.* hidden;

Tagdán, *n.* flagpole;

Taghóy, *n.* lamentation;

Taginting, *n.* noise made by tow metallic objects tinkling;

Taglamíg, *n.* winter;

Tagpî, *n.* patch;

Taguán, *n.* hide and seek;

Tagubilin, *n.* recommendation; instruction;

Tagumpáy, success; victory;

Tagurî, *n.* nickname;

Tahán, *v.* to stop crying;

Táhanan, *n.* home;

Tahî, *n.* sewing;

Tahiín, *n.* to sew;

Tahilan, *n.* beam of the house;

Tahimik, *adj.* peaceful;

Tahíp, *n.* palpitation;

Tahipin, *v.* to winnow;

Tahol Nang tahol, *adv.* keeps on barking;

Tahól, *n.* bark;

Tahulán, *n.* to bark at;

Taibós, *n.* young leaves;

Taimtím, *adj.* devoted;

Taká, *n.* longing desire;

Takal, *n.* measure; price in selling;

Takalan, *v.* Takalan mo ngâ siyá ng dalawáng salóp na bihgás;

Takalin, *v.* to measure;

Takapán, *v.* to bawl out;

Takbó, *v.* run;

Takbuhín, *v.* Takbuínm mo ang kaniyáng

Takdâ, *n.* limit;

Takdáng-aralín, *n.* assignment;

Takes, *n.* escape;

Takip-Silim, *n.* twilight;

Taklób, *n.* covering;

Takot, *n.* fear;

Taksil, *adj.* traitor;

Takulubán, *n.* to put cover;

Takutin, *v.* to frighten; to make afraid of ;

Talá, *n.* a big star;

Talâ, *n.* notation;

Tálaan, *n.* list; writing book;

Talagá, *adv.* naturally; intentionally;

Talagá, fate;

Talahiban, *n.* a place overgrown with talahib;

Talaksán, *n.* pile of firewood;

Talambuhay, *n.* biography;

Talampás, *n.* level area on top of a hill;

Talastas, *v.* understand; knew;

Talatà, *n.* paragraph;

Talátinigan, *n.* dictionary;

Tali, *n.* knot; tie;

Talian, *v.* to tie;

Talibà, *n.* guard;

Talibaan, *v.* to guard; to watch;

Talikdán, *v.* to turn one's back to;

Talím, *n.* blade;

Talinghagà, *n.* Parable; allegory;

Talino, *n.* talent; intelligence;

Talipandás, *adj.* fickle; not constant;

Talón, *n.* falls; waterfalls;

Talóng, *n.* egg plant;

talóp, *adj.* skin peeled;

Talós, *n.* comprehended;

Talsík, *n.* splash;

Talsikán, *v.* to splash;

Talu-Salig, *adj.* temperamental

Taludtód, *n.* lene (as in verse);

Talukab, *n.* crab shell; eyelid;

Talukbóng, *n.* veil;

Taluktók, *n.* summit; top;

Talulot, *n.* petal;

Talumpatí, *n.* speech;

Talupan, *v.* to peel;

Talusin, *v.* to understand;

Talyasè, *n.* vat;

Tamà, *adj.* correct;

Tamarín, *v.* to be lazy; to feel lazy;

Tanán, *pron.* everyone;

Tanáw, *n.* sight; outlook;

Tanawag, *v.* called;

Tanawan, *n.* a point from wjere pme voews'

Tánawin, *n.* scenery;

Tanawin, *v.* to look;

Tandâ, *n.* sign; mark; age;

Tandaán, *v.* to remember;

Tangd, *n.* confirmation by nodding;

Tanggál, *adj.* loose; disconnected;

Tanggáp, *v.* acceptaed receive;

Tanggapan, *n.* office; reception room;

Tanggapín, *v.* to accept; to receive;

Tanggulan, *n.* defense;

Tanghalì, *n.* noón

Tanghalian, *n.* lunch;

Tanghaling-Tapát, *n.* midday;

Tangì, *adj.* special;

Tangkaín, *v.* plan; intend;

Tangkás, *n.* bundle;

Tangkáy, *n.* stem;

Tangkilik, *n.* support; care;

Tangkilikán, *n.* mutual aid;

Tangkilikin, *v.* to support; to care for;

Tangláw, *n.* light; lamp;

Tanglawán, *v.* to light;

Tanim, *n.* chain;

Taním, *n.* plant; planting;

Tanóng, *n.* question;

Tanyág, *adj.* weell-known; famous;

Tapa, *n.* dried meat; smoked meat;

Tapahin, *v.* to make tapa out of;

Tapák, *adj.* barefooted;

Tapak, *n.* footsteps;

Tapang, *n.* bravery; courage; strength;

Tapát, *adj.* faithful;

Tapatan, *adj.* sincere; frank;

Tapatín, *v.* to confess; to talk frankly;

Tapón, *n.* cork;

Tapon, *n.* oucast;

Tapós, *v.* finished; concluded;

Tarangkahan, *n.* gate;

Tarukín, *v.* to fathom;

Taták, *n.* stamp;

Tatay, *n.* father; appelation for father;

Tatay, *n.* stamp;

Tawa, *n.* laugh;

Tawag, *n.* call; name;

Tawang-Aso, *n.* sarcastic laugh;

Tayd, *v.* stand up;

Taye, *pron.* we;

Taynga, *n.* ear;

Tayuán, *v.* to stand for; to guaranty;

Tibay, *n.* strength; durability;

Tibayan, *v.* to strengthen to be courageous;

Tibók, *n.* palpitation;

Tibukan, *v.* to feel; to palpitate;

Tigil, *v.* stop; suspend;

Tigíng, *adj.* dry;

Tigmak, *adj.* soaked; wet;

Tigpasín, *v.* cut off;

Tikas, *n.* bearing; form; figure;

Tikmán, *v.* to taste;

Tinapay, *n.* bread;

Tinatamasa, *v.* is enjoying;

Tindahan, *n.* store;

Tindíg, *v.* stand erect;

Tingin, *n.* look;

Tingkád, *n.* brightness (as of color);

Tingnán, *v.* to look at;

Tinidor, *n.* fork;

Tinig, *n.* voice;

Tiník, *n.* thorn;

Tinitirhan, *n.* address; place where one lives;

Tinubuang lupà, *n.* native country;

Tinuhog, *v.* slung together;

Tinuran, *v.* mentioned;

Tirá, *n.* left over;

Tiwangwáng, *adj.* widely open; totally exposed;

Tiya, *n.* aunt;

Tiyagâ, *n.* perseverance;

Tiyak, *adj.* certain; sure;

Tiyakin, *v.* to ascertain; to be sure of;

Tiyán, *n.* stomach;

Tiyani, *n.* tweezers;

Tíyapan, *n.* appointment;

Tiyo, *n.* uncle;

Tnghál, *n.* show; display;

Totohanin, *v.* to make true;

Totoó, *adj.* true;

Trahedya, *n.* tragedy;

Troso, *n.* timber;

Tsiko, *n.* delicious brown sweet fruit;

Tsino, *n.* chinese;

Ttalukbungán, *v.* to put a veil on;

Tubig, *n.* water;

Tubigan, *v.* to put water on;

Tubo, *n.* chimney;

Tubò, *n.* gain;

Tubó, *n.* sugar cane;

Tubuan, *v.* to have sprout;

Tubusan, *n.* pawn shop;

Tubusínm, *v.* to redeem;

Tudík, *n.* accent;

Tudlâ, *n.* aim;

Tudling, *n.* furrow;

Tugkulin, *n.* duty; obligation;

Tugmâ, *n.* rhymes;

Tugón, *n.* reply; answer;

Tugtugin, *n.* music;

Tuhod, *n.* knee;

Tukâ, *n.* bill;

Tukaín, *v.* to peck;

Tuklás, *n.* discovery;

Tukláw, *n.* bite (as a snake);

Tuksó, temptation;

Tulâ, *n.* poem;

Tulalâ, *adj.* ignorant; simple;

Tuláy, *n.* bridge;

Tulayán, *v.* to cross the bridge;

Tuldikán, *v.* accént;

Tulíg, *adj.* deafened by shock;

Tuligín, *v.* to render deaf;

Tuligsâ, *v.* criticism;

Tuligsaan, *n.* and exchange of destructive criticism;

Tulis, *n.* point;

Tulisán, *n.* robbers;

Tulisan, *v.* to make pointed;

Tuló, *n.* leak; drip;

Tulod, *n.* banana shoot;

Tulóg, *adj.* asleep;

Tulog, *n.* sleep;

Tuluan, *v.* to be wet because of drips;

Tulugán, *n.* bedroom;

Tulugan, *v.* to sleep on

Tuluyan, *n.* prose;

Tulyá, *n.* small clams;

Tulyapis, *n.* unsubstantial grain;

Tumabì, *v.* to get out of the way;

Tumagistis, *v.* to fall freely (as of tears);

Tumalikod, *v.* to turn one's back;

Tumalima, *v.* to obey;

Tumalungkd, *v.* to squat;

Tumanà, *n.* vegetable patch;

Tumanod, *v.* too keep guard;

Tumantiyá, *v.* to estimate;

Tumbalík, *adj.* inverted;

Tumbás, *n.* equivalent;

Tumbasan, *v.* give the equivalent of;

Tumbukan, *n.* collision;

Tumbukín, to strike against anf object;

Tumimó, *v.* to lodge;

Tumpák, *adj.* correct;

Tumugot, *v.* to yield;

Tumulóng, *v.* to stand on;

Tumumbá, *v.* to tumble down;

Tumunggâ, *v.* to drink;

Tunáw, *adj.* dissolve;

Tunay, *adj.* true;

Tunggák, *adj.* unfit;

Tunggalian, *n.* conflict;

Tungkabín, *v.* to open forcely;

Tungkód, *n.* cane;

Tungkól, *prep.* with reference to;

Tungó, *adj.* bowed, stooped;

Tunóg, *n.* sound;

Tuód, *n.* stump;

Tuók, *adj.* burned;

Tuós, *n.* settlement;

Tupa, *n.* sheep;

Tuparín, *v.* to fulfill;

Turnalón, *v.* to jump;

Turnilyo, *n.* screw;

Turnips, *n.* singkamas,

Turó, *n.* teachings;

Tusino, *n.* bacon;

Tuso, *adj.* astute; wily;

Tusok, *n.* prick;

Tustós, *n.* allowance;

Tustusán, *v.* to support;

Tusukin, *v.* to prick;

Tutól, *n.* opposition;

Tutóng, *n.* burned part of boiled rice;

Tutóp, *n.* trimmings;

Tutubí, *n.* dragon fly;

Tutukan, *v.* to point a gun on somebody;

Tutulí, *n.* ear wax;

Tutupán, *v.* to put trimmings on;

Tuusín, *v.* to settle; to liquidate;

Tuwâ, *n.* gladnessa;

Tuwâ, *n.* happiness; joy;

Tuwalya, *n.* towel;

Tuwangan, *n.* coordination;

Tuwangán, *v.* to help;

Tuwî, *adv.* often;

Tuwíd, *adj.* straight;

Tuyâ, *n.* sarcasm;

Tuyaín, *v.* to mock to make fun of;

Tuyót, *adj.* totally dried;

Uu

Uban, *n.* white hairs;

Ubanin, *adj.* full of white hairs;

Ubas, *n.* grapes;

Ubó, *n.* cough;

Ubod *n.* Core; Pith; center;

Ubusin, *v.* to consume;

Udyók, *n.* inducement; urge;

Ugit, *n.* rudder;

Ugnáy, *n.* connection;

Uhaw, *n.* thirst;

Ukâ, *adj.* worn out; dug up; rotten;

Ukà, *n.* part dug;

Ukol, *prep.* in connection with

Ulam, *n.* viand; dish;

Ulî, *adv.* again;

Uli-Uli, *adv.* next time;

Uli-Uli, *n.* eddying water;

Ulikbâ, *adv*: black;

Ulila, *n.* orphan;

Ulilahin, *v.* to cause to be an orphan;

Ulinigin, *v.* to listen; to hear;

Ulirán, *adj.* ideal;

Ulit, *n.* repetition;

Ulit, *n.* something stolen;

Ulo, *n.* head;

Ulok, *n.* incitement;

Ulól, *adj.* insane;

Uluhán, *adj.* with a big head;

Uluhan, *v.* to cut off the head;

Uluín, *v.* to fool;

Ulukán, to incite;

Ulupón, *n.* direction of the head;

Ulupóng, *n.* posisonous snake;

Umaga, *n.* morning;

Umagahin, *v.* to be aught by dawn;

Umagtig, *v.* to vibrate;

Umalalay, *v.* to support; to prop;

Umalingasaw, *v.* to spread out;

Umalingawngáw, *v.* to be repeated in whispers;

Umalís, *v.* went away;

Umaliw-íw, *v.* to bubble like the brook;

Umibis, *v.* alight;

Umidlip, *v.* to take a nap;

Umigib, *v.* to fetch water;

Umilag, *v.* to avoid;

Umilandáng, *v.* to be throwr away or far;

Umilap, *v.* to become wild;

Umiling, *v.* to shake one's head;

Uminit, *v.* to become hot;

Umisip, *v.* to think of;

Umit, *n.* pilfered goods;

Umitim, *v.* to become black;

Umitin, *v.* to pilfer; to steal;

Umudlót, *v.* to fall back;

Umulán, *v.* to rain;

Umumbók, *v.* to swell;

Umuntág, *v.* to remind;

Umurong, *v.* to go back; to retreat;

Umuslî, *v.* to stick out;

Umuwî, *v.* to go home;

Una, *adj.* first;

Unahán, *n.* fornt;

Unan, *n.* pillow;

Unat, *n.* straightness;

Unatin, *v.* to straighten;

Unawa, *v.* to comprehend;

Unawain, *v.* to understand;

Ungal, *n.* howl;

Ungás, *adj.* simpleton; stupid;

Unggd, *n.* monkey;

Unós, *n.* strong breeeze;

Unsiyamî,. *n.* stunted growth;

Unti-Untî, *adv.* little by little;

Untóg, *n.* bump;

Uod, *n.* worm;

Upa, *n.* payment; fee;

Upd, *v.* to be seated;

Upo, *n.* white squash;

Upós, *adj.* exhausted; consume;d

Ûpuan, *n.* seat;

Uri, *n.* quality; kind;

Uriin, *v.* to classify;

Urungan, *v.* to back out;

Usá, *n.* deer;

Usad, *v.* crawl;

Usap, *n.* conversation;

Usapín, *n.* case in court;

Usbong, *n.* young shoot;

Usbungán, *v.* to cut young shoot;

Uso, *n.* mode; style;

Usok Nang Usok, *adv.* keep on smoking;

Usok, *n.* smoke;

Usukan, *v.* to smoke;

Utak, *n.* brains;

Utang-Na loób, *v.* please;

Utangin, *n.* to be in debt;

Utangin, *v.* to be in debt;

Utasín, *v.* to finish;

Utos, *n.* order; command;

Uturuj, *v.* to make stand; to erect;

Uurin, *v.* to be filled with worms;

Uwák, *n.* crow;

Uwáng, *n.* beetle;

Uwî, *v.* to return home;

Uyamín, *v.* to be sarcastic;

Wa ;ás, *adj.* faithful; sincere;

Wagaywáy, *v.* fulttering;

Waglít, *v.* mislaid; missed:

Wakás, *n.* end;

Wakasán, *n.* to end;

Wakwák, *adj.* torn;

Walâ, *adj.* not available;

Waláng anumán, you are welcome;

Waláng habas, *adj.* unrestrained;

Waláng hanggán, *adj.* eternal;

Waláng hiya, *adj.* shameless;

Waláng-Bahalà, without value; carefree;

Walang-Habas, *adj.* careless;

Waláng-Humbáy, without ceasing;

Walis, *n.* brom;

Walisÿn, *v.* to sweep;

Walo, *adj.* eight;

Walumpû, *adj.* eighty;

Wastd, *adj.* correct;

Wastuín, *v.* to correct; to put in order;

Watak-Watak, disunited; scattered;

Watawat, *n.* flag; emblem;

Wawi, *n.* rivulet;

Wikaing, *n.* dialect; adage;

Wikia, *n.* language;

Wiligán, *v.* to sprinkle water on;

Wiling-Wili, feeling at home;

Windang-Windáng, *adj.* torn; tattere;

Wisik, *v.* spray; sprinkle;

Yy

Yabág, *n.* footstep;

Yabang, *n.* pride;

Yabong, *n.* growth;

Yagít, *n.* rubbish;

Yakag, *n.* inducement;

Yakagin, *v.* to induce; to ask;

Yakapin, *v.* embrace;

Yakayík, *adj.* crestfallen;

Yaman, *n.* riches;

Yamang, inasmuch as;

Yamót, *n.* annoyance;

Yamungmóng, *n.* expansion enlargement;

Yamutin, *v.* to annoy;

Yanigin, *v.* to shake; to virate;

Yantók, *n.* rattan;

Yaón, *pron.* that;

Yapak, *n.* footprints;

Yapakan, *v.* to step on;

Yapós, *v.* embraced;

Yapusin, to embrace;

Yari, *adj.* manufactured; made; finishe;

Yari, *n.* product;

Yariin, *v.* to finish; to make;

Yatà, *adv.* may be; perhaps;

yayà, *n.* invitation;

Yayain, *v.* to invite; to persuade;

Yayamang, *conj.* since;

Yayát, *adj.* emaciated;

Yese, *n.* chalk;

Yoye, *n.* toy;

Yugto, *n.* brief stop in a drama;

Yugyugin, *v.* to shake;

Yukd, *adj.* stooped;;

Yukód, *n.* salute; stoop;

Yukuÿn, *n.* shaking; shake;

Yumakag, *v.* to invite; to call;

Yumao, *v.* died;

Yumì, *n.* modesty; meekness;

Yungib, *n.* cave;

Yungyóng, *n.* shelter; shad:

Yungyungán, *v.* to shelter : to shade to protect;

Yupì, *n.* dislocation;

Yupí_Yupî, *adj.* distorted; flattened;

Yupiín, *v.* to distort;

Yurak, *n.* trampling;

Yurakan, *v.* to trample;

Yutà, *n.* a hundred thousand;

Yutyót, *n.* shake, shaking;

Yutyutín, *v.* to shake;

Printed in the United States
151924LV00005B/85/P

9 781843 560449